SEXUAL BLACKMAIL

ANGUS McLAREN

SEXUAL BLACKMAIL

A

MODERN HISTORY

HARVARD UNIVERSITY PRESS

CAMBRIDGE, MASSACHUSETTS

LONDON, ENGLAND

2002

Library of Congress Cataloging-in-Publication Data

McLaren, Angus.
Sexual blackmail : a modern history / Angus McLaren.
p. cm.
Includes bibliographical references and index.
ISBN 0-674-00924-X (alk. paper)
1. Extortion—United States—History.   2. Extortion—England—History.
3. Sexual ethics—United States—History.   4. Sexual ethics—England—History.   I. Title

HV6688 .M394 2002
364.16′ 5—dc21   2002068726

#496277757

CONTENTS

ILLUSTRATIONS

ACKNOWLEDGMENTS

So many years have passed since I first began to mull over the ideas that provide the framework for this book that I am afraid I no longer recall all of those to whom I have subjected my pet theories and endless string of anecdotes. I do know that I owe a special debt to Brian Dippie, Constance Backhouse, and Lesley Hall—experts in American, legal, and English history respectively—who read complete drafts of the manuscript. Their close readings made this a better book. The press's three anonymous readers provided penetrating and thoughtful suggestions for revisions. I am especially grateful to Joyce Seltzer, my editor, whose patience, keen eye, and energetic prodding helped me clarify my arguments. Donna Bouvier did a wonderful job in helping me polish my prose.

Being made a visiting fellow of Clare Hall, Cambridge, in 1998 provided me with the perfect setting in which to begin the writing stage of the project. My repeated trips to London were brightened by Richard and Susannah Taffler's hospitality and kindness. Danny and Judy Walkowitz's generosity made a research trip to New York City both possible and pleasurable. At Berkeley Martin Jay and Paul Thomas were as bemused about what I was up to as they had been in grad school. The support of the Social Science and Humanities Research Council of Canada enabled me to make the numerous overseas trips that this project required.

I much appreciate the suggestions made by those who listened to portions of the work at the University of Victoria; the annual meeting of the

Acknowledgments

Victorian Studies Association of Western Canada; the University of Umeå; Clare Hall, Cambridge; the University of California at Berkeley; and the William Andrews Clark Memorial Library at UCLA. George Alter, Donna Andrew, John Beattie, Catherine Ellis, Ginger Frost, Gert Hekma, David J. Langum, Steven Maynard, Robert Nye, Michael Sibalis, Margaret D. Stetz, and Nikki Strong-Boag offered me the benefit of their expert advice.

Some of the material contained in this book first appeared in *Sex, State, and Society: Comparative Perspectives on the History of Sexuality* (Stockholm: Almqvist and Wiksell International, 2000). I thank the editor, Lars-Göran Tedebrand, and the publishers for permission to reprint this material. For their unflagging assistance I am grateful to the staffs of the University of Victoria Library, Cambridge University Library, the British Library, the Wellcome Institute for the History of Medicine, the Canadian Lesbian and Gay Archives, the New York Lesbian and Gay Community Services Center Archive, and the Kinsey Institute. At the History Department of the University of Victoria Eric Sager has been an understanding Chair and Karen McIvor an ever helpful departmental secretary. Robert Moyes has provided skilled research assistance.

I am particularly indebted to Brian and Donna Dippie, whose boundless generosity makes my continual shuttling between Victoria and Vancouver possible. The appearance of this book—and so much more—is due to Arlene and Jesse's faith and encouragement.

SEXUAL BLACKMAIL

INTRODUCTION

On January 16, 1997, the world was stunned by the news that Ennis Cosby, son of Bill Cosby, the beloved television comedian, had been shot to death in Los Angeles. The comedian's tragedy was compounded when two days later the United States Attorney's Office reported that a woman claiming to be Cosby's illegitimate daughter had been arrested for attempting to blackmail him out of millions of dollars. Autumn Jackson, the young woman in question, and three confederates were charged with menacing Cosby and the executives of companies with which he was associated. In the next few days the story slowly came into focus. Twenty years earlier Cosby had had a brief affair with a woman named Shawn Thompson. She later gave birth to a child. Cosby was not sure if the girl, Autumn Jackson, was his; but to keep Thompson from going to the press, he had over the years given her approximately $100,000 in "loans." He had also aided Autumn Jackson with her college expenses. In the past year she had begun making more demands. By a cruel coincidence, it was on the very day of the shooting of his son that Jackson and her colleagues faxed Cosby that if they did not receive $40 million they would sell to the tabloids the story that he had an out-of-wedlock daughter. When he refused to pay, Jackson replied that she would have to use "the only property I have to sell in order to survive."[1] Cosby at that point contacted the FBI. Agents there told Cosby's lawyer to arrange to have Jackson come to New York. FBI agents taped the January 18 meeting at which Autumn Jackson agreed to accept $24 million as the price of her silence; they then arrested her and her accomplices and charged them with extortion.[2]

2   At the trial in July 1997 the prosecution argued that blackmail was a form of robbery—"your money or your reputation." But the prospect of a possible twelve-year prison term for a poor daughter who had made demands on her wealthy father made some commentators queasy. Did not lawyers regularly threaten lawsuits in order to force compensation? In divorce cases were not threats of exposure often used? Jackson's demand for millions of dollars was unreasonable, but did she have no rights at all? Bill Cosby was the best-paid African-American entertainer on television. Moreover, as author of the best-selling book *Fatherhood* and star of *The Cosby Show* he had built his reputation exalting family life. In his folksy comedy routines he was renowned for carefully avoiding sexual innuendo. He had perfected the role of the patient, understanding parent both in his sitcoms and on a range of lucrative advertisements aimed at children. Segments of the American public were disturbed by the apparent revelation that this man seemed to care more about his fictional TV children than about his real child—indeed, that he would be willing to see that child sent to prison.

The scandal forced on the public some appreciation of the complexities and possible inequities of the law on blackmail.[3] Autumn Jackson's lawyer said he would prove in court that Cosby was the young woman's father, though he later said that he would prove only that she believed that Cosby was her father. Did the argument that she was acting in good faith justify blackmail? The press made it clear that the American public felt that paternity was relevant; the judge said it was not. Who, the defense asked, was the real victim? Had not Bill Cosby harmed Autumn Jackson? She was homeless and penniless, while he was a multimillionaire. Those facts too, according to the judge, were not mitigating circumstances. Legal experts explained to a confused public the paradox of blackmail. It was not a crime to ask for money. Nor was it illegal to tell the truth about a person's past. But putting the two acts together as a threat constituted blackmail, a criminal offense. Indeed, threatening to tell the truth about a person made the menace all the more dangerous. And for doing just that Autumn Jackson was found guilty and sentenced to twenty-six months in prison.[4] The case provided a classic demonstration of the enormous value modern society attributes to reputation. It also revealed the seriousness with which twenti-eth-century American law regarded unwarranted demands.

When the Cosby scandal broke I was in the midst of reading the accounts 3 of sensational sexual blackmail trials of the 1920s and 1930s. I was struck by the fact that in the 1990s, on hearing of the Bill Cosby case, the public had to learn from legal experts what exactly blackmail was. Past generations were far more aware of the classic blackmail scenario—demanding money in return for not telling about someone's sexual past. But in the 1990s if one looked up "blackmail" on the Web one found far more references to political blackmail, nuclear blackmail, and emotional blackmail than to sexual blackmail. Here was confirmation of my central premise: sexual blackmail has a history. The crime emerged at a certain time, as did the "blackmail story," a narrative device that legitimated the discussion of a range of issues that were otherwise excluded from public discourse, such as homosexuality and abortion.

Blackmail and the stories it generated were implicated in the creation and policing of a certain set of sexual standards. Modern blackmail first emerged when criminals in the eighteenth century recognized that the laws against sodomy provided them with the means by which they could extort money from those whom they could entrap. Such opportunities expanded in the Victorian age. In focusing on sexuality as the key determinant of one's personality and redefining gender relations by stressing male and fe-male differences, nineteenth-century middle-class society made a fetish of the cult of sexual respectability.[5] At the fin de siècle those made anxious by such social transformations as the changing nature of men's work, the re-duction of the birth rate, and women's entry into higher education and the professions propounded new scientific norms of male and female sexuality. This attempt to define and demarcate the "truth" about sex had as an unin-tended consequence the propagation of dangerous secrets and lies. Notions of respectability and deviance were inextricably entwined; the more rigid the moral standards, the more certain they were to be violated.

The moralists' strenuous attempts to organize, police, and control het-erosexual desires provided blackmailers with an expanding pool of poten-tial victims. As legal and social disapproval of certain forms of sexual be-havior rose, so did the profitability and frequency of blackmail. The growth of blackmail in turn prompted rearguard action by police and authorities to repress a crime made more widespread by the criminalization of sex. Laws had traditionally been confined to handling injury to public reputation, as in cases of defamation. By the turn of the century the middle classes were demanding the legal protection of privacy.

In the first decades of the twentieth century, which witnessed unprecedented class mobility, social anonymity, increased leisure time, and a steady blurring of class, gender, and racial lines in major cities, preoccupation with sexual blackmail peaked. Modern men and women were abandoning the older notion of sexuality as necessarily linked to reproduction and moved toward acceptance of a nonprocreative model of marriage and even the notion of the relative harmlessness of sexuality outside of marriage. Women were moving into the public world as never before and engaged with men in new forms of sexual bartering. The old moral standards were increasingly flouted, but the new standards would not be socially sanctioned until the 1960s. The growing gap between nineteenth-century laws and twentieth-century behavior created contradictions that both the desperate and the unscrupulous could exploit.

Studying the accounts of blackmail trials allows a plotting of the cresting of such sexual tensions in the first half of the twentieth century and their decline in the second half. The activists of the 1960s, in bringing the statute books closer in line to actual behavior by reforming the laws on abortion, divorce, and homosexuality, went a long way in disarming extortionists. Such reforms did not end blackmail—many types of deviant behavior were still stigmatized—but made certain key forms of it less likely. Once sexual mores changed and more open discussion of sexuality was possible the once revelatory blackmail stories lost much of their interest. Actual attempts at sexual blackmail did not end—they may even have increased—but blackmail stories were displaced by the tabloids' exposés in the narrating of sexual secrets and threats of exposure.

This book charts the history of the practice of blackmail and explores the narrative forms through which that history unfolded. An analysis of blackmail stories reveals the changing public sentiment on blackmail and on the individuals and actions that attracted blackmailers. Seeing where sympathy and opprobrium fall over time allows us to follow the ebb and flow of public and official acceptance of different forms of sexual behavior and personal identity. Womanizing males, homosexuals, women who sought abortions or had adulterous affairs, those who dared to cross racial boundaries in pursuit of sexual pleasure are all key characters in such accounts. What follows is an examination of sexual blackmail and the meanings that were attributed to it. I begin by tracking the activities of criminals and victims 5 through the stylized and structured stories told in court. Most of these have been garnered from the *New York Times* and the *Times* of London. Leading cases have been followed through the English Law Reports and the reports of the state and federal courts of the United States. In turning to accounts in the tabloid press and the depictions of blackmail found in novels, plays, and films, my goal has been to set the legal contests in their cultural context.[6]

Though financial and political extortion occur, the public has always been more preoccupied by sexual blackmail. The law on blackmail is an apparent paradox.[7] It declares that threatening to tell the truth is a crime. It raises the question of what is just: to pretend to be a moral person while leading a double life, or to gain by exposing another's guilty secrets? Because of the questions they raised, blackmail cases fascinated the American and British public for much of the nineteenth and twentieth centuries. During that time, blackmail trials revealed that one's sexual reputation—that vague entity—had, in an increasingly commercial age, a definite monetary value. And as middle-class notions of sexual respectability emerged, so in tandem did sexual blackmail.[8] Chronicling the emergence of this particularly parasitic form of crime casts a fresh light on the history of sexual assault, prostitution, divorce, abortion, and homosexuality and provides striking evidence that when morality was made the law's business it often became the criminal's business as well.[9]

Though other forms of larceny far outnumbered the instances of blackmail, it was blackmail that struck a nerve. Blackmail stories allowed a range of anxieties relating to the exposure of sexual secrets to be played out. Regarding privacy and secrecy as both precious and dangerous, the middle classes found such accounts hypnotically preoccupying. The propertied no sooner felt protected from crude and violent crimes than they were alarmed by more sophisticated assaults, such as fraud, embezzlement, forgery, and especially blackmail.[10] The nightmarish scenario of the exposure of a dangerous sexual secret haunted the anxious; it was a demon, which the court accounts, like the sensationalist novels and melodramatic films, attempted to exorcise. Yet, depending on the time and social context, blackmail stories resulted in different morals, produced different warnings, elaborated different myths, and came to different conclusions. They had a social role; they reflected and spoke to the interests of different communities.

6   A titillated public enjoyed blackmail stories because they revealed dangerous sexual secrets that remained otherwise hidden. Wealthy men felt themselves particularly at risk. In the eighteenth century English men were so alarmed by the thought of criminals extorting money by threatening to accuse innocent victims of sodomy—which at the time was a capital offense—that the government made the leveling of such charges a felony. In the nineteenth century men began to fear that even their heterosexual peccadilloes could put them at the mercy of a blackmailer. With the increasing centrality of family life, an unsullied sexual reputation increased in importance. Realistic middle-class males were well aware of the existence of a sexual double standard. Hypocrisy created fear of exposure, and the threat of exposure was accordingly criminalized. But the wealthy and the respectable were not the only victims. The homosexual man was the classic prey of extortionists, and by the twentieth century the woman in the public world also drew their attention.

Blackmail stories told in the courts and other such official forums served a repressive purpose, especially in major cities such as New York and London, where new forms of sexual identity appeared. As relationships between men and women shifted and sexual behavior altered, blackmail trials became a theatrical expression of the culture's preoccupation with the relationship of the private life to the public. The law on blackmail appeared at times to be one more defensive weapon used by the powerful to protect themselves. Blackmail accounts raised the specter of the young, the female, and the poor deviously plundering older, wealthy males. Official stories told about blackmail often had the apparent task of castigating some adventurers and thus deterring others. Reflecting a male perspective, these tales aimed to impress on society the necessity of respecting the power represented by age, gender, and wealth. Moreover, as some blackmail was a sort of private law enforcement, the establishment felt as much affronted by it as did the individual victim, and all the more intent on extirpating it.

The press appeared both to support and to undermine the courts' attempts at deflecting attention away from sexual improprieties. Journalists recognized the prurient appeal of a crime that broached the boundaries separating private and public, male and female, poor and wealthy, respectable and rough, and that revealed complicated and at times shocking relationships. Reporting blackmail allowed the press to indulge in a prurient presentation of transgressors for consumption by a purportedly respectable readership. Writers' occasional claims that decency prohibited full discussion of some cases fueled rather than dampened public interest. Scandalous trials allowed newspapers to expose the "problems" of abortion, adultery, and homosexuality and to depict subjects otherwise taboo. The justification was that readers were being warned of the dangers of urban life, thus allowing them to recognize the threat posed by the eavesdropping servant, the designing woman, and the overly attractive young man.

What newspaper readers actually thought of sexual blackmail is hard to determine. Each story contained layers of meaning that allowed varying interpretations. The evidence suggests that the public actively studied the evidence given in court and reported in the press.[11] The public wanted to see and hear what was considered so shocking. One of the reasons why it was fascinated by blackmail cases was that, despite the best intentions of the court, subversive rather than conservative readings of the facts were always possible. The result could destabilize rather than affirm the moral status quo. Trials allowed people to conceptualize a range of taboo behaviors and gave them insights into the ways in which both the rough and the respectable participated in such activities. Such cases were rarely the simple cases of robbery the prosecutor sought to present; they often demonstrated the intertwining of sexuality with race, class, and gender. They offered furtive glimpses into the private lives of the powerful, their secrets and shame. Judges presiding over blackmail trials reminded the public that new laws pertaining to divorce, age of consent, prostitution, abortion, and homosexuality had brought many sexual issues under public scrutiny. Blackmail cases revealed how difficult it was to split neatly the private from the public.

Blackmail trials were not only reported; they also shaped the public's notion of sexuality. Though judges and journalists might seek to turn blackmail cases to purposes of maintaining the boundaries of the status quo, the mere descriptions of the behavior that led up to the blackmail threat demonstrated how boundaries were broached and moralizing warnings flouted. In court abortionists or adulterers who had been victimized by blackmailers naturally had to go along with accounts that minimized their guilty activities, but what readers made of the information on where abortifacients were purchased or how affairs were conducted was not predetermined. And though cases of homosexual blackmail were presented by the press as a sign of the danger and degeneration of the "perverted," they were also evidence of the existence and resistance of a sexual minority. Sex scandals thus dramatically demonstrated the corrosive power information enjoyed in the modern world.

A well-managed trial was supposed to result in guilt punished and innocence protected.[12] The nature of the sexual blackmail trial—the fact that the victim had a "guilty secret"—often prevented such a satisfying conclusion from being achieved. Rather than silencing sexual subversives the court accounts led to the airing of embarrassing questions: Did a man who seduced a woman "owe" her anything? Why should homosexuality be criminalized? Should women be permitted to abort? Blackmail stories were the product of a culture going through important transformations in attitudes toward sex and gender. Society preferred to blame the eruption of blackmail on certain "dangerous" women and men rather than come to terms with the tension between the laws and the sexual practices that often provided temptation to unscrupulous individuals. In the Anglo-American world blackmail stories were employed to discuss and define what was moral and immoral, what was natural and what was perverted. These stories shocked, they educated, they entertained; by negotiating the parameters of what was acceptable and tolerated they helped redefine modern sexuality.

At times blackmail cases also had important legal ramifications, sparking calls in the early twentieth century for reform of the laws on age of consent, divorce, and breach of promise, and in the latter twentieth century of the laws on abortion and homosexuality. Certain cases can be seen as turning points. For example, fear of "gold diggers" in the 1930s led many American states to revoke laws—known as "heart balm statutes"—that provided compensation for the jilted. In the 1950s and 1960s British parliamentarians, claiming that the existing law encouraged the blackmailing of homosexuals, succeeded in the partial decriminalization of that sexual activity. Panic over a specific type of sexual blackmail often signaled the end of one era of sexual rights and the beginning of a new.[13]

In this book I compare the blackmail stories produced in the United States and England over two centuries. The two nations' legal systems were based on English common law, but their different legal developments led to publicity being given to different forms of blackmail. After 1925 English courts usually provided the victim with anonymity. Officials assumed that this policy would make victims of blackmail more likely to lay charges. Certainly English papers carried far more references to homosexual blackmail than did their American counterparts. In the United States, by contrast, the 9 Mann Act—aimed at ending interstate prostitution—led American papers more often to report cases of heterosexual males who were subjected to shakedowns by prostitutes' bullies. And because the names of United States blackmail victims were allowed to be published, the American evidence provides more detailed depictions of extortion practices. This book draws on the strengths of both English and American sources. Sexual blackmail stories were obviously not the only means employed by past generations to understand the changing cultural meanings of sexuality, but they played a unique and as yet unappreciated role in forcing both America and England to examine and redefine the relationships of sex, crime, and privacy.

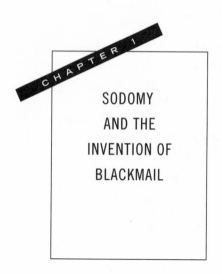

CHAPTER 1

SODOMY
AND THE
INVENTION OF
BLACKMAIL

In 1822 Robert Stewart, Viscount Castlereagh, Great Britain's foreign secretary and leader of the House of Commons, committed suicide by plunging a small knife into his throat. Rumor had it that he was driven to take his own life by blackmailers who were threatening to charge him with being a sodomite. His fate had been sealed when, according to one account, he had made the mistake of going to a brothel with someone he took to be a female prostitute.

> In a very short time he found to his horror that his companion was not a female, as he had supposed, but a youth dressed in female attire, and disguised to pass as female. He had no time for reflection or delay as to what course to take; the door of the room was forced open, a couple of villains rushed in, and accused him of being about to commit an act from which nature shrinks with horror; adding at the same time, that they knew perfectly well who he was. The purport of this accusation was palpable, and, unfortunately, in the intensity of the crisis, the Marquess lost his presence of mind and his courage. He adopted the course which they suggested, and gave them all the money he had about him to secure his immediate escape. This course was precisely what they had plotted to bring about; they had secured their victim; he was in their power; and they were resolved to let him know that their silence could only be obtained by full compliance with their extortionate demands.[1]

Whether or not this obviously melodramatic tale—written thirty years after the fact—was true is not all that important. The point is that nineteenth-century English gentlemen could envisage such a chilling, career-destroying scenario. 11

In both England and America attacks on one's sexual reputation had always been taken seriously. A woman called a whore could go to court to seek redress. Similarly, a man accused of being a thief, rascal, rogue, or cuckold might file suit. The community took such disputes seriously. Stigmatized individuals who were the victims of malicious libel could find themselves shunned, their work prospects destroyed, and their families marginalized. The courts regarded it as their duty to prevent or punish scandalous attacks on the innocent. The larger interests of the community were also at stake. By impressing on the public the importance of reputation—as manifested by the behavior deemed appropriate for one's class and gender—the authorities attempted to maintain social order and police sexual conduct. But the laws on libel and slander were designed to patrol only the boundaries of *public* speech.[2] The courts understood that individuals could be wounded by something untrue or maliciously said or published about them. It took some time for legislators to recognize that the respectable might regard *private,* as yet unpublished, information in the wrong hands as potentially even more disturbing and threatening.

To understand the origins of the law on blackmail under which women like Autumn Jackson would be prosecuted in the twentieth century it is necessary to begin by reviewing statutes that set out to protect eighteenth-century Englishmen from being accused of sodomy. The criminalization of blackmail was first used to deal with the specter of well-off men being plundered by so-called perverts, of the mysterious metropolis witnessing an unnatural mixing of the rough and the respectable, and of ruthless miscreants driving members of the social elite to murder or suicide. Sexual blackmail was first and foremost a symptom of a heightened concern with stigmatized homosexual acts. The crime and stories told about it were in short narrowly focused on one sort of sexual secret, and this linkage of homosexuality and blackmail was far more pronounced in England than in America. Only in the latter half of the nineteenth century, when the concern for sexual respectability was further ratcheted up, was the legal definition of blackmail extended to cover the exploitation of heterosexual secrets.

"Blackmail" originally had nothing to do with either reputation or the sending of letters. When the term was first used, in Tudor times, it referred to the extortion Scottish barons levied on farmers in the north of England. Scotland passed acts against blackmail in 1567 and 1587; the Tudors in 1601 sought to prevent the ransoming of subjects in border areas of Northumberland, Westmoreland, Cumberland, and Durham. The act made the demand for protection money, or "black mayle" ("mail" being the Anglo-Saxon word for tribute or rent), a capital crime. Right through the eighteenth century the word "blackmail" was simply used to describe protection money paid to robbers. In Sir Walter Scott's *Waverley* (1814) the hero does not understand the term. A lovely lassie explains that it is "a sort of protection-money that low-country gentlemen and heritors, lying near the Highlands, pay to some Highland chief, that he may neither do them harm himself, nor suffer it to be done to them by others; and then if your cattle are stole, you have only to send him word, and he will recover them; or it may be, he will drive away cows from some distant place, where he has a quarrel, and give them to you to make up your loss." In 1853 an English inspector of prisons would recall that in Scotland this "tax to robbers" was paid partly in oatmeal as a sort of feudal due.[3]

The next stage in the evolution of the concept of blackmail occurred in eighteenth-century England when the sending of menacing letters—that is, the power of a new, anonymous method of communication—caused disquiet. For example, in 1767 Sir Richard Betensen received a graphic, if grammatically flawed, depiction of what would happen if he did not remove his steward: "You may Look to Your House being sett on fire if Stones will not Burn You damned Sun of a hoare You shall have your throat cutt from Ear to Ear except You Lay £50 under the Second tree of Staple Nashes."[4] Written threats sent anonymously by ruffians were an innovation and, because their authors were harder to track down than those who made oral threats, all the more feared. Accordingly the English government's passing of the Waltham Black Act in 1722, aimed at bands of men in the countryside known as the "blacks," made it a felony to extort money or venison by the sending of threatening letters. Though the 1722 act was meant to be only a temporary measure, its provisions were extended through the course of the century. The statute, however, still represented property owners' fears of robbery and arson and not an individual man's worries about his reputation.[5] Eighteenth-century legislators, thinking of conflicts between poachers and gamekeepers, generally assumed that to be a true menace a letter had to contain threats of personal violence or attacks on property.

A second concern of the authorities was not the new medium of the letter, but the new message—the sort of menace a man might have to face. For most of the eighteenth century extortion by simple threat was not considered robbery. As the century progressed, however, judges began to extend the notion of "robbery" to include giving up property out of fear of being accused of a serious crime such as rape, buggery, or bestiality. In 1757 a statute specifically declared that sending a letter threatening to accuse a person of a serious crime with intent to extort money or valuables was a misdemeanor punishable by seven years in a penal colony. Potential victims most feared being accused of the "unnatural offense" of sodomy. This was a very serious crime, punishable by death; naturally enough an accusation so easily made and so difficult to disprove raised anxieties. Originally proof of penetration and emission were needed in both rape and sodomy trials; in practice the law was far less demanding.[6]

It says something about the eighteenth century that most men at the time regarded sodomy as a far more serious charge than rape. In earlier centuries powerful members of the male elite ran few risks in carrying on passionate affairs with other men. But in the early 1700s a new, middle-class model of domestic heterosexuality emerged, and Englishmen became increasingly concerned with maintaining a reputation of being attracted only to women. Historians have attributed this new sensitivity to the decline of an older sexual culture in which same-sex passions had not been as negatively viewed. In addition, the model of the "manly" Englishman may have been constructed to counter the "effeminate" French. Some have also suggested that the rise of evangelical religion was responsible for a new stress on decorum. Others have noted that an economic view of the world that lauded thrift and self-control necessarily spurred on men to assert their masculinity.[7] In this new cultural climate gender relations were redefined and sharply differentiated—men were to be active and women passive. A woman's honor was defined almost exclusively by her sexual respectability. She was enjoined to feign an ignorance of sex: "A woman without delicacy is a beast; a woman without the *appearance* of delicacy is a *monster*."[8] A healthy man, by contrast, was expected to provide public displays of his passionate interest in the opposite sex. He did not have to worry

13

that his respectability would be compromised by extramarital liaisons; indeed, the courts had difficulty in imagining that a man called a whoremonger had been libeled. What men did fear was being defamed as a sodomite or bugger.

The irony was that in the very years when reforming societies in England were seeking to marginalize and demonize effeminate males, London was home to an emerging homosexual subculture, with meeting places and social networks. Criminals were quick to exploit the situation. As early as the 1720s references were made to the organized blackmail of sodomites in London. In 1751 John Cather was tried and found guilty for conspiring "to procure money" by preferring an indictment for sodomy against Edward Walpole. Cather was sentenced to the pillory and a year's hard labor. In 1759, having heard Henry Morice's wife call him a buggerer, two men attempted to extort money from him. They were sentenced to three years' imprisonment and the pillory. Morice was a member of Parliament; the case accordingly highlighted the extent to which people in public positions were put at risk. In 1776 a discharged servant preferred a bill of indictment for criminal assault against Samuel Foote, one of the leading actors of the day.[9]

In the first half of the eighteenth century, the punishment for oral threats was relatively light. By the 1770s, however, the climate had changed, and false accusations of sodomy were punishable by death. In the case of the *King v. Thomas Jones,* the court heard from Mitchel Newman that in September 1775 he had accidentally touched Jones's breeches in the press of the crowd in the upper gallery at the Covent Garden Playhouse. After the play Jones claimed to be insulted and threatened to raise a mob. The terrified Newman gave him three guineas and twelve shillings to silence him. The next day Jones extorted a further £40. Finally in January 1776 Newman had had enough. He apprehended Jones and took him before Sir John Fielding, the famous Bow Street magistrate, who committed him to trial for highway robbery. "The prosecutor [Newman] swore, that at the time he parted with his money, he understood the threatened charge to be the imputation of sodomy; that he was so alarmed by the idea, that he had neither courage nor strength to call out for assistance; and that the violence with which the prisoner detained him in the street, had put him in fear for the safety of his person."[10] The jury found Jones guilty, but the case was reserved to determine if it was in fact a case of robbery. The judges meeting at Serjeants' Inn Hall concurred that when Jones first held Newman by the arm "a sufficient degree of force" had been employed to constitute the offense of robbery; accordingly, Jones in May 1776 was sentenced to death.

In 1779 the court heard that Charles Fielding, son of the earl of Denbigh, had been accosted in Soho Square by James Donnally, who demanded a present. When asked why, Donnally replied, *"You had better comply, or I will take you before a Magistrate, and accuse you of an attempt to commit an unnatural crime!"* Fielding gave him half a guinea. Two days later Donnally made a further demand. Fielding's claim was "that he was exceedingly alarmed at both times, and *under the alarm gave the money;* that he was not aware what were the consequences of such a charge, but apprehended that it might cost him his life." The judges again had to decide if this were a case of robbery. Citing the Thomas Jones case, Mr. Justice Willes delivered their decision: a robbery did not have to involve actual violence. "A reasonable *fear of danger,* caused by the exercise of *constructive violence,* is sufficient; and where such a terror is impressed upon the mind as does not leave the party a free agent, and in order to get rid of the terror he delivers his money, he may clearly be said to part with it *against his will . . .* What can operate more powerfully on the mind than a menace to do that, which, in its consequences, would blast the fairest fame, and ruin for ever the brightest character?"[11] In short, the court was stating that robbery could result from simple fear; Donnally, who had employed neither force nor violence, was found guilty, though apparently not executed.

In 1783 Daniel Hickman was tried for robbing John Miller of two guineas. Hickman, a guard at Saint James's Palace, after having spent an evening with Miller, had demanded money from him, saying, "I am come for satisfaction; you know what passed the other night; you are a *Sodomite;* and if you do not give me satisfaction, I will go and fetch a serjeant and a file of men, and take you before a Justice." Hickman seemed to know his law, because after taking the money he further stated, "Mind, I don't *demand* anything of you." Miller asserted that he gave the money not out of fear of violence but out of a concern for preserving his reputation. Hickman was convicted; but, as he had not exercised the force that Donnally had, the twelve judges had to consider if this also was robbery. In 1784 their decision was given by Mr. Justice Ashurst, who stated: "To most men the idea of losing their fame and reputation is equally, if not more terrific than the dread of personal injury . . . [A] threat to accuse a man of committing the greatest of all crimes, is, as in the present case, a sufficient force to constitute the crime of robbery by putting in fear."[12] In so exalting the importance of sexual practices the courts not only bolstered the norms of middle-class conduct and behavior, they also established the grounds for the ways in which blackmail would develop—as a potent way of leveling a tax on reputation.

Jeremy Bentham, the utilitarian philosopher, was one of the rare individuals to observe how the law against sodomy provided the criminal with "an instrument of extortion." In the notes prepared for an unpublished essay entitled "Paederasty" around 1785 he wrote:

> In England the severity of the punishment and what is supported by it, the moral antipathy to the offence, is frequently made use of as a means of extorting money. It is a most terrible weapon that a robber can take in hand; and a number of robberies that one hears of, which probably are much fewer than the ones which one does not hear of, are committed by this means. If a man has resolution and the incidental circumstances are favourable, he may stand the brunt and meet his accuser in the face of justice; but the dangers to reputation will at any rate be considerable. Men of timid natures have often been almost ruined in their fortunes ere they can summon up the resolution to commit their reputations to the hazard of a trial. A man's innocence can never be his security; knowing this it must be an undaunted man to whom it can give confidence; a well-seasoned perjurer will have finally the advantage over him. Whether a man be thought to have actually been guilty of this practice or only to be disposed to it, his reputation suffers equal ruin.[13]

As if to bear out Bentham's warnings, in the early nineteenth century James Cook, the owner of a pub where men made assignations, struck on a new form of extortion. He had a handbill printed letting "Peers, Footmen and Foot-soldiers" know he was producing a book in which—if they did not pay—their perverted passions would be depicted. Cook was jailed, but a friend repeated the menace in *Phoenix of Sodom, or the Vere Street Coterie* (1813).[14]

Sodomy continued to be considered an extremely grave charge right through the nineteenth century. Fifty sodomites were executed in England between 1805 and 1832. A repressive law created a climate in which blackmail would thrive, which in turn meant that to protect well-off men's reputations, judges had to bring about a major change in English law. They did so by extending the notion of robbery to cover giving up property out of fear of being accused of sodomy; but the felony of menacing a victim's reputation to extort money was at first narrowly restricted. Moreover one should not exaggerate the practical effects of these changes. The notion of "constructive robbery" was not greatly extended. Indeed in the early nineteenth century only a handful of blackmail cases went to court, though in 1829 the two men and a woman who had extorted over £100 by threatening to accuse a man of an "abominable offence" were reported by the press to be members of a gang of up to a dozen culprits. Until 1837 the crime of wielding such a menace was a capital offence. In February 1833, for example, William Thomas Attrell was sentenced to death for preferring an infamous charge against Mr. Pearsall of the India House. In December 1838 the court heard the case of James Norton, who had warned a clergyman, "If you do not assist me, I will say you took indecent liberties with me some time ago." In sentencing Norton to fifteen years' transportation the bench told the prisoner how lucky he was. If he had been found guilty of that crime a year earlier he would have been sentenced to death. Indulging in the melodramatic stereotypes of the time, the judge damned the lax age in which craven crimes flourished. "The robber on the highway who was bold and wicked enough to hold a pistol at the head of his fellow-man, and demanded his money or his life, was an innocent offender, compared with the cowardly assassin of honour and reputation, who sheltered by darkness and secrecy, would seek in cold blood to gratify his sordid views by wounding the peace and blasting the happiness of his terrified victim."[15] Incorporating bourgeois norms, the official blackmail story held that no crime was worse than an attack on reputation.

Thereafter sentences of fifteen years' penal servitude appear to have been the norm as punishment for such methods of extortion.[16] Such cases provide only a vague and not necessarily trustworthy account of London's homosexual subculture. On the one hand, the ruthless recognized how they could turn the law to their own advantage by entrapping the innocent; on the other hand, a man who was in fact guilty of an unnatural act that was brutally punished would naturally attempt to counter his accusers' story by claiming they were motivated by hopes of being bought off.

No one was executed in England for sodomy after 1836, but even after the criminal law reforms of 1861 the offense could still be punished by imprisonment from ten years to life. The 1885 Labouchère Amendment to the

17

18 Criminal Law Amendment Act, which more vaguely criminalized all "indecency between males," put far more men at risk of both prosecution and extortion. Common prostitutes could fall foul of vagrancy acts, but the law specifically decreed that men who prostituted themselves—unlike their female counterparts—were criminals. It was hardly surprising that some would move on to blackmail—they had little to lose and much to gain. The older law had targeted the specific act of buggery, but now homosexuals who would not have identified themselves with sodomites found themselves cast into the same camp.

Between 1885 and 1900 there was a surge in the reportage of attempts at blackmail, which in turn precipitated the emergence of the first blackmail stories told from the homosexual's point of view. The vagueness of the law made it, in the words of John Addington Symonds, an "incitement to false accusation." Some frightened victims, it was claimed, were driven either to kill their harassers or to commit suicide. An American writer cited one turn-of-the-century suicide note reported in the English press: "I have been for two years at the mercy of a rascal, without honour or pity, who has driven me now to my death. God help me! I cannot struggle any more, and my means to keep him at bay are gone. I prefer death to disgrace."[17]

Few writers of fiction could have been ignorant of homosexual blackmail, but only after 1885 did it begin to be depicted in novels and plays. In Robert Louis Stevenson's *Strange Case of Dr. Jekyll and Mr. Hyde* (1886) one character wonders—while passing Jekyll's laboratory—if the doctor might be the victim and Hyde the homosexual blackmailer. "Blackmail, I suppose; an honest man paying through the nose for some of the capers of his youth. Blackmail house is what I call the place with the door, in consequence." In *The Picture of Dorian Gray* (1890) Oscar Wilde has his hero threaten to expose a male friend's past. In 1893 Wilde and several anonymous homosexual writers produced *Teleny*, a pornographic work in which the hero receives a threatening letter: "To-day you are a man of spotless reputation; tomorrow, a single word uttered against you in the street by a hired ruffian, a paragraph in a ranting paper by one of the modern *bravi* of the press, and your fair name is blasted forever." References to homosexual blackmail were not supposed to appear in respectable fiction. André Raffalovich and John Gray used their play *The Blackmailers*, presented at the Prince of Wales Theater on June 7, 1894, to glamorize the relationship of a man of the world and his handsome young disciple. The *Times* tartly declared that it was "a sordid and repulsive picture of blackmailing practices carried out in society," adding that it was a work without precedent and hopefully without imitators.[18] What the paper failed to observe was that fictional depictions of homosexual blackmail—even when produced by homosexuals—only served to reinforce the public's notion that a variety of punishments awaited immoralists.

A study of late nineteenth-century press reports of homosexual blackmail suggests that the law continued to be concerned primarily with the victimization of well-off men with a reputation to worry about. One man, who was convicted of having menaced a doctor with a sodomy charge, was released from prison in 1888, having served a twenty-year term. Others who committed the same crime received life sentences. In 1886 an impoverished patient who threatened to accuse a Willesden surgeon of "an infamous offense" was sentenced to ten years in prison. "The crime was a very bad one when it was committed against any one," Mr. Justice Field stated, "but when it was committed against a medical man, whose whole life and fortune depended on a good character, especially for morality, such a charge might simply blast him for life."[19]

The official blackmail story was unabashedly constructed to defend the propertied, but the courts on occasion had to admit that the "better sort" might also themselves be blackmailers. In 1889 a dismissed schoolmaster in East Anglia sent a letter to the clergyman of the parish accusing him of "hellish and beastly practices," which he would report to the police if not paid £300. Perhaps the most brazen case of extortion came to court in December 1895. Having prepared the defense of a young Huddersfield man tried for homosexual offenses in 1894, the solicitor decided that, as the case had been so "unpleasant," he had not been paid enough. When the father of the young man refused to hand over an additional £150 the solicitor sent him a threatening letter. "We have in our possession at the present time a confession in G. W. Hirst's handwriting of indecent conduct with thirteen other lads other than those for offences against whom he has already been convicted, and your present conduct towards me now is ill-calculated to induce me to keep such information to ourselves." The father still refused to pay. He was "anxious to save what reputation his son had left, but he was not to be imposed upon." In describing the solicitor's letter as "scandalous," the judge sentenced him to twelve months in prison and suggested that he be dropped from the profession.[20]

The courts sought to protect the wealthy from the poor and men from boys. Judges distrusted poor children who claimed to have been abused and took an obvious delight in sentencing young men who attempted to extort a few pounds to up to ten years in prison. The police and the courts made it clear that homosexual blackmail stood out from other forms of extortion in that it was institutionalized with gangs of "blackmailing boys" working in specific areas of London. In 1889, for example, two men walking along Oxford Street were accosted by two youths who asked for a match. The youths then demanded money, presumably with a threat. They were sentenced to five years in prison. Not all blackmail victims were wealthy. In 1887 John Richardson proposed to a young man named Tibbut that they go to some public house or place of amusement. Richardson and a second man, thereupon claiming to be detectives, threatened that if Tibbut did not pay them £2 they would accuse him of indecent assault. They followed him until he pawned his watch. Both youths were sentenced to ten years' penal servitude. The same year George Gray and William Markham were tried for a series of extortions. The court heard that they had gone to the place of employment of the under butler of Earl Stanhope and threatened to charge the servant with an infamous offense. He handed over £3. The accused worked with a nineteen-year-old boy, who met both Thomas Treherne, a cook, and William Copeland, the butler of the Marquis of Bristol, in Hyde Park. Gray and Markham, pretending to be brothers of the boy, subsequently obtained ten shillings from Treherne and blackmailed Copeland for £40. In sentencing Gray and Markham, Mr. Justice Stephen made the remarkable assertion that they were the two worst men who had ever stood in the dock. "A man who used violence, who garroted people or used other similar cruelty, did almost nothing in comparison with a person who used this mode of torturing others in order to extort money from them."[21] He decreed they would serve their time on each charge consecutively, not concurrently, which resulted in the extraordinary sentences of twenty-nine years for Gray and twenty-four years for Markham.

Blackmail cases also provided the courts with an occasion to defend the prerogatives of the police. In sentencing three conspirators to five years' imprisonment in 1895, Mr. Justice Wright declared that blackmail was "one of the worst offenses known to the law."[22] What especially outraged such judges was the fact that in many homosexual blackmail cases the accused presented themselves as policeman or detectives, thereby bringing the law into disrepute. Judges did not, however, call for the reform of the criminal statutes that facilitated the blackmailing of homosexuals.

How did the trial accounts portray same-sex relations? The courts for the most part did not want to know if the blackmailers made up their stories or if the victims actually had engaged in homosexual practices. Most who committed "indecencies" would obviously have thought twice before going to the police. The same was true of men who had been simply robbed by male prostitutes. Sir Melville MacNaghten, chief of the Criminal Investigation Department of Scotland Yard, recalled that in the spring of 1897 the police stumbled across what he called a ring of "blackmailing boys" after a gentleman reluctantly reported that two youths he had met on the Embankment had stolen his fur coat. Victims who appeared to have engaged in same-sex activities put the courts in a potentially awkward position. On the one hand the law stated that the truth of the blackmailer's accusation in no way mitigated the offence. On the other hand the courts did not want to be seen as defending immoralists. The way out for the prosecution and judge was to assert that there were was no truth to the charge. One observer noted that on the continent trials were "managed" so that the victim would not incriminate himself. Similar attempts were made in England, but not all ambiguities were obliterated. In 1898 twenty-year-old Frank Simms, the "body servant" of a major in the militia, threatened to accuse his master of an "abominable crime" if not paid £50. "You can clear the country," wrote Simms, "for I swear I will do what I say, if only to ruin you." He was found guilty and sentenced to three years in prison, but it was brought out in court that the major admitted that he himself had had to resign from the militia and that he wrote to Simms as "My dear Frank." In 1899 a nineteen-year-old youth, claiming to be a policeman, threatened to charge a sixty-year-old man walking on the sands at Blackpool with having committed an "abominable crime." The victim immediately paid £1. The youth received £10 at a second meeting and went on to demand £100 at a third. The judge, in sentencing him to four years, noted that some "indecency" might have occurred but held that it did not justify such extortion. The courts were certainly heterosexist and homophobic, but the evidence suggests that their concern for maintaining propriety and protecting property could override their desire to root out indecency.[23] The heaviest sentences were levied on men who preyed on the servants of the rich. Such "pests" were warned that their harassing of gentlemen and their retainers would not be tolerated.

Given the English courts' concern to protect the reputations of elite males, it was all the more shocking for the public to learn in 1895 that the extortionists who had preyed on Oscar Wilde, the country's most successful playwright, would testify to his perverted sexual practices. Wilde had many brushes with extortionists, as did his young friend, the golden-haired Lord Alfred Douglas, to whom in 1892 Wilde humorously dedicated a copy of his poems

From Oscar
To the Gilt-Mailed
Boy
At Oxford
In the heat of June
Oscar Wilde[24]

Just as Castlereagh might have been an unintended casualty of England's sodomy law, Oscar Wilde was an accidental victim of the Labouchère Amendment. Gentlemen were not supposed to be charged with indecency between males; why Wilde's case ended so disastrously has never been satisfactorily explained. What is clear is that his sensational 1895 trials focused renewed attention on the issue of homosexual blackmail. At first not appreciating the gravity of the situation, he wittily described in court what is probably the most famous blackmail attempt in history. "He [Allen, the blackmailer] said, 'A very curious construction can be put on that letter.' I said in reply, 'Art is rarely intelligible to the criminal classes.' He said, 'A man has offered me sixty pounds for it.' I said to him, 'If you take my advice you will go to that man and sell my letter to him for sixty pounds. I myself have never received so large a sum for any prose work of that length; but I am glad to find that there is someone in England who considers a letter of mine worth sixty pounds.'"[25]

In his defense of Wilde (which he produced under a nom de plume), Lord Alfred Douglas claimed that Piccadilly harbored twenty to thirty blackmailers, "the very children of vice." Sir Edward Clarke, Wilde's counsel, protested that these criminals were appearing as witnesses: "This trial seems to be operating as an act of indemnity for all the blackmailers in London." Yet Clarke called Frederick Atkins to the stand to admit that he had been used by James Burton to extort money from a number of men. In 1891 Atkins had brought back a man from the Alhambra music hall, and

the landlady found them in bed together. She called the police, who arrested Burton and Atkins. Alfred Wood testified, "When I occupied rooms at 72 Regent Street, Chelsea, Charles Parker behaved indecently with a gen-   23
tleman in my bedroom. Allen, Charles Parker, and I obtained money from the gentleman, I got £175 out of a sum of £400 or £500."[26]

Wilde was strangely fascinated by the enormous risks run by these young men and perversely excited when he "feasted with panthers." Few others took the blackmailing of homosexuals as a joke. Henry James was panicked by Wilde's open sexuality and avoided writing publicly on the issue, but in his private letters he referred to Wilde as an "unclean beast." When Wilde went on trial James wrote to a friend about his horror at the appearance of the "little beasts of witnesses. What a nest of almost infant blackmailers." André Raffalovich, though homosexual himself, believed that Wilde's behavior simply confirmed the public's disgust for same-sex love. "The man of the world who addresses himself to one of these [boy prostitutes] knows the hazards and scarcely merits the pity he receives were one to imagine the consequences of his folly."[27] Sentenced to two years' hard labor, Wilde learned too late the consequences of his behavior. This brilliant writer's fall from grace impressed on the entire English-speaking world the lesson that same-sex relations led to blackmail, which in turn led to disaster.

The blackmail story in England from the mid-eighteenth to the mid-nineteenth century focused on the threat of the charge of sodomy. Such cases were not reported in the United States until the late 1890s. Although as early as the 1840s there were reports of male prostitutes in New York City, sodomy was rarely prosecuted in America. Historian Michael Lynch reviewed 75,000 New York indictments for the years 1796 to 1893 and found only thirty pertaining to sodomy. Though the vast majority of these were not consensual acts and in fact involved violence, only two resulted in guilty verdicts. A further indication of Americans' liberal view of the effete (and perhaps same-sex practices) was their ambiguous reaction to the western world's best known aesthete, Oscar Wilde. During his 1882 lecture tour of America, some took the opportunity to attack the "feminized" gilded youths who feted him, and the press on occasion disparaged the poet as a "Mary Ann" or a "Miss Nancy." Yet much of the criticism of Wilde took the form of friendly banter. The *National Police Gazette*, a crime and sporting tabloid founded in 1845, preferred to spend its time criticizing the hypocrisy of do-gooders and clergymen who opposed blood sports and music hall entertainments. Its report that a religious editor had in a railway sleeping car mistaken Wilde's legs for a woman's was telling. "The revulsion of feeling he [the religious editor] says was awful . . . We suspect the truth is that our religious editor got pretty badly sold on Oscar's legs and his talk about revulsion of feeling and all that moral guff is in the nature of what we tough worldlings in the other departments of this great journal would call a 'dead give-away.'" The tabloid assumed that Wilde was effeminate but proceeded to attack not the "great aesthete," but those who guiltily refused to admit that they found him physically attractive.[28]

In the 1880s the sexualization of identity appears to have been still in the process of taking place in the United States. By the time Oscar Wilde went on trial in 1895 for indecency it had begun to jell. In 1898 C. S. Clark told North Americans that they had their own "sinners of Oscar Wilde's type." He reported hearing from a bellboy of a large Toronto hotel how he had blackmailed a judge caught in an act of indecency. "This is one case only, but they are countless."[29] Boys all over the city knew of such goings-on.

A similar note of alarm was struck by the New York authorities at the time of the trials of William E. Hall for sodomy and extortion. Given "the disgusting and revolting character of the testimony," the judge in Hall's 1897 trial stated that neither spectators nor reporters would be allowed to attend. Hall was found guilty of extortion. His counsel in January 1898 successfully appealed, arguing that the enforced secrecy had rendered the trial unconstitutional. At a new trial in April 1900 the public finally learned that Hall and three fellow conspirators had accused a priest of sodomy. Hall and a man named MacIntyre on June 18, 1897, had caught Father Fidelis C. Oberholzer in a compromising position with a young man. The gang demanded $2,500 from Oberholzer; they immediately received $250 and a further $200 a few days later. Oberholzer, a weak old man, denied their charge and protested that he paid because of fear that their story would be published in the press. The court, in affirming Hall's conviction, noted that a judge did have the right in certain cases to exclude the public.[30]

The Hall trial was one of the few homosexual blackmail cases reported in the American press. Members of the homosexual subculture had a far better sense than did the general public of the extent of such practices. Henry Blake Fuller was unusual among American fiction writers in referring explicitly to homosexuality. In his short play *At Saint Judas'* (1896) a man is made so distraught by the idea of his best friend's marriage that he attempts to stop it by in effect "blackmailing" him with anonymous let- 25 ters.[31] Edward Prime Stevenson, an expatriate American who wrote under the name of Xavier Mayne, was more impassioned.

> Blackmailer!—the blackmailed!—tyrant and writhing victim! In all sorts of relations where human rashness, passion, folly, weakness, carelessness, sordid mercenariness or vengeance attack the individual, we meet this dark process. But nowhere else does blackmail operate with such terrible alertness as in the uranian [homosexual] world . . . No female blackmailer, however audacious and cruel, ever has shown herself quite so torturing in shattering nerves, happiness, fortune, courage, social quietude, and life as has the the methodical, homosexual blackmailing demon proved himself, time and again, the world round.[32]

With this dramatic salvo Stevenson began the last portion of *The Intersexes: A History of Simisexualism as a Problem in Social Life,* a book privately printed in Rome sometime after 1908. Drawing on his own experiences and the works of sex reformers such as Magnus Hirschfeld in Germany, Stevenson set out to demonstrate that the laws against homosexuality in Britain, the United States, and Northern Europe were a disaster. That society condemned some sexual desires as depraved and degenerate was bad enough. When it criminalized them, Stevenson argued, it armed the blackmailer.

Stevenson gave examples of American travelers victimized in Germany and Italy. Because adult same-sex relations were not criminalized in Italy, the country was a mecca for homosexuals. Nevertheless Stevenson provided accounts of the "social terrorizing" to which even in southern Europe men could be subjected. And tourists could find themselves pursued back to North America. Stevenson cited the case of an American banker who passed a pleasant few weeks with Vasco G. in Venice and with Nazzareno S. in Sorrento. To his horror, on his return to New York the American was contacted by a third man who threatened to expose the banker's activities. Over the course of two years he was bilked out of thousands of dollars.[33]

Stevenson lamented the ease with which men allowed themselves to be plundered. They were cowed by fear of scandal. Too often they lacked strength, courage, and some knowledge of the law. He optimistically assured his readers that the police and magistrates would be on their side. "Immediate recourse to legal help, to betake oneself to the nearest police-court, to call the nearest police-officer, to face down the blackmailer with rudest or calmest contempt and with counter-threats and action—these are not only the first defenses but often perfectly efficient ones."[34] Given the trap in which homosexuals found themselves, Stevenson claimed that it was not uncommon for some to murder their assailants; many more committed suicide.

In constructing his accounts Stevenson drew most of his examples from Europe. "In England and America [he explained] there are plenty of current cases, more or less of the same stamp. But in England and America the publication of legal or other proceedings that bear on so-called 'unnatural offences' is not encouraged by the press, nor often detailed as in Continental Europe." Yet while criticizing such prudery he worried about the noxious effect of the publicity given blackmail trials. "The unlucky fact has been observed that legal proceedings necessary for the rescue of some victim of blackmail on homosexual grounds (even cases in which blackmailers are punished) seem to do more harm than good toward obstructing this vile 'business.' They suggest to the mob the ease with which timid victims can be bled, and they teach the technique of blackmail."[35]

Reportage did indeed lead to copycat crimes. In the spring and summer of 1870 when the English papers were filled with accounts of the trial of two transvestites named Ernest Boulton and Frederick William Park, John Elliott, a twenty-two-year-old schoolteacher, wrote an acquaintance: "Unless you pay me by the 7th of June the doctor's expenses I have been put to, and also my solicitor's and others, amounting to 1£. 19s. 6d., I shall expose you and punish you in the same way as Boulton and Park will be. You have injured me, and I will be revenged." On the same page of the *Times* for May 8, 1895, which reported Oscar Wilde being released on bail, was the story of two men posing as detectives who tried to extort money from an Oxford Street hairdresser. A third man had accosted him coming out of a lavatory and then the others appeared and claimed that if not paid they would arrest him for "some Oscar Wilde business."[36] It was futile, if not counterproductive, argued Stevenson, to convict the individual extortionist while leaving in place the statutes that his imitators could exploit.

The first sex reformers took up this argument and pushed it to its logical conclusion. On the continent as early as 1869 Karl Heinrich Ulrichs had asked: "Whoever does his duty as a human being and state's citizen, who faithfully carries out the duties of his profession, should he, just because he is an urning [homosexual], be allowed by the turn of the hand of a scoun- 27 drel or some dumb boy to have his honor and personal happiness thrown aside?" In England this line of argument, which was to be so central to those calling for decriminalization of homosexuality, was taken up in the 1890s by Edward Carpenter and Havelock Ellis, who succeeded in making the Labouchère Amendment known as the "blackmailer's charter." The amendment had, according to Carpenter, "opened wider than ever before the door to a real, most serious social evil and crime—that of blackmailing." Oscar Wilde could be included in this group of polemicists because as his biographer has noted, "Puritanism, as Wilde never tired of showing, produces its viciousness as much as debauchery."[37]

Homosexual blackmail trials performed a variety of functions. They were used by the defenders of bourgeois respectability to depict the horrific fate of both the extortionist and the man who had been so incautious as to fall into his snare. In fin de siècle London and New York judges told men as well as women that they had to be wary of strangers, in particular young men. The press reported miscreants who threatened to charge men with "infamous crimes" and the courts dealt openly with accusations of sodomy, yet in generally asserting that the extortioner's threat was not only illegal but untrue, judges sought to make it known that they had no intention of protecting perverts. The courts and the press carefully tried to avoid using blackmail cases to explicitly discuss same-sex passions, while they implicitly warned the adventurous of the dangers of giving way to temptation. Interestingly enough, the court and press reports did not suggest that dangerous youths would necessarily appear effeminate; the stereotyped "homosexual" had not yet fully emerged. Yet because the accused included male prostitutes, the trials no doubt confirmed the popular notion of the homosexual as villainous blackmailer, not as the blackmailer's victim.

Despite the courts' efforts, an unintended outcome of these trials was to focus attention on homosexuality. Sexual blackmail trials dealt with daring issues that Victorian novelists could do no more than hint at. Victimization was made visible, and the existence and resistance of sexual outcasts were demonstrated. Some have argued that one effect of Oscar Wilde's trial was that the homosexual came to be seen as an older, decadent, upper-class male. The boys with whom he consorted were simply coded as immoral or mercenary. In most of the blackmail trials, however, a different story was told. The well-off victim was portrayed as naïve or foolish; the boys as perverse. This was a more satisfying account, as morality and property were lined up on one side and vice and poverty on the other. But whatever story was told, new sexual practices and relationships were acknowledged.

Blackmail stories broke the silence in which same-sex practices had been shrouded. "What is called blackmail in England," noted Havelock Ellis, "*chantage* in France, and *Erpressung* in Germany—in other words, the extortion of money by threats of exposing some real or fictitious offense— finds its chief field of activity in connection with homosexuality." The irony, as Ellis noted, was that an unexpected consequence of criminalizing certain forms of male sexual behavior was the spawning of a new form of crime. The magistracy, in Edward Carpenter's words, had "undertaken a censorship over private morals (entirely apart from social results) which is beyond its province, and which—even if it were its province—it could not possibly fulfill." Though the press and the courts sought as best they could to turn the trials of blackmailers to the purposes of boundary management, the mere descriptions of the behavior that led up to the extortion threat demonstrated how boundaries were broached and moralizing warnings flouted. In court the homosexual man who had been victimized by a blackmailer naturally had to go along with accounts that minimized his guilty activities, but what did readers make of the reports of how and where young men were picked up? Trial proceedings broadcast the very information that the blackmailer threatened to reveal. They introduced the general public to new social actors and sexual categories. Morris B. Kaplan has pointed out the authorities' caution in dealing with reports of the homosexual practices of elite males: "even the highest legal officials deliberated whether it might not be better to allow the guilty to go uncharged rather than publicize the commission of such acts."[38] Blackmail put in jeopardy this implicit policy of "don't ask, don't tell."

The most important effect of the blackmail trials associated with sodomy and homosexuality was that they familiarized the public with a frightening new scenario. Wretches who obtained incriminating information could destroy the reputations of the wealthy and the powerful. The first victims were accused of perverse sexual practices, but as standards of sexual propriety were raised in the nineteenth century it was possible to imagine that criminals would next turn on the respectable. The courts had for centuries reassured the latter that their good names were protected by the laws on libel and slander. The publicity given to the emergence of the black-mailer raised the horrific possibility that the pillaging of the propertied could be carried out by those who threatened not to tell hurtful lies, but obscene truths.

CHAPTER 2

THE MODERN
MANIA
FOR MORALITY

In 1797 Alexander Hamilton, the recently retired Secretary of the Treasury, printed a remarkable pamphlet. A journalist had accused him of being involved with John Reynolds in "pecuniary speculation." There was evidence that Hamilton had sent money to Reynolds, and some thought that the Secretary of the Treasury had in some way abused his position. Hamilton responded that they were wrong. "My real crime," he announced to a startled public, "is an amorous connection with his [Reynolds's] wife." To clear himself of what he called the more "serious stain" of corruption Hamilton spelled out in detail how the affair had commenced. In 1791, when he had visited her at her home to lend her money, she had made it clear that "other than pecuniary consolation would be acceptable." He could not resist. Though Hamilton claimed that he sought to disentangle himself from her embraces, "intercourse" with Mrs. Reynolds continued for over a year, with some of the encounters occurring in Hamilton's home when his own wife was away with the children. Looking back on his relationship with Marie Reynolds, Hamilton suspected that her husband had arranged matters "with the design to extort money from me." In the summer of 1792 John Reynolds, posing as the wounded spouse, did indeed begin to make demands for "forced loans." In his pamphlet Hamilton included examples of Reynolds's letters, complete with their grammatical errors and misspellings: "I should take it as a protickeler if you will Oblige me with a loane of about thirty dollars." "Under duress for fear of disclosure," Hamilton made a number of such payments, which amounted in all to around $2,000. When in 1792 hostile congressmen, including Senator James Monroe, wanted to know why the Secretary of the Treasury was consorting with a known scoundrel like Reynolds, Hamilton told them in confidence of the affair, and they agreed to keep silent. Nevertheless the story was passed from Monroe to Thomas Jefferson to the sensationalistic journalist who used it in 1797 to accuse Hamilton of corruption. In 1792 Hamilton had told three congressmen of his affair with Mrs. Reynolds; in 1797 he told the whole world.[1]

The Hamilton affair was America's first sex scandal. Two hundred years later, when President Clinton denied his relationship with Monica Lewinsky, conservative critics attempted to score points by asking why he had not demonstrated Hamilton's candor. They assumed that Hamilton had told the truth. But had he? Many at the time thought he was using the affair as a red herring. "His willingness to plead guilty to adultery," wrote Jefferson, "seems rather to have strengthened than weakened the suspicions that he was in truth guilty of speculation."[2] As our interest in this book is with sexual blackmail stories, whether or not the account Hamilton produced was true is largely irrelevant. The story Hamilton told is nevertheless important for two other reasons. First, he not only admitted that he had been carried away by his passions, he also provided a detailed account of where and when—even as he claimed that he wanted to spare his wife and family the knowledge of his "amorous connection." He did so because he regarded the charge of speculation as posing a far more serious threat to a politician's reputation than that of being an adulterer. Contemporaries who also had a weakness for the ladies, such as George Washington, Jefferson, and Aaron Burr, no doubt shared his view. The difference was that they understood that adultery was not the sort of thing one paraded in public. Second, although Hamilton presented himself as a victim of extortion he never thought of seeking a legal remedy. He knew that none existed. Eighteenth-century Americans—like their British cousins—assumed that if a man compromised himself in a heterosexual relationship he either had to face down his assailant or pay up. The courts would not protect him.

According to eighteenth-century English law, taking by simple threat was not robbery unless the perpetrator also accused the victim of a serious crime, such as rape, buggery, or bestiality. In practice the courts rarely recognized anything other than an accusation of sodomy as being so frightful and intimidating to the normal man as to justify his seeking the protection of the law. Only in the mid-nineteenth century do we begin to find evidence of individuals being convicted of threatening to reveal heterosexual improprieties. The fact that it took some time before the courts and the press would view a man accused of adultery or promiscuity as seriously defamed demonstrates that although a middle-class model of sexual respectability had been in the process of formation since the 1700s, it only crystallized in the 1800s. As an ever increasing percentage of the population began participating in the political process, the notion that men of every class could and should act as gentlemen—that is, manifest civility, manliness, and morality—became more popular. The idea that one's character, rather than one's birth, should determine the public esteem one enjoyed was logical enough. But when character was narrowly equated with sexual respectability the private acts of public men were subjected to unprecedented scrutiny. Only the rare observer noted that while the first generation of blackmailers had exploited the laws against sodomy, the second turned to their own purposes the stigma associated with sexual indiscretion.

Legally, the notion of heterosexual blackmail did not exist in the eighteenth century. This is made clear when one turns to the question of what happened to women who menaced men. According to the *Oxford English Dictionary* the adjective "designing" was first used to describe men; the term "designing woman" appears only to have emerged in the eighteenth century. The notion that the unscrupulous woman might employ her sexual wiles to extort from men illegitimate gains has of course a longer history. But women's attempts at extortion were not treated as crimes until the later nineteenth century. For example, in the 1740s Constantia Phillips (1709–1765) wrote a shocking autobiography modestly entitled *An Apology* (1748–49) as part of a campaign to blackmail her ex-lovers. They included Lord Chesterfield, the famous author, whom she claimed had made her his mistress when she was only thirteen. Nearing middle age, she let Chesterfield and her other wealthy ex-paramours know that in return for a life annuity she would omit from her memoirs any details they might find unpleasant. Of one ingrate who failed to pay she wrote, "It is evident that he loves his money above reputation." Phillips was a member of what historian Lawrence Stone describes as a "select army of pretty young ladies of good family and good breeding, but who lacked the money to make a respectable marriage." In the eighteenth century it was hardly surprising that

32

such an intelligent and enterprising young woman, facing the prospect of a life of poverty, opted to become the kept mistress of a series of wealthy men. Stone has painted a sympathetic portrayal of Phillips, pointing out that her ribald autobiography, though "certainly initially intended as blackmail," was also an attack on the sexual double standard of the time.[3]

Similarly astute was Mary Anne Clarke, the mistress of the Duke of York, who in 1809 threatened that, if not paid £10,000, she would produce her scurrilous *Recollections*, which would provide a detailed account of their sexual relationship. Harriet Wilson likewise announced in the 1820s that her forthcoming memoirs would name names. The veiled warning immediately threw George IV, as well as a large contingent of aristocrats, into a panic. The Duke of Wellington responded to Wilson's threat of embarrassing disclosures with the famous response "Publish and be damned!" Many of his colleagues were not so brave; Wilson purportedly extorted huge sums of money from her old flames.[4]

Many men would have liked to have silenced these women, but it could not be done through the courts because the women had not committed any crime. Indeed, in the latter decades of the eighteenth and the first decades of the nineteenth century such mercenary stratagems received a degree of support from a radical reading public imbued with the populist notion that the corruption of the upper classes should be exposed. This was a world in which only a hazy line separated blackmail from political exposé. As one historian has pointed out, this sort of literary extortion was, "if not respectable, then at least a tacitly accepted and widely practised political mode."[5] Women like Clarke and Wilson were able to demand hush money from ex-lovers without fear of prosecution.

The legality of such tactics was tested in 1844. Between 1839 and 1843 the son of the Bishop of Petersborough, a rector himself, was repeatedly hounded for money by a French "actress" whom he had first met in a London brothel. She threatened to make a series of charges against him, including "administering drugs to procure abortion." He paid the woman over £1,200 during the four-year period. When he finally refused to pay any more the woman descended on his village and described to him in minute detail how she would blacken his reputation:

Firstly I will go into your church on Easter Day and, reckoning from that evening, I will go into your village, from cottage to cottage, to inform them all of that which has passed. Afterwards I will go to the magistrate at Stamford, from clergyman to clergyman at Petersborough, to all the chapter, and to the bishop. I will take afterwards the names of all the bishops, and cause you to be inserted in all the newspapers; afterwards I will go to find the Archbishop of Canterbury, who, being equally instructed, and I will go again to London to the magistrates . . . I may not be more rich for it; but at least I shall be revenged for all that you have made me suffer.[6]

She was tried for demanding money with menaces, and there is no doubt that that is exactly what she had done. Yet her counsel successfully played the image of the "starving girl" against that of the promiscuous minister "clothed in purple," referred to the law's stipulation of "reasonable and probable cause," and won her acquittal "amidst loud and reiterated cheers." When the Libel Act of 1843 was debated in the House of Lords Sir James Graham had similarly suggested that it would be wrong to prosecute a girl who demanded money from her seducer with the threat of blackening his character. "Such a threat," he stated, "might be conducive to good order, morality, and just and proper feeling on the part of the person so injured."[7]

It should not be thought, however, that before 1844 men did not fear women's demands. The passage of a number of other laws in the nineteenth century explicitly shored up the sexual double standard. The Bastardy Clause in the Poor Law Act of 1834—which forbade an unwed mother from seeking an affiliation order to force the father to pay support—disarmed women who sought legal redress from their seducers. This change was the work of reformers relying on unsubstantiated reports that the old Poor Law gave women the ability to blackmail wealthy men into bearing responsibility for spurious offspring and had accordingly played a major part in promoting female promiscuity. The Poor Law commissioners asserted that the new regulations, which made unwed mothers solely responsible for their offspring, would both protect male honor and stimulate female virtue. The courts' suspicion of female demands was exploited by male defendants in rape trials claiming that they were being blackmailed. Any evidence offered that suggested that the victim had requested or been paid compensation could result in her being condemned as a prostitute, blackmailer, or "designing woman."[8]

The best-known example of legal support of the sexual double standard came with the 1857 Matrimonial Causes Act, which made divorce available to the middle classes. The act stipulated that while a wife's adultery provided sufficient grounds for divorce, simple adultery by a husband—unless it was accompanied by cruelty or desertion—did not. The law offered men 35 a degree of protection from the exposure of a liaison that was denied women. Neither partner was offered an easy way out of an unhappy marriage. Subsequent legislation created the office of the Queen's Proctor—dubbed the "Official Peeping Tom"—who could annul a divorce if he discovered a man and a wife had colluded.[9]

The Contagious Diseases Acts, enforced between 1861 and 1883 and having as their purported aim the elimination of venereal disease, called for the medical investigation of only poor prostitutes, not their clients. The authorities always suspected prostitutes of extortion, and the proponents of the acts argued that the policing of prostitution would not only protect men's health, it would also counter such criminal practices as the "badger game," in which the male customer was suddenly confronted by the prostitute's bully, claiming to be her indignant spouse and demanding reparation.[10]

Opinion was divided on the law on breach of promise cases, which could be pursued by jilted women whose marriage prospects had been blighted by the refusal of their prospective mates to commit themselves. A number of these suits were undertaken by raped women who felt they had no other option than to marry the men who had assaulted them; when the men refused, the women then turned to the courts. Breach of promise suits thus were utilized for the moral purposes of legitimating a relationship, but many legal commentators condemned the women who brought them as mercenary and the process as a legal form of blackmail.[11]

Nineteenth-century English society was characterized by men who on the one hand maintained a sexual double standard while on the other paraded a chivalrous concern for the weaker sex. The Select Committee of the House of Lords that prepared the 1843 Libel Act spent much of its time imagining how the law could protect women from blackmail. "I will suppose the case of a woman who, early in life, when a girl of sixteen, in Cornwall, has a bastard child," mused one member. "She is then reclaimed, and becomes a respectable person; removes herself to another part of the country, and when she is the mother of a family, to make the case stronger, some man with whom she has refused to lie shall then say, 'If you do not, I shall publish your shame, by letting that be known what happened in

Cornwall.'" Or "Take the case," suggested another, "of a woman of character, who had to defend herself against imputations, which however successfully rebutted, would leave a stain on her character forever." A colleague declared himself revolted by the notion of "dragging [even] one woman before the public gaze." Robert Peel, the prime minister, conjured up the image of a newspaper threatening to publish something about the marriage of a woman "of the greatest delicacy."[12] That such examples were mentioned was curious, not just because of the prospect of elite men being overly anxious about the well-being of poor, provincial women, but because almost every reported blackmail case involved a *male* victim. These politicians were not so much responding to the plight of their female constituents as indulging in the pleasing fantasy of honorable men such as themselves coming to the defense of besieged womanhood.

When in the nineteenth century English judges began to extend the notion of "demanding money by menaces" and envisaged the need to protect the sexual reputation not just of those accused of being sodomites but of every person whose reputation was at risk, men were the main beneficiaries. The government appreciated that in a society increasingly peopled on the one hand by professional men whose reputation was their chief asset and on the other hand by journalists seeking to sniff out indiscretions, steps had to be taken to prevent mercenary invasions of privacy. The first step was the Libel Act of 1843, which stated that those who "shall publish or threaten to publish any libel upon any other person, or shall directly or indirectly threaten to publish it, or shall directly or indirectly propose to abstain from printing or publishing, of any matter or thing touching any other person, with intent to extort any money or security for money, or any valuable thing shall be guilty of a misdemeanour and liable to three years' imprisonment."[13]

The man who threatened to expose William Gladstone's dealings with prostitutes was prosecuted under the Libel Act of 1843. Gladstone, a future Liberal prime minister, had the politically dangerous habit of attempting to rescue streetwalkers. Coming across the politician in Leicester Square in conversation with a prostitute, a man by the name of William Wilson threatened that unless he were given a government post he would write to the *Morning Herald* of Gladstone "being in company with the woman for an improper and immoral purpose." Gladstone immediately handed Wilson over to the police. The trial account demonstrated that the idea of heterosexual blackmail was in 1853 still regarded as something new. "It was," the judge noted, "only very recently that such a proceeding was made to amount to a distinct substantive offence." He sentenced Wilson to a mere 37 twelve months in a house of correction as his was neither a premeditated act nor "part of a system put into practice to obtain a guilty livelihood." Nevertheless the bench felt obliged to assert that blackmail was "a form of robbery the most fatal not only to the general interest of society, but to the peace of those, including their family, upon whom the attack was made."[14] Blackmail by threat to one's sexual reputation in the middle of the nineteenth century was just emerging as a crime, still only treated as a misdemeanor, and clearly not regarded as serious as extortion by threat of violence, damage to property, or accusation of an infamous crime such as sodomy.

The first important legal reference to a woman being blackmailed occurred in *Regina v. Hamilton* (1843). George William Hamilton threatened Miss Jessie Hopper that unless paid he would tell her father, brother, and friends and notify the *Satirist* newspaper that she had been at a brothel with an officer. Hamilton then wrote her father, an architect, stating that the daughter was to be subpoenaed as a witness in a trial of the brothel, which he claimed she had frequently visited. Hamilton was prosecuted, found guilty, and sentenced to fourteen years' transportation. His counsel protested that the woman neither testified nor denied the accused's charge. Her evidence was not necessary, responded Mr. Justice Rolfe; that is, the truth of Hamilton's charge was immaterial. The judge's point was that the accused did not have a "reasonable and probable cause" to demand the money. The judge also stated that Hamilton's threat "was very nearly as bad as those charges of a most dreadful character against the other sex."[15] That is, by the mid-nineteenth century some judges regarded accusing a woman of immorality as almost on a par with accusing a man of being a sodomite.

What constituted blackmail was slowly clarified. A variety of menaces, both written and oral, were consolidated in the Larceny Act of 1861. Section 44 of one of the law's statutes held that "whosoever shall send, deliver, utter, or directly or indirectly cause to be received, knowing the contents thereof, any letter or writing, demanding of any person with menaces, and without any reasonable or probable cause, any property, chattel, money, valuable security, or other valuable thing, shall be guilty of a felony." Section 45 dealt with demanding property by force or threat; section 46 made the menace of accusing one of any serious crime a felony; and section 47 included the menace of accusing of "infamous" crimes a felony.

38   The issue of what was "reasonable or probable cause" was tested in an 1867 case when John Chalmers was tried for demanding money from a draper whom Chalmers claimed had seduced his wife. Defense counsel argued that the accused honestly believed he had the right to make his demand; the Court of Criminal Appeal, responding that there were no grounds on which such a belief in a right to compensation could be based, confirmed Chalmers's conviction. But the draper clearly had not seduced the wife; if he had, would Chalmers have had "reasonable" cause? In many trials judges told the jury that they had to determine whether the blackmailer's charge were true. In 1861 John Whitlock, a solicitor's clerk, blackmailed the Reverend John Armstrong for the rape of Armstrong's nineteen-year-old maid. Whitlock threatened to go to the police but gave the minister time "to offer any adequate monetary compensation to the poor thing whose life-long prospects you have so cruelly blighted." "To blast the character of a minister of the Gospel," thundered the prosecution at the trial, "was worse than death." In this case the judge interpreted "reasonable and probable cause" to mean that if the rape had occurred compensation could have been rightfully demanded and an acquittal would be necessary. The trial focused on the purported rape, not on the subsequent threat.[16] In short, the law was still primarily intent on punishing the leveling of *false* threats and only slowly came round to punishing those who threatened to reveal the truth.

Only in the 1890s did the English law on heterosexual blackmail become fully formed. In 1895 a farm laborer by the name of Tomlinson was, as the courts quaintly put it, caught in his employer's stable "in the commission of an act of immorality" with a maid, Kate Youde. John Thomas Morgan, the employer and apparently also a paramour of Kate, dismissed Tomlinson, who sometime afterward retaliated by sending Morgan a letter demanding money with the threat "if I do not get it on or before Tuesday morning I shall let Mrs. Morgan and your friends know of your doings with [Kate Youde]." Tomlinson was found guilty of demanding money with menaces, but the case was sent on to the Queen's Bench Division to determine if indeed a simple threat to reputation was covered by section 44 of the Larceny Act of 1861. Tomlinson's defense counsel argued that only a direct "menace or threat" to property or person was covered by the law.

The fact that so few cases of heterosexual blackmail in England were reported prior to the 1890s appeared to bear out the contention that the courts assumed that only the threat of either violence or the accusation of a 39 heinous crime such as sodomy would intimidate the average man. But in confirming Tomlinson's guilt, Lord Russell declared that the threat to expose a man's relationships with his maid was considered "much more serious than many cases of injury to person or property."[17] An "accusation of misconduct" leveled at a "reasonable man" could "deprive him of his volition and put a compulsion on him to act as he would not otherwise." Noting that some blackmail victims might not have "average firmness," Mr. Justice Willis called for an even more liberal interpretation of the act. English judges at the turn of the twentieth century were declaring that as the value of sexual reputation had increased in importance, the greater the protection the law owed to it. The case of Tomlinson thus made clear that a "menace" did not have to be either the threat of personal violence or an accusation of having committed a crime. A menace of exposing simple sexual misconduct was sufficient. The definition of "menace" was given a much wider meaning. Judges by the 1890s were viewing as extortionate "any menacing action or language, the influence of which no man of ordinary firmness or strength of mind can reasonably be expected to resist."[18]

It was also in 1895 that Oscar Wilde presented *An Ideal Husband*, in which Mrs. Cheveley, an extortionist, informs her prey that if he does not pay he will be ruined:

> Remember to what a point your Puritanism in England has brought you. In old days nobody pretended to be better than his neighbours. In fact, to be a bit better than one's neighbours was considered excessively vulgar and middle class. Nowadays, with our modern mania for morality, everyone has to pose as a paragon of purity, incorruptibility, and all the other seven deadly virtues—and what is the result? You all go over like ninepins—one after the other. Not a year passes in England without someone disappearing. Scandals used to lend charm, or at least interest, to a man—now they crush him.[19]

As Wilde and the Tomlinson case indicate, the modern notion of heterosexual blackmail was a product of the late Victorian period. What a literary critic says of the importance of scandal in fiction applies to that of blackmail in life as well: "At a moment when distinctions between private and public life are increasingly scrutinized . . . and in which private subjectivity is consolidating around a core of sexual identity, scandals about sex come to be the characteristic type of the genre."[20] Regarding privacy and secrecy as both precious and dangerous, the middle classes found blackmail cases captivating.

In 1871 a representative of the Prince of Wales, the future Edward VII, paid the brother of an Italian courtesan for the return of incriminating letters. The prince was reported to be "strongly opposed to B. [the courtesan's brother] appearing before any tribunal (police or otherwise) as the case would then immediately get about." In 1914 the countess of Warwick, yet another ex-mistress of Edward VII, attempted to use the threat of publishing her batch of his love letters to win the financial support of the royal family. Dreading a scandal, the government employed the Defense of the Realm Act—passed in 1914 to deal with threats to national security—to remove from the public record all accounts of the legal action used to counter her demands.[21] As fascinating as such high-profile blackmailing attempts are, they are of limited value. To gauge the social responses to extortion it is necessary to examine cases that came to public notice. Court accounts, press reports, and fictional depictions not only inform us about the ways in which a particular type of crime was carried out, they also demonstrate how society used blackmail reports to debate and make some sense of changing sexualities.

Not until the late nineteenth century did criminal courts assume the task of defending the respectable from those who sought to exploit their victims' sexual past. The law made it clear that legislators took very seriously the idea that as the result of a minor transgression—perhaps in his youth—a rich man could be plundered by a lower-class ruffian or a "designing woman."[22] Protection was seen as particularly necessary for upwardly mobile professional men, who took great pride in an unspotted reputation while having to live in a world of divorce courts, private investigators, and newspaper reporters all seeking to ferret out sexual secrets.

In the forensic literature mention of blackmail was usually followed by the assertion that women and girls, claiming to have been sexually assaulted, commonly preyed on men. Railway compartments, which threw the sexes together, were decried by the nervous as a dangerous space in which a designing female might accuse a naïve male of assault. A legal text reported that a woman seated herself opposite a businessman and said, "'I want a five pound note.' 'What do you mean?' said the astonished passenger. 'You have taken liberties with me,' and at once she proceeded to let her hair down and disordered her dress [and threatened to call a policeman] . . . Seeing that this evidence would be very formidable he preferred submission to a police court and paid her demand." Women frequently made false 41 rape accusations as part of blackmail conspiracies, claimed A. S. Taylor. In *A Manual of Medical Jurisprudence* he estimated that doctors could expect to hear twelve false claims for every true one. Medical experts rebuffed even reports of child abuse as usually no more than crude attempts orchestrated by mothers and girls to blackmail innocent men. Accordingly, the journal *Truth* warned in 1885 that the proposal of raising the age of consent to sixteen would place men further at risk and could not be construed as improving public morality: "The Bill now before the House of Lords would be more correctly described as a measure for facilitating every sort of extortion and blackmail." Convinced that at least 95 percent of girls fifteen and under who claimed to have been assaulted made up their stories, Lawson Tait, a leading gynecologist, opined that it was "an open question as to whether it would not have been far better that many of these children, and the mothers and women concerned with them, aiding, abetting and originating their vile sins . . . had been prostitutes openly plying for hire in the market place than have been the vile conspirators and blackmailers that many of them, the great bulk of them proved to be."[23] Tait claimed to have uncovered twenty cases of deliberate blackmail in Birmingham alone. Strangely enough, he could give no details.

In literature one noted a shift away from the early nineteenth-century tragic tale of the "kept" or "fallen" woman. By the 1890s the emergence of the New Woman, a respectable female with an enlightened view of sexuality, was a sign that the old paradigm was breaking down. The cultural shift could be detected in the popularization of the vampire theme in the 1890s, which exploited the notion of men being dragged down by women (hence the term "vamp"). Actresses in particular, if not suspected of being actual prostitutes, were at best regarded as using their clothes and looks to ensnare men. In Arthur Pinero's *The Second Mrs. Tanqueray,* first performed in 1893, one of the male characters says of a woman with a past that she "was a lady who would have been, perhaps has been, described in the reports of the Police or the Divorce Court as an actress." A world that publicly adulated the helpless, passive female was all the more perturbed by the idea of the sexually aggressive and calculating woman.[24]

Despite such alarmists, however, a perusal of the London *Times* indicates that in the late nineteenth century cases of blackmail based on claims of assault were rarely prosecuted or even reported. In 1895 thirty-seven-year-old Agnes Royce was charged with blackmailing her doctor. He had attended her for a "painful malady peculiar to her sex." The paper said little else except that she threatened to claim that he had assaulted her. The doctor had at some stage given her money, but he eventually went to the police. The authorities found the case embarrassing inasmuch as both the doctor and the patient were from the same class. It was ultimately resolved by the court's attributing the woman's accusation to her "hysterical condition" and releasing her into her father's custody. When the accused was from a lower class, however, the punishment was far harsher. Mr. Justice Day, famous for the enthusiasm with which he sent off prisoners to hard labor and floggings, in 1888 sentenced a woman to twelve years' penal servitude for having falsely accused a grocer's manager of criminally assaulting her.[25] These were both unusual cases in that men were far more likely to be blackmailed by other men than by women.

The courts were happiest when it could be proved that the extortionist's accusation was obviously false. James Slater in 1895 ambitiously claimed to be the illegitimate son of a member of Parliament. Slater was only fourteen years younger than the man he asserted was his father, but he threatened that, if not compensated, he would broadcast the guilty relationship in the columns of tabloids such as *Truth* and *Reynold's Weekly*. The indefatigable Slater concluded his early letters to the MP "Your affectionate son" and later, when rebuffed, "Your determined son." He was ultimately convicted and sentenced to eighteen months in prison. In 1885 an apparently mad Englishman living in Vienna threatened Prime Minister Gladstone that if he did not pay £300 he would be accused of "infamous crimes." The culprit also wrote to a number of newly marrieds—whose names he drew from the newspapers—threatening to accuse them of "misconduct before marriage." In 1897 Florence Stansfield was prosecuted for sending demanding letters to Earl Carrington whom she claimed had "visited" her. At trial she pleaded that she had mistaken Carrington for another man. When it came out that she had sent such letters to other peers she was found guilty. Well-publicized divorces naturally drew extortionists' interests. In 1886 a nineteen-year-old youth, hearing of Lord Colin Campbell's divorce proceedings, attempted to extort money from him. Campbell was willing to see it as a "joke," and the youth was released on his own recognizances. Maitland Morland, a sixty-five-year-old Oxford tutor, brazenly sought to compromise a number of wealthy men by pretending to be a young woman willing to sell her sexual favors. Those to whom he wrote suggestive letters in 1891 included Lord Hothfield, Lord Ormathwaite, and the Earls of Lindsey, Carnarvon, and Aylesford. At the same time Morland's wife, Ruth, 43 wrote to Earl Russell—then embroiled in a messy divorce—to demand £100 in return for letters that she claimed were proof of their adulterous affair. The journalist-politician Henry Labouchère exposed the Maitland Morland hoax in *Truth* in August 1891. Though not a penny had been exchanged, the judge was so affronted by Morland's hounding of members of the elite that he sentenced him to twelve years in prison.[26] As Morland claimed to have written all the letters, his wife walked free.

Though some charges were false, blackmail trials did turn up evidence of real sexual improprieties. Servants and employees with knowledge of household secrets posed an obvious threat. In 1885 the gamekeeper of Lord Clifden was sentenced to five years' imprisonment for blackmailing the peer. The nature of the threat was discreetly not specified. In 1890 the wife of a dismissed coachman sent a letter to his ex-employer in Kensington warning that if she were not given money she would "disclose certain matters [which she had learnt from the cook] to his wife." Oscar Wilde tapped into such bourgeois fears when he had a character in *The Picture of Dorian Gray* state, "It was a horrible thing to have a spy in one's house. He had heard of rich men who had been blackmailed all their lives by some servant who had read a letter, or overheard a conversation, or picked up a card with an address, or found beneath a pillow a withered flower or a shred of crumpled lace."[27]

Blackmail trials led to old sexual relationships being unearthed. In 1895 Geoffrey Perkins, having discovered that an Exeter College undergraduate, the son of a clergyman, had impregnated a young woman, tried to extort £1,000 from the student's father. Perkins, who pretended at times to be an attorney and a policeman, went so far as to threaten to notify the Archbishop of Canterbury. Outraged by such predatory attacks on a Christian minister, the judge sentenced Perkins to ten years in prison. In 1898 the court heard that an actress in 1867 had had an affair with the Marquis of Worcester. He thought he had bought her off in 1869 with £250, but three decades later she was making new demands. Also in 1898 a Sheffield solicitor paid £250 to silence a man who accused him of bigamy.[28]

In some of these cases the courts advanced a script in which the blackmailer's accusation was depicted as either false or delusional. In others the courts defended the sexual double standard to the extent that they reassured men that though they had an affair or had sired an illegitimate child the law would protect them from extortionists. At the same time the sort of punishment convicted blackmailers received depended not simply—as the law stipulated—on what they had done, but why. Sentences were savage for mercenary men like Perkins and Morland, who sought to use knowledge of other men's sexual peccadilloes. But when a woman was tried under the Libel Act for blackmailing a vicar, the court was more sympathetic. Her defense was that in spending two nights at her temperance hotel with a maid, he had injured the reputation of her business. In a confusing fashion the judge tried to spell out the freedom he felt he had in interpreting the law. He instructed the jury that the truth of the accusation was both not at issue and that it was "also to a certain extent relevant."[29] In the end, it was clearly because the vicar admitted to having seduced the maid fourteen years previously that the accused was found not guilty.

Judges were especially likely to parade their chivalry in their handling of women who sought some compensation for past affairs. As with "crimes of passion," in the right circumstances society would accept that a woman might have been pushed to private justice by the inadequacy of public remedies. At the same time judges pointed to the evidence that some men had been bilked out of money by blackmailers to warn others to spurn sexual temptation. Such cautionary accounts were taken up by medical and religious writers. A contributor to the *Lancet* claimed: "It is difficult to prove the prevalence of blackmail for obvious reasons, but it is known to be a means of livelihood for many persons in London and elsewhere who are never convicted, and we believe it to be an important source of income to most of those persons who carry on businesses connected with sexual vice, such as, for example, and not to exhaust the list, indecent exhibitions, the sale of alleged cures for defective virility, and so-called massage establishments." The White Cross League distributed pamphlets in which it warned young men that quacks preyed on fear of sexual weaknesses and disorders in hopes of bilking or blackmailing their customers.[30]

What of the woman as blackmail victim? In 1891 John Smith threatened Euphemia Williams that he would tell his own wife of their affair. "I now, although repulsive to my feelings, ask you for the last time to make it worth my while to leave this part of the world . . . If you wont bring or send to me a sufficient sum to last me a while, and to leave the country, I must communicate, first with my wife, who will at once make you a party to a divorce suit, which would cost you at least £50, and I must make all that past known to Mr. W., all your relatives, and Doggy acquaintances." In sentencing Smith to five years for his cowardly act, the presiding judge stated that 45 whether adultery occurred was immaterial, as "a man has no right if he had illicit intercourse with a woman to trade upon the fact and make it the means of enforcing demands of money."[31]

English women in fact could only expect the full support of the law if they were chaste. Moralists were fond of noting that though much was asked of males, chastity was the only virtue looked for in females. "Husbands and fathers generally expect but one virtue to adorn the character of women," declared a minister in a sermon lamenting sexual immorality. The laws on seduction and abduction were passed with such views in mind. A special Slander of Women Act came into effect in 1891, which held that a woman did not have to prove special damage in suing those who might have imputed to her unchastity or adultery.[32] Why were nineteenth-century women not likely to be blackmailed for sexual indiscretions? Two reasons suggest themselves. First, subjected so much more to family surveillance, women simply could not be as promiscuous as men; second, being much less wealthy, they were less prone to attract the attention of blackmailers. As a result, judges could, without fear of undermining public morality, indulge the odd woman whose indiscretions had left her open to menace.

Across the Atlantic in the United States, it was only in the 1870s that heterosexual blackmail emerged as a preoccupation of public commentators. A New York paper declared that no crime except perhaps kidnapping was so cowardly: "If there is a crime viler, baser, more anti-social than . . . blackmailing, . . . it is the crime that has been committed in Philadelphia . . . blood-mailing." The press reported that in June 1874 two "colored boys" delivered to the Honorable Fernando Wood in Washington, D.C., a threatening letter from Samuel B. Murdoch, which read: "Sir, I am satisfied as to your guilt. I have one reason for not shooting you. I will settle for $50,000, you to take the woman and keep her. The alternative—I will empty seven chambers of a Colt revolver into you on the first opportunity. Answer immediately in writing to messenger. If you do not comply with these terms I will publish you in all the New York papers and write to your wife." In its report of the case the *New York Times* noted that it was of special interest because the defense argued that such a threat to reputation was not recognized in the United States as an indictable offense. The district attorney countered that such threats had in fact been established as indictable fifteen years earlier in a Delaware court. In October Murdoch was found guilty and sentenced to three years in prison.[33]

There appear to be no reports of heterosexual blackmail trials going to court in the United States in the first half of the nineteenth century. Only in the 1870s did the blackmail story suddenly blossom in America. Blackmail statutes varied by state. Some demanded completion of the extortion; others criminalized simply the attempt. The states enumerated threats to person, to property, and to reputation. Section 519 of the California penal code, for example, passed in 1872 (amended in 1933 and 1976), dealt with fear used to extort by the threat to use violence, to accuse of a crime, to expose or to impute to the victim or the victim's family any deformity, disgrace, or crime or to expose any secret affecting victim or family. A "good faith" defense was not allowed, just as in England there was no "just cause." When in 1888 in New York a blackmailer appealed his conviction, arguing that the letters he sent threatening to reveal that his victim had sex with a woman were too vague to constitute a menace, the court ruled that the law did not insist on the demand being precise.[34] The court was similarly rigid when in 1890 in Pekin, Indiana, William Motsinger was found guilty of blackmail for sending the following letter to James Barnet:

> Mr. Barnet
> Sir
> You can come up and settle with me for the way you talked to my wife, or go to court, just as you like. I will tell it all over the country. It is a note [sic] that a woman can't go to a milk without being insulted. Come up right away.
> Yours,
> William Motsinger
> If you will pay what I think is right I won't say anything about it to any body. $10 will do.

Barnet, Motsinger argued, had only been asked to make amends for propositioning his wife. He asserted that he had not—as the law stipulated—accused Barnet of immoral conduct or attempted to disgrace or subject him to the ridicule and contempt of society. Nevertheless the court affirmed Motsinger's conviction, stating that the ambiguity of a letter did not offer its sender protection.[35]

In the United States the first references to heterosexual blackmail had be- 47 gun to appear in the 1860s. They primarily reflected a discovery by those worried over the rise of urban anonymity of the "social counterfeits" and confidence men who lurked in large cities. Such villains posed a threat to what a professional man most treasured: his reputation. Also dangerous were sex radicals and proponents of free love, who condemned the sexual hypocrisy of the middle class, and journalists on the lookout for juicy stories. The most sensational sex scandal of the century took place in 1875 when Henry Ward Beecher, the nation's leading minister, was tried for having committed adultery with the wife of his best friend, Theodore Tilton. Victoria Woodhull, free-lover and spiritualist, had exposed Beecher four years earlier by informing the New York press that she knew "a public teacher of eminence, who lives in concubinage with the wife of another public teacher of almost equal eminence. All three concur in denouncing offenses against morality." The Beecher-Tilton trial impressed on the American public the devastating impact of the uncovering of sexual secrets. Those who threatened to exploit them had to be silenced. Woodhull was, of course, not a blackmailer; but Anthony Comstock, the puritanical "Secret Agent of the Post Office," used her sensational disclosures to have her convicted on obscenity and slander charges. The message appeared to be that those who revealed vice were worse than those who engaged in it.[36]

As in England the courts in America took some time before they discriminated between a threat to one's reputation and a threat to one's person. Many of the first American descriptions of blackmail—unlike the English—included references to the brandishing of weapons. In 1867 a Dr. Alexander and his wife were charged in Eugene, Oregon, with extorting money from a Dr. Renfrew. Mrs. Alexander sent a note asking Renfrew to visit her. Her husband hid in a closet, reported the *Oregon State Journal*, "to 'bag' his game." When Renfrew was about to leave he was confronted by a revolver-toting Alexander, who forced him to sign a note for $2,000 payable the next day. In 1874 the New York police arrested Mrs. Annie M. Baker for blackmailing Mr. J. B. Johnson. In her letters Baker threatened to tell her husband that Johnson had insulted her in the train from Washington. The chief threat appeared to be that of the violence that would be unleashed by her spouse if she were not paid $50,000. That same year the press reported

48   the case of a Philadelphia woman who lured a doctor to her room. Her husband then appeared with a pistol, threatening to kill the physician unless he signed a confession of improper conduct. In the ensuing scuffle the victim was shot in the leg, which had to be amputated.[37]

Unlike England, the reported blackmail cases in America were overwhelmingly heterosexual in nature and frequently involved the use of firearms. The *New York Times*'s first reference to sexual blackmail occurred in February 1872, when the police charged George A. Banks of Boston with attempting to extort money from William L. Lutz for criminal conduct with Banks's daughter. The usual scenario in such cases was for a man to

For much of the nineteenth century American commentators assumed that a blackmail attempt would involve threats to person as well as to reputation. (From "The Result of Following a Street Walker," James McCabe, *Lights and Shadows of New York Life,* Philadelphia: National Publishing Co., 1872.)

find himself the victim of a shakedown. In March 1872 James Bell threatened Thomas Crawford that he had letters, which would be revealed to Crawford's wife, showing that Crawford kept a woman in an apartment. The threat was a ploy on Bell's part—or so he claimed—to force payment of a debt. A man identifying himself as Henry Boyle of the *New York World* in November that same year threatened Thomas Brown, owner of the Pavonia Ferry, that he had evidence of Brown's frequenting houses of "ill fame." When the two met at Delmonico's Restaurant to settle up, the police arrested "Boyle," who proved to be Charles S. Bogart. The press reported that a banker and a broker had also been victimized by the same individual.[38]

Blackmailers often pretended to be the police. In 1875 a man representing himself as a detective attempted to blackmail a man with information pertaining to the latter's son. In 1883 the *National Police Gazette* claimed that criminals were seeking to compromise men with women in Lover's Walk in Central Park. The paper later complained that real Central Park policemen, instead of cracking down on such criminals, were themselves blackmailing respectable couples.[39]

Although most blackmailers in both America and England were men, the blackmail stories constructed in United States fixated on the threat posed by unscrupulous females. In "Love Is Not Enough," a piece of fiction that appeared in *Harper's Monthly Magazine* in 1884, a female charity patient was portrayed as transforming herself into a "virago" and threatening a doctor with a malpractice suit. His wife ultimately dealt with the "blackmailing vixen." As early as March 1872 the *New York Times* ran an editorial entitled "Female Blackmailers" in which it applauded the Reverend Dr. Carter, who had had arrested a woman who attempted to victimize him. "Few persons," the paper editorialized, "have any idea of the extent to which the female practitioners of this act of blackmailing victimize timid and nervous men. Not only do they persecute clergymen, whom they find their easiest prey, but the physician and merchant are also made to contribute to their shameful gains." Women lay in wait and then made a false claim. They were always believed. The victim feared loss of reputation. Paying only encouraged such women; and Carter, the paper asserted, had carried out his Christian duty in prosecuting. In a subsequent letter to the editor one man agreed that thousands of men were "being bled." It did not matter if they had violated the "laws of chastity"; that was merely a fault, whereas blackmail was a crime.[40]

Another writer of letters to the *New York Times* in 1872 complained that women had become so rapacious that men needed the help of lawyers. Yet
50   not long after this letter was printed, the press was fulminating that many lawyers were in fact aiding female extortionists in carefully navigating the fine line between legitimate negotiation and extortion. In 1877 Mr. Aeneas Yamada, a Japanese-born lawyer, and a law student were charged with blackmail after agreeing to accept $200 to stop the prosecution of Daniel O'Connell for an indecent assault on Mary Coyle. In 1887 Andrew J. Wightman, the lawyer representing Mary Thatcher, reportedly told her seducer that he had the option of either paying or having his misdeeds made public. The New York court declared that the attorney, in attempting to obtain money by accusing a man of making pregnant an unmarried woman, was guilty of extortion. Lawyers could get into trouble by compounding a felony—that is, seeking compensation for a crime rather than reporting it to the police. After W. N. Crane apparently assaulted a fifteen-year-old girl, Joseph D. Hart launched both criminal and civil proceedings against Crane. Hart had the story of the assault planted in the press and the alarmed Crane settled for $2,500, half of which was kept by Hart. The court, in disbarring Hart, stated that lawyers were acting unethically in threatening criminal proceedings in order to extort settlements.[41]

In the 1880s stories of the avaricious female blackmailer became a staple of the *National Police Gazette*, which played up both the sexual power of the predatory, working-class femme fatale and the gullibility of men. "The Blackmailer and His Prey" formed part of the paper's 1881 series "The Man Traps of New York":

> Few persons have any conception of the extent to which blackmailing is carried on in this metropolis, or of the bold and unscrupulous operators who have reaped rich harvests from timid and conscience-stricken men, who, in an evil hour, may have committed some indiscretion, an exposure of which would bring ruin and misery to themselves and their families. The blackmailer is the meanest, vilest, and most treacherous, enterprising, intelligent, and patient of the *chevalier de industrie* class. Their ways are dark and they seldom strike without accomplishing their end.[42]

After this melodramatic introduction highlighting the mysteries of city life, the author explained the operations of blackmail gangs. The underlying assumption was that the victim would be a man. Mercenary women played the central role in such plots, abetted by male accomplices. The victim's lack of courage was presented as essential to the villains' success.

Yet the *National Police Gazette* used the blackmail story in a variety of 51 ways. Priding itself on its racy character, the paper in 1896 regarded it as a joke that a man who attempted to rescue prostitutes would become himself the victim of a "badger game." As a resolute opponent of religious hypocrisy the sporting paper was happy to cite as another victim "a pillar in one

The popular press played up the notion that professional men—particularly ministers—whose reputations were their most precious asset had the most to lose in being sexually compromised. (From "Almost Trapped: An Episcopal Minister in New York Just Misses Becoming the Victim of a Horrible and Scandalous Blackmailing Racket," *National Police Gazette*, Sept. 18, 1886.)

of the most aristocratic up-town churches." It also reported on wealthy businessmen who purportedly paid up to $55,000 in hush money and social frauds who were driven to suicide. The tabloid warned its readership that "first class hotels" were the hunting ground of the female blackmailer. "She either secures temporary quarters through references, some of which are obtained by compulsion from influential victims, or manages to gain free access to the parlor through other influences." In pointing out that the modern large hotel provided a site for a dangerous mixing of the sexes, the *Gazette* reminded its readership that hotel managers were for decades obliged to police (sometimes with their own detectives) the morality of their clientele. The criminals' plan usually involved a "fascinating" woman, who would allow herself to be seduced by some "susceptible gentleman." An accomplice posing as the woman's husband would then show up, threatening a messy divorce and possible violence. To prevent the courts and the press from broadcasting his shame, the victim would pay off the man, perhaps never realizing the swindle that had been perpetrated.[43]

On the other side of the country in 1899 a California court dealt with such a typical shakedown. Elsie Williams and a Mr. Azhderian were convicted of threatening to reveal the adultery of W. A. Melville in order to extort $2,000 from him. Section 518 of the California penal code stated that force or fear had to predominate for such a demand to be construed as extortion. The defense argued that Melville had several motives for paying. Nevertheless the accused were convicted, perhaps because Azhderian reportedly said that he was building a home for Williams and other women "so that when we leave the Paragon [Melville's farm] we can go there. Then I will bring business men out there and we will get them full of wine and afterward blackmail them." The Irish-born woman known as Chicago May provided a first-person account of carrying out such shakedowns in the 1890s. "I caught them all," she gloated, "University Professors, ministers, priests, gamblers, country yokels, sports, 'gentlefolk,' and visiting grandees from foreign parts." Although the public had no way of gauging the truth of the story of her life of crime, it is clear that they were fascinated by the possibility of role reversal when "weak" women like May used photos, letters, and breach of promise suits to extort money from "powerful" males.[44]

Commentators employed a variety of blackmail stories to force their readers to review the complicated state of marriage laws in late nineteenth-century America. Divorce was difficult to obtain, especially for a woman, as a court would generally not regard a husband's affairs with servants, prostitutes, or slaves as constituting adultery. Unwary men were warned that they could become embroiled in suits for seduction, alienation of affection, criminal conversation, breach of promise, and bigamy. A man who sought to extort money from Albany, New York, bureaucrats in 1874 included the charge that one had a bogus marriage. In 1875 showman P. T. Barnum obtained a warrant for the arrest of J. H. Meller, who ran the *Bridgeport Lance.* Meller mistakenly believed that he had information proving that Barnum had married another man's wife and was threatening if not paid to make the story part of "newspaper tattle."[45]

In January 1882 Louis S. Ward was arrested in New York for demanding $1,000 in return for keeping silent about a man's having married a sixteen-year-old girl without her parents' consent. Later that May, under the title "Whispers of Scandal," the *National Police Gazette* reported that Lieutenant Governor Tabor of Colorado had been blackmailed for having had an affair. When in 1894 Senator Stewart of Nevada was cited in a divorce case he claimed it was part of a badger game. The press also reported some breach of promise suits as possible cases of blackmail, such as the 1894 case against the son of the vice-commodore of the New York yacht club, who was pursued by a young woman he had impregnated.[46]

Wealthy families learned to use blackmail charges to beat off interlopers. In 1893 at the age of twenty-four Lillian A. Ashley moved to California with the sixty-five-year-old Elias J. Baldwin, who claimed to be divorced. He talked of adopting her at one time; later they completed an "informal marriage." Baldwin, who made his first million providing the bricks for the construction of Alcatraz prison, moved on to successful real estate and mining speculations. On his death in 1909 he left a huge estate. When Beatrice Anita Baldwin, his daughter by Lillian Ashley, sought her share, his family successfully argued that she should receive nothing as her mother was simply a blackmailer and had never been legally married to Baldwin.[47]

The question of blackmail also arose in rape and sexual assault cases. In 1877 three men and a woman were charged with conspiring to accuse Dr. Howard F. Damon with the "seduction and procuring of abortion of Miss Adie E. Ward, a school teacher." The papers described the doctor as an excitable and sensitive man who had been badgered by the gang for three months. He had left Boston but was convinced by his friends to return and fight the accusation. Earlier the same year the court had declared in-

sane the woman who attempted to extort money from a General Paxton of
Vermont with a claim of indecent assault. In 1884 an Illinois appeal court
ruled that the unfortunately named Permolia Slutz had "purely for blackmail" charged Nathaniel J. Austine with rape. In 1899 an Indiana court
ruled that a Stella Cooper and her male accomplice were guilty of blackmailing Everett Sheeks. They had demanded $500 to keep secret his pur-
ported rape of Cooper. Depending on one's sex, each of these accounts
could be interpreted differently. Even the male tabloids recognized that a
man accused of sexual assault would naturally claim that he was being
blackmailed. Under the title "Villainy or Blackmail?" the *National Police
Gazette* in 1879 reported the story of a woman who stated that the doctor
who had raped her warned her that her account would not be believed in
court. She quoted him as saying, "I am a reputable man and if you say anything everybody will believe you are blackmailing me, and will set you
down as a lewd woman."[48]

The power of the sexual double standard was reflected in the courts' regarding a married woman's loss of chastity as far more serious than a
man's. The middle classes' ideology of domesticity and their lauding of
companionate marriage were accompanied by the imposing of restraint
and decorum on women. One indication of the success of process was that
in America, as in England, only a few "respectable" women appeared in the
press as blackmail victims. In 1878 the *National Police Gazette* reported that
a clerk first seduced his employer's wife and then threatened to expose the
affair if she did not pay for his silence. In 1888 the clerk of a Lake George,
New York, hotel demanded $250 for the letters sent by a married woman to
her paramour. In an unusual 1882 case an Ohio man blackmailed a wealthy
widow who had sent him love letters by having his wife threaten the
woman with an alienation of affection suit. As it was assumed that no jury
could ever imagine that a man would be the passive rather than the active
partner in a seduction, such suits aimed at women were customarily dismissed.[49]

When well-off women were victimized it was sometimes because they
acted as protectors of men. In 1873 the *New York Times* reported that Joseph McLaughlin came to tell Mrs. Cecilia Slater that a former servant girl
of hers had had an abortion. The girl was now about to marry and needed
money to buy furniture. "Mrs. Slater said, 'Do you want me to give you

$25?' 'Well, yes,' said McLaughlin, 'I think I can avoid exposure for $25.'"[50] Mrs. Slater had told the police that McLaughlin had been making demands on her. Detectives, having hidden themselves in her home, overheard the conversation and arrested the young man. The press did not explain whom the blackmailer was threatening to expose. Was it Mrs. Slater's husband? Her son? Obviously it could not have been her.

The American press reported that even more humbly situated women were on occasion victimized. In 1877 men pretending to be detectives attempted to extort money from the proprietor of a "disreputable house." Prostitutes always had to fear the demands of the police or those who pretended to be in a position of authority. Given its interest in women who appeared on the stage—the *National Police Gazette*'s pages were filled with illustrations of chorus girls as well as sports heroes—it was not surprising to find that it was also sympathetic to victimized showgirls. Claques, it claimed, demanded money for applauding certain performers. Actresses' love letters, it asserted, were stolen by agents in order to compromise them. One of the tabloid's cartoons showed an actress holding such a villain upside down and shaking from him the incriminating notes.[51]

Victorian novelists anticipated judges and journalists in recognizing early on the dramatic appeal of stories of blackmail conspiracies. Given the age's preoccupation with protecting family privacy, writers of nineteenth-century romances, mysteries, and melodramas drew on the public's fascination with sexual secrets and mysterious demands. The nineteenth-century novel almost by definition dealt with the unraveling of secrets, the notion being that what was secret was the real, the most important, and possibly the most dangerous truth.[52] The phrase "skeleton in the closet [or cupboard]" meaning "a secret source of shame or pain to a family or person" was, according to the *Oxford English Dictionary*, brought into literary use in the 1840s. Whose secrets would criminals most likely exploit? Though men—enjoying greater wealth—would be the extortionists' most obvious blackmail targets, Victorian writers were more given to portray women as victims.

In cautionary novels about blackmail, writers warned women that just one slip made them susceptible to attack. In Edgar Allan Poe's "The Purloined Letter" (1845) a government minister steals an incriminating letter from a woman of high station. Detective Auguste Dupin knows that to divulge its contents would "bring into question the honor of a personage of the most exalted station; and this fact gives the holder of the document an ascendancy over the illustrious personage whose honor and peace are so jeopardized." Nathaniel Hawthorne's *The Scarlet Letter* (1849) presented Roger Chillingworth as a blackmailer of sorts who uses the secret of Reverend Arthur Dimmesdale's adultery to torment him and Hester Prynne. In

56

Commentators assumed that actresses, having ventured into the public world, would naturally draw the attention of extortionists. (From "An Actress's Love Letters: How a New York Artiste Dropped to Her Agent's Game, Got Her Letters Back from Him and Avoided a Scandal," *National Police Gazette,* Nov. 4, 1882.)

Charles Dickens's *Bleak House* (1853) Lady Dedlock is threatened with blackmail when Mr. Tulkinghorn discovers she has visited the lodgings of an old lover. Fortunately Tulkinghorn is killed off by a maid.[53]

Several sensational novels of the 1860s, in using a blackmailer's threat to reveal a woman's unintentional bigamy, found a moralizing way to titillate readers with the notion of a proper female's unintentionally having two spouses. Authors crafted such books to exploit the public's preoccupation with the legal complications of marriage and the hundreds of bigamy cases that went to court. In Mary Elizabeth Braddon's *Aurora Floyd* (1862) the heroine is blackmailed by her first husband after she discovers he did not die as she supposed and thus her second marriage is bigamous. He uses the threat of "a nice bit of gossip for the newspapers" to demand money. When he is found dead the wife is the obvious suspect. In *No Name* (1863) Wilkie Collins has Mrs. Vanstone paying the scoundrelly Captain Wragge to keep silent because he knows that she is not legally married.[54]

The blackmailed-woman theme lent itself to comedy as well. Decadent poet Algernon Charles Swinburne wrote a salacious play, meant for a small coterie of friends, entitled *La Soeur de la reine*, in which Queen Victoria is blackmailed by Lord John Russell, her supposed ex-lover. Victoria's secrets—at least in Swinburne's fertile imagination—were many. Her sister, the play's title character, is a prostitute. Having been debauched by Wordsworth, the Queen becomes addicted to "nameless practices." Her courtiers include the Duchess of Fuckingstone, Miss Sarah Butterbottom, the Marchiness of Mausprick, and Miss Molly Poke. Ironically Swinburne was himself a victim of blackmail of a sort. In the 1870s George Redway, a bookseller, came into possession of some of Swinburne's sadistic flagellation fantasies. Redway made the poet an offer he could not refuse. As his biographer noted, "They would be returned in exchange for the copyright of one of Swinburne's more respectable works. It was not, technically, blackmail since Redway had bought the manuscripts and they were in his possession. In moral terms, however, Swinburne's indiscretion had laid him open to the blackmailer's art."[55]

When novelists portrayed men being blackmailed little was said of their sexual foibles. The theme of a threatened inheritance was central to Anthony Trollope's *Castle Richmond* (1860), in which Mollett attempts in some mysterious way to extort money from Sir Thomas Fitzgerald. The blackmailer is described as a bloodsucker. "Mr. Prendergast knew that such

57

leeches as Mr. Mollett never leave the skin as long as there is a drop of blood left within the veins." In Trollope's *John Caldigate* (1877) the hero's alleged first wife threatens to go to court and charge him with bigamy. If he does not pay her off the story will be circulated in the newspapers. His brother-in-law protests, "'There can be no circumstances—' and as he spoke he dashed his hand down upon the table—'no circumstances in which a man should allow money to be extorted from him by a threat.'" Caldigate knows that paying will not bring peace, but he gives the money anyway. In George Eliot's *Middlemarch* (1872) Nicholas Bulstrode is blackmailed by Raffles, whom he has paid to keep quiet about a lost stepdaughter. Bulstrode's dream of Raffles's death comes to pass when Bulstrode allows his nurse to give the ill Raffles more opium than necessary.[56]

In general, however, writers of late nineteenth-century fiction continued to portray women as the blackmailer's preferred prey. Continental imports were especially daring. *Le Dossier No. 113* by Emile Gaboriau, who has been called the father of French detective fiction, appeared in its English translations as *File No. 113* and later as *The Blackmailers*. The story revolved around letters that revealed a woman had had a child by her lover. In Fortuné du Boisgobey's *The Red Lottery Ticket* (1887), a young man finds letters that if exposed by a blackmailer could result in a husband's murder of his adulterous wife. Ibsen ended *Hedda Gabler* (1890) with the lead character's realizing that Brack has her in his power. He knows that she is in possession of the gun with which her ex-lover killed himself. The police have found it.

HEDDA: What will they do?
BRACK: Try to trace the owner.
HEDDA: D'you think they will succeed?
BRACK: (bending over her, whispering) No, Hedda Gabler. So long as I hold my tongue.
HEDDA: You . . . own me.
BRACK: (low whisper) Hedda darling, trust me. I won't take advantage.
HEDDA: I'm still in your power. At your disposal. A slave.

Hedda feels she has no option other than to commit suicide. Life copied art in 1898 when Eleanor Marx, daughter of Karl Marx, took her own life. Though contemptuous of bourgeois morality, she was said to have paid Edward Aveling, her common-law husband, hush money to keep secret either his having "bigamously" married an actress or the fact that Karl Marx had fathered by his maid an illegitimate child. Another popular fictional outcome was for the victim to kill the blackmailer. In "Charles Augustus 59 Milverton" (1899) Sherlock Holmes and Dr. Watson stand by while a lady finishes off her tormentor: "I will free the world of a poisonous thing. Take that, you hound, and that!—and that!—and that!—and that!"[57]

The fin de siècle's most penetrating analysis of the risks run by the straying wife was provided by Edith Wharton in *The House of Mirth* (1905). Having accidentally acquired the love letters of Mrs. Dorset, Lily Bart—a beautiful but poor and unmarried woman of twenty-nine—ponders their destructive potential.

> The letter before her was short, but its few words, which had leapt into her brain before she was conscious of reading them, told a long history—a history over which, for the last four years, the friends of the writer had smiled and shrugged, viewing it merely as one of the countless "good situations" of the mundane comedy. Now the other side presented itself to Lily, the volcanic nether side of the surface over which conjecture and innuendo glide so lightly till the first fissure turns their whisper into a shriek. Lily knew that there is nothing society resents so much as having given its protection to those who have not known to profit by it: it is for having betrayed its connivance that the body social punishes the offender who is found out. And in this case there was no doubt of the issue. The code of Lily's world decreed that a woman's husband should be the only judge of her conduct; she was technically above suspicion while she had the shelter of his approval, or even of his indifference. But with a man of George Dorset's temper there could be no thought of condonation—the possessor of his wife's letters could overthrow with a touch the whole structure of her existence.[58]

If the public accepted these fictional accounts as accurate, it had a skewed notion of extortion. The evidence suggests that in reality men (and in particular homosexual men) were far more likely to be blackmailed than women; thus, it appears that a form of displacement took place when writers chose to portray women as the extortionists' prey. According to the melodramatic script the woman's natural role was that of victim; writers such as Eliot presented their Bulstrodes, but the unimaginative found the idea of portraying a cowering male victim too distasteful to contemplate.[59]

Moreover, respectable Victorian women were not supposed to be sexual creatures. A cultural shift had occurred from the eighteenth century's cynical portrayal of the mistress to the nineteenth century's tragic tale of the "kept" or "fallen" woman and the many paintings of the period that portrayed the adulteress. Women could be depicted as being at risk, falling, and being redeemed. There was no male equivalent.[60] Yet the press did report that men were accused of infamous crimes. If the vast majority of Victorian novelists did not refer to homosexual blackmail it could not be because they were unaware of its existence. Rather the stories they chose to tell were crafted to ignore same-sex attractions and shore up heterosexuality. Yet these writers anticipated and provoked the late nineteenth-century middle-class fear that every family harbored some dangerous secret. Fact and fiction at times interacted. The press kept the general public informed on how blackmail was practiced, and judges often grumbled that books and newspapers contributed to the number of such crimes. In 1826 London police found a copy of the *Memoirs of Harriet Wilson* in the possession of a fifteen-year-old boy whom they charged at the Bow Street court with having menaced a gentleman. The magistrate ordered the book thrown into the fire.[61]

Blackmail trials, like novels, were also scripted. In both America and England they played out in a theatrical fashion a central fin de siècle cultural preoccupation: the relationship of the private to the public. Though the courts sought to blame blackmail on certain "dangerous" types of women and men, trials frequently led to the airing of embarrassing questions and the revelation of the victim's own "guilty secrets". Judges—with their extravagant claims that blackmail was worse than murder—therefore attempted to construct a narrative that magnified the evil of the extortionist in order to deflect attention away from the dangerous sexual secrets he or she threatened to expose.

In spite of the authorities' attempts to construct stories to defend respectability and social stability, blackmail trials proved to be the site of gender, sexual, and social conflict. The nineteenth-century bourgeoisie claimed to regard sex as a taboo topic; but, as Michel Foucault has pointed out, they were fixated on its surveillance, regulation, and control. This was an age that sought to split the public and the private, spoke of "secret parts" and "secret diseases," and produced such works as *My Secret Life* (1880). The preoccupation with patrolling the boundaries of sexual respectability was a symptom of the central role sexuality had come to play in western culture as an indicator of individual worth.

In the later 1800s the courts raised the warning that an individual did 61 not have to commit a heinous crime in order to draw the attention of extortionists; a minor sexual transgression would suffice. Middle-class moralists attempted to distinguish pure and healthy sexual relationships from secret, dirty, and dangerous ones and in so doing created new boundaries, which were inevitably broken. The emerging popular press was, extortionists pointed out, only too eager to broadcast supposed transgressions. The fear of the reaction of others no doubt outweighed any personal guilt or shame experienced by the exposed individual. An individual's public reputation had always been important, but for mobile and ambitious members of the nineteenth-century middle classes, sexual respectability rivaled financial probity and eclipsed (in theory at least) every other virtue.

In increasingly open and democratic societies claims to sexual respectability served to locate one in the class hierarchy and so were embraced as essential props by those worried over the prospect of a downward social and economic slide. Particularly in the congested urban centers where classes and genders mixed, where the possibility of a confusion of identities arose with prostitutes taken for respectable women and male "pests" as gentlemen, it was essential that one's character be defended. Moreover in an age that rigidly demarcated the genders, men had to prove their masculinity and women their femininity. An elaborate vocabulary—of male "bounders" and "fallen" women—was used to describe those who had lost respectability or concealed a shady past. The perceptive noted that as reputation became ever more crucial, young men would instruct themselves on what rules to follow so they could "pass" for respectable. But as the gap between appearance and reality grew, the explosive potential of sexual secrets necessarily increased. Indeed as the social importance of sexual respectability was inflated, so too—as journalists, detectives, and blackmailers quickly recognized—was the spectacle of its public loss.

The story is told that Samuel D. Warren, annoyed by the intrusive accounts the Boston newspapers gave of his daughter's wedding, was enraged to discover that he had no legal right "to be let alone." He turned to his brilliant law partner (and future Supreme Court justice) Louis D. Brandeis. Together they produced the classic 1890 *Harvard Law Review* article "The Right to Privacy."[62] The fact that there was no legal way of responding to the disclosure of embarrassing private material was, they argued, evidence of a gap in the law. Privacy deserved the same protection as that offered property and the person. Libel and slander laws were insufficient, as they dealt only with malicious or untrue statements, not with the publication of material that simply exposed personal secrets. New laws were therefore required to shore up the boundary separating the public from the private, a boundary that in a modernizing world was being seriously eroded.

> The press is overstepping in every direction the obvious bounds of propriety and decency. Gossip is no longer the resource of the idle and of the vicious, but has become a trade, which is pursued with industry as well as effrontery. To satisfy a prurient taste the details of sexual relations are spread broadcast in the columns of the daily papers . . . The intensity and complexity of life, attendant upon advancing civilization, have rendered necessary some retreat from the world, and man, under the refining influence of culture, has become more sensitive to publicity, so that solitude and privacy have become more essential to the individual; but modern enterprise and invention have, through invasions upon his privacy, subjected him to mental pain and distress, far greater than could be inflicted by mere bodily injury.[63]

Warren and Brandeis deftly portrayed what was to become a central cultural preoccupation of the early twentieth-century world. The same fear of the exploitation of secrets fueled both the passage of invasion of privacy laws in a number of American states and the explosion of sexual blackmail stories on both sides of the Atlantic.

The law on blackmail had evolved from being first focused narrowly on protecting men from being slandered as buggers in the eighteenth century to protecting primarily the heterosexual reputations of elite males in the later nineteenth century. By the 1890s the world was on the cusp of a new century in which discussions of sexuality would be framed by concerns of increased class mobility, social anonymity, and the general blurring of class, gender, and racial lines. Reports of sexual blackmail would peak in the early twentieth century. This curious crime and the stories the popular press told about it increasingly fascinated the public. Blackmail accounts not only provided sensational disclosures; they provided a safe way for people to acknowledge and come to terms with a range of distinctly new and troubling sexual personas and practices.

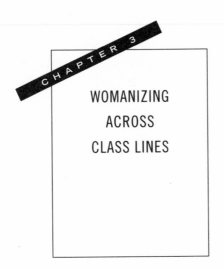

WOMANIZING
ACROSS
CLASS LINES

In the first decades of the twentieth century the reportage of sexual black-mail accelerated. Blackmail stories became a standard narrative device of those seeking to make some sense of both the liberalization of sexual beliefs and practices and the controversies sparked by this development. Shifting gender expectations at the turn of the twentieth century began undermin-ing the notion of separate sexual spheres and the cult of the passionless fe-male. World War I broke the repressive Victorian code of morals and man-ners. Feminist women on lecture platforms and unchaperoned youths in dance halls and movie theaters challenged the sexual status quo. Activists launched campaigns for divorce reform, sex education, and birth control. But if social mores were dramatically changing, the laws were not. Unlucky adventurers could find themselves entangled in statutes pertaining to sex-ual behavior that had been passed in the 1800s while technological ad-vances permitted the unscrupulous to intercept information relayed by telegraph or telephone or photograph and threaten to broadcast it via the tabloid press or radio. The result was a surge of blackmail scandals that peaked in the interwar decades of the 1920s and 1930s.

The discussions elicited by such scandals helped people to clarify many of the key sexual issues of the twentieth century, and the stories themselves cast a revealing light on the supposedly giddy 1920s and impoverished 1930s. They warned of the dangers of anonymous encounters in a destabilized urban world. Such accounts may speak to fears of a loss of male power. They offer evidence of men's resistance to the encroachments of women and youths and of a blurring of the boundaries and categories of class, gender, and race. But many of the same stories could also be taken as a sign of women's greater social and economic activity, women's attempts to control their fertility, the increasing visibility of homosexuals, and a greater mixing of the races. Thanks to these tales the public became familiar with a host of twentieth-century sexual characters—the flapper, the gold digger, the gigolo, the playboy, and the pervert—all of whom we will turn to in subsequent chapters. But an account of early twentieth-century blackmail necessarily begins with the portrayal of the male victim, who remained, as ever, the courts' first concern.

More than anything else, twentieth-century blackmail trials reveal how male sexual adventuring was constructed and perceived. The pursuit of sex was one way modern men demonstrated their power and established their identity. As the more economically powerful partner in a relationship, a man could take more risks than a woman in the pursuit of sexual gratification.[1] Laws, social values, and traditions shaped men's promiscuity, their patronizing of prostitutes, and their exploitation of female employees. Such activities all had their risks. There was in effect a "male route" to being blackmailed. The lessons that Americans and the British drew from blackmail differed, however, with Americans regarding the crime primarily as a symptom of the subversive power of sex and the English preoccupied by the way in which extortion eroded class boundaries. This chapter is devoted to the English male victim; the following chapter will examine the fate of his more adventurous American counterpart.

The English fixation on class relationships—the rich versus the poor—was repeatedly brought out in the fictional portrayals of extortion. The victims in such stories were always well-off. "Whoever read a detective story about poor people?" asked G. K. Chesterton. "The poor have crimes; but the poor have no secrets. And it is because the proud have secrets that they need to be detected before they are forgiven." In Henry James's *In the Cage* (1898) a wealthy man living in London's West End is appalled to discover that a young woman who works in a telegraph office knows of his adulterous affair. For her the secret information promises an entrée to another world. "She quite thrilled herself with thinking what, with such a lot of material, a bad girl would do. It would be a scene better than in her ha'penny novels, this going to him in the dusk of evening at Park Chambers and letting him at last have it. 'I know too much about a certain person now not to put it to you—excuse my being so lurid—that it's quite worth your while to buy me off.'" In an insightful 1923 short story John Galsworthy portrayed on the one hand a pauper justifying his demands by asserting that the wealthy by their misdeeds were "askin' for it" and on the other hand a middle-class man musing, "No wonder blackmail was accounted such a heinous crime. No other human act was so cold-blooded, spider-like, and slimy; none plunged so deadly a dagger into the bowels of compassion, so eviscerated humanity, so murdered faith!" Only a socialist like George Bernard Shaw dared present the bilking of gentlemen by the poor as comedy. In *Pygmalion* (1913) Henry Higgins is asked by Alfred Doolittle for five pounds for his daughter, Eliza. Higgins accuses him of blackmail. Higgins's friend Pickering then tries to intercede: "I think you ought to know, Doolittle, that Mr. Higgins' intentions are entirely honourable." Doolittle replies, "Course they are, Guvernor. If I thought they wasn't, I'd ask for fifty."[2]

When less subversive and less accomplished authors attempted to treat extortion in a lighthearted fashion, their blackmailers were inevitably presented as well-born if momentarily hard-up members of the social elite. Such stories patently served to defend the social status quo. For example, in a short story by Saki (H. H. Munro) an enterprising young man discovers a list of people involved in scandalous activities. Telling him he should destroy the information, his aunt asks him to think of "'all those poor unfortunate people who would be involved in the disclosures.' 'Unfortunate, perhaps, but not poor,' corrected Vasco; 'if you read the list carefully you'll notice that I haven't troubled to include anyone whose financial standing isn't above question.'" E. F. Benson's female blackmailer, a countess, likewise has no trouble in rationalizing her taxing of the nouveau riche. "She looked upon the payments they made as a sort of insurance against indiscretions on their part in the future. She protected them against their own lower instincts."[3]

More often, however, the image of the blackmailer that English authors conjured up was of a lower-class ruffian or foreigner who threatened the elite. William Le Queux, author of popular pre–World War I invasion scare stories, exploited the class aspects of extortion in *The Man About Town: A Story of Society and Blackmail* (1916), portraying the naïve Lord Sidcup as the victim—threatened with divorce proceedings—and a disloyal maid with access to letters as the blackmailers' accomplice. In *Radio Blackmail* (1936) L. G. Redmond-Howard's villains threatened both an English girl's marriage into the Waldavian royal family and the takeover of the country by the "Reds."[4] Such fantasies of the gentry personally warding off plagues of criminals were pushed to laughable lengths in a 1935 Herbert Jay short story. Tall, beautiful Lady Lessingham runs into her cousin, tall, athletic Percy Stanhope:

> "Hullo, Steph, this is luck! I'm delighted to see you. Where are you off to? And, by the way, what's the matter with you? You look worried, dear."
>
> "I am, Percy. I've just had an upsetting interview."
>
> "With a doctor, or a money lender?"
>
> "With a blackmailer."
>
> "A blackmailer, eh? Gad, that sounds bad! Curiously enough, I'm in the same boat myself. There seems to be an epidemic of it."[5]

Stanhope finds it great "sport" to retrieve his cousin's letters from the extortionist, who is described as being fat and piglike and having avoided war service.

The fate that awaited the perpetrators of what the writers of interwar thrillers called the most cowardly of crimes can be imagined. "Sapper" (H. C. McNeile) took a sadistic delight in describing the killing of an extortionist who, as the hero tells the narrator, was an antimonarchist and

> ". . . a foul blackmailing swine. He was a man dead to even the twinge of a decent instinct, a loathsome brute, a slimy cur. And though I realize quite fully that legally speaking I've committed murder, from every other point of view I have merely exterminated a thing that had no right to live."
>
> "Granted, old man," I said helplessly . . .
>
> "Bill, sometimes now I see the look in his eyes of cringing hideous terror when he first realized it wasn't bluff. And I glory in it. He gave a sort of stifled scream, and reached for the bell, just as I plugged him through the heart."
>
> "Then I locked the door and I burnt the films and I knew that my darling was safe. Old friend, wouldn't you have done as I did?"[6]

Similarly in a 1926 short story the loyal family retainer, after having disposed of the body, reassures his master that he was right to murder the man who sought to exploit a dangerous secret. "'He got all he deserved, Sir William,' I answered, 'and I'm very pleased to hear how well he deserved it, because that'll put you in a better appetite, I dare say, and you won't feel too vexed when you look back.'"[7]

67

Fiction writers were not alone in viewing extortion as a key symptom of social conflict in early twentieth-century Britain. The *New York Times* in 1908 carried a report on England by "A Veteran Diplomat" entitled "Men

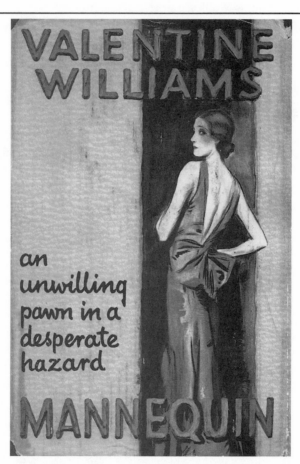

In the 1920s and 1930s popular novelists cranked out countless thrillers in which sexual secrets led to blackmail. In this British example the reader is promised a racy account of "love and blackmail in Cannes and Monte Carlo." (Valentine Williams, *Mannequin*, London: Hodder and Stoughton, 1930.)

68 Who Trade in the Secrets of Others." It attributed the "phenomenal growth" of blackmail to the press's appetite for scandal and "an ever increasing class of men whose intelligence has been developed by free education sufficiently to give them a distaste for the manual labor of their fathers."[8] Every new school produced more recruits for crime, anarchy, and "social piracy." It says something of the antiquated mind-set of the author that he was so preoccupied by the notion of overeducated and ambitious servants unscrupulously selling household secrets.

World War I exacerbated such fears. On March 10, 1925, Captain Arthur Hope, a Unionist MP, rose in the House of Commons to table a resolution calling for the more vigorous prosecution of blackmailers. The social dislocations caused by the war had, he maintained, led the unsavory to attempt to live by their wits. The favorite victims of such extortionists were professional men, such as doctors and clergymen, who risked emerging from even a successful trial with a tarnished reputation. If a doctor's name had been dragged through the mud, cautious men would not allow him, even if proved guiltless, to attend their wives and daughters. Captain Hope accordingly sought to have blackmail trials held in camera. His proposal was supported by Conservatives but immediately countered by Labour MP Rhys Davies, who asserted that one should not feel undue sympathy for wealthy men because "a common cause of blackmail is that of a woman who may have been seduced by the prodigal son of a rich man." Responding to his opponents' cries of "No!", Davies insisted, "Yes, that is a common cause." He went on to argue that in camera trials "would tend to shelter the rich to the disadvantage of the poor." Thomas Johnson, another Labour MP, was even more vociferous in objecting to any changes in court procedures that appeared to give rich men special treatment. Though acknowledging the fact that the tabloids exploited divorce and blackmail cases, he believed they served a useful educational function. "If only the 'muck' could have been kept out of them [the newspapers], recent cases would have been an aid to public morals. They had led millions of decent people who produced the wealth of the country—the backbone physically, mentally, and morally of the country—to see how the idle, useless, parasitic rich spent their time. Letting daylight into such cases would do more than anything towards cleansing the social structure."[9] It was right and proper, Johnson concluded, that the public should know what princes and rajahs were up to.

In response to the request that the press be forbidden to publish the names of blackmail victims, Sir William Joynson-Hicks, the Home Secretary, replied that it was impossible to have a closed court, even for incest 69 cases. Judges only had the discretion of asking the press to be discreet. Some judges believed that anonymity created greater, rather than lesser, interest in blackmail. A magistrate in a 1927 case left it to the press to decide whether anonymity would be granted. In the main, however, after 1925 English courts routinely suppressed victims' names; they would be described in the press as, for example, Mr. A or Mrs. X. Thirty to forty cases were brought to the attention of the police each year before World War I. The numbers crept up to one hundred a year by 1932. The general public assumed that the granting of anonymity contributed to the rise in the number of blackmail charges, but the courts chiefly attributed the surge to the moral fecklessness of women and workers.[10]

In England both the left and the right's notions of blackmail were framed by class preoccupations. No doubt there were few crimes that so clearly targeted the better off. Even the royal family was not spared. In the 1930s a deranged man, claiming to be the illegitimate son of the Duke of Clarence, wrote Buckingham Palace that if he were not given £600 a year he would tell the world of his parentage. Ramsay MacDonald, the Labour Party leader, was also targeted. MacDonald had written some pornographic letters to a Viennese woman, and when he became Prime Minister for the second time in 1929 she threatened to have them published in the French press. Eventually the British Embassy in Paris purchased the letters for £20,000 and they were destroyed. The public was never informed of this particular incident, but the press let it be known that other men in the public eye were at risk. One such distinguished victim was Colonel James Robert Bain, Conservative MP for the West Division of Cumberland for the period 1900–1906. In 1911 the court heard that thirty-three years earlier Bain, then a fresh subaltern, had met in Carlisle a young woman "with the result that in the following year she said she was *enceinte.*" He made provisions for her, which he maintained until her death in 1908. Then a woman claiming to be her sister and a male accomplice showed up demanding money for her letters. Under a barrage of phone calls, visits to his club, and four or five postcards a day, Bain paid out over £1,500. Finally, when the pair threatened to go to his constituency office, Bain informed the police.

In sentencing the accused to prison terms, the judge attempted to down-play their damaging revelations by praising Bain for having acted "hand-somely."[11]

A similar situation occurred in 1929. Two actors, using information about the seduction of a woman and the birth of her baby, blackmailed a Conservative candidate during a parliamentary election. They presented themselves as private investigators working for the Labour Party and on the day of the election threatened to distribute an embarrassing leaflet. The same year a forty-eight-year-old woman began sending demanding letters to Philip Snowden, a leading Labour MP. When they became "rather warm" he informed the Home Secretary, and she was arrested. The judge was not impressed with her claim that she had the victim confused with another "Philip Snowden" and sentenced her to eighteen months.[12]

Judges and politicians worried that blackmailers not only bilked the rich but also exposed secrets that could not fail to undermine the public's confidence in the ruling class. In 1930 the international press carried the story of attempts made to extort money from Sir J. B. Robinson in Johannesburg. An enthralled readership learned of Robinson's debauched existence, his naked dance parties, his long affair with a married woman, and his purported rape of her younger sister. The magistrate called it the "filthiest case I've heard" and described Robinson as a "peculiarly natured man." The defense's argument was that the mistress and her lawyer were not trying to blackmail but rather sue Robinson for his assault on the younger sister. His lawyers replied that launching such a scandalous civil suit was in fact a scare tactic. The court agreed that issuing a summons of claim based on false facts of such a nature that it would inspire fear in the ordinary reasonable man as to his reputation and good name and result in his paying to avoid publicity amounted to extortion.[13] But could other rich men take comfort from a legal victory when it was purchased at the price of one's reputation?

Both the courts and the press informed the public that those most at risk were not the representatives of old wealth, but professional men. The popular tabloids always liked to play up accounts of compromised country vicars; this may explain the large number of reports of church ministers targeted by extortionists. The clergy, as public officials, had to be concerned about what was said about them. The expectation that they would cleave to a higher morality also put them at risk. In a bizarre 1914 case William Davis, a twenty-five-year-old wastrel, attempted to blackmail his own father, the Reverend W. L. Davis. The son sent postcards that could be read by all, stating, "Preach better sermons. You have made my mother's life a hell." 71 Another was addressed to "Revd. W. Davis, Money Grabber Twister and Deceiver Greedy Guts." "You have twisted me out of my money and abused me," he wrote. "You are a dirty scoundrel, and caused me great expense. I expected it from a pig. You ought to be in a pigsty." He also wrote to the archbishop. Eventually arrested, he claimed that William Davis senior was not his real father.[14]

The courts repeatedly reminded the public that churchmen's occupation put them in contact with a needy clientele who could turn nasty. In 1902 a vagrant threatened Dean Hole of Rochester that unless paid, the clergyman's youthful indiscretions would be reported to the archbishop. In a 1930 case, an ex-convict, whose wife worked for the chaplain of Holloway prison, claimed that the wife and the chaplain had had an affair. The blackmailer was sentenced to five years in prison. Some threats were simply manufactured. In 1931 an unemployed man threatened the Bishop of Manchester with revealing his relationship with a young woman. In court the accused admitted that he had made up the story. "He says he was desperate," noted the magistrate, "and had seen in a newspaper of a case of blackmail and thought it would be a good opportunity to demand some money from the bishop." A seventeen-year-old youth claimed in 1933 to have photos of a rector with women. The judge concluded that this too was a ridiculous attempt at blackmail and gave the young man a suspended sentence.[15]

Despite the courts' explicit attempts to protect the reputations of clergymen, some trial accounts revealed that ministers had clearly broached expected bounds. In 1914 a woman claimed that the Reverend Arthur Wilde had followed her to the top of an omnibus and then home and threatened, if she were not paid, to give the story to the tabloid *John Bull*. While admitting that the law was confusing, the judge refused to allow her defense of reasonable or probable cause. The woman might well have been harassed; but that, the judge was happy to note, gave her no right to make a claim. In 1930 a churchwarden was sentenced to seven years for extorting £1,600 over the previous few years from the Reverend H. E. Dunn, rector of a village in Cornwall. The rector claimed he only kissed the churchwarden's wife, but the warden threatened to report the rector's indiscretions to his bishop. In another case in January 1931, Mr. Justice Wild imposed an extraordinary ten-year sentence on a laborer for having blackmailed a clergyman. While up a ladder the workman had accidentally caught sight of the minister in a compromising situation and used the threat of reporting him to his bishop to milk the minister out of £100.[16] Though judges did what they could to defend the clergy against charges of hypocrisy, the fact that many paid out large sums of money over long periods of time confirmed popular suspicions that some clergymen did not practice what they preached.

The press gave the impression that, after ministers, medical men were most likely to be targets of blackmailers. The professional journal the *Lancet* leapt to the defense of doctors accused of sexual improprieties and made clear its suspicion of complaining female patients. In 1904 it described as "A Vile Conspiracy" the attempt of the evocatively named Mrs. Faithful to claim she had been seduced by Dr. A. D. Griffith of Bridgend, South Wales. Every practitioner, the journal warned, ran the risks of unfounded assertions made by female patients. Suffering from "hysterical hallucinations," women sometimes thought a gynecological examination was an assault. More often, claimed the journal, it was a case of calculated blackmail, as in the case of Mrs. Faithful, who telephoned her victim to say she would withdraw her summons if provided travel money. In 1913 a twenty-year-old woman admitted that her fiancé forced her to claim that her doctor had assaulted her. "I wrote the letter, but he dictated it to me. He is always asking me to get money for him." She had threatened the doctor with a £2,000 suit but offered to drop it for £100. The Medical Defense Union prosecuted, and the truth came out.[17]

Members of the legal profession appeared in court as both blackmailers and victims. A solicitor's clerk who in 1911 was refused a letter of reference sent scurrilous postcards to his employer. In 1928 another clerk threatened Mr. Z with publicizing a document he had signed in 1922 admitting to an indecent assault on a girl. The case was unusual enough to be reported in the international press. Mr. Z had first been blackmailed in 1922 by his solicitor, Percy Burnett. When Burnett died the blackmailing scheme was taken over by his clerk, who wrote the victim: "I have no doubt that you would like to have these papers, particularly one document which might be very injurious if it got into the hands of certain people."[18]

Judging from press reports, the classic heterosexual male blackmail victim was thus not the country gentleman so beloved by mystery writers, but the professional man. The class stereotype did appear to hold regarding 73 blackmailers, however; in the main they came from the lower echelons of society. The English upper classes had complained for centuries that their indiscretions were exploited by their domestics. Now servants were accused of turning to blackmail. In 1928 a manservant was sentenced to three years for blackmailing Mr. B and Miss A—who were about to be married—with the exposure of their letters. In 1935 a twenty-five-year-old chauffeur was found guilty of extorting money from Mr. X and taking his cigarette case and gold watch. In 1937 an ex-employee of another Mr. X took letters and papers from his flat that could ruin him and then demanded £250. "This is my birthday," he called to say on the phone. "How are you feeling? Did you notice anything wrong with your flat?" The fact that so many servants continued in the interwar years to show up in court accused of extortion serves as a reminder of how slowly social relations had evolved in England. A vivid portrayal of the yawning gulf that continued to divide the classes was provided by an account of the 1931 trial of a nineteen-year-old gardener who attempted to extort money (though not by a menace to reputation) from Lady Cave. The youth's naïve threat—to kill her dog—was sent via the butler and began "My lady." Lady Cave, who employed six members of the accused's family, had her own quaint explanation of the youth's behavior: "He was smoking far too much, and she thought he was getting a swollen head and things of that sort."[19]

Warning employers of the danger posed by employees who had access to compromising documents was yet another way in which the courts raised the specter of subservients exploiting sexual information. In 1930 the press reported that two youths threatened Mr. T that if he did not pay, they would show his wife an incriminating letter of his that they had intercepted at work. In 1931 a man attempted to get a job by threatening the manager of Britivox that he would publish an article in *John Bull* about the manager's association with prostitutes. In 1936 a judge sent to prison for twenty months a hotel worker who made "certain allegations" against his employer. Some commentators believed that poverty was often a precipitating factor in such cases. A contributor to the *Police Journal* in 1931 wrote that the recent economic crash had led to an upsurge in crime: "In these days of acute industrial depression, of the many persons who are in want of money a few have no fundamental sense of honesty to keep them straight."[20] But the admission that some blackmail threats made by workers were precipitated by poverty was rarely made by either the courts or the English press; they unreservedly sided with the well-off victims.

English blackmail cases revealed generational as well as class tensions. One of the arguments used by Conservatives to oppose the Punishment of Incest Act (1908) was that it would enable scheming mothers to use their children to entrap and blackmail incautious males. In 1917 it was asked in the House of Commons how many cases of blackmail were brought by girls under sixteen years of age using the Criminal Law Amendment Act of 1885. Sir George Cave, the Home Secretary, stated that no trustworthy figures were available, but that in the previous ten years twenty-two cases of false accusations were reported to the Commissioner of Police. The worrying implication of both the question and the answer was that new laws subjected men to new threats from heartless young women who sought to compromise them.[21]

Most young men cited in blackmail cases had attempted to shake down homosexuals. The smaller number of youths charged with blackmailing heterosexual men were frequently presented by the courts as deluded fantasists, obviously influenced by thrillers and mystery stories. In April 1912 a seventeen-year-old tailor's assistant was charged with having sent a letter to a man demanding £10. The letter, emblazoned with skull and crossbones, warned that if the money were not sent the "Black Hand" would strike. The judge, giving the accused a suspended sentence, ridiculed him for being too avid a reader of penny dreadfuls. In 1925 seventeen-year-old Septimus Toyne sent letters in the name of the "Lincoln Branch of the Crimson Triangle" to Harry Winkle, a dispenser at a doctor's office. Toyne claimed that the mysterious 15,000-strong organization had been established by Lord Kitchener to suppress immorality in the United Kingdom. Having discovered that Winkle had "acted as a rotter" toward a girl some three years previous, Toyne demanded £50 in restitution. The chivalrous youth concluded that the poor girl needed fresh air. His fantasy was to spend the money on a motor bike on which he would take her for rejuvenating rides. Toyne was given a suspended sentence.[22]

In 1926, at the time of the General Strike, a seventeen-year-old Oxford solicitor's clerk sent threatening letters to Lord Townsend, Lord Churston,

Lord Cadogan, Lord Bute, and other peers, introducing himself as a "British Communist" and demanding £5,000. He was obviously well connected; the sympathetic judge, blaming the rash act on "sensational literature," gave him a suspended sentence. British judges took a dim view of such reading matter. Though a sexual accusation was not involved in the case of the two youths found guilty in a 1931 trial, they were described in court as threatening a man in the style of an "Edgar Wallace" thriller. A Scottish judge sneered that a seventeen-year-old apprentice's silly act of trying to blackmail a surgeon (by claiming that his nurse was his mistress) was prompted by his reading or hearing about extortion plots. In January 1937 police searched the room of a seventeen-year-old footman and member of a "Communist Club" who had demanded £5 from a wealthy woman residing in Eaton Square, London. "In his room," the prosecution reported, "were found a number of books of the 'thriller' type from which Wilcox said he got his ideas." In July of the same year a Scottish judge, in sentencing a twenty-one-year-old man to three months in jail, berated him for reading too many detective novels.[23]

In 1931 the *Times* carried an editorial entitled "Animal Blackmail" in which it related the story of a German blackmail gang that used a homing pigeon to carry the swag. The gang tried to claim that the bird was not theirs, but it kept returning to them. "There is a simplicity about pigeons," the *Times* concluded admiringly, "that makes them unfitted for a life of deceit."[24] Many wished modern youths were as honest. Judges, in attributing a rise in crime to the unfortunate reading habits of the poor, were tapping into the old notion that a little knowledge was a dangerous thing. Would mass education produce more conscientious or more cunning young people? Twentieth-century English society, which thought itself largely protected from the violent depredations of the ignorant, worried that the price of a more knowing youth might include their exploitation of dangerous sexual information.[25] The pessimistic assumed that cheap paperbacks and popular films, in carrying out an unprecedented diffusion and commercialization of sexual knowledge, were further incitements that steered youth toward crime.

Yet the forms of blackmail carried out against English male victims do not appear all that new, especially when compared to what was occurring in America. In England much blackmail appeared to be fairly amateurish, even in cases of the "badger game" in which a husband or male relative de-

75

manded compensation. William Ball claimed in 1938 that his daughter was thirteen, not eighteen as she looked, in demanding money from Mr. X. A milkman who kissed a woman found himself in 1931 blackmailed by her husband. In 1939 a transport worker similarly demanded money from a professional man he believed had improper relations with his wife.[26]

Among the professional blackmailers the police included, as always, prostitutes' bullies and pimps. In 1919 a victim, given anonymity, testified to meeting "a woman well-known in the West End." He visited her several times and paid her £30. John Knight appeared, claiming to be her husband, and demanded £500 in return for some letters and the dropping of a divorce suit. In 1921 a Pall Mall caretaker who went to a prostitute was shaken down by her partner, who claimed to be a police constable. A married man was a victim of badger game in 1927, as were Mr. Y and Mr. Z in 1932 and a retired colonel in 1940. Nevertheless a police inspector noted that female prostitutes were far less likely than male prostitutes to turn to blackmail. Those who did sometimes posed as virtuous women, he noted. They might fake a pregnancy and as a veiled threat claim they needed a "loan." As a last resort a bully could be called in to threaten or coerce.[27]

The courts and the press warned that even those men who shunned prostitutes still had to be careful. Blackmailers attempted to exploit every stage of the heterosexual courtship cycle. Premarital escapades were exploited. In 1932 a laborer threatened to publish compromising pictures and letters of the wife of Mr. A before they were married. In 1925 Samuel Taylor was found guilty of sending blackmail letters to Lord and Lady Terrington. Taylor had been engaged to Lady Terrington's sister. When Lady Terrington heard of the relationship she threatened to make her sister a ward in chancery. In revenge Taylor, claiming to be a private inquiry agent, threatened to make public that Lord and Lady Terrington had lived together before their marriage and subsequently had affairs. On being arrested Taylor admitted that it had all been a hoax and apologized. He was sentenced to nine months in prison.[28]

Blackmail accounts provided men with repeated warnings that their adulterous affairs could end disastrously. In 1914 two eighteen-year-olds were sent to a reformatory for demanding £30 from an electrical engineer for "ruining a typist." A man warned Frank Howard in 1920 that if he did not pay £50 he would be "exposed" to his wife. In 1921 photos were taken of a businessman and the threat made that his company directors and his mother would be informed. In 1922 a man was sentenced to four years in prison for threatening a solicitor that his affair would be revealed to his wife. In 1930 a Manchester theater owner was threatened that his adultery 77 would be revealed. In 1932 an ex-policeman threatened a merchant that he would tell the merchant's wife of his spending nights with another woman. In 1934 a man and wife to whom love letters were accidentally delivered blackmailed both Mr. A and Mrs. X. In 1938 a woman who had years previous been intimate with a certain man began to demand money. She told him that she was being blackmailed herself, a not uncommon ploy.[29]

Blackmailers so shared society's notion that a man's honor was preeminently important that they on occasion threatened a wife with the menace of revealing not her, but her husband's, sordid secrets. In 1921 two men tried to get money from Mrs. Florence Blake, saying they had a photograph and a dictaphone recording of her husband with other women. In 1931 a man threatened a woman to expose the secret of a male relative. In 1933 Albert Daly demanded £3,250 from a widow, Mrs. X, saying he had evidence of a relationship between her late husband and Daly's daughter.[30]

Trial transcripts make it clear that the married Englishman's most common fear was that if his spouse were informed of his affair she would demand a divorce. A judge noted in 1937 that despite the many causes of marital unhappiness adultery was almost the only grounds for divorce. Men were to a degree protected from having their extramarital liaisons revealed inasmuch as until 1923 a woman in England could not obtain a divorce simply on the basis of her husband's adultery. Nevertheless being cited by another man as correspondent in a divorce case and having one's name in the paper could have serious consequences and was a threat frequently brandished by extortionists. Some politicians accused journalists who reported such divorces as thereby assisting blackmailers, but the papers replied that if the divorce courts were closed to them even more blackmail would result.[31]

In divorce blackmail a man would simply threaten to cite his victim as the correspondent in the legal proceedings. In 1937 a bigamous couple employed a more elaborate plot to extort money from Mr. X, an army officer. He had had an affair with the woman; her husband then turned up with her "confession" and threatened divorce proceedings. Another member of the gang impersonated a solicitor, and the group met several times with Mr. X in London. In the trial that eventually took place the judge noted that

Mr. X had not been accused of "ordinary acts of misconduct but extraordinary facts, foul things which were quite untrue." Sometimes divorcing couples blackmailed each other. In 1925 Colonel Denniston's counsel accused Denniston's ex-wife of attempting to obtain more alimony by threatening to publicize letters that showed that Lady Carnarvon—his current wife—had previously been his mistress.[32]

Adopting the same inflammatory vocabulary fiction writers used to portray extortion, judges on the bench warned well-off English men that every sexual temptation could be a trap. Mr. Justice Wild, in sentencing a laborer to four years' penal servitude in 1923, referred to blackmail as "moral murder." In a later trial, the same judge stated that if the victim had paid "he might as well have cut his throat, as he would have been bled and bled and bled." In 1931 a colleague stated that "the offence of blackmail was only next to murder in its gravity." Another agreed that "blackmail was morally indistinguishable from murder." Yet another judge lamented that even innocent victims paid, since they knew "that mud, when it is flung, will stick."[33]

In response to these attacks on the propertied, the bench first called for stricter enforcement of the law. At the 1931 Leeds assizes Mr. Justice Swift even defended police entrapment. "If you see the traces of a rat running about your sitting-room, you set a trap. There is no other way of catching it." Second, judges called for harsher laws. In 1916 reputational blackmail was defined clearly in England by statute as a separate offense that could be either a misdemeanor or a felony. Earlier punishable threats had to be to person or to property and had to be direct and immediate. As late as 1898 a payment made not to report poaching had been called a "business transaction." With the passage of the Larceny Act of 1916 threats and menaces could be punished with anything up to a whipping and life imprisonment. The act drew together the various types of blackmail. Crimes defined in section 29 (to menace and/or to threaten to accuse of a serious crime such as rape, buggery, or bestiality) were felonies punishable by up to a life sentence; those in section 30 (extortion by other threat) were felonies punishable up to five years; those in section 31 (which originated with the Libel Act of 1843 and covered any libel) were misdemeanors punishable by up to two years. Unfortunately, the new act caused some confusion to remain, as it left the authorities to decide under which section a given offense should be prosecuted. Moreover, judges did not always understand its provisions.

For example, in 1922 a man was tried for threatening a solicitor that his affair would be revealed to his wife. The judge seemed to think that a "menace" had to be a false accusation and instructed the jury to determine if 79 "misconduct" took place. Only after the jury unanimously said that misconduct had not taken place did the judge sentence the accused to four years in prison. Like many of his fellows, the judge was as eager to defend the reputation of the victim as he was to punish the villain.[34]

In peculiarly English fashion the third response of judges to what appeared to be a rising incidence of blackmail was their plea for a return to corporal punishment. In sentencing an ex-convict in August 1930, the *Times* reported, Sir Ernest Wild "said it was a great pity blackmailers could not be whipped . . . His particular form of blackmail only allowed a sentence of five years penal servitude, and it gave him [the Recorder] great pleasure to pass on him the maximum sentence." Later the same year Sir Henry Dickens, the Common-Serjeant, joined in the call for flogging and whipping to be extended to those convicted of blackmail, which he described as "the most serious, and certainly the most cowardly, offence we have to deal with."[35] The judiciary's hankering after flogging was a nostalgic yearning for a time when attacks on the character and honor of gentlemen were dealt with peremptorily.

In interwar England judges were literally trying to beat back the threats posed to well-off men by the poor and the young. The bench's perception of the "normal" blackmail victim was of the well-off, white, heterosexual male. The villain was poor or young or female or all three. Mixing of the classes was inherently suspect. In a 1933 Scottish case, the guilt of the seven men and one young woman accused of extorting money from an Edinburgh cashier was clinched when the judge asked the jury if they could believe that a man would simply give money to "strangers who were not of his class." The prudent were instructed to draw from blackmail trials the moral that an increasingly dangerous age had emerged, an upside-down world in which "natural" power relationships could be easily reversed. The "weak" or naïve man could easily succumb. This loss of confidence was captured by Mr. Justice Wild, who in sending to prison in 1923 a villain who had compromised a "good Samaritan" felt obliged to caution adult males not to talk to strangers. Such counsel had once been reserved for children.

Both real and fictional accounts of blackmail of the period reveal a sense of the predicament in which interwar middle-class Englishmen purportedly found themselves.[36] They were warned that their success, chivalry, and wealth—all of which should have brought peace and happiness—made

80 them the obvious targets of criminals. Blackmail scandals exacerbated old fears the well-off had always had of being robbed by their staff, while introducing the new and more menacing notion that the exposure of a man's sexual secrets could lead to his complete ruin. Such stories served as cautionary tales to warn men in both England and America of the dangers that surrounded them; but the English discussions were marked by laments for a lost world in which women, workers, and servants had known their place.

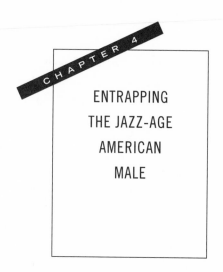

CHAPTER 4

ENTRAPPING
THE JAZZ-AGE
AMERICAN
MALE

When Warren G. Harding, the twenty-ninth President of the United States, suddenly died in 1923 few Americans knew of the irrational risks he had run in his zealous womanizing. Enlightenment was offered in 1927 when Nan Britton published *The President's Daughter*, which provided a detailed account of her seven-year adulterous affair with the married Harding. Thirty-one years younger than her lover, Britton had posed as his niece. Their frantic lovemaking often took place in hotels (in one they had to pay to silence two house detectives). She recalled that because she had no "preventive facilities" her daughter was conceived in an office of the United States Senate in January 1919. After Harding became President the following year, they had sex in a small anteroom off the Oval Office. Though he promised to provide for her, after Harding's death Britton found his family deaf to her appeals. They regarded her as an extortionist, but she insisted that it was only her concern for her daughter's well-being that had led her to write her exposé. She knew women who had been paid off, she asserted. Harding's friends had earlier drawn $20,000 from a special fund to silence another mistress.[1] Few read Britton's account. Agents of the Society for the Suppression of Vice attempted to prevent the book's appearance. When it was published the major newspapers refused to review it. Only a small coterie initially would know how well President Harding matched the media's portrayal of the early twentieth-century American male blackmail victim.

A review of the stories of the blackmailing of the American male suggests that their primary purpose was to act as a deterrent; but they were also constructed to titillate. The public's fascination with such sexual blackmail cases lay in their revealing the amazingly dangerous activities into which otherwise intelligent men would plunge when moved by lust. They blundered on, seemingly moved by a sense of infallibility or entitlement, blind to the dangers posed. What began in a spirit of euphoria or risk-taking ended in bitterness. What men naïvely assumed was a fling, a romance, or an adventure turned into a nightmare. In England the reportage of the blackmailing of men was framed by backward-looking class concerns; in the United States such cases were largely read in the context of a modern recognition of the social potency of sex.[2] They functioned as an implicit critique of twentieth-century Americans' throwing off of the restraints of the Victorians. Men might relish the excitement of a world of dynamic capitalism where consumption and possessiveness were lauded, but the notion that everything had its price—even one's reputation—could, they were warned, come back to haunt them.

Another important purpose of the blackmail trial and its fictional depictions was to demonstrate how a victimized man might salvage a reputation, defend his character, and win sympathy. The courts and the press began with the assumption that men would naturally wander and should be chastised, but they concluded with the injunction that men should not be exploited. The blackmail stories revealed key middle-class values—privacy, trust, and confidentiality—being transgressed and violated; the courts and the press took as their duty to defend and restore these values.

American blackmail trials were presented by some politicians and newspapers as evidence that prudish laws aimed at imposing antiquated moral codes and restraining male lust actually provided criminals with the weapons with which they could fleece both the imprudent and the innocent. Critics cited in particular the Mann Act and the "heart balm statutes" dealing with seduction, alienation of affection, and breach of promise of marriage. The moral was that if American blackmailers—like American bootleggers—appeared to be far more professional than their English counterparts, it was because the legal codes of the United States unintentionally provided them with a more supportive environment.

Even before the Mann Act of 1910, early twentieth-century America labored under a patchwork of obscure laws, which meant that a sexual adventure could have significant legal consequences. Some states criminalized simple fornication—that is, extramarital intercourse. Rape and sexual assault were more serious charges. Only men were prosecuted for such crimes, and several states referred to penetration or specifically stated that rape was a male act. When an older male had sex with an underage female

83

In the interwar decades American journalists repeatedly warned male readers that their love letters could be employed by unscrupulous women to extort financial compensation. ("When Cupid Goes A-Profiteering," from Delancy Cox, "The High Cost of Loving," *Forum*, June 1919.)

it was classified as statutory rape. The age of consent was set at ten in the nineteenth century but by the early twentieth century had crept up to six-
84 teen in most states. Incest, by legal definition, was another felony that could only be committed by men, usually by a father or stepfather against a daughter or stepdaughter. Bigamy, not uncommon before divorce was lib-eralized, was a crime. Men and women could both be charged with bigamy, but in practice it too was an overwhelmingly male offense, as were the crimes of abduction and seduction. The male clients of prostitutes were also at some risk. Prostitution was a crime in many parts of the United States; in England, by contrast, solicitation was a crime, not the act of pros-titution itself. Patronizing a prostitute was not often prosecuted, but was possible in the states of Connecticut, Illinois, Indiana, Minnesota, Pennsyl-vania, and New York. And while adultery was not penalized in England it was a crime (though rarely prosecuted) in more than a dozen states, includ-ing Massachusetts and Michigan. In Massachusetts even a cohabiting di-vorced couple could be found guilty of adultery. In almost every state adul-tery provided grounds for divorce, and the guilty party could lose out in property distribution and child custody decisions. Usually only the ag-grieved spouse could initiate divorce proceedings, though a few states, such as Oklahoma, allowed third parties to do so if the couple were living openly in adultery. It took little imagination to envisage how blackmailers might exploit this complex web of statutes.[3] For progressives the interwar black-mail trials presented America with the question of which could be more easily changed—the laws or human nature?

Although American commentators provided a less class-conscious ac-count of extortion than their English counterparts, the press made note of rich and powerful men who were preyed on by blackmailers. Some journal-ists were themselves suspected of being extortionists in all but name. Most claimed to follow an implied code of honor that prevented them from ex-ploiting intimate information, but the code was very flexible. Colonel Wil-liam D'Alton Mann, the publisher of *Town Topics,* successfully sued *Col-lier's Magazine* in 1906 for calling him a blackmailer, yet it was common knowledge that the Vanderbilts, Whitneys, and Morgans paid to keep com-promising stories out of his magazine. In the 1920s gossip columnists con-tinued to be accused of "kid glove" shakedowns, in which they threatened the rich with embarrassing publicity.[4]

Unlike in England, in America when a wealthy man went to court the news could not be suppressed. In 1905 the public was informed that the courts had sentenced Paul de Hart to ten years in prison for the blackmailing of C. S. Mellon of the New York, New Hampshire, and Hartford Railroad. In 1918 the police arrested two nineteen-year-old boys who had written L. F. Loree, president of the Delaware and Hudson Railroad, that if not paid off they would make "sensitive disclosures" concerning Loree's son, who was about to be married. In 1925 Louis Gimbel, Jr. (of the department store dynasty), received three letters threatening "distasteful disclosures" if he did not pay $15,000. The two youths whom the police arrested convinced the authorities they were only go-betweens and were released. In 1929, in an attempt at extortion, a young woman made demands on James S. Cushman, a sixty-year-old financier, threatening to tell his church pastor of their relations. Cushman took her demand for $20,000 seriously enough to retain as his lawyer former New York governor Charles S. Whitman. Though America prided itself on its egalitarian ethos, commentators used blackmail reports to highlight the way in which those possessing large fortunes predictably attracted the mercenary attentions of the less well advantaged.[5]

America, like England, had experts in the "badger game." Fans of popular stage actor Raymond Hitchcock were relieved to hear in 1907 that the four young girls who claimed that he had assaulted them were part of a blackmail scheme. In 1916 the *New York Times* reported that a husband "caught" his wife with a wealthy man and threatened him with a revolver as he demanded a check for $30,000. In March 1917 the police charged one man and three women with using the claim of "misconduct" to blackmail Dr. David Tobey. In 1918 J. W. Cook was sentenced to a year on the chain gang and a $1,000 fine for blackmailing Asa G. Candler, mayor of Atlanta, Georgia. Cook had tried to turn to his own purposes the sixty-seven-year-old Candler's relationship with thirty-eight-year-old Margaret Hirsch. Hirsch herself, who had purportedly demanded half a million dollars in hush money, was sentenced to a year in prison. In an editorial entitled "They Didn't Know Their Man" the *New York Times* continued its line of praising those who faced down blackmailers. "The plot was the familiar one that involves the use of an unscrupulous woman to manufacture a seemingly compromising situation and the sudden breaking in on that situation of a man who violently asserts the right to resent it."[6]

Coincidentally in 1922 Walter Candler of Atlanta, Georgia (possibly a relation of the mayor), claimed that he was badgered into signing a check for $25,000 by Clyde A. Byfield, who had caught him in a ship's stateroom with

Mrs. Byfield. Candler asserted that he was drunk. In 1921 two men and two women were arrested for conspiring to accuse Dr. Harry Schneider of assaulting a seventeen-year-old girl in the back seat of a car. The doctor had initially paid out $13,000, but had then gone to the authorities; and the girl, denounced as incorrigible by her mother, finally admitted that there had been a plot. The courts were happiest in dealing with charges that were obviously trumped up, as they could draw the simple moral that the good had to be protected from the evil.[7]

When the man's immorality was demonstrated, the meaning of the blackmail charge could be contested. Men who claimed they had been blackmailed included those who had no other way of countering a rape charge. In 1906 Charles Barrett, a Chicago saloon owner, was arrested along with two others for the gang rape of fifteen-year-old Nora Sherrill. Barrett argued that Sherrill's claim was a pure invention, and she was initially jailed. He also produced one witness who asserted that Sherrill was out to blackmail him. The Illinois court, however, was more impressed by the doctor who testified that the physical signs indicated that the girl had in fact been assaulted. Barrett was convicted. In 1918 a California court heard Wallace Preston, a forty-five-year-old married man, claim that the story of his having had sex with a twelve-year-old girl had been constructed by her mother for blackmail purposes. The child testified that Preston had said he would marry her and that she had even given him measurements for a wedding dress. She had kept the affair a secret from her family, she said, passing notes to Preston, and was with him on nineteen occasions. She naturally found it embarrassing to say just what occurred during those times and would only acknowledge in court that "he put his thing in mine." Despite the defense's objection that the statement was too vague, the court ruled that Preston—even if blackmailed—was guilty of statutory rape.[8]

In the United States the risks of innocent men falling into "badger games" rose in 1910 when the Mann Act, passed to stop the "white slave trade," made it a federal offense for any man to travel with a woman other than his wife for sexual purposes across a state line. Consequently a man who took a woman, say, from New York City to Atlantic City for an overnight fling was technically committing a crime. This provided enterprising criminals with new opportunities. A woman would lure her victim across a state border and then her male confederates would appear, either pretending to be police officials or threatening to go to the police. The press

86

realized something was amiss when wealthy men began finding themselves entangled in a law that was supposedly meant to target pimps. In February 1914 San Francisco police arrested J. Parker Whitney, a wealthy clubman, 87 under a Mann Act warrant for having brought Genevieve Hannan from New York to California. Whitney claimed that she was part of an underworld blackmail conspiracy. In December 1914 Jessie A. Cope, a "comely brunette," was arrested in Chicago for attempting to bribe an official to assist her in the blackmail of Colonel Charles Alexander of Providence, Rhode Island, on a white slavery charge. Cope and Alexander had met in Los Angeles two years previous and, after he promised to divorce his wife and marry her, the two had traveled together. When he attempted to leave her she and her mother pursued him to Providence. After consulting lawyers in Providence and Los Angeles she brought charges in Chicago. In 1921 the press reported that T. Coleman Dupont and Alfred Gwynne Vanderbilt, who died on the *Lusitania* in 1915, had also been the victims of such extortionists.[9]

As such shakedowns came to light the *New York Times* became a resolute campaigner against the Mann Act. In 1915 the paper published an editorial pointing out how the act led to extortion. In 1916 it labeled the Mann Act "The Blackmail Act," noting that its dangers had been clear from the start. "White slavery"—that is, the notion that women were shanghaied into prostitution—was, the paper insisted, a myth, but the existence of syndicates of blackmailers was not. For six years the government had been the "pal" of such villains. In an editorial of September 1916 entitled "Government and Blackmail" it argued that the act made a harmless spree or simple elopement a crime. The blackmail that resulted from the Mann Act was far worse than the prostitution it sought to suppress. Moreover, the paper pointed out, the act's penalties were so harsh that few juries were willing to convict. It noted that one enterprising individual even tried to blackmail the *New York Herald* newspaper, claiming that its advertising columns contributed to white slavery.[10]

"Dapper Don" Collins (whose real name was Robert A. Torbillon) epitomized the professional criminal who used the Mann Act for extortion. Between 1908 and 1923 he was arrested thirteen times and convicted on four occasions. In 1916 the *New York Times*, in a front-page story entitled "Blackmail Rich Man by White Slave Act," reported that Collins, who was out on bail for a previous shakedown, had been arrested again. Federal officials stated that his gang of four men, posing as U.S. marshals, had obtained more than $200,000 from wealthy men. Four women were used as bait to entrap the victims. To avoid arrest the victims paid from $500 to $20,000 in hush money, one such transaction having taken place in the Federal Building in Philadelphia. Collins was caught by chance when police, looking for a gang stealing nickels from pay phones, raided an apartment and found in the trash federal warrants issued by the Department of Justice in Philadelphia. Because of fear of divorce and disgrace, two victims would not identify Collins.[11]

A 1916 *New York Times* editorial entitled "Government Aid to Blackmailers" disingenuously argued that it did not require the activities of the Collins gang to demonstrate that the Mann Act incited crime. "But if no such gang had ever existed, it would still be true that the Mann Law is chiefly a bid for blackmail and serves no other purpose worth mentioning." It made immorality, if participants crossed a state line, a crime and, for criminals, it was a "business opportunity." In fact Collins—described as a handsome, clean-cut young man of refined appearance, held on $50,000 bail—nicely personified for the press the sort who turn a misguided law to their advantage. By April 1916 the *New York Times* was claiming that his gang consisted of ten to twelve individuals who knew how to exploit the fears of the small-town businessmen who were brought to New York by wartime prosperity. Women would pick them up in Manhattan and lure them to Atlantic City. On their return to New York they would be accosted by "marshals" and the woman's lawyer. Up to $2,000 would be requested as hush money, the woman receiving only $10 to $50. In November 1916 a man named George Bush was arraigned for extorting $18,000 from men at Atlantic City. The police estimated that only one out of fifty victims ever lodged a complaint. Collins's victims—"wealthy and eminently respectable men"—were usually too afraid to come forward. Ironically the chief complaint against him was actually filed by a woman, Mrs. J. Bolten Winpenny of Philadelphia, whom Collins had blackmailed out of $8,000 in 1915.[12]

Collins was found guilty of extortion and spent two years in Sing Sing. In 1921 he was again in the news after John H. Reid, a wealthy silk manufacturer, was shot five times in the New York apartment of Hazel Warner on the night of May 5. She claimed that she saw nothing. Though he had bullets in his head, mouth, eye, neck, and thigh, Reid made the unlikely claim that he had shot himself; then he refused to make any further statement and was held as an uncooperative witness.[13] The police, finding letters to the twenty-seven-year-old Warner written by men from Palm Beach, Miami, Daytona, and Atlantic City, concluded she was part of a badger game 89 that worked the transatlantic liners. Such women made pickups at sea and then the male gang members made their demands in New York. The police believed that Collins, who was part of the gang, had shot Reid. By late May, however, the district attorney admitted that there was no proof of blackmail. Warner, while conceding to the grand jury that she knew another man who had been shot, insisted, "The allegation of a blackmailing ring is all bunk." The attempted murder of Reid was never solved, but the press would not let go of the story, describing Hazel Warner as "Collins' alleged accomplice in numerous blackmailing schemes which are said to have netted Collins' 'blackmailing syndicate' over one million dollars yearly."[14]

Just as the Mann Act created opportunities for criminals, so too did Prohibition. The press reported that Collins and Warner moved from the badger game to rum-running. Collins's whiskey-laden submarine-chaser was seized only after it had unloaded the 1,800 cases it had brought from the Bahamas to Philadelphia. In February 1922 Collins was arrested in Miami and indicted for violating the Volstead Act, but he managed to flee to France. His extradition in 1924 offered the press yet another occasion to recount his life of crime. The hordes of reporters who awaited his disembarkation from the *Paris* described him as the "real Raffles," a smooth talker and dresser, the head of a blackmailing ring that bilked victims out of hundreds of thousands of dollars. Collins served a year in prison and returned to France. He was soon back in the United States, however, and until 1937 the *New York Times* continued to report his brushes with the law. His reputation was such that he figured centrally in a 1933 *Collier's* magazine article exposing blackmail attempts entitled "Millions for Tribute." The newspaper-reading public was fascinated by Collins. The journalists who helped to construct the image of this enterprising rogue could not conceal their admiration for a figure who made such good copy.[15]

Chicago was also the focus of a major national blackmail conspiracy that exploited the Mann Act. In September 1916 the press reports of the arrests of a "Blackmail Trust" was front-page news for much of the month: "$250,000 BLACKMAIL ARRESTS" (September 16); "BLACKMAIL PLOT SPREADS" (September 25); "BLACKMAIL VICTIMS NAMED" (September 26). Federal agents were reported as conferring in Washington on the violation of section 145 of the Penal Code as they were allowed to involve themselves in state cases pertaining to the Mann Act and the impersonating of federal agents. One paper ran the story of the federal dragnet under the racy title "Government Extends Its Search for Love Pirates." It reported that the story broke after attempts were made to blackmail a Philadelphia congressman. In the winter of 1915 a young man had introduced the legislator to three women in Atlantic City. A week later two men claiming to be the police made an extortion demand. A trap was set for them, but they failed to show up. Bureau of Investigation head A. Bruce Bielaski launched a national search that turned up six hundred phony warrants and nine secret service badges. A gang of four men and three women had victimized at least fifteen men—the most prominent being a judge—in Chicago, New York, Philadelphia, and Atlantic City. The press claimed that the gang also worked on sleeping cars. Its victims included Francis Junkerman, a Cedar Rapids wholesale druggist, who believed that it was the authorities who had caught him with two women. To ensure that his prosecution would not take place until after his daughter's wedding, he paid out $10,000.[16]

The Collins gang was jailed only because a woman brought charges. Similarly Mrs. Regina A. Klipper was the first victim to come forward to testify against the Chicago syndicate. Four Chicago men had extorted $500 from Klipper, a Philadelphia department store buyer whom they caught in a room in the Empire Hotel in New York City with a confederate of theirs, Frank Crocker. In an attempt to prevent her from testifying in Chicago, Crocker kidnapped her and took her to Montreal for seven weeks. She eventually appeared in court where, despite fainting in the process of making her declaration, she identified several members of the gang. Crocker also helped the police, who made their swoop on September 16 on the "social gangsters" at the Tyson Apartments in Chicago.[17]

Another account of the gang's activities came from Edward R. West, the vice-president of a New York tea and coffee company. After traveling with Buda Godman from Chicago to New York he found himself arrested by "detectives" in the Ansonia Hotel. They threatened to charge him with violating the Mann Act if he did not pay $15,000. They all returned to Chicago, Godman hysterically demanding that West protect her reputation. West finally paid and was released. His evidence led to the indictment of Buda Godman (who proved to be the wife of Tell Taylor, a Chicago songwriter) and three men. The other victims' names, the press reported, were not to be released. It also noted that if witnesses were needed, discretion required that the unmarried would go first. The victims were said to include a Pennsylvania judge, a Philadelphia broker, and a Republican congressman entrapped in a badger game at his party's convention in Chicago.[18]

The press played up the notion of the villains being good-looking, fastidious "gentlemen crooks," one of whom disdainfully denied being part of any gang: "Pretty women and slick men! Say, did you see those cheap looking fairies? Who would fall for them? No live one would. It's a joke." The gang purportedly kept a card index on those Chicago citizens with money and an interest in "the gay life." Newspaper reports that the gang had up to sixty members and that its loot amounted to a million dollars were clearly exaggerated. In the end, few went to jail. In October 1916 Homer T. French was sentenced to eighteen months in Atlanta prison for impersonating a government official in order to blackmail West. His associates went to trial in December. In Chicago, Edward Donohue pled guilty and was sentenced to eighteen months in prison.[19]

The major gangs who exploited the Mann Act were broken up by the 1920s, but individual cases continued to surface. In 1921 Lyle Chastine was held on a Mann Act violation. Living on the avails of May Gallagher in Montreal and New York, he tried to shake down a movie businessman who had been with Gallagher at a Brooklyn apartment. In August 1928 the press reported that yet another man who took a woman from Atlantic City to New York found himself the victim of a badger game. Her husband and a "Pinkerton agent" demanded $1,000. The victim paid $500 and went to the police, who arrested the couple. In 1937 Sol Campo was victimized when two real policemen surprised him at a Long Beach, Long Island, hotel with a twenty-two-year-old woman. "We've been looking for you for a long time," they said. "You're both married and we're going to lock you up." Campo agreed to pay them $2,500 in installments. When the woman arrived at the first scheduled meeting with the two patrolmen, Campo realized that she had been part of the conspiracy. He went to the authorities, and at a second meeting the conspirators were arrested. The woman was given fifteen years' probation and was banned from New York City. Though the two patrolmen were sentenced to long prison terms, the judged stayed the execution pending their good behavior.[20]

In 1917 the United States Supreme Court concluded by a vote of five to three that the Mann Act applied "to individual escapades as well as to commercial vice." The result, protested Justice McKenna, was that "blackmailers of both sexes have arisen who use the terrors of the construction now sanctioned by this court as a help for their brigandage."[21] Lawmakers admitted that their fear of being seen as soft on vice prevented them from amending the law. The Mann Act remained on the books until 1986. Although press reports of blackmailers' exploitation of the act tended to wane in the later 1930s, such scenarios continued to be played out through the 1940s and 1950s.

American men were warned by the press and the courts that the Mann Act was not the only law with which the blackmailer could menace them. Various laws pertaining to adultery, divorce, alienation of affection, and breach of promise also lent themselves to similar purposes. In most states prosecution for adultery could occur only if the injured party complained, but once the suit was launched it could not be stopped. The courts feared that some might attempt to use the charge for purposes of extortion. For example, in Washington state in 1919 Laura B. Wilcox's husband charged her with having committed adultery with Joe H. Astin. Sometime later Mr. Wilcox, realizing that the case would bring disgrace and ridicule on all concerned, attempted to stop the proceedings. He found that he could not. A Washington appeals court judge declared that once such a suit was filed it had become a public offense and therefore could not be stopped. To allow private individuals to threaten or drop prosecutions for adultery, he warned, "would open the door of a treasure room for a horde of blackmailers . . . In no other class of litigation is the opportunity for blackmail already so great, and to increase it [would] add to its immense possibilities for the evilly disposed."[22]

Although cruelty was replacing adultery in America as grounds for divorce, cases involving adultery still occasioned opportunities for blackmail.[23] In 1919 Betty Inch, a young movie actress, was tried twice for blackmailing Eugene P. Herrman, president of an automobile company. He stated that she said that if she were not paid she would support Mrs. Herrman's divorce suit against him by stating that he was with two women while his wife was in Atlantic City. In court it also came out that Inch had made an affidavit in another divorce case, which the judge ordered to be identified only as involving Mrs. X and Ensign Y. The first Inch jury could not come to a decision, so a second trial was necessary. Convinced that the sight of the actress's legs had affected the men on the first jury, the district attorney had the bottom of the witness box closed in. Nevertheless the second jury also failed to reach a verdict. In 1921 Betty Inch appeared in another divorce trial, in Denver, Colorado, presided over by Judge Ben Lindsey, America's most famous divorce expert. This trial, which began in 1919, was a long-drawn-out affair in which the wealthy W. E. D. Stokes cited a dozen male friends of his wife as correspondents. The wife called his statements "filthy charges." Inch testified that Stokes had offered her $1,000 to testify against his wife. Stokes retorted that Betty Inch had asked for $10,000 to give evidence about certain happenings in the life of his wife, but that he had refused to pay. Stokes lost the divorce case and Inch was not prosecuted, but a man was found guilty of seeking to blackmail Stokes with letters that were supposedly incriminatory.[24]

Blackmail trials revealed that unscrupulous divorce lawyers exploited the lucrative possibilities that alienation of affection suits offered. In 1907 Lulu Grimes told an Indiana court that she had been used by a lawyer to extort money from well-off men. She was too good-looking to be working, the lawyer told her. "He said I could make my living easily by pulling people's legs."[25] The plan was for her to compromise a man and then for the lawyer to show up, announce that she was married, and, on behalf of her husband, threaten an alienation of affection suit.

"Rich Man Accuses Woman" headlined a 1918 press account of the claim made by Paul Edward Heller, president of the Heller Brothers Steel Company of Newark, New Jersey, that he was a victim of such a blackmail conspiracy. "Dandy Phil" Kastel, a well-known New York curb broker, named Heller in an alienation of affection suit and demanded $200,000 compensation. Heller, a bachelor, claimed that when he first met Maud Kastel he believed she was unmarried. When Heller learned otherwise he asked her husband if Heller's "social attentions" were acceptable. In response Kastel launched a divorce suit citing Heller as the correspondent; but a go-between came to tell Heller that if he paid $20,000 the suit would be dropped. The Kastels were indicted for blackmail, but the judge eventually threw the suit out for lack of evidence. Nine years later, in 1927, Kastel was found guilty of using the mails to defraud. Though the jury called for leniency, Judge Learned Hand sentenced him to three years in prison.[26]

A blackmail ring of Boston divorce lawyers was brought to light in 1922 by Mrs. Esther Levy (also known as Marion Sanders). The gang's leader, W. J. Corcoran, ex-prosecutor of Middlesex county, used women as lures and the threat of alienation of affection suits as weapons. Levy testified that in 1920 Victor Albert Searles, a Boston artist, paid $50,000 to Corcoran after a raid on a Back Bay apartment. In 1921 Corcoran, claiming to represent an injured husband, demanded $35,000 to withdraw a complaint against a hotel in which the man's wife had had unlawful intercourse. Ultimately the Commonwealth of Massachusetts brought down fifty-seven indictments, citing an attorney, a former state legislative representative, and the manager of the Copley Square hotel. In July 1923 Corcoran was jailed on seventy-four counts of extortion, conspiracy, and procuring.[27]

Alarmed by such revelations, the state of California in 1927 passed a law to prevent divorce blackmail. Without such a law, lawmakers asserted, "legal blackmail" was possible, as an individual could threaten to name a prominent person as a correspondent. In future, the law stipulated, if such allegations were not verified the libel laws would apply to the persons making the allegations. Yet the problem continued to be reported. In 1930 actor Harry Langdon, in fear of having his career destroyed, handed over $15,000 in cash and a $11,500 promissory note to stop a $250,000 alienation of affection suit against him threatened by Thomas J. O'Brien. Langdon subsequently discovered that he had been defrauded—Helen Walton O'Brien had left her husband years earlier. In 1933 Mrs. Frances King was tried for extorting $50,000 from Bruce Barton, an advertising executive. His story was that when she began working for him in 1928 she pretended to be single. They had an affair, which allowed Hugh King, her husband, to begin a divorce and alienation of affection suit. Barton paid $25,000 for a promise of no further demands. Nevertheless Frances King, who profited from the suit, then wrote a book that she threatened to publish if she were not paid an additional $50,000. Her story was that Barton was devoted to her between 1925 and 1928 and had her marry King to protect Barton's career. When King's husband—who appeared for the prosecution—denied her story, the jury found her guilty, but strongly recommended mercy. The *New York Times* reported that Barton's wife forgave him; and the judge went so far as to congratulate Barton as one of those men who "admit their mistakes, who keep women of this type from going on forever."[28]

Herman C. Pollack, Frances King's lawyer, was very much involved in pressuring Barton. Pollack himself paid the printer of the galleys of the book to show that the threat was serious. As a result he was disbarred in 1936 for having conspired with his client to attempt to force a cash settlement of an action for slander by the threat of publication of a book. "We are too frequently reminded in recent times," the judge concluded, "of the fact that some members of the bar have very little conception of true ethical principles. An attorney who lends himself to any such attempt at blackmail as here shown should not be permitted to remain a member of an   95 honorable profession."[29]

Breach of promise suits, like alienation of affection cases, attracted increasing amounts of the newspaper press's ire in the early twentieth century. The notion that a man could be sued for having reneged on a marriage promise was attacked by reformers as an antiquated and inequitable law that put only men at risk. Enrico Caruso, the famous opera singer, was entangled in just such a suit in 1912. In 1915, in another case, police charged Franklin D. Safford, a hotel clerk, for perjury and Miss Rae Tanzer for using the mails to defraud for launching their suit. Safford had assisted Tanzer in her breach of promise case against James W. Osbourne by asserting that Tanzer and Osbourne had been in the same hotel room. The prosecution portrayed Tanzer as a prostitute and attacked her lawyers as blackmailers, noting that if they "had gotten away with the Tanzer case they would have risen to the top of the blackmail bar." "How would you like to have any of this class of lawyers and this class of women get after you?" the district attorney asked the jury. "And if you don't do justice in this case you will give such lawyers and such women opportunity to ply their trade." Safford was found guilty and received a stiff prison term. In his summation Judge Hough, the press noted, made a point of underscoring the dangers posed by "entanglements" with women "to pocket, to reputation, and sometimes even to life."[30]

In July 1925 Evan Burrows Fontaine, a dancer, hit Cornelius Vanderbilt Whitney with a $1 million breach of promise suit. His counsel, John W. Davis, the recent Democratic Party candidate for president, called it blackmail and noted that Fontaine had lost a similar suit in California. Perhaps the most famous of the interwar breach of promise cases came to light in 1929 when Gene Tunney announced that Mrs. Katherine Fogarty was attempting to extort from him $500,000. On September 23, 1925, Tunney had become the world heavyweight boxing champion by defeating Jack Dempsey in Philadelphia. In 1927, when a rematch was being organized, Fogarty claimed that Tunney had promised to marry her, but had later wed another. His lawyer stated that threats of "damaging publicity" were made immediately before Tunney's last fight. In July 1928, two days before boxing Tom Heeney, Tunney paid Fogarty $35,000 for an affidavit disavowing any claim and the return of his letters. Interestingly, the affidavit also stated that Tunney "has at no time harmed or injured her [Fogarty] either physically or mentally" and that their relationship was "strictly impersonal." Once retired, Tunney declared that he would pay no more.[31]

If the laws on courtship and marriage put some men at risk, even more were compromised by their own foolhardiness. Such a lesson was unavoidably drawn by an enthralled American reading public that in the late 1930s followed the convoluted plot of what was probably the most sensational and complicated set of interwar extortion trials. On May 15, 1936, the *New York Times* reported that a grand jury would investigate the charge leveled by Alfred E. Smith, Jr., that he had been blackmailed. This was big news. Smith was the thirty-five-year-old son of Alfred E. Smith, Sr., the four-time governor of the state of New York, the 1928 Democratic Presidential nominee (the first Catholic of either party to be so honored), and now the chief booster of the newly built Empire State Building. His son, vice-president and general counsel of the Golden Stakes lottery corporation, moved in well-off if less exalted circles.[32]

Smith had trouble with women. He had married his wife, Betty, in 1924 after a whirlwind romance. They soon began to bicker over money, and she testified that he twice threatened to kill her. They divorced in 1932. Smith told the authorities that in May 1933 he met at a party a slender twenty-five-year-old blonde, Catherine Marie Pavlick. They spent a night at a hotel. Thereafter Smith had been milked out of $13,000 by Max Krone, a detective, and A. Henry Ross, a Brooklyn lawyer. Smith finally appealed to his father, who took him to the district attorney's office. When the police arrested Ross they discovered that he was the brother of Dr. Maxwell Ross, the Democratic Party leader of Brooklyn's 23rd Assembly District. In Krone's Dixie Hotel office they found a camera, wire-tapping equipment, a .38 pistol, clippings pertaining to breach of promise suits, and a picture of ex-Governor Smith inscribed, "To my friend Mr. Krone, Alfred E. Smith." The police had stumbled onto "a real nest of extortionists."[33]

Smith's story was that sometime after he had met Pavlick, Ross presented himself as her legal representative and stated that she needed $1,000 for an "illegal operation." Smith paid, but was told more money might be necessary to keep the secret abortion out of the press. He then paid $9,000 in cash and $4,000 in promissory notes, naïvely demanding in return a release. On the basis of Smith's testimony Ross, twenty-eight, and Krone, thirty-three, were indicted on May 16, 1936, for having extorted $12,900 from Smith with the threat of exposing his relationship with Pavlick. They pleaded not guilty. Pavlick admitted to the grand jury her part in the plot, asserting that she only expected $75 but received $1,000. Newly wedded and sobbing, she was released.[34]

The grand jury was not finished. Assistant District Attorney Harold W. Hastings informed it that Krone had for some time organized "champagne parties" at which well-off men were assured of meeting attractive young women. The police wanted to know if he and Ross had used these women to institute court actions against other men besides Smith. The press recalled that a young woman had recently cited Jefferson Wynne, son of the New York City health commissioner, in a suspicious $100,000 assault suit, which Judge John F. Carew had thrown out. In December 1934 Wynne had brought Helen Bray, a salesclerk, back to his apartment for a drink. She claimed that he had assaulted her. In dismissing her suit the judge told the court that Wynne was lucky: "He is not going to pay for this lesson, but if he doesn't learn maybe he'll pay for the next. That's all."[35]

Helen Bray, one of five women the police interrogated in 1936, admitted that Krone had forced her to bring actions against two men; one had settled out of court. Jack Dempsey, the ex–heavyweight champion, was also called before the grand jury, as his name had appeared in Krone's letters to Rosa Bianca Griffith, who had filed a breach of promise suit against another man. Dempsey had been the target of such a suit himself years earlier, but denied knowing either Krone or Griffith.[36]

Samuel C. Stampleman, president of the Gillette Safety Razor Company of Boston, then came forward to state that Krone and Ross had victimized him. He had to pay them $5,000 to halt a suit threatened by Helen Conboy of Kingsbridge, New York. Stampleman, who was subpoenaed to appear in Ross and Krone's trial, testified that in October 1933 he had been introduced by a friend to Helen Conboy in Boston. A week later he ran into her—by accident, he thought—on a train to New York and they had had dinner. On October 13 Krone, identifying himself as "Mr. Harris," phoned to set up a meeting at which he stated that the woman would claim that Stampleman had drugged and assaulted her in a New York hotel room. Ross, presenting himself as the woman's lawyer, offered to settle out of court. Stampleman, insisting that there was no truth to the allegation, nevertheless in December 1933 gave them two checks worth $5,000 to stop the suit. Conboy testified that she and the businessman did not have "improper relations," but that Krone, by threatening to tell her parents of her trip to Boston with Stampleman, had forced her to sign the four-page affidavit used to blackmail Stampleman. Conboy stated that Krone had similarly used her when threatening William D. Thomas, president of Stanwix Steel, with a $100,000 suit.[37]

Pietro Aria, identified in the press first as an opera singer and later as a concert violinist, came forward to lodge a complaint against a third black-mailer, Ernest Desmond de Hagen. Aria held Desmond (who called himself Lord Desmond) responsible for a threatened $5,000 suit launched by Anna Graef Drouillard. On hearing of the charges, Desmond, a habitué of Park Avenue bars, immediately fled New York in the company of twenty-three-year-old Marie Nielsen. When she eventually returned to New York, Nielsen, a former showgirl and Miss America of 1931, was jailed as a material witness. The police finally caught up with Desmond on June 22 in Los Angeles. By July 11 the portly middle-aged man with the fake British accent was back in Manhattan, residing in the Tombs Prison, where it was ascertained that his real name was Ernest Behagen. Originally from the Virgin Islands, he had passed himself off on various occasions as a barrister and a doctor. In 1924 he had been sentenced to a year in the St. Louis workhouse for unlicensed practice of medicine; but he had managed simply to walk away. He had run into similar legal problems in Winnipeg and Chicago. Since 1931 he had lived on $40,000 "borrowed" from Mrs. William H. McKelroy, widow of an Alabama banker, of East 48th Street. Desmond admitted to being twice married, siring an illegitimate child, forging a passport, and pretending to be a lawyer, doctor, and lord. He had conned Mrs. McKelroy out of $40,000 with the story that the money was needed to save his relatives' chateau in Bordeaux, France. Marie Nielsen, with whom he had fled, told the court that all she had ever got from him was a diamond that turned out to be glass. "You are a gigolo lord!" she cried, to which Desmond, still in character, tearfully responded, "That wounds my heart excruciatingly."[38]

Desmond was even reported to be sending extortion letters from the Tombs. Miss Nielsen visited him several times, and a keeper was suspended for his lenient treatment of the con man. In November 1936 he was tried and convicted for stealing $4,177 from Mrs. McKelroy, though her lawyers asserted that the actual amount was closer to $80,000. Desmond admitted to knowing Krone, Ross, and their stable of attractive young women, and in an attempt at plea bargaining said that he had found the woman for Ross and Krone who sued Aria and was willing to turn state's evidence against them. In the end he did not provide any help and was sentenced to two and a half to five years in Sing Sing.[39]

The fourth member of this New York gang was a well-known midtown lawyer, Jerome A. Jacobs. He had provided a reference when Krone applied for his detective license. In mid-June 1936 Paul J. Bonwit, former president of Bonwit Teller, testified that in the spring of 1933 Krone and Jacobs extorted money from him with the threat of launching a $100,000 suit on behalf of yet another wronged young woman. Apparently Bonwit had been on friendly terms with her in June 1932. In January 1933 Jacobs served a summons on Bonwit, and proceedings were actually begun in the New York Supreme Court. Krone and Jacobs demanded $1,000 to stop the suit against Bonwit, but eventually accepted $600. Jacobs, when indicted, attempted to suggest that the charge was politically motivated, protesting that "he would not be the goat for Governor Smith or anybody else."[40]

The authorities decided to try Jacobs in August 1936 for extorting money from Harry Bannister, the former husband of movie actress Ann Harding. Bannister testified that Jacobs and Raymond Derringer (a projectionist who posed as a police officer) in November 1934 tried to extort $1,800 from him with evidence that would endanger his child custody battle with Harding. (Their 1932 divorce had led to a nasty fight over their child.[41] Indeed, Bannister himself had to deny in court that he had attempted to blackmail his wife by linking her name to that of Hollywood playwright Gene Fowler.) Jacobs purportedly had evidence on Bannister's conduct after his divorce that would jeopardize his child custody suit. The prosecution also implied that Jacobs had attempted to extort money from Henry Huddleston Rogers, Jr. (grandson of one of the founders of Standard Oil), following the suspicious death of a showgirl in Rogers's home.[42] In October Jacobs was found guilty of extortion and sentenced to four to eight years in Sing Sing.[43]

In December 1936, because of a technicality, the first trial of Ross and Krone ended in a mistrial. Their second trial began in January 1937. Al

Smith, Jr., again described how he had met Catherine Pavlick at a party on Riverside Drive on May 3, 1933. She testified that after she had been to a hotel with Smith on May 6, Desmond, who had also been at the party, sent her to see Krone. He had her sign a paper, which she claimed she did not

As was the case in the Al Smith, Jr., scandal, the press reported that blackmail gangs commonly used pretty young women as bait with which to hook wealthy men. (Herb Roth illustration for John B. Kennedy, "Millions for Tribute," *Colliers,* March 25, 1933.)

read. Two weeks later Krone gave her $100, which he said was from Smith. Under questioning by the prosecution she admitted that there was no reason why she should have received $1,000 in total. Throughout 1933 Ross 101 kept up the pressure on Smith. The latter recalled Ross saying, "It's too bad you, your father, and your family must be brought into a matter like this." He told Smith that Pavlick would accept $7,000, but as she was in a "delicate condition" she also needed an extra $250 for a trip to Bermuda to see a doctor. The demands continued, and it was only a year later, after Krone began to badger Smith's father that Al Smith, Jr., decided to stop paying and contact the police. A detective sat in a phone booth in a restaurant where Smith and Krone had their last meeting. The detective heard Krone say to Smith, "You had better pay up or I'll take you over the jumps." In the final days of the trial, as the evidence piled up, Krone and Ross accused each other of being the brains of the gang. They were both found guilty and sentenced to three to eight years in Sing Sing.[44]

In the meantime, in August 1936 Betty Smith, in an attempt to make her ex-husband resume alimony payments, which he had stopped in July 1935, alleged that Al Smith, Jr., paid Pavlick over $12,000. Smith, Jr., whose admitted monthly income ranged anywhere from $1,000 to $30,000, was ordered to pay $150 a month to his ex-wife.[45] The press reported that she was an attentive spectator at Krone and Ross's trials.

Beginning in the 1920s New York tabloid newspapers such as the *Daily News,* the *Daily Mirror,* and the *Daily Graphic* (popularly known as the "Porno-Graphic") fed the public a constant stream of sensational stories under headlines ablaze with references to "love-pacts," "love-nests," "love-children," "love-thieves," "love-slayers," and "love-cheats." Dismayed commentators pointed to the appearance of the tabloids, as well as men's magazines such as *Hot Dog, Red Pepper,* and *Snappy Stories,* which specialized in off-color stories, as signaling the end of American prudery.[46] Such views could only be confirmed by the extraordinary series of interlocking blackmail trials precipitated by Alfred E. Smith, Jr., going to the authorities. The resulting trials revealed a modern America of promiscuous businessmen, shady lawyers, and sexually adventuresome young women. The latter were the focus of the concluding remarks of the judge who presided over the Krone and Ross trial. Ignoring all the evidence of male philandering, he presented the case as a lamentable demonstration of the decline in female morality. The testimony of Miss Pavlick, he said, was a "sad commentary on the custom of this age that girls do so much drinking."[47] What of the men who had pursued them? Erstwhile respectable men who were very much in the public eye, while claiming to be innocent, had put themselves in positions in which they appeared to be involved in adultery, seduction, sexual assault, and abortion. Were these powerful and wealthy men sexual predators? Were they gullible victims? Were they both? Strangely enough, neither the courts nor the press made much of the men's ambiguous activities. No doubt the simple narration of their fate was taken as a sufficiently sobering lesson for others who might think of giving in to temptation. The courts were not going to add insult to injury by dwelling on the misconduct of the men who had been swindled.

Moviemakers were equally circumspect. It is hard to think of many films that portrayed the straying male. *Philadelphia Story* (1940)—George Cukor's comic classic starring Katherine Hepburn, Cary Grant, and James Stewart—touches on the issue in an often overlooked subplot. A scandal sheet is threatening to expose the affair Hepburn's father is having with a showgirl, but the blackmailer is himself in effect blackmailed into silence. What is surprising is that the mother is portrayed as loyally taking her husband's infidelities in stride.[48] Eight years later Alfred C. Kinsey's famous sex survey would reveal that 50 percent of American husbands had been unfaithful at least once. Well before his book came out, the interwar blackmail cases were implicitly used by the press to show that America was no longer the repressed society it was once reputed to be.

It was only fitting that Peter Arno, the *New Yorker* cartoonist best known for his risqué depictions of gold-digging showgirls and their sugar daddies, found himself in January 1939 at the center of a blackmail scheme. The superintendent of Arno's studio on East 56th Street found a photograph, which two other men used to demand from Arno a "reward." The public might have wondered if it was a coincidence that in March, Mary Lansing Arno filed for divorce in Connecticut, citing Arno's intolerable cruelty. Arno did not contest the ending of the four-year marriage. The public must have also wondered about the nature of the mysterious photograph. All it learned was that the superintendent was given a suspended sentence for possession of an obscene picture, and the other two men were sentenced to three years in prison for extortion. On the very same page of the April 13, 1939, issue of the *New York Times* that reported their trial was an account of Arno sketching Miss Cobina Wright, whom the illustrators of New York had chosen as the city's most attractive and talented girl.[49]

Arno, according to the authorities, had acted wisely in going straight to the police. The first lesson drawn from extortion cases by legal experts and journalists was that men who were menaced had to prove their mettle. In 1918 the *New York Times* warned that cowardice made blackmail possible. In 1920 the paper launched the curious idea of organizing a "league" of men who would take a solemn vow not to pay bribes or blackmail. Cowardice stimulated crime; honesty and courage would defeat it. The police were eager to help, so a 1933 *Colliers'* magazine article reported, but fear still prevented the plundered from complaining. Such men were assured that if they showed courage there was no doubt as to whose honesty and whose honor the courts were most likely to support.[50]

Blackmail stories peaked in the interwar period because they fulfilled a social role. English accounts centered on class preoccupations. The American trial reports differed from the British in that they provided an arena in which male anxieties created by the greater sexual temptations and sexual dangers of modern life could be aired. When filmmakers and novelists produced accounts of the blackmailing of women they tended to be moralizing tales, warning women of sexual dangers. Men were far more likely to be blackmailed, but in fictional accounts there was no male equivalent of the "fallen" woman. Though there were, of course, innocent male victims, blackmail trials revealed that many erstwhile respectable men were accused of adultery, sexual assault, and even rape.

The blackmailing of American men cast a searching light on male privilege in the interwar years. Yet few victims seem to have appreciated the changing dynamics of gender relations that resulted from the increasing numbers of women entering the public sphere. Well-off men continued to assume they had the right to use their economic power to pursue and possibly extort sexual favors. The courts' response to such evidence was to position the men as victims, not aggressors. In reaffirming the naturalness of gender norms, blackmail accounts were in effect employed to support the call for men to be more manly than ever. Yet individual courage was not sufficient. Real change could only be accomplished if the lessons drawn from such trials led to legal reform. America had to free itself from antiquated laws that put men at risk and armed gold diggers and their confederates. That raised an obvious question: What view would American and English courts take of the laws that criminalized homosexuality and thereby armed the most ruthless gangs of extortionists?

THE
HOMOSEXUAL
TARGET
BETWEEN
THE WARS

Men who were victimized by pimps and prostitutes were customarily portrayed in the press as having been betrayed by their natural inclinations.
Men chased women. That such behavior was gaining a new level of explicit
social acceptance in the first decades of the twentieth century was a
reflection of the decline of the Victorian model of masculinity that had
stressed self-control, discipline, and delayed gratification. This older model
was slowly being replaced by notions of an elegant, sensual manliness,
personified by Rudolph Valentino in *The Sheik* (1921). The new male
model of gentle eroticism and athleticism as popularized by the matinee
idols clearly appealed to women. Men, however, were undecided about this
new image. Indeed, when the "slick and satiny" style of sophisticated masculinity associated with actors such as Noël Coward emerged, some commentators worried that it could lead to a potentially dangerous blurring of gender roles.[1] Anxieties elicited by the sense that in a white-collar world it was
no longer always obvious what constituted true manliness led some fiction
writers to create a caricature of the effeminate homosexual as the antithesis
of the "real" man. Interwar homosexual blackmail trials should be read
with this cultural context in mind. They threatened to destroy the clear de-
marcations supposedly separating the healthy from the perverse, and
thereby to expand the meanings of sexuality. Responding to the challenge,
the authorities and the press constructed accounts of blackmail that were
designed to limit as much as possible the damage such cases might cause.

In England the number of reports of homosexual blackmail was such that the newspaper-reading public could easily have concluded that almost every reference to "threats" or "menaces" related in some way to a same-sex encounter. The desire to prevent such scandalous accounts being multiplied led the House of Commons in March 1925 to engage in a remarkably candid discussion of homosexual blackmail, a discussion that would have been unthinkable in the United States House of Representatives. The topic was broached by a Unionist member's assertion that rapacious women were increasingly compromising professional men. Sir William Joynson-Hicks, the Home Secretary, responded that the police had informed him that in fact they were aware of few cases of poor girls extorting money from wealthy men. Most blackmail attempts involved what Joynson-Hicks described as the "far worse crime of sodomy, the threat of exposing which is the foundation of a very large proportion of the blackmailing that goes on in this country. It is a most disgusting and terrible thing that that should be the case."[2] He suggested flogging be added as a punishment to those miscreants who "seduced" men into a crime in order to blackmail them.

Mr. George Buchanan, a Labour MP from Scotland, concurred that in Glasgow the seduction of girls "never" led to blackmail. He, like other Labour members, opposed any extension of corporal punishment, but agreed with Joynson-Hicks that extortion was usually linked to gangs of male prostitutes. In Glasgow, he reported,

> They were without dress, or any male attire, but with tight fitting jackets; and all that; with their hands finely chiseled [nails filed]—or far more chiseled than, say, the hands of my wife; who called each other by female names, used the scents common to women, and even painted [wore make-up]. They were known to the police. In nearly every charge of blackmail, or in nearly every case where blackmail was suspected, it was a comparatively well-to-do man who was concerned. It is very rarely that there is blackmail amongst the poor. I have my own ideas as to that, and I will merely say that I think working people are more moral. They do not lend themselves to this sort of thing.

After noting that one well-known gang of Glasgow youths called themselves the "White Hats," Buchanan insightfully went on to note that repressive laws and stigmas combined with widespread poverty provided fertile ground for the growth of blackmail.

The problem is that, generally speaking, the ordinary crime as between men and women is not the heinous offense that men need to be ashamed of so much as the crime known as sodomy . . . Every one of the men who follow   107 this trade of sodomy—and it is a trade, I am sorry to say among some men—an occupation—every one of those men is, more or less, the product of the cruel sort of social life in which they are brought up. It has partly grown up out of social conditions and I do not think you will stamp it out merely by repressive punishments like flogging.

With better economic conditions Buchanan was hopeful there would emerge "a type of men who will rebel against selling themselves in this cruel and fearful fashion."[3]

In the following decades the English police would regularly report that they regarded male prostitutes as the most likely blackmailers. One police detective who contributed to a 1938 discussion of extortion stated: "Without doubt immorality of some kind forms the basis of most kinds of extortion. Either the victim has been guilty of some immoral act or has been indiscreet enough to make associations which have exposed him to accusations of such conduct. Hence we find that most professional blackmailers are either prostitutes, male or female (and the former predominate), or those who live upon the proceeds of prostitution, directly or indirectly." Sex for the male prostitute was a means to an end. Once he saw his opportunity of using the power he had over his client he turned to extortion. A 1949 police report on male prostitution stated that blackmail was its most dangerous feature. Male prostitutes tended to be "clannish," hanging out at cafés and milk bars (called soda fountains in America). Yet how "homosexual" such men were was difficult to determine; of the fifty cited in the 1949 sample over a third were married. William Jowitt, the Lord Chancellor, later stated that 95 percent of the blackmail cases that came to court when he was attorney general between 1929 and 1932 involved homosexual threats.[4] This was clearly an exaggeration; but certainly the single largest category of blackmail cases that the British press reported concerned same-sex activities.

One reason why so many homosexual blackmail cases were reported in England, especially as compared to the United States—yet a fact not reported by British commentators—was that after 1925 all English blackmail victims were given anonymity in court. This must have led to a larger percentage of homosexuals going to the police, though it is difficult to determine exact numbers. What is clear is that the English press carried numerous accounts of such cases, their numbers climbing in the Depression years of the early 1930s. Even so, the ordinary citizen had no idea of the full extent of the victimization of homosexuals. Fortunately we can have some sense of the gap between what the police knew and what came out in the press because the Public Record Office has the full file of the activities of what appears to be the most aggressive of the English homosexual blackmail gangs. A comparison of the published and unpublished accounts of homosexual blackmail gives some sense of the degree to which the authorities constructed an account of homosexual blackmail suitable for public consumption.

On October 23, 1937, the *Times* reported that Harry Raymond, a thirty-seven-year-old café proprietor, and Alfred Bird, a twenty-one-year-old club secretary, had been charged at the Westminster Police Court with demanding £5,000 from a man identified only as Mr. A. The police had been waiting at the Empire Restaurant near Victoria Station on October 21 when the three men had met at a prearranged rendezvous. There the authorities overheard Raymond threatening the victim with the words "You know I can ruin you unless you pay." Raymond and Bird were remanded and further charged with having on a previous occasion demanded £3,000 from their victim. The two were committed for trial on November 2, the crown counsel indicating that the case involved "certain acts of misconduct" that had taken place between Alfred Bird and Mr. A. The magistrate refused to permit either bail or legal aid for the prisoners. At their trial the prosecuting counsel explained to the jury that the prisoners were charged with what "was commonly known as blackmail." Raymond and his accomplices had, the crown alleged, entrapped Mr. A in a compromising situation with Bird. Raymond had pretended to be Bird's brother and the other men (who had not been arrested) detectives. Threatening to make public Mr. A's "misconduct," they sought to extort large sums of money from him. Bird gave no evidence. Though Raymond admitted to being part of a conspiracy, he denied making any threats. The jury needed just thirty minutes to find both men guilty. On December 4 the press reported that Raymond, the "lank-haired and glassy-eyed" mastermind of the gang, had been sentenced to ten years' penal servitude; young Bird got twenty months.[5]

The *Times*'s account was typical of interwar press reports of such crimes. The paper made no explicit mention of homosexual acts. It assumed that the ordinary reader knew that male "misconduct" could only mean one thing. The *Times* was certainly not going to refer to "the love that dare not speak its name." British judges' practice of asking the press not to reveal the identities of blackmail victims further shrouded such trials in mystery. This was ironic. In bewailing the alarming rate at which the crime of blackmail was growing and in depicting the hordes of ravenous criminals waiting to pounce on the respectable man who gave way to temptation, the authorities were clearly seeking to shore up the sexual status quo. But the courts' desire to protect the reputations of victimized middle-class men resulted in their providing the public with only the sketchiest account of the blackmailers' activities. What did the general reading public make of such slim, tension-ridden reports? Were they alarmed or mystified? Did they identify with the well-off, incautious victims who enjoyed anonymity or with the vicious young men whose names, ages, and addresses were publicized? Was public morality improved by the press's broadcasting the fact that areas of London such as Piccadilly Circus were notorious hunting grounds for male prostitutes? These questions are not easy to answer, but the fact that they even come to mind indicates the difficulty the courts and the press had in seeking to depict homosexual blackmail in ways that were neither sexually nor socially subversive. By first tracing Scotland Yard's investigation of the Raymond gang and then comparing the detailed information of this one case with the reports of fifty or so others that occurred in England between 1900 and 1939 it is possible to see what the public was told and what it could only guess.

The police had known of Raymond's activities for some time before he was charged in the Mr. A case. In May 1937 they received an anonymous letter stating that Raymond was a "ticket of leave man," or parolee, having earlier been sentenced to five years for blackmail. He now ran a café in Berwick Street, Soho, and moved in rough circles. "He is regularly seen in Tattersall's Enclosure at the various London Race meetings in company with obvious sodomites who [*sic*] he uses as pawns in his nefarious game."[6] The Metropolitan Police noted on June 8, 1937, that they knew he was blackmailing a number of men. The problem was that all the victims had a "skeleton in the closet" and so would not want to appear in court.

109

Unbeknownst to her son, a Mrs. Giveen of Belfast wrote Scotland Yard in August 1937 that Raymond, whom she knew as "Mr. Gould," was blackmailing her boy, who enjoyed a good position in society. Scotland Yard assembled a long list of the victims of Raymond's extortion attempts and assigned code names for those whom they thought might appear as witnesses. The files contain little more than the names of some of these men. Mr. G was Mr. Insole of Hastings, Mr. H was Patrick Wise (son of Sir Frederick Wise, Unionist MP), Mr. K was a Mr. McLean, and Mr. L was Joseph Britland.

The police collected full statements from ten others. Rather confusingly the police referred to two different victims as Mr. A. The first was a young artist by the name of Edward Seago. In October or November of 1936 at the Café Royal he had met Desmond Nils (who was in fact Thomas Desmond McNally), a young American. Seago told the police that he and his new friend discussed the French Impressionists and visited the Burlington gallery. They had dinner at Seago's club and though he admitted that they had later shared a room at the Tuscan Hotel he insisted that they had had separate beds. After their third meeting Desmond was allowed to borrow Seago's car and was introduced by Seago to his mother. The artist told the police that the relationship was quite innocent and described himself as acting as a "Dutch uncle." When Desmond said he needed money to return to the United States Seago gave him £35. Desmond subsequently attempted—or claimed he attempted—suicide (a common ploy), and Seago provided him with a further £45 and paid his rent. Raymond then showed up at Seago's country house and made further demands, but without success. Seago's relationship with Desmond came to the police's attention in September 1937 when the youth was arrested for a theft and was found to be carrying a revolver. He was sentenced to three years in Borstal.[7]

Mr. B was the seventy-year-old Frederick Simmons. The Caithness-shire constabulary informed Scotland Yard in April 1937—by letter, there still being no telegraph connection to the Shetland Islands—that two "sodomites" by the names of Harry Raymond and Frank Wright were making demands for money on a local man, presumably using the threat of exposing "some guilty association between the parties." Simmons made a statement to the Shetland police that in October 1936 while visiting London he had met the nineteen-year-old Frank Wright. They struck up some sort of friendship. After Simmons returned north they corresponded, and he agreed to hire on Wright, who had asked for work. Wright arrived with his "brother" Leslie, who announced that the boy was in trouble. Simmons related that, as Frank was in tears, he gave Leslie Wright a £100 check and agreed that Frank could stay at the farm while Leslie returned to England. The latter soon wrote, however, stating that a further £250 was required to ensure Frank's safety. "Now once more I beg of you to do everything in your power. I can only say I thank you from the bottom of my heart for all you have done. Please don't mention anything to Frank about this, the best thing to say is that everything is settled, otherwise he will worry himself to death. Tell him I hope he is a good lad and working hard and doing as you tell him." Simmons sent the money. Why did he make these large payments? Simmons's line was that it was simple charity. "I never had any relationship with these men," he asserted, adding that he "believed they were brothers." The Shetland police claimed to believe Simmons and concluded its factual report with the curiously moralizing statement "He does *not* appear to have had any vile dealings with the above named."[8]

Leslie Wright was in fact Harry Raymond. His continued demands finally drove Simmons to contact the police. At the beginning of June the Lerwick force sent Scotland Yard a copy of Raymond's photo. The local police spoke again to Simmons in August. His complaint was that Leslie Wright (Harry Raymond) and Frank Wright (whom the police also knew as Frank Cotteril and Danny O'Neil) had attempted to obtain money from him by menaces. The superintendent of Lerwick cautioned Scotland Yard that Simmons's account "may be deemed useless." Nevertheless on August 11 the Shetland county police sent Simmons to London to talk to the officers of the Criminal Investigation Department. Simmons now told them that he knew Raymond as "Leslie Wright" and that he was a "sodomite." He admitted giving Raymond £250. He did not want, he insisted, his name linked in public to Raymond in any way.[9]

Harold Vernon, a retired Indian judge living in Taunton, reported that he had been subjected to similar demands. Sometime in 1935 at about 10:30 at night, having left the Palladium Music Hall and walking down Regent Street, he met a youth, seventeen or eighteen years of age, who appeared down and out and who called himself "Harry Green." He was about five foot five, fair-haired, and had a cockney accent. Vernon went back to the young man's room on Panton Street, Haymarket. Vernon claimed that all he did was give the youth £1 and advise him to stop loitering, but he also admitted, "I probably gave him my London club address and telephone number." Moreover months later Vernon wrote the young man to say he was coming to London and would like to see him. Shortly thereafter another man (probably Raymond) called Vernon and asked for a meeting at the Leicester Square tube station. He told Vernon that the youth was in trouble and "made some suggestions to me as to my relations with Harry Green." Vernon reported that he angrily left. Nevertheless on October 20, 1937, he met Harry again near Leicester Square and gave him a few shillings. The next month when Harry phoned him Vernon refused to speak to him and insisted that Harry write him. On November 22, Harry sent Vernon a telegram saying he needed money to go to Ireland. Vernon agreed to pay for his fare, but then someone calling himself Andrews phoned, identified himself as a friend of Harry, and asked for a "loan." On November 25 Harry came to Vernon's house with the story that Raymond—who was now in police custody awaiting trial—had wanted to use him to blackmail Vernon. Harry said that he refused and was now on the run and needed money. Vernon would not advance any cash, and he and his wife subsequently received threatening phone calls. After an unidentified man rang, insisting on knowing what Vernon had done to the caller's "brother," claiming to have proof that he had "interfered" with Harry, and demanding money, Vernon went to the police.[10]

Captain Richard Dixon, a retired officer of the Royal Engineers, lived in fear of being victimized by someone just like Raymond. A decade earlier a gang had extorted over £10,000 from Dixon. On May 20, 1927, its six members were convicted. The leader, George Taylor (purportedly the son of a high-ranking British civil servant in Egypt), was sentenced to life and the rest received prison terms of eight to thirteen years. Their jury heard that the gang had used as bait twenty-six-year-old Norman Stuart, a musician who, telling a tale of distress, had lured Mr. X (Dixon) to his flat. The other gang members barged in claiming to be the young man's irate father and brothers and demanded hush money. Arthur Brown, who had not even been part of the original gang but simply heard that the captain was an easy mark, pursued him to Amsterdam and, claiming to be a detective specializing in blackmail, also extorted money. The demands had been continually pursued over the course of three and a half years. In handing down such severe sentences the presiding judge castigated the accused; he also upbraided the victim for not coming forward sooner.[11]

Nine years after the convictions, in 1936, one of the gang members who had blackmailed Dixon had the effrontery to write him to ask for money to hire a lawyer. Worse, some of the gang members still in prison passed on their information to Raymond, who was also serving time for a 1933 conviction. In 1937 Dixon was seventy-two years of age and still in mortal fear of further extortion demands. The trappings of wealth—his house in Cornwall, his servants, his eighteen-ton yacht the *Sea Crest*—provided little protection. His fears were justified. In July 1937 Raymond and three other members of the gang—John O'Neil, Leslie Crawford, and Harry Davis— tried to contact Dixon. They descended on Falmouth, saying they were old friends of the captain and asking his whereabouts. The Cornwall constabulary got wind of the affair and in the town of Flushing used the excuse that the Londoners' car was illegally parked to question its occupants. They looked, the constabulary reported, like bookmakers. Fortunately Dixon was away on his yacht and could not be contacted. Scotland Yard apparently hoped to use Dixon as bait in order to entrap Raymond. On their instructions Dixon's servant Albert Corke in September 1937 was sent to Raymond's café on Lisle Street in London to ask why he was looking for Dixon. Arrangements were made for Raymond to come to Dixon's London club. For some reason—possibly because he suspected a trap—Raymond never showed up, and the ensnarement failed.[12]

Francis Lawrence Walsh, a fifty-year-old unmarried sales representative of the Country Machine Corporation in Sittingbourne, also managed to avoid paying Raymond. Walsh told the police that it was his custom to spend Saturdays in the neighborhood of Charing Cross Road. There in May 1936 he met in a café a dark-haired, nineteen- or twenty-year-old "decent sort of fellow," Frank Cotteril (actually Danny O'Neil, and known to Frederick Simmons as Frank Wright), who said he was hoping to work as an extra in the film industry. Walsh's story was that they became friends and he started to pay for Frank's meals. Then, in December 1936 someone began to make inquiries about Walsh at both his home and his business. The day before Christmas Harry Raymond, claiming to be Frank's brother, turned up with the sad news that Frank had been involved in a robbery and needed help. Walsh was suspicious and uncooperative. Frank then called asking for financial assistance. When he was refused he dropped his whin-

113

ing tone and turned nasty. On December 26 Walsh sent a letter describing the shakedown to Scotland Yard.[13] He noted that Raymond had a list of names and addresses and assumed that he was also blackmailing others.

Francis Berkeley Hyde Villiers, who lived in Mayfair and worked for Imperial Chemical Industries, had a similar experience. His story was that in March 1937 at Russell's Bar in Leicester Square he met a "lad" by the name of Frank Neale. Villiers told the police he went back to the young man's flat on the Gray's Inn Road only "for the purposes of examining references the youth said he held." Three days later a man calling himself Dillon called, claiming to be Frank's brother and demanding money. Villiers contacted his solicitors, they wrote to the "brother," and nothing more was heard of it.[14]

Mr. C (Captain Harold Godwin, a retired officer of the Indian Army) was one of the few victims to be quite open about his homosexuality. The file does not explain why he failed to employ the customary narrative form of the gullible innocent. Godwin, who worked as a theatrical agent in Bolton, in September 1936 recalled meeting at the Haymarket Fun Fair "Jim," a slim, dark young man, eighteen or nineteen years of age. Godwin candidly reported that they went to a hotel near Waterloo Station, where they spent a half hour masturbating each other. Jim said he could usually be found around the Fun Fair. They continued to meet through November and December, Godwin paying Jim fifteen to twenty shillings each time. On February 1, 1937, they were together in a flat in Whitfield Street when suddenly a man claiming to be a policeman (actually Villiers' Dillon, who was also known as John Michael Conner) burst in. After insisting that Godwin identify himself he told Godwin he would have to come to the police station. "I'll have to take you along there. I suppose you know that this boy is on probation as being suspected of being a male prostitute and I am a probation officer who is responsible for his conduct." Jim was allowed, however, to telephone his brother. Shortly thereafter the brother, "John Stone" (actually Raymond), arrived. Godwin recalled him bouncing about the room in an excitable manner, shouting at Jim: "Where have you been, we've been looking for you everywhere, your mother is very anxious about you." He apologized to Godwin on behalf of Jim and said that he could "square it" with the probation officer. He calculated that £50 would be needed both to pay off the officer and to send Jim to Leicester. Godwin realized that he was caught in a badger game, but afraid that if he was uncooperative the three men might turn violent. Regretting that he did not have much money on him, he gave them £1, promising that more would be forthcoming. Instead he went to the police the next morning.

Godwin was not otherwise a cooperative witness and had no desire to appear in court. Having made his initial complaint he fled the country for Cyprus. Only on his return to England in the fall of 1937 did the police track him down in Newcastle. The Department of Public Prosecutions was not impressed by the statement he gave in October 1937, complaining that there was no corroborating evidence.[15]

The police described all of these victims of Raymond's gang—even the candid Captain Godwin—as men of "good social standing." But Ashley Pearce, whom the police code-named Mr. F, was in their eyes "a very weak effeminate type of individual." He was the only victim so described. This judgment appears to have been at least partly based on the authorities' distaste for Pearce's low social status. They were certainly not as condemnatory of the wealthier victims, who had presumably committed similar "indecent acts." Pearce, a single twenty-nine-year-old, was the caretaker at a Stratton Street block of flats just off Piccadilly. In September 1936 in Piccadilly Circus he met Leslie Simmons (Benyman), a smartly dressed man in his early thirties. Pearce told the police that the next night they had sex in his flat. Simmons wanted to bugger Pearce but the latter did not like it. "In my rooms we masturbated each other. It was his suggestion in the first place but I agree that I was willing for it to be done. After the acts described he told me he was hard up, stuck for rent and asked me to lend him a pound." Thereafter Pearce had to pay £1 for each sex act.

After a few weeks Raymond showed up at Stratton Street and took over Pearce's flat as a second home, sleeping on the floor and at least once sharing Pearce's bed. "On the one occasion Raymond slept in my bed with me he asked whether I wanted to 'do it' to him (meaning of course to commit buggery with him). I told him I was far too tired and would have nothing whatever to do with him."[16] Despite the fact that he was scraping by on a mere twenty-seven shillings a week, Simmons and Raymond ruthlessly used the threat of exposing Pierce's homosexuality to take all of his cash. They even had him raise £4 on his life insurance policy. In the meantime they used the flat as a meeting place to plan sting operations, including extorting money from Edward Seago. Simmons told him that Seago was in love with Thomas Desmond McNally (whom Seago knew as Desmond

Nils). When Seago visited the Stratton Street flat, Raymond pretended to be the caretaker.

116   Pearce was in the peculiar position of being the one victim of Raymond's gang who viewed its operations from the inside. He saw Raymond playing the role of caretaker when Seago visited Desmond at the Stratton Street flat. He watched the gang when they went off in their rented automobile—complete with a chauffeur in livery—to track down Seago at his country house. The gang members openly told Pearce of their scams: "Grahame [another member of the gang] and McNally told me they associated with men and committed acts of indecency with them for money and that they had no difficulty in getting money from them as they could bring pressure to bear by threatening to expose them." At the same time the gang ruthlessly exploited Pearce. When he was slow in paying Raymond threatened him. "You wouldn't like your Mother to know what you are doing up here. You're nothing more than a bloody fucking prostitute and I am going to tell your Mother unless you give me money."[17] When Pearce tried to keep the young thugs out of the flat Raymond simply kept on ringing the bell and made a disturbance until Pearce was forced to respond. Raymond beat Pearce for not trusting him, and the abusive Simmons reduced him to tears. When Pearce's cash supply was finally exhausted, he was assaulted by Simmons, who even stole his clothes and then pawned them for thirty-nine shillings. Pearce found himself in effect a prisoner in his own flat from June 1936 to May 1937, when, in his own words, he finally "escaped." The man whom the police interviewed in September 1937 had been reduced to a nervous wreck.

By the fall of 1937 the police had no shortage of information on Raymond's hectic round of blackmailing attempts. Lloyd's Bank informed them of the large checks he deposited in his account. The Department of Public Prosecution's problem was that his victims were either men of good social standing who refused to testify or an abject creature like Pearce in whom the crown counsels had no confidence. Finally the prosecution found in the second Mr. A the sort of witness they needed, a man of sufficient wealth to impress a jury and the willingness to admit his homosexual practices. This Mr. A, the man Raymond threatened at the Empire Restaurant, was Ian B. Fraser, a wealthy fifty-one-year-old retired businessman who lived in Kensington. After twenty-six years in India Fraser had returned to London in 1932. He met at the bar of the Palladium Music Hall a young man who introduced him to his brother, Alfred Bird. They discovered they shared a common interest in automobiles, soon became friends, and Fraser began to take Alfred with him on visits to Blackpool and Brighton. He allowed the young man to drive his Riley, but cars were not their main interest. The first time they met, Fraser told the police, "We played about together and he masturbated me." He admitted that "indecent conduct" took place thereafter (by which he meant mutual masturbation), he paying £1 or more per session. He gave Alfred clothes and money; the youth got to know everything about Fraser. In particular he knew of the other young men to whom he introduced Fraser—young men who went back to Fraser's Westminster flat for sex in return for money.[18]

On May 2, 1937, Harry Raymond, posing as "Vincent Axford," burst into Fraser's flat while Alfred was there. Raymond claimed that he had had detectives watching them because Alfred had procured Raymond's brother for a sadistic homosexual client who had savagely whipped him. All these sordid details were now going to be presented to the police. Fraser was alarmed, and Alfred advised him that it would be best to silence Raymond by paying him £450. Raymond agreed to accept the money, saying it would be spent sending his brother to Ireland, and signed a statement promising to drop all further proceedings. Fraser in addition gave Alfred £200 to open up his own business. Three days later Alfred was back saying that he needed more money to call off the detectives. Fraser, still trusting the youth, gave him another £350.

Fraser left London for his house in Bath. Raymond and Bird were soon in hot pursuit. They made it an excursion of sorts, Raymond bringing along his sister and his nephew. Bird now claimed that, given the social prominence of the sadist whom they were investigating, the "detectives" were demanding a further £3,000 to drop the case.[19] Fraser was badgered by the hysterical Bird, who cried that if his scandalous life were made public it would kill his mother. Fraser drew £2,500 on his life insurance and once again received a receipt and the promise that the detectives would be called off. But at this late stage Fraser began to have doubts and, when he could find no reference to the detective agency in the business directory, stopped payment on the check. Bird came round immediately, now protesting that if the news of his activities got out he would be jailed as a procurer. Fraser caved in yet again and reversed the stop order. At long last, in the fall of 1937, when Raymond and Bird renewed their demands yet again, Fraser finally went to the police. They were accordingly waiting at the Empire Restaurant when the extortionists made their demand for £5,000. At this last meeting Raymond brazenly admitted to Fraser that there had never been any detectives but that he and Bird now had to leave the country, possibly for South Africa. Raymond reminded Fraser that his homosexuality still placed him at risk: "You know I can ruin you unless you pay." Raymond further cited the fact that he had served time as evidence that he was not intimidated by the law: "So you see prison means nothing to me." Chief Inspector William Parker overheard the conversation and made the arrests as the culprits left the restaurant.

At the trial the police were preoccupied by the nervousness of their star witness. Fortunately Fraser persevered, and Raymond soon crumpled. The Chief Superintendent of Scotland Yard was very pleased with the outcome of the case. He noted the difficulty of obtaining evidence in blackmail attempts and the months of work required to assure a conviction. In January 1938 Chief Inspector Parker and Detective Inspector Thorp received commendations for their masterly handling of a difficult undertaking. The outcome of the investigation, according to Scotland Yard, represented more than anything else the triumph of dedicated police work. What the documentation in the police file does not disclose is as interesting as what it does. It neither directly mentions the laws against homosexuality that gave rise to blackmail nor even alludes to the possibility that the upper-class men who engaged in "vile dealings" could be prosecuted.

So much for the victims and the police. Who were the blackmailers? The police files referred to a total of eleven gang members, but only two men were tried—Raymond and Bird. Harry Raymond's original name was Arthur Gould. He had been an actor, appearing in the West End in the 1920s in such plays as *The Ringer, Firebrand,* and *Rising Generation;* "Harry Raymond" was his stage name.[20] Even after turning to crime he remained an actor. He took on the various roles of outraged brother or father or probation officer with obvious zest. He spent some time in South Africa in the late 1920s and returned to England in 1929. Somehow by 1931 he had acquired the money to buy a Carnaby Street café in Soho that became a meeting place for a shady crowd. According to his brother-in-law: "This was frequented by Moral Perverts. Whilst he was in this business he was convicted at the Old Bailey and sentenced to five years penal servitude." In January 1933 Raymond had indeed been sentenced to five years for the blackmailing of Mr. W. The press accounts of the trial were very discreet, but it was reported that though given £75 Raymond had threatened his victim that if more money were not forthcoming damaging information would be given to his wife.[21]

119

While in prison Raymond was schooled by the gang that had milked Richard Dixon for over £10,000. On his release in October 1936 Raymond took over another Soho café, Harry's Restaurant, and threw himself back into a hectic round of extortion attempts. Vernon, Walsh, Godwin, Pearce, and Fraser had all been involved with young men while Raymond was in prison. It was only after he returned to the streets in October 1936 that he transformed these male prostitutes into accomplices in his blackmailing scheme. The police knew that Raymond had attempted to extort money from over a dozen victims during a single year. There were no doubt others who did not come forward.

Those who simply read the newspapers had no idea of how many victims of blackmail there were; they also had no idea of how many blackmailers were at large. In this particular case the police felt they only had sufficient evidence to convict Raymond and Bird. Most of the men associated at one time or another with Raymond's activities were not prosecuted. The gang consisted of two types. One included attractive young men like Alfred Bird, who acted as bait. Bird, to whom Fraser had given £1,200 between 1932 and 1937, lived on the Pentonville Road and, according to Scotland Yard, had a girlfriend in Brighton. When the police pounced, Raymond's first thought was for his confederate. "Can't you leave Bird out of this?" he asked the constables. In the police court Bird's main concern was if he could see his mother. The others of this sort in Raymond's gang included Leslie Benymam (also known as Simmons); Thomas Desmond McNally (Desmond Nils), who was convicted in 1937 along with Frank Grahame for a confidence trick involving a jade necklace but because of his youth was sent to a reformatory; and Frank Bernard Neale, who had been convicted with Raymond in 1933 for blackmail and sentenced to three years in prison. Neale was described at the time by the police as a "dancing partner." A good many of the blackmailers who preyed on homosexuals passed themselves off as artists, actors, and musicians or as being in some way connected to the entertainment industry. The police simply stated in court that Neale was a "pest," having been sentenced for homosexual offenses in 1926, 1929, and 1930.[22] John (or Danny) O'Neil (known also as

Frank Wright and Frank Cotteril) lived with Raymond. The police regarded him as a "sexual pervert," but he insisted that he had never acted indecently with Raymond. "He has tried but I would not stand for it." O'Neil claimed to be only a friend and chauffeur, driving the gang to the Shetlands, Hastings, and Cornwall. He lied like a trooper, claiming to have no idea why such trips had been undertaken.

The second type of criminal associated with Raymond were prison-hardened toughs, whose job it was to pose as policemen or detectives and frighten the victims into paying up. Harry Richard Davis (also known as Burgess) had been charged with assault and receiving stolen property; John Michael Conner (also known as Dillon) had a thirty-year-long record that included housebreaking and larcenies; Frank Grahame had been convicted of robbery; Leslie Crawford had served time in prison for stealing. Crawford on occasion had the temerity to call himself "George Ives," an apparently mocking tribute to George Cecil Ives, one of England's most active campaigners for the decriminalization of homosexuality. The one thing that both the reformer and the criminal shared was the knowledge that the existing law made homosexuals the prime victims of blackmailers. In the late nineteenth century the police had reported the existence in parts of London of "blackmailing boys"; thanks to twentieth-century advances in communication and transportation Harry Raymond's gang was able to pursue its prey across the entire country.

Though the newspaper-reading public knew little of the machinations of Harry Raymond's gang, those who closely scrutinized the short newspaper accounts of other criminals who victimized homosexuals were provided with remarkably similar scenarios. But what did the public know of the victims? Alan Sinfield has argued that Oscar Wilde's trials "helped to produce a major shift in perceptions of the scope of same-sex passion. At that point, the entire vaguely disconcerting nexus of effeminacy, leisure, idleness, immorality, luxury, insouciance, decadence and aestheticism which Wilde was perceived as instantiating, was transformed into a brilliantly precise image."[23] But no such homosexual blackmail figure ever appeared in a twentieth-century English court. Middle-class men were more careful after the Wilde debacle; so were the authorities. In 1930 the press reported that a man had been tried for exploiting two boys who went to hotels with gentlemen. In 1915 he had provided boys for army officers and dabbled in blackmail as well. The irate judge, in sentencing the accused to five years in prison, pointed out that the 1885 Criminal Law Amendment Act only made it a crime to procure girls, as the Victorians could not imagine one to be "so black as to live on the immoral earnings of young men."[24] He said nothing of the morals of the officers and gentlemen.

121

Somerset Maugham's biographer notes that the police did not want to see well-known people in court, and Maugham's "fame and family connections almost guaranteed him immunity unless he behaved with Wildean stupidity." Given that youthful homosexual experimentation was ubiquitous in the English public schools, it is hardly surprising that the elite would close ranks to protect its own. When Bobbie Shaw, Nancy Astor's son, was arrested in 1931 for a homosexual offense Waldorf Astor used his influence to have the press provide a cover-up. Yet E. M. Forster's homosexual novel *Maurice* (written in 1913 but published in 1967) captures what must have been the worry of many well-off men. The guilt-ridden hero mistakenly believes that a note which a friendly gamekeeper has sent him contains a threat. "It contained every promise of blackmail, at the best it was incredible insolence . . . He [Maurice] had gone outside his class and it served him right." W. H. Auden, however, claimed that he regarded extortion as a joke. He asserted that in 1929 he had to pay £5 to the Oxford college scout who discovered him in bed with future poet laureate John Betjeman. Auden liked to end the story with the punch line: "It wasn't worth the £5." The wealthy were presumably the most tempting targets for extortionists, but if they were extremely wealthy the news of their victimization never got to court. On April 28, 1932, Sir Robert Bruce Lockhart wrote in his diary, "In the afternoon Randolph Churchill came to see me. He tells me there has been a scandal about Prince George—letters to a young man in Paris. A large sum had to be paid for their recovery."[25] The prince, younger brother of the future King George VI, was known to be bisexual, his lovers including Noël Coward and Florence Mills, an African-American singer who toured England in 1926.

Judging from the published reports the typical victims of homosexual blackmail were professional men—barristers, civil servants, clergymen, pharmacists, businessmen, army officers, hotel managers. Sometimes they were referred to in court simply as "gentlemen." Such accounts confirmed the English reading public's notion that churchmen particularly risked being compromised. In 1921 the public followed with fascination the sordid details that emerged from a Worcester trial. Charles and Ernest

McClausland were charged with threatening the Reverend George Featherstone, curate of St. Martins, Worcester. The court heard that Charles, twenty-three, had from the age of twelve been in the employ of Featherstone at the latter's Irish estate. Charles had been treated as a son and taken to Corsica at the age of sixteen by the cleric, who credited him with the photographs in his book *Through Corsica with a Pencil*. When eventually replaced with a younger boy McClausland began to make threats: "You know our past relations, and it is your duty to help me. I am penniless . . . I blamed you for my ruined life, and you may have to pay for it . . . I shall have a nice tale to put before your bishop . . . I hate to annoy you but what can I do?"[26]

Charles and his brother faced twelve charges of accusing of an abominable crime, conspiracy, and defamation libel. The jury, which purposely contained no women, heard that Featherstone gave the McClauslands £1,000 to leave the country. They had not been satisfied and demanded a further £5,000 from the seventy-one-year-old cleric. The crown stressed that the "guilt" of the victim was immaterial in a blackmail case. The defense nevertheless managed to ask a number of damaging questions about Featherstone's other young male friends, his being asked to leave a Dublin hotel, and his addressing one of the accused as "My darling Charl." The judge said he would not allow the defense to present evidence of Featherstone's having committed sodomy, since "neither the jury nor I have any right to inquire into that part of it and your questions must not tend to show that he did except in so far as he may give evidence and you may want to discredit him." Nevertheless the court seemed to be impressed in hearing that Charles wrote, "I swear to God you shall not ruin any others . . . I am doing this to purify the Church. You bastard, I shall get you." Though found guilty, Charles McClausland was sentenced to only eighteen months and his brother to six.[27]

At a different trial, in 1927, it was revealed that over the course of three years a chauffeur had extorted £1,367 from a sixty-eight-year-old Norwich clergyman identified as Mr. X. In 1923 the accused was given £60 after first meeting the clergyman for tea. The chauffeur then claimed that detectives saw the two of them together and wrote "Dear Montie" in 1924, 1925, and 1926, first saying he needed money to enter the army, then to go to America, then to Australia, and finally to New Zealand. To the cleric's horror the young man broke every promise. "But you are still in England poisoning my life," wrote the cleric, "though you promised faithfully to go abroad and try and repay me."[28]

In another case, the Leeds police court heard in 1934 that the vicar of 123 Hunslett had been badgered for money by a young man who had once been in his Sunday school. He had allowed the accused to live in the vicarage and paid his hotel bills and gambling debts. He even admitted to kissing the twenty-six-year-old man goodnight as, he said, it had been his parents' custom. The accused finally threatened that if more money was not forthcoming he would say "indecent behavior" had occurred (this despite the fact that he had signed a declaration that no "improper relations" had taken place); but when he made renewed demands the vicar finally went to the police.[29]

One English blackmailer actually posed as a churchman. Introducing himself as the "Reverend Williams," Raymond Mullineux in 1932 contacted in Piccadilly a businessman identified as Mr. A. The latter had been indiscreet with a youth named Stanley Keary, and Mullineux presented himself as trying to save both the youth and Mr. A. He prayed with Mr. A in his office and asked for money for Keary. In June Mr. A tried to break the relationship off, but Mullineux and Keary pursued their victim to his country home, where on October 12 they received £750. Two weeks later they demanded a further £200 to send Keary to Australia. This too was paid, but further demands led the victim to consult his solicitor. When Mullineux returned to the village again in July 1934 he was arrested. He and Keary were both sentenced to four years in prison.[30]

The unimaginative Mullineux reappeared in court in 1939, having been out of prison for little over a year, charged with exactly the same offense: demanding money with menaces. His new victim was Mr. X, an Enfield man. In early 1938 Mr. X had met a youth in the Haymarket and had brought him to his home. Though Mr. X claimed nothing improper had occurred, shortly thereafter Mullineux, posing now as the "Reverend Francis," appeared, asking for £200 to keep the boy out of prison. Mr. X reported that he did not mind giving £160 in June, as he believed that Mullineux was "a pukka padre." To his shock, in August Mullineux returned, admitted who he really was, and demanded £700; in November he asked for a further £1,000. Mr. X eventually went to the police, who found in Mullineux's Upper Berkeley Street flat a New Testament, a rosary, seven clerical collars, a cloth front, and a black homburg. He admitted to not being a clergyman but claimed that he had been a novice in a monastery some years earlier. Whether the stress of the ordeal contributed to the victim's poor health is unclear, but Mr. X died halfway through Mullineux's trial. The latter's assertion that he had been corrupted by an older man did not impress the judge. The victim's dying deposition was read in court, which led to Mullineux receiving a stiff ten-year sentence.[31]

Although the public must have noticed what appeared to be an undue interest taken in young men by blackmail victims, the prosecution would usually only admit that the victims had acted foolishly. For example, in 1902, according to his counsel, when Mr. Austin Neame "was coming out of the lavatory at Victoria Station, the prisoner stepped up to him and asked for assistance. Mr. Neame, who was a gentleman greatly interested in the working classes, listened to him, and, with the utmost foolishness, offered to take him down with him that night to Balham to see if they could find some clothes for him." A bachelor, Neame had given a meal to the prisoner, who then threatened to accuse Neame of an infamous act; Neame gave him £2. The next day he came back for a further £2 and a week later for another £5, supposedly to get his clothes out of hock before leaving for Manchester. Finally Neame went to his solicitor. When the accused turned up again he was arrested and ultimately sentenced to ten years in prison.[32]

The prosecution went to enormous lengths to avoid any discussion of homosexuality. The victims of blackmail—even when they had paid repeatedly—were presented in court as gullible rather than as perverse. Neame, for example, was portrayed by his lawyer as foolish. The RAF lieutenant who in 1919 went back to the room of a nineteen-year-old youth "to play cards" was upbraided by the judge for being "very foolish." A Scottish judge stated in a 1937 case that the victim was "an innocent citizen, who had unfortunately not the strength of character to resist those menaces on the first occasion." In their memoirs judges continued long after the fact to insist that it was not lust but kindheartedness that led older men of "wealth or position" to stumble into young men's traps.[33]

But the public knew that not all victims were "innocent." In January 1931 the trial began of a schoolmaster and a hairdresser who had "indelicate" photographs of "Mr. X" taken two years earlier at an escapade in Maidenhead. Mr. X had posed in a "disgusting way," and the two accused threatened to send out 1,300 copies of the picture to all the members of his club. In another case in 1937 two men in their mid-twenties successfully blackmailed an elderly Mr. A out of £3,100 with the threat of revealing "certain incidences at a cinema." Only after they demanded a further £10,000 did he go to the police.[34]

The rare occasions homosexuality was openly discussed in court occurred when defense counsels succeeded in questioning the morals of the victim. The judges—not wishing to appear indifferent to parental concerns—tended to allow such liberties when parents claimed to be protecting their sons from a seducer. John and Rose Powers were prosecuted in 1911 for threatening to tell William Cronshaw's relatives and the codirectors of his Manchester firm of his guilty relationship with their boy. The mother castigated Cronshaw as a "blackguard" who had ruined two or three other young men and demanded £10,000 for herself and her son. Cronshaw, a forty-nine-year-old bachelor, had been introduced to the young Frederick Powers by an actor, Reginald De Veulle. The defense counsel asked Cronshaw about De Veulle.

Has he had large sums of money from you?—Yes, very large sums.

Thousands?—No: perhaps £2,000.

What for?—Generally to pay his debts.

What claim had he on you?—Nothing except friendship.

Have you been paid back any of the money?—No.

Do you expect to be?—No, I am afraid not. He has been abroad in America for some time.[35]

When the case went to trial Rose Powers pleaded guilty and stated that her lawyer had explained to her that she had no legal claim. She therefore withdrew her imputations and expressed her regrets. The prosecution accepted that she had acted under excitement and agreed that her statement did not have the "criminal complexion" it appeared to have. The *Times* reported that Mr. Justice Darling was also of the opinion that these were not ordinary circumstances. "He was not dealing with a case of people such as they are accustomed to see there who brought absolutely baseless charges simply in order to extort money. She [Mrs. Powers] was under a complete delusion produced by her having received untrustworthy information. She was, he was satisfied, acting not in order to extort money primarily, although that entered into her threat, but in order to protect her son against what she imagined to be the evil company into which she supposed he had got."[36] Darling therefore gave her a suspended sentence. Given the evidence this looked very much like a cover-up by both sides. Indeed Cronshaw's friend De Veulle was to later figure centrally in the 1918 Billie Carleton cocaine scandal. When the socialite died of a drug overdose he was prosecuted for drug dealing. The press made its distaste clear in describing his "effeminate face and mincing little smile." The *Daily Sketch* published photographs of him in women's clothing. Although its relevance to drug use appeared remote, the coroner at Carleton's inquest made a point of asking De Veulle about the Cronshaw case and other "curious friendships" he had had in his youth with older men. "Were some of these friendships with men much older than you very remunerative for you?" he was asked.[37] De Veulle was eventually sentenced to eight months in prison on the drug charge.

Judges made their class biases apparent in the short shrift they gave to poor parents. In 1913 a mother was tried for blackmailing a wealthy man who had purportedly ruined her son some ten years earlier when he was about sixteen. Under an agreement managed by a solicitor the man had given them £150 in 1912 in return for a letter withdrawing their allegations. Her demand for an additional £150 resulted in her being sentenced to five years and the son to twelve months. After Mr. X, a West End shopowner, struck up a friendship with a seventeen-year-old youth, his father and another accomplice, who claimed to be a solicitor, demanded £250 for the man's having acted like a "filthy swine." In cross-examination at the 1928 trial the defense counsel tried to break the victim: "I am suggesting that you are a man whose word cannot be relied upon, that you are a degenerate and a vagabond." Why, he was asked, did he take shop assistants to lunch? Why did he write letters to working-class boys? Nevertheless the father, condemned by the judge as mastermind of the plot, was found guilty and sentenced to three years; his confederate was labeled a "jackal" and got eighteen months.[38]

These cases were unusual in that real family members were involved. Most homosexual blackmail schemes reported in the press followed a familiar scenario in which villains played a variety of roles. Piccadilly, Hyde Park, and Soho were blackmailers' favored hunting grounds, and night was their favored time. Most who were charged with attempting to extort money—such as Robert Owen Phillips, an eighteen-year-old messenger, who was sentenced in 1935 to three years in a reformatory for demanding money with menaces—were young and poor. Any article of clothing that might suggest a man's effeminacy was presented by the authorities as con-

clusive evidence that he was a male prostitute. For example, in 1914 the po- 127
lice let it be known that they had found a woman's wig and makeup in the
flat of a valet whom they described as a blackmailer who annoyed gentlemen in the West End. In February 1924 the *Times* reported that two members of a blackmail gang who were sentenced to seven and six years in
prison called themselves by girls' names when working the West End at
night, where they targeted drunks near lavatories. It was preposterous,
complained the judge, that men could not use public conveniences without
fear of such "pests and parasites of society." In December 1924 Mr. Justice
Wild sentenced William King to eighteen strokes and nine months in
prison for importuning. The police found on him face powder, scented
handkerchiefs, and two photos of himself dressed as a woman. King had
been previously convicted in 1921 and was described by the police as a
member of a blackmailing gang.[39] The public could be forgiven for assum-
ing that a man who used makeup was committing a crime. Cross-dressing
was not an offense per se, but had become freighted with dangerous conno-
tations.

The twentieth-century press popularized the notion of the effeminate
homosexual. Blackmail reports also—if unintentionally—presented an
unflattering portrait of the "manly" sort of man. Men with a military or
police background were well represented among the ranks of those who extorted money from homosexuals. In 1921 a twenty-year-old naval deserter
was reported as having accosted and extorted money from a frightened
civil servant. In April 1926 two men (one an ex-guardsman) were sentenced to five and three years respectively for menaces. The following December two Bradford police constables were sentenced to four years for extorting money from a solicitor who, they claimed, had made "certain
overtures" to them. In December 1933 Sidney Madden, purportedly a
member of a gang of grenadier guards, received a ten-year sentence for extorting £200 from a man whom he had accosted in Green Park. Judge
Avory denied his appeal, stating that Madden was known as one of the
"pests" of a certain part of the metropolis. In 1938 two more ex-guardsmen
were sentenced to three years in prison for demanding £200 from Mr. A
whom they had caught with a youth in a Chelsea flat.[40]

Assiduous newspaper readers learned that such bullies customarily employed an attractive young man to entrap the victim; then, sometimes representing themselves as the police, they would show up and surprise their

target. On February 9, 1924, for example, John Clark was accosted at London's Marble Arch by George Whiteside, who suggested they go into Hyde Park. Once there Whiteside said he had to urinate and undid his fly. Out jumped George Robson and William Doyle, who shouted at Whiteside, "We have got you, you old offender!" and to the victim, "Do you know that you are with a man of immoral character? . . . Do you know what this will mean for you? . . . it means six months without the option of a fine . . . I warn you that anything you say will be used in evidence against you." When the case was eventually reported two other men came forward with similar tales. The police described Whiteside, Robson, and Doyle as "clever members of the young school and apt pupils of the old West-End blackmailers." In April three other members of the gang were also tracked down. The court heard that the names and addresses of victims were always carefully recorded so that the "slow death" of extortion could be pursued. Judge McCardie sentenced the six to a total of thirty-one years in prison.[41]

In the depths of the Depression reports of homosexual blackmail gangs peaked. In early 1932 a man who picked up eighteen-year-old Rupert Starling in Piccadilly and went back to the boy's flat in St. Martin's Lane found himself threatened by an accomplice of Starling's: "You have come around expecting a bit of fun . . . How much is it worth for you to offer us to keep quiet?" The victim handed over a gold watch and £40. When the authorities eventually raided the flat they caught Starling with an undergraduate. Starling and his accomplice were arrested, and two more members of the gang appeared in court a week later. The publicity led to another victim's coming forward, but a man whom the police saw fleeing the St. Martin's flat with the laughing Starling in pursuit refused to cooperate. Three of the four gang members were found guilty and sent to prison, the judge threatening to order a whipping for such offenses.[42]

Four members of yet another gang appeared in court on September 23, 1932, charged with extorting money from a Mr. X of Peckham. One explained, "We went to see him about his interfering with my brother, whom we took to his rooms." He said he thought—erroneously—that the victim would be too frightened to go to the police. The sentencing of the eighteen-year-old "chicken," whom the judge felt had been led astray, was postponed; he sentenced the three others to eleven to eighteen months in prison. "The accused," he summed up, "had ruined the nerves of Mr. X for life. Had he not had the courage to go to the police for protection he might as well have shot himself."[43] It was no accident that the judge should have referred to suicide. It was, according to the moralists' overheated rhetoric, the only imaginable fate of harried homosexuals.

When a homosexual blackmail case came to court the judge typically berated the victim for not having immediately gone to the police. "It is difficult to understand why persons who are tortured in the way the victim in this case has been tortured, do not come forward and lay the facts formally and fully before their solicitors or the police, or both. They can, then, I am sure, rely upon the discretion of the Press; and if they are prepared to take that course they will have done something to stamp out one of the worse pests of contemporary civilization." In implying that lack of courage prevented some men from reporting their victimization, judges reinforced the stereotype of the timid homosexual. But it was not just the fear of social disapprobation that prevented victims from going to the authorities. Given that buggery was a felony punishable by up to ten years in prison, while fellatio and mutual masturbation were misdemeanors that could lead to two-year sentences, what obviously prevented victims from going to the police was good common sense. Despite lack of cooperation from victims, the police congratulated itself for occasionally stumbling upon extortion plots. The bungled suicide attempt of sixty-four-year-old Mr. X in 1930 brought to light the fact that he had been bilked out of over £500 by a twenty-seven-year-old man and an accomplice who posed as his father.[44]

That homosexuals could be robbed with impunity was in itself a sort of blackmail, a fact the police did not dwell on. In 1929 Philip Eaton, a professor of chemistry at a Massachusetts college, took a flat in Half Moon Street, Piccadilly. He later claimed that he had not sought a homosexual encounter; but, feeling lonely and "interested in the guards," he met and brought back to his flat Roland Bateman, an ex-soldier who had been "looking for a mug." Bateman's story was that Eaton got him drunk, took him to his bedroom, and attempted to indecently assault him. In revenge and "in defense of his honor" Bateman admitted beating Eaton and stealing his clothes. The next morning the maid was horrified to discover Eaton covered in blood and excrement. Eaton first tried to stop her from reporting the matter to the police. When that failed, he told the police that a second man had entered the flat and robbed him. The police, who expected to be lied to by homosexual victims, ignored Eaton's story and easily tracked down Bateman, who was sentenced to three years in prison. The papers reported it as a simple robbery. The sexual side of the story was not divulged, but coincidentally the tabloid *John Bull* claimed a few weeks later that all guardsmen were libeled by reports of soldiers being involved in blackmail gangs.[45]

The constant stream of homosexual blackmail trials and the heavy prison sentences levied on the accused were no doubt meant by the authorities to deter others from entering a life of crime. But the other message that came through was that homosexuals were fair game. According to a 1931 account, young men compared notes on "how very easy it was to earn a living compatible with personal liberty by permitting gentlemen of position to commit indiscretions with oneself of an illicit kind, and then to scare them with threats of exposure to the police unless they were prepared to make one a suitable allowance as the price of one's silence." This was obviously the view of a laborer charged in 1938 with having demanded £5 from Mr. X, who had given him a ride in his automobile. When charged with uttering threats, the laborer, who already had a police record, boldly asserted, "His type ought to be made to pay."[46] In *Low Company* (1936), the autobiography of a young man who had spent time in a reformatory, author Mark Benney provided a sense of the same moral self-righteousness that many blackmailers employed as a way of rationalizing their crimes. Shy and awkward with girls, Benney recalled convincing himself that if he somehow obtained the money to buy proper clothes he would succeed:

> And slowly, fostered by the dark humidities of the Marble Arch atmosphere, an idea grew in me. There were elegant young epicenes who walked out of the park with arms linked in the arms of crapulous burghers, and contrived to buy suits in the process . . . I was, I felt, as physically attractive as they. I too would walk out of the park linked arm in arm with some rich and crapulous burgher, take him to a quiet spot, and knock him down and take his wallet. If the thought revolted me at first, it also excited me. And I was supported by a feeling of moral justification. These old men seemed placed by their practices beyond the pale of social consideration. Whatever one did to them, they deserved. And they wouldn't dare to go to the police.[47]

Benney made his first and only such attempt at Hyde Park Corner. To his dismay he discovered that the man he had picked up was almost his mirror image. "He was so lonely in London, he said, and he wanted a woman and he couldn't afford it and he was shy with them and he wasn't really a homo and sometimes he wished he was and London is a dreadful place if you don't know anyone who understands you."[48]

As Benney's account suggests, the working class could draw on reports of homosexual blackmail to have its opinion confirmed that only the upper classes were "queer." The middle class, for their part, might take such trials as further evidence of the immorality of the lower orders. Only by being arrested for public indecency did one become a "homosexual," and only working-class men were so charged. Accordingly many educated, middle-class men had only the foggiest notion that their relationships with other men could be construed as criminal. Few in England (aside from sex reformers such as George Ives, Havelock Ellis, and other progressive members of the British Society for the Study of Sex Psychology) noted that the confused notions the English public had of homosexuality were largely the result of the laws that criminalized it.[49]

Though there were fewer reports of homosexual blackmail in the United States, they followed the English pattern. In June 1908 Carl Fischer-Hansen, a New York lawyer, was tried for extorting several thousand dollars from Joseph E. O'Brien, a Philadelphia decorator. Evidence was heard that Antonio Macaluso, an Italian "boy," had come to the lawyer in December 1907 to complain that he had been ill treated by O'Brien. The youth, Fischer-Hansen was pleased to discover, had "incriminating letters" written by O'Brien. "Well, you leave this thing with me," he was reported as saying. "Why, man, you ought to be rich."[50] Through Francis Dowling, a friend of O'Brien's, Fischer-Hansen threatened the decorator that if he did not pay up he would face the prospect of being sentenced as a sodomite to a twenty-year prison term and of "hungry" newspapers getting the story. In exchange for Macaluso's providing the letters, a diary, an affidavit recanting his charges, and a general release, the terrified O'Brien handed over $15,000.

If the conspirators had not fallen out the public would never have heard of this crime. O'Brien had no intention of lodging a complaint, and one can only guess at how many other shakedowns of wealthy American homosexuals escaped notice. As it turned out the authorities stumbled upon this case when the naïve Macaluso, to whom Fischer-Hansen had given a measly $140, filed a court order for a larger share of the loot. The district attorney immediately proceeded to have Fischer-Hansen, who already had an unsavory reputation in the New York legal world, charged with blackmail.

The story made the front page of the New York papers. The son of the leader of the Left in the Danish parliament, Fisher-Hansen had earlier made a successful career in the United States; his marriage in 1896 to the daughter of Isaac V. Brokaw, a wealthy businessman, had been attended by members of New York's finest families, including the Goulds and the Rockefellers.

At the trial the prosecutor instructed the jury to ignore the issue of homosexuality: "It is in no way material whether the crime charged against O'Brien is true or not; you are dealing only with the crime charged against Fischer-Hansen." Nevertheless the defense's tactic was to attack the evidence and the character of both O'Brien and Dowling. The latter was asked by Fischer-Hansen's lawyer if he had been known as "Miss Dowling." Had Dowling told O'Brien that he would have to choose between Dowling and the boy? The defense then subjected O'Brien to a savage cross-examination. Forced to say why he had paid out so much money, he admitted, "I wanted to put an end to the whole thing: I was afraid of exposure: my social life, business, everything—and I thought it would kill my mother." In the end, the prosecution's case was destroyed when Macaluso, the key witness, changed his story. He had originally told the authorities that Fischer-Hansen had talked him into blackmailing O'Brien; now he supported the lawyer's claim that the money exchanged was owed him as a debt. Fischer-Hansen was duly acquitted.[51]

The fact that Fischer-Hansen had been let off—though the press, the prosecution, and the judge considered him guilty—was attributed by some to American middle-class bigotry. But the story did not end there. In January 1909 Fischer-Hansen and his law partner were rearrested. The police now had evidence that the lawyer had won his earlier acquittal by bribing a process server and Macaluso. Fischer-Hansen pleaded guilty to the bribery charge, was disbarred, and was sentenced to a year in prison.[52] The fall of this once-eminent attorney was dramatic; his reputation dropped farther when in the midst of his 1909 trial Charles Warner, a well-known English actor, committed suicide in the Seymour Hotel. In the suicide note that Warner left he accused Fischer-Hansen of blackmailing him. The two men's relationship was never clarified. Warner's son claimed that the two had never met and that his father was deluded. Fischer-Hansen, not surprisingly, denied blackmailing the actor, but did admit that Warner had paid him for legal advice.[53]

Men like O'Brien and Warner had good reason to fear being branded ho-   133
mosexuals. It was difficult to disprove a charge of indecency.[54] Those found guilty of the "abominable and detestable crime against nature" faced long prison terms. Under Rhode Island's 1896 act, for example, sodomy was punished with a minimum seven-year sentence. In New York State the accused in a sodomy case had the odds stacked against him. As in forgery, counterfeiting, false pretenses, rape, and blackmail trials, he could be required to "refute evidence of crimes not charged in the indictment."[55]

But the Fischer-Hansen trial was unusual in its level of publicity. Though homophobia was rife, respectable American newspapers at the start of the twentieth century carried only rare references to either homosexuality in general or to sodomy trials in particular. This was intentional. The Vice Commission of Chicago reported in 1911 that the city harbored "colonies" of those addicted to "perversions," but doubted that "any spread of the actual knowledge of these practices is in any way desirable." *Town Topics*, a tabloid that in the decade prior to World War I blackmailed socialites into paying for the suppression of embarrassing stories, was one of the rare publications that went after homosexuals. One popular singer, for example, found himself subject to such an attack. "Harry Lehr's proud parade of his many sissy qualities . . . his pink complexion and golden hair, his thin voice, his peculiar gestures, the feminine prettiness of his general make-up . . . has gone beyond the limits of tolerance by decent society."[56] But in the first half of the twentieth century far fewer cases of homosexual blackmail were reported in the United States than in England. Not being assured anonymity, victims were reluctant to go to the authorities. At worst, they would be jailed. At best, they might find themselves meeting the fate of O'Brien, their character and reputation torn apart by merciless defense attorneys. The fact that a blackmailer like Fischer-Hansen was finally imprisoned offered scant compensation. The general public no doubt felt that the victim as well as the villain got what they deserved.

In the few cases that were reported in the United States the authorities and the press appeared to have assisted wealthy victims of homosexual blackmail in shrouding their affairs in secrecy. Indeed press accounts of extortion were at times so brief that the American reading public would have had difficulty in determining just what threats the extortionists had made.

In 1915 the *New York Times* reported that George Bancroft, a banker, had told the police that three men had forced him at gunpoint to sign two $2,500 drafts. Bancroft had gone to the University Hotel with Don Collins (whose nefarious activities were noted in Chapter 4). While Bancroft was in a hotel room with a second man a third appeared, identifying himself as a policeman, and a threat to Bancroft's reputation had been made. Bancroft did not go straight to the police. He first consulted his lawyer. The public had to work out for itself what so frightened the banker. Collins meanwhile felt so sure of himself that he remained in New York and was not arrested until two weeks later.[57]

In 1922 and 1923 the U.S. press gave similarly vague though extensive coverage to the murder trial of Walter S. Ward. He admitted to having killed Clarence Peters, a young sailor near White Plains, but claimed that it was in self-defense. Peters's body had been found on May 16, 1922. Turning himself in three days later, Ward stated that Peters was blackmailing the Ward family and he had acted from a concern to protect his family. According to Ward's defense attorneys, Peters and two other young men had set out to obtain $70,000 by blackmailing George S. Ward, owner of the Ward Baking Company. They threatened to expose the "immoral acts, practices and disgrace of his son," Walter. On May 15 Walter met the gang and, according to him, in the struggle that ensued he shot Peters while the other two extortionists escaped. Thanks to the Ward money, the trial was repeatedly postponed. When it finally was held in September 1923 the details of the blackmailers' threat were not revealed and, to the cheers of the spectators, Walter Ward, who did not even testify, was acquitted of murder. To prove his respectability his lawyers had his wife come to court, and they showed the jury photos of his children. No one was more vile, Ward's lawyers argued, than the homosexual blackmailer who sought to prey on respectable young men. And Ward, being married, clearly could not be a homosexual, while Peters, a young sailor, presumably was. The public appeared to agree with the defense's argument that blackmail was worse than murder and that Ward had acted heroically in facing down his enemies.[58]

Every cryptic report of young men pressuring the sons of wealthy fathers could be read as further evidence of the blackmailing activities of homosexuals and their confederates. In 1931 Theodore Schweiner's chauffeur attempted to blackmail Theodore's father, Carl, a wealthy West Orange, New Jersey, printing executive. The same year a twenty-year-old Berkeley student tried to extort money from a plumbing contractor with scandalous information about his son, who was a student at Dartmouth. In 1944 a man posing as a FBI agent attempted to use information regarding an old incident to blackmail Stanley Stegall, the valet of Hollywood actor Dudley Digges.[59]   135

The fact that so many more homosexual blackmail cases were reported in the British press no doubt played some role in reinforcing the American notion that homosexuality was an English vice. In American films and theater productions the "nance" was inevitably presented as English. Many male novelists tapped into the theme that homosexuality was foreign to middle-class American life. In Floyd Dell's *The Briary Bush* (1921), for example, the main character asks a girlfriend about an effeminate fellow whom he has just met in Chicago:

> "But are these airs natural to him or is he just putting them on to impress people? Where is he from?"
>
> "Guess?"
>
> Felix thought he saw a light.
>
> "London?"

White male writers who helped construct the twentieth-century image of healthy American masculinity were particularly prone to play it against stereotyped portrayals of homosexuals. F. Scott Fitzgerald, Ernest Hemingway, and Sinclair Lewis used effeminate characters to highlight the virility of their heroes. The narrator in James M. Cain's *Serenade* (1937) is repelled by something he says is "unhealthy" about the people he meets at a musician's party: "young girls looking each other straight in the eye and not caring what you thought, boys following men around . . . everybody coming out in the open with something they wouldn't dare show anywhere else." The depiction of homosexual blackmail offered the most obvious way of portraying the dangerousness of homosexuality. In John Dos Passos' *The Big Money* (1933) the aptly named Dick Savage makes the mistake of inviting back to his apartment "Gloria Swanson," a cross-dressing black male prostitute, and another "buck." Blackjacked, Savage wakes up the next morning to find his watch and money gone. "He sat on the edge of the bed. Of all the damn fools. Never never never take a risk like that again. Now they knew his name his address his phone number. Blackmail, oh, Christ. How would it be when Mother came home from Florida to find her son earning twenty-five thousand a year, junior partner of J. Ward Moorehouse being blackmailed by two nigger whores, male prostitutes receiving males? Christ."[60]

In Raymond Chandler's *The Big Sleep* (1939), the best known of the 1930s hard-boiled detective novels, private investigator Philip Marlowe is told that General Sternwood is being blackmailed by men who have information on Carmen, his thumb-sucking, nymphomaniacal daughter. Geiger, the extortionist, is a "queen" who owns a Hollywood Boulevard bookstore that carries a stock of "indescribable filth." He also lives with a "punk" or, as Marlowe explains to the police in nudge-nudge, wink-wink fashion: "I mean living with him, if you get the idea." To find out what is going on in the store the rugged detective goes incognito. "If you can weigh a hundred and ninety pounds and look like a fairy, I was doing my best." Failing that, he goes to Geiger's stylishly furnished house, which our hero recognizes as radiating "a stealthy nastiness, like a fag party." Marlowe finds that Geiger—who has drugged, stripped naked, and photographed Carmen—has been killed. Who is the murderer, and who has the photos? Is it the "boy" from Geiger's store? Marlowe describes him lovingly: "Moist dark eyes shaped like almonds, and a pallid handsome face with wavy black hair growing low on the forehead in two points." He even more lovingly describes his fight with the youth.

He stood with his fist on his hips, looking silently at the house above the top of the ridge.

"All right," I said, "You have a key. Let's go in."

"Who said I had a key?"

"Don't kid me son. The fag gave you one."

It [the punch] caught me flush on the chin. I backstepped fast enough to keep from falling, but I took plenty of the punch. It was meant to be a hard one, but a pansy has no iron in his bones, whatever he looks like . . .

He shot at me like a plane from a catapult, reaching for my knees in a diving tackle . . . [and used] his hands on me where it hurt. I twisted around and heaved him a little higher . . . and turned my right hipbone into him and for a moment it was a balance of weights. We seemed to hang there in the misty moonlight, two grotesque creatures whose feet scraped on the road and whose breath panted with effort.[61]

Chandler desperately sought to parade his loathing of homosexuality; despite his best intentions, however, the fascination it held for him shines through. In popular literature, as a rough rule of thumb the more hard-boiled the hero, the greater his hatred of "fairies." Chandler, the most critically acclaimed of the interwar writers of detective stories, was laughably 137 addicted to hard men. In *The High Window* (1943), which also has a convoluted blackmail plot, Marlowe modestly protests, "I'm not tough . . . just virile."[62]

African-American writers did not feel the same need to trumpet their masculinity, though they may have had a better sense of the sexual dangers of city life. In the mid-1920s Wallace Thurman, one of the leading writers of the Harlem Renaissance, was arrested for having sex with a white hairdresser in a 135th Street subway washroom. He was obsessed thereafter by fears that his past would come back to haunt him. Indeed his wife later threatened to use his homosexuality as grounds for divorce. Claude McKay, the Jamaican-born writer, reportedly had an "unlikely relationship with a young Irishman who made his living as a blackmailer of 'respectable' gay men caught in compromising situations."[63]

Despite the homophobia so widespread in American culture, the 1930s witnessed the appearance of a handful of sympathetic fictional portrayals of homosexuals. Not surprisingly, blackmail themes surfaced in some of these accounts. In Mrs. Blair Niles's *Strange Brother* (1931) Mark, the main character, who works in a settlement house, is threatened with blackmail when he is seen with an effeminate man. Rico, the local fruit seller, says that he *knows:* "My uncle told me. He said I could make it hot for you at the settlement. Said if I needed money you could be my bank now. That's what my uncle said."[64] Citing sex reformers to make the case that society has to show more understanding of homosexuals, Niles ends her well-intentioned but heavy-handed novel in predictable fashion, with the "innocent" Mark committing suicide.

Niles was obviously acquainted with European writers such as Sigmund Freud, Havelock Ellis, and Magnus Hirschfeld, who provided sophisticated explanations for same-sex attraction. Ellis and Hirschfeld portrayed blackmail as a scourge created by the criminalization of same-sex practices. Most American doctors were far less sympathetic, but they increasingly tended to regard homosexuals as sick rather than criminal. Dr. Samuel Kahn, having used Blackwell's Island as a "welfare laboratory" in which he could diagnose criminals, concluded that the prognosis of his sample of five hundred or so homosexuals ceasing to be deviant was poor. Dr. Joseph Collins began his 1926 discussion of sexuality with the curious statement that the problem with perverts was that they tried to put square pegs into round holes. Homosexuals, according to Collins, were not so much degenerates as victims of fate, doomed to lived in fear of blackmail. "To get that for which their nature clamors they must, as a rule, go furtively beyond their own social and cultural circles, and they must forsake their souls for they put themselves into another's power." Dr. Aaron J. Rosanoff agreed that homosexuals' "clannishness" was due to their fear of extortionists.[65]

The little Americans knew about homosexuality came mainly from press reports of "shakedowns," not from medical texts or novels. In *The Professional Thief* (1937) Edward H. Sutherland claimed that organized shakedowns of homosexuals in New York began in 1909–1910 around the subway stations at 51st and at 43rd Street and Broadway. Thugs first simply broke into toilets and robbed their prey. They moved on to employ a "muzzle," "mug," or "mouse" to entice a victim into a compromising position. Such "professional steerers" who helped entrap victims were not, Sutherland claimed, "highly effeminate, berouged characters" because the mob would not accept such types. An older gang member's job was to impersonate a policeman and threaten the arrest of the mug and his victim if not provided a "bond," or bribe. Mobs spread such schemes to major cities across the country. "The muzzle is," Sutherland asserted, "one of the few rackets in which a go-back (second attempt) can be successfully staged."[66] He reported that a Philadelphia department store owner paid out $35,000 and that, until he moved to Europe, a New York businessman had had to pay off not only crooks, but also his parents, policemen, anti-vice officials, and journalists.

The first report of a major gang being broken up came in 1922. Newspapers stated that the seven members of an Atlantic City blackmail ring preying on homosexuals had been charged. Robert L. Haney, a wealthy Philadelphia man, told the police that on July 4 he was approached by Charles Mercer (calling himself Wood) with the "friendly offer of an umbrella." Haney went to Wood's hotel room on South Tennessee Avenue. There he was set upon by four men impersonating federal officers, who accused him of an offense. He handed over a check for $100. The police reported that the gang, equipped with revolvers and handcuffs, preyed on visitors along the East coast. In reporting the case in July the *New York Times* noted that the seven men who were charged—out on bail of $1,000 each—were unlikely to go to jail, as witnesses were too afraid to give evidence. In fact,

138

however, the courageous Haney did testify. The American papers—not employing the discretion of their English counterparts—published both the victim's name and his address in Philadelphia. Wood turned state's evidence, and four of the gang received two- to seven-year prison terms.[67]

Sutherland claimed that few of the blackmailers of homosexuals were arrested. This appeared to be borne out by the rarity of references to such cases in the U.S. press. In 1927 detectives hiding in the Shelburne Hotel in Atlantic City arrested three men who were heard to threaten Jacob Factor, a New York broker. He had previously given them $1,500. In 1937 in California Edward Jones and Fred Cabany conspired to extort $250 from William J. Hayman. Cabany, showing Hayman a badge, stated, "You are under arrest." He presented a fictitious warrant for Hayman's arrest on a sodomy charge and stated that $2,500 was needed for his release. Americans abroad were warned that they too were at risk. In April 1930 the *New York Times* reported that three English youths had been arraigned for blackmailing a Harvard student (identified only as Mr. H) who was studying at Cambridge. The young men whom he had considered as his friends had compromised him at a party in Pimlico. After the party the three drove up to Cambridge to say that one of them had been arrested for indecency and that Mr. H would be called as a witness in the trial unless he paid them off.[68]

In New York, as in London, the Depression saw the peaking of newspaper coverage of homosexual blackmail gangs. In the late 1930s the press repeatedly referred to the "Forcier gang," a collection of petty criminals who from time to time cooperated with each other in the blackmailing of homosexuals. Though some of the gang had no doubt been involved in shakedowns for some time, they first came to public attention in 1938. That year, the *New York Times* reported, Edward Watson was the victim of several men. All the evidence suggests it was a case of homosexual blackmail, but no doubt because the victim had been named the authorities declined to reveal the nature of the threat. All the public learned was that in November 1938 a man posing as a detective demanded $1,600 from Watson. A week later the "detective" returned with a "lieutenant" and the two extorted a further $5,120. When a third man came around pretending to represent the district attorney the police were finally alerted and arrests were made.[69]

Only at the trials in 1939 did the authorities finally produce an account that gave the public a clear idea of the blackmailers' modus operandi. The gang members sought out their prey at New York bars, restaurants, railway stations, and an area near the lake in Central Park. A common ploy was for one of the gang's younger members to strike up an acquaintance with the intended victim at a nightclub. He would get himself invited to the victim's home, have sex with him, and steal a readily identified object. A few days later men pretending to be the police, or even agents of District Attorney Thomas Dewey, would show up at the victim's home with a photo of the thief, saying that they had heard of the robbery and that the victim would have to testify. "The circumstances in which the property was stolen would be hinted at, and money accepted to 'kill the case' and avoid publicity."[70] The implied threats to bring discreditable public attention to the victims intimidated even those who knew or suspected they were dealing with criminals. After the first payment, the "go-backs" would begin. Other men claiming to represent the district attorney, the chief inspector, the police commissioner's office, or some newspaper would show up. In some cases as many as ten different demands were made. Violence occasionally resulted.

In most crimes the victim would go to the police, who then would track down the perpetrator. In the case of the Forcier gang—or so the police claimed—the scenario was reversed. A gang member turned stool pigeon informed the authorities that a bank official was being blackmailed. The police questioned the victim, who at first refused to cooperate. The police, one reporter noted, were not surprised. "They had long ago learned that in cases of assault, robbery, etc., in which the complaining witness was a homosexual, the lawyer for the defense invariably would discredit and humiliate the complainant, and the case would be thrown out of court without any chance for a complete presentation of the facts."[71] The police finally managed to get the information they required to begin an investigation. Individual gang members were then picked up and subsequently ratted on each other, providing the authorities with the names of even more victims and villains.

By December 1939 twenty men, having pled guilty on lesser charges to protect the complainants from publicity, were jailed. Ten others had fled. In late December the three leaders of the gang—Charles Forcier, Salvatore Andenocci, and Edward F. Sheehan—were tried on blackmailing charges. At the trial only one complainant, whose name the district attorney asked not be released, came forward. He testified that he had given $1,000 to Sheehan, who passed the money on to Charles Forcier. Sheehan and

Andenocci turned state's evidence and testified against Forcier, who was found guilty and sentenced to six to twelve years in prison.[72]

But even with Forcier in prison the gang continued to operate. In March 1940 the press, in reporting that Richard Thompson had just been sentenced to two and a half years in prison, noted that he was a member of the Forcier gang that had supposedly extorted over $1 million. In 1941 Robert Gaffney, a fugitive since 1939, was apprehended by Dewey's men in Washington and pleaded guilty to having acted as a fake detective for the gang. He was sentenced to two and a half to six years in Sing Sing. According to Frank S. Hogan of the district attorney's office, "Many of the victims of his gang were visiting Europeans, some of them of the nobility. Although in one instance the blackmailers obtained more than $85,000, all the victims were reluctant to testify against the gang. This was because they feared the disgrace it would bring on them among their friends in this country or in European countries."[73] It was reported in 1942 that thirty-two of the estimated total of thirty-four gang members had been apprehended.

Patrick Rafferty (or O'Rafferty), implicated in the 1938 blackmailing of Edward Watson, was arrested again in 1942. In court he was identified as an ex–Irish Republican Army member who had joined the gang that since 1938 had focused on "men prominent in academic, artistic, and business circles." His job was to pose as a police constable. For the blackmailing of a prominent writer Rafferty and his colleague were sentenced to three to six years in Sing Sing. Finally in 1943 the police arrested three more men, who had used a trumped-up morals charge to attempt to extort $10,000 from a "prominent American fiscal representative here for the British government." Pretending to be police, two of the men had accosted the victim at Washington's Union Station on February 5, 1943. He arranged to pay them in New York, and a trap was set by the police. When arrested the three brazenly attempted to bribe the police to release them. According to the assistant district attorney the accused were "remnants of an old gang of Washington blackmailers which was broken up in this city in 1939, when thirty-four of the gang were arrested. All were later sentenced to long state prison terms for extorting about $1,000,000 from numerous men here under threats to arrest them on framed morals charges."[74]

At least three sorts of stories may be drawn from these American reports of blackmail. It is difficult not to call them cases of "homosexual blackmail," but most accounts were so cryptic that the uninitiated would not

142 know what had really taken place. The press clearly connived in fostering a protective public ignorance. Thus, one type of story ignored the homosexuality of the victims. For example, in 1939 the *New York Herald Tribune* declared that the Forcier gang had "tricked" their victims into compromising situations.[75] In 1943 the victims were said to have been "framed." The blackmail victims were not described as homosexuals. Such accounts permitted naïve readers to assume that they were not really reading about the same-sex passions of the wealthy. They could embrace the vaguer and less alarming belief that the consumerism of the 1920s and the destabilizing effects of Prohibition, which supposedly relaxed all moral strictures, were responsible for well-off men unwittingly finding themselves entrapped in compromising situations.

In the second type of story, where it was hard to ignore that the victim was a homosexual, a cautionary account was constructed, the moral being that homosexuality was inevitably punished, either by society or the underworld. William Peer took this approach in a 1953 article written for the *American Mercury.* Beginning with the false claim that the press in the 1930s and 1940s had not even reported the Forcier gang's activities, Peer categorically stated that most of those subjected to shakedowns were "more or less obvious and notorious homosexuals," though the "peculiar inclinations" of some had not been previously suspected. All were wealthy. All demanded anonymity. Some threatened suicide. Peer portrayed the typical homosexual victim as a coward. "Thoroughly frightened," on the way to the police station he "would lose all control and commence frantically pleading with the two 'detectives' to drop the matter." The "sweating victim" would be allowed to post bail for the gang member who had acted as bait and be promised that nothing more would be heard of it. In this rendition, the police are seen as patient professionals. When the first victim of the gang refused to cooperate they subjected him to a necessary grilling. Happily "the wretched deviate broke down and told his story." Without (rather than because of) the assistance of the victims, the police broke the case. "Getting information and co-operation from the blackmailers was a simple matter compared to that of inducing the victims to file complaints and agree to appear before the grand jury."[76] Ignored in such an account were the disastrous social consequences awaiting any man exposed as a homosexual.

In constructing their accounts of homosexual blackmail public commentators in both England and the United States—police, judges, doctors, and novelists—were intent on portraying homosexuality as a pathological disorder. Americans in particular worked at creating an image of the effeminate deviant.

143

It requires a sensitive reading of the court records and press reports to distinguish a third type of story, a narrative that reflected the homosexual man's perspective. Nevertheless, homosexual men constructed from the reports of extortion cases their own story. Newspaper accounts identified certain public sites—Riverside Drive and Central Park in New York City; Lafayette Square in Washington, D.C.; Atlantic City—where homosexual activity took place. They also publicized the dangers associated with chance encounters. Interestingly the press in the interwar years did not present homosexual men as seducing innocent youths. In fact, the blackmail stories presented just the opposite scenario: the young thug seducing the older homosexual into a compromising situation. For some, such reports reinforced the idea that homosexuals should stay in the closet. Others came away thinking that safety in numbers might prevent violence and blackmail, and that the long-term goal should be decriminalization of homosexuality.[77] Blackmail stories played a part in expanding the meanings of sexuality, but most people assumed that the possibilities of real change lay in the distant future, given that public reports of same-sex practices, like those of interracial relationships, continued to be colored by a voyeuristic mix of revulsion and curiosity.

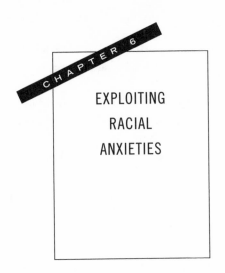

CHAPTER 6

EXPLOITING
RACIAL
ANXIETIES

Late nineteenth-century blackmail trials revealed unexpected class and gender entanglements, but said nothing about the crossing of racial boundaries. That was to be expected, given that in England there was only a tiny nonwhite population and that in America Jim Crow segregation made interracial relations unlikely. In the twentieth century, however, with the mixing of races and sexes in the cities came heightened concern over possible confusion of identities. Blackmail stories by the early twentieth century did more than warn middle-class men that if they sought sexual adventures outside their class they ran the risk of being compromised. In a radical departure from the older script, sensational cases in the both the United States and England demonstrated that those who dared to cross racial lines could also find themselves victimized.

In 1904 eighty-four-year-old John R. Platt charged in a New York court that Hannah Elias, a "negress and courtesan," had extorted from him the enormous sum of $685,385. Platt, the last president of the New York volunteer fire department, which had been legislated out of existence in 1865, was an eminent figure. He first met his "octoroon girl" in the Tenderloin in 1884 when she was only sixteen. Their paths crossed again in 1896 when he went to a massage parlor (because of his rheumatism, he said), and at this point he became "interested in her welfare." He claimed that he believed she was single and set her up in a boardinghouse. She said that she loved him; but, he told the court, she later threatened to tell his married daughters and her Pullman porter husband of their adulterous affair. As a result

Platt felt obliged to give her money, including the lawyer's fee for her divorce.

The press informed the public that what began as a private romance 145 ended in sensational public scandal. Platt had sometimes called himself "Mr. Green" when secretly visiting Elias at her fashionable home on 230 Central Park West. In the fall of 1903 Cornelius Williams, a discarded and insanely jealous "Negro" admirer of Elias, mistakenly murdered an Andrew H. Green, believing him to be Platt.[1] Elias threatened to use the sensational circumstances of the murder, Platt asserted, as yet another weapon with which to extort money from him. He finally had had enough.

Hannah Elias defied Platt's June 3, 1904, civil order for her arrest and barricaded her home. Given the press coverage the story had received, her besieged residence immediately attracted crowds of curious onlookers. Tourists were taken by it on sightseeing coaches, and it was circled by the members of a local African-American cycling club. Finally on June 8 the police prevailed upon Platt to swear out a criminal warrant. Thousands watched as four policemen broke into Elias's home and arrested her. The press gave a detailed account of the appearance of the short, self-possessed, elegant woman—whose race, it declared, was "obvious"—and of her three-month-old baby, the baby's white nurse, and Kato, the Japanese houseboy.[2]

Elias's position plummeted dramatically, as the *New York Times* maliciously noted, from Central Park West to the female tier of "Coon Row" in the Tombs Prison, where she was held on $50,000 bail. Kato, "the Jap," insisted to reporters that Platt had showered Elias with money but that she never resorted to extortion. Indeed, according to Kato, she had been the victim of white men (including the lawyer who handled her divorce) who threatened to make public her irregular relationship with Platt. Elias took the moral high ground and said that despite Platt's vindictiveness she felt sorry for the octogenarian and saddened by the press's fixation on the color of her skin: "I have all my life made white people my friends and have never had much to do with my own race." At the arraignment Platt—clearly under the hectoring pressure of his children to pursue the case—appeared confused and embarrassed at having to testify, and in the end stubbornly refused to admit to being "bled." The case against Elias collapsed. When Platt left the courthouse a large crowd jeered and catcalled.[3]

Platt's family were not through with Hannah Elias. They proceeded to file a civil suit against her, which came to court in 1905. Once again huge crowds turned out to hear how Elias had made her way from being a cook earning $3 a week to being the mistress of a man who paid $20,000 to the lawyer who secured her divorce. Elias, represented by former New York state governor Frank S. Black, insisted that she had been Platt's devoted mistress and friend, pointing out that he had even given her his deceased wife's watch and pocketbook. The court again found in Elias's favor, concluding that there was no proof of undue influence and that Platt had given her the money out of affection. An appeals court agreed in 1906 that it could find no proof of threats. Moreover it stated that judges did not have the duty of enforcing immoral contracts.[4] John R. Platt admitted to being a fool, getting the very publicity he had paid hundreds of thousands of dollars to avoid.

By presenting to the public such issues as adultery, abortion, and homosexuality, blackmail trials offered a forum in which sex and class relationships could be analyzed and debated. As mentioned earlier, however, the question of race rarely emerged in such court cases in either America or England. This silence could simply be taken as evidence that interracial sexual relationships were uncommon. Yet we know that, given the sexual double standard and racist prejudices, society turned a blind eye to white men's sexual exploitation of black women. White men's patronizing of black prostitutes, for example, as W. E. B. Du Bois noted on another occasion, was generally ignored.[5] Presumably such encounters rarely gave rise to blackmail because black women's marginal position deprived them of the ability to proffer serious threats.

The Platt case was precipitated by his advanced age and his family's greed. Until Platt's family prevailed upon him to launch his ill-fated blackmail charge, the keeping by a wealthy white man of an African-American mistress had easily escaped public attention. The fallout that resulted from the levying of Platt's blackmail charge could be read in a variety of ways. The optimistic could point out that Hannah Elias ultimately triumphed and thereby proved the "fairness" of New York state law. The pessimistic could counter that her trials demonstrated that if and when men such as Platt sought to discard their paramours the charge of blackmail could be backed up by their playing the race card.

The press coverage of the case reminded the American reading public that an interracial relationship, if not criminal, was "unnatural." This was true even if the relationship was mistakenly sanctioned by marriage vows. In 1921 an Arizona man argued that his marriage to a woman who he claimed was black was illegal because of the state's miscegenation law. Indiana was the only northern state to carry the ban on interracial marriages into the twentieth century, but in 1910 James J. Walker—future mayor of 147 New York City—supported a New York State bill that would have defined mixed marriages as "incestuous and void." The bill failed, but Leonard Kip Rhinelander's family—one of the oldest and wealthiest in the state— sought in 1924 to have his marriage annulled on the grounds that he had failed to realize that his wife was black. She suffered the indignity of having to partially disrobe in court. His lawyer's appeal to the jury was shockingly blunt: "There isn't a father among you who would not rather see his own son in his casket than to see him wedded to a mulatto woman." Unfortunately for the Rhinelanders, "passing" was not a crime. Despite their argument that a white man should not be "chained" to a "mulatto," that her refusal to accept an annulment quietly was in effect blackmail, the Rhinelanders' suit failed.[6]

In the Platt case, the New York press was more amused than shocked to discover that an old white man had a young black mistress. In the northern states, economic disparities, de facto segregation, and laws pertaining to abduction and prostitution made the opposite situation—a wealthy black man having a white mistress—highly unlikely. The very notion acted as a spur to the campaign against the "white slave" traffic. One of the purposes of the Mann Act was to criminalize the relationships of black men and white women. Its most famous victim was Jack Johnson, the first black heavyweight champion, who was convicted in 1913 for having a white mistress, or as the court preferred to view it, having transported a woman across a state line for "immoral purposes."[7]

In the southern states, laws against miscegenation were passed after the Civil War. In the twentieth century, moralists and eugenicists continued to publicly condemn racial mixing. Led by the Ku Klux Klan, those fearful of blacks' potential political and economic power exploited whites' sexual insecurities. The horrific work of lynch mobs resulted in over 3,800 black victims, though only one-quarter of the vigilante episodes were motivated by any evidence of sexual activity.[8]

Given the near impossibility of a wealthy black man's having a white mistress, newspaper readers in America, as in the rest of the western world, were shocked by the news that began to leak out in the fall of 1924 that an upcoming trial in London would reveal something like the Platt-Elias affair, with the difference that the racial roles were reversed: an incredibly wealthy "Oriental" had handed over huge amounts of money to keep the news of his adulterous affair with a white, married woman from being made public. The judge insisted that in the court proceedings and in newspaper accounts the mysterious victim was to be identified only as Mr. A, not because of his rank or status but for reasons of state: "It is very important that a scandal should not be caused where this potentate lives."[9] Though the India Office hoped thereby to protect the "potentate" from publicity, its clumsy attempt at secrecy simply increased the curiosity of journalists, and the case received unprecedented international attention. The flood of stories it generated demonstrated the interwar world's heightened preoccupation with the dangerous possibilities of race mixing.

Mr. A was in fact Sir Hari Singh, the wealthy and indolent twenty-four-year-old heir presumptive and nephew of the Maharajah of Jamma and Kashmir. In 1919 he was caught in a Paris hotel in bed with a woman by an enraged Englishman who claimed to be her husband. The story of how the gang of blackmailers had extorted £150,000 (the equivalent of $690,000) from an unidentified and unwitting "Eastern potentate" only broke five years later, in 1924, but when it did it was for weeks front-page news. The *Times* judged the conspiracy set up to blackmail Hari Singh unprecedented in its boldness and daring: "Vice and folly are common to all ages and all climates . . . Great writers have sometimes sought to paint the 'under-world.' Not the most daring among them have put upon the canvas scenes more revolting or more despicable in the cold-blooded and sordid vices they display than several which the evidence in this case has depicted."[10]

Two trials took place. In the first, the jury found that Mr. A had been victimized by blackmailers but held that Maud Robinson (the woman used as bait) and her husband were not party to the plot. In the second, Thomas Hobbs, a solicitor's clerk who was regarded as the chief culprit, was found guilty and sentenced to two years' hard labor. Some felt that a two-year term for the sixty-year-old and apparently ill man was too severe a sentence. Mr. Justice Avory, however, believed he was being lenient. In his summing up he made it clear that he was unhappy that the Robinsons, who had obviously been involved in the crime, had been allowed to walk away. Why, despite such overwhelming evidence of their complicity, were they let off? One lawyer's opinion was that the crown felt there was no point in trying to prosecute Maud Robinson because "the jury in a criminal case would regard the woman as a mere pawn in the game."[11] That did not explain, however, why her husband was not tried. Sex, class, and racial concerns did.   149

Most blackmail trials provided the public with a degree of both entertainment and education. The public's fascination with the Mr. A case was first framed by the notion that the robbing of an individual who was so incredibly wealthy that he did not even know he had been robbed could be treated as a sort of joke. Indeed comics, who were always on the lookout for topical concerns they might exploit, immediately sought to extort whatever humor they could from the trial. Music hall audiences had, of course, long

The trial of the conspirators who blackmailed Sir Hari Singh made the front pages of the international press. ("The Leading Figures in the 'Mr. A.' Case," *Daily Chronicle*, Dec. 4, 1924, by permission of the British Library.)

enjoyed representations of the "toff," or gent, being taken down a peg or two. Popular entertainers accordingly had no difficulty in incorporating the story of the blackmailing of the rajah in their stand-up routines and reviews. In *Patricia*, at His Majesty's Theater, Billy Leonard included in his song "I'm a Dancing Man" the verse

> I've danced at Ciro's and at the Albert Hall
> I've danced a gay grasshopper's hop whilst at a Victory Ball
> When, early in the morning, to flag the fun began
> I said "Good Day" to Mr. A; for I'm a married man

David Burnaby joked in *The Co-optimists* "Hullo everybody! I'm not so well today/I've just been to the bank to cash a cheque for Mr. A." When Hobbs was laughed at in court he had responded by calling his tormentors "baboons." Billy Merson, the music hall comedian, garnered laughs by shouting back at rowdy Palladium audiences, "You baboons, you baboons." Also at the Palladium other jokes included: "We haven't a bedroom left—the last went to Mr. A"; "I've written to my solicitors—Hobbs, Newton and Hobbs"; and "He was gone before you could say 'Jane Robinson.'" Music hall comedians particularly treated the rajah as a figure of fun. The song in one revue had the verse:

> I shan't go away for Christmas
> In London I shall wait;
> But I am going to Paris with
> An eastern potentate

While Blaney and Farrer sang in *Gonna Rain No More,*

> We've got a friend named Harry
> Who talks like anything
> But we have to go to India
> To hear our Hari Singh.

The music hall treatment of the Mr. A case, which allowed audience members of modest means to enjoy jokes about the bilking of a wealthy man, had an obvious class dimension. Though no one attempted to give the story an explicit "Robin Hood stealing from the rich and giving to the poor" gloss, the humor nevertheless had a mildly subversive edge.[12]

But Hari Singh was not just a rich man, he was a rich *black* man, and the racial and sexual aspects of the case were what the public found most scintillating. For the English of the 1920s all nonwhites were categorized as "black." And though music hall jokes about the trial were allowed, full-length revues dealing with black-white sexual relations were not. The Lord Chamberlain, charged with granting licenses for public entertainments, turned down Albert de Courville's outline for a play entitled *Mr. A, or a Matter of Taste*, in which each character was to be identified as a letter and comedian Billy Merson was to play the role of judge. The Lord Chamberlain—Lord Cromer, son of the British imperialist who "made" modern Egypt—forbade all plays on the subject of Mr. A. One reporter noted that "naturally any black-and-white sex intrigue would stagger him, especially if it were so talked about as this one."[13]

If the trial drew attention because it depicted the crossing of class boundaries, it gained its greatest notoriety because it dealt with the taboo subject of the crossing of racial boundaries. Hari Singh was the victim of an enormous fraud, but could an Englishman feel sorry for a black man who slept with a white woman? Whatever else divided the participants in the trial, they all shared the view that the races should not mix. In England's most prestigious court, witnesses and barristers did their part to maintain race barriers by employing astonishingly crude racist epithets to describe the foreign prince who had dared to violate the color bar. The editor of the trial account sneered that Singh's secretary was "a man of the same race and hue as himself," a man "who rejoiced in the name of Maboob." Charles Robinson reported that Montagu Newton (a coconspirator) came to tell him "that there was an affair between my wife and a nigger; I might say a nigger or a black fellow." Robinson stated he accused her of "misconducting herself with a black man or nigger."[14] The elite barristers used language as crude as Robinson's. He was asked whom his wife had been with in Paris:

A. He [Newton] simply told me he could get all the necessary information, and he played on the fact of Mr. A being a nigger, and so on. That is all the evidence I had got and all the information I had got at that period.

Q. It would not have done you much good in Divorce Court to simply come and merely say on your oath, that Mr. A was a nigger?

A. No, I was relying on Mr. Newton.

Sir John Simon pointed out to Robinson that he had to know with whom his wife had been if he were to cite him in a divorce proceedings: "one cannot cite as correspondent 'a nigger, unidentified.'"[15]

The judge was as disturbed as the barristers by the notion of the races' promiscuously mixing. Counsel asked Robinson if he thought a friend of his wife could be considered virtuous, given that she slept with Hari Singh's secretary. When Robinson replied he was not sure of either woman's virtue Mr. Justice Darling upbraided him: "Do consider it! Your own case is that these conspirators, of whom you were not one, got these two women over to Paris and that one of them slept with the master while the other one slept with the secretary, both of these being people of a different race, a coloured race." All the court participants unselfconsciously used racial epithets. Newton, when asked how Mr. A acted when caught in bed with Maud Robinson, sought to raise a cheap laugh. "Well, if it was possible for a coloured man to turn green, he did." Mr. Justice Darling, who considered himself a wit, tried to drag in references to Othello. Hobbs claimed that two gang members considered returning the money to Hari Singh but were afraid that he could not be trusted not to go to the police. "You don't know these niggers as well as I do," Hobbs reported Newton's saying. "They go back upon their word." The only one to protest the use of such derogatory terms was a barrister who appeared in Robinson's appeal trial. He noted that the prince, who had been described in court as a "nigger black man" and a "green shivering wretch," in fact had acted as a gentleman in trying to protect a married woman's reputation.[16]

The Mr. A trial is a forceful reminder that the word "nigger" was used in polite society in 1920s England. In some ways hostility to blacks was greater in the early twentieth century than it had been earlier. Liberals in the nineteenth century, such as John Stuart Mill, attributed what they viewed as the effeminacy and brutality of Indians' sexuality to its primitive state and assumed that their behavior could be improved. Later social Darwinists, however, adopting deterministic views of racial difference, held that natives would always be in a sense naturally perverted and inevitably driven by their lust to pursue whites. Whites, for their part, would always find blacks repulsive. Such obsessions were not confined to the colonies. With the ending of the wartime economic boom and the start of the demobilization of troops after World War I, race riots took place across Britain. In January 1919 Cardiff was swept by riots after white American soldiers claimed that blacks had insulted white women. On the Tyneside in February white sailors attacked Arab seamen. There were also confrontations in London; in April the *Illustrated Police News* published a cartoon entitled "East End Riot between Arabs and Sailors." In May a riot took place between black and white Americans at the Winchester repatriation camp, the whites resenting the African-Americans' associating with English women. The largest confrontation occurred that same month in Liverpool when a crowd of up to 10,000 whites besieged hundreds of blacks who were forced to seek shelter in jails.[17]

The clashes between sailors were caused mainly by competition for work, whereas the problem with soldiers originated with white Americans, who were unused to seeing race mixing and instigated a number of conflicts. The press played up the theme of sexual animosity. In the docklands, according to the *Liverpool Courier*, "You glimpse black figures beneath the gas lamps, and somehow you think of pimps, and bullies, and women, and birds of ill-omen generally, as now and again you notice a certain watchful callousness that seems to hint of nefarious trades and drunkenness in dark rooms . . . One of the chief reasons of popular anger behind the present disturbances lies in the fact that the average negro is nearer the animal than is the average white man, and that there are women in Liverpool who have no self-respect." The *Manchester Guardian* reported a policeman as stating, "The negroes would not have been touched but for their relations with white women. This has caused the entire trouble." Sir Ralph Williams, ex-governor of the Windward Islands, wrote to the *Times*, "To almost every white man and woman who has lived a life among coloured races, intimate association between black or coloured men and white women is a thing of horror . . . It is an instinctive certainty that sexual relations between white women and coloured men revolt our very nature."[18]

Through the 1920s the British press carried stories of whites in the American south lynching alleged black rapists, which helped inflame racial anxiety. The *Illustrated Police News*, a sensationalist tabloid, provided grisly cartoons with captions such as "Negro Abductor Lynched" and "Human Gorilla's Ghastly Crime." Closer to home E. D. Morel harped on the image of the black rapist in *The Horror on the Rhine* (1920), which attacked France's stationing of Senegalese troops in Germany. The "sex instincts" of the troops, Morel wrote, would inevitably be "satisfied upon the bodies of white women."[19]

The English preoccupation with sexually dangerous black men was exacerbated in 1920 by the investigations of the Hunter Commission into the
154   massacre at Amritsar, India. There, in April 1919 natives had knocked a Miss Sherwood off her bicycle and beaten her; the local white community immediately transformed this assault into the myth that she had been raped. General Dyer, the local military commander, imposed a series of humiliating punishments on the entire native population. When protesters assembled he ordered his troops to fire into the unarmed crowd, to continue firing after it began to disperse, and to give no assistance to the wounded. The butchery resulted in an estimated one thousand deaths. It was months before the British government learned of the extent of the bloodshed and set up a commission of inquiry. The final report of the Hunter Commission called for some minimal sanctions against Dyer, but even these were repudiated by the House of Lords. The tabloid press lauded Dyer's bloody defense of white womanhood as a "Horrible Duty."[20]

The hardening of racial attitudes in the 1920s was in part a reaction to the campaigns for civil rights by nationalists in India and African-Americans in the United States. In America the racist musings of Madison Grant in *The Passing of the Great Race* (1916) and Lothrop Stoddard in *The Rising Tide of Color* (1920) were published. British eugenicists bewailed the dangers of racial mixing. At a discussion entitled "Eugenics and Imperial Development" one contributor treated the notion of intermarriage as a joke: "I am quite ready to look upon the coloured races as our brothers, I do not want to look upon them as our brothers-in-law. I think that is a very different matter. (Laughter.)"[21]

The idea of the dangerous, racially erotic "other" was thus very much in the air in the 1920s. And Hari Singh, as a wealthy, young South Asian, far from home, was the quintessential "other." His blackmailers knew that the sensitivity of the British to racial mixing made him all the more susceptible to coercion. Hari Singh's solicitor recalled that the prince was willing to pay almost anything to avoid publicity and scandal. "I was given to understand that for political reasons in his own state there should be no scandal of that kind connecting the name of Sir Hari Singh with a white woman." Another concurred that the prince was at the gang's mercy because "any breath of a scandal hinting at relations with a white woman would be absolute ruin to him."[22]

The press, in speculating that news of the liaison could imperil Singh's succession to the throne, recalled that in 1911 the Gaekwar of Baroda had been cited as a correspondent in a divorce case. The irate husband with- 155 drew his charges only after the Gaekwar paid £5,700. It was not unknown for maharajahs to form liaisons with European women, but it horrified the British government. The British—in particular the officials in the India Office—were more concerned by such entanglements than their Indian counterparts were. Indeed Lord Curzon, Viceroy of India, fearing that de-signing English women would pursue wealthy maharajahs, sought to allow only the most respectable to visit England.[23]

The prince, then, clearly was seen as the "other"; but how was Maud Robinson portrayed? Whites were both titillated and appalled by the fan-tasy of a black man having sex with a white woman—they assumed it had to be rape. The Mr. A case introduced a curious twist. The rajah had indeed slept with a European woman; but in doing so he had been entrapped.[24] Was she to be viewed as his victim? The public could not make up its mind. The ways in which the court and the press portrayed Maud Robinson re-veal much about society's preoccupation with the "New Woman."

To the early twentieth-century reading public, reports of English women who were involved with black men immediately conjured up images of "white slavery" and Oriental dope rings. The *Illustrated Police News* repeat-edly carried cartoons of opium dens occupied by cunning Orientals and drugged women. The authorities wanted both vices subjected to surveil-lance. Prewar accounts of "white slavery" had portrayed blacks and Jews as the most likely pimps and procurers. Such sentiments continued to be ex-pressed into the 1920s. Tabloids described blacks as having a "subtle attrac-tion" that allowed them to keep women in slavery. Some of the barristers in her case seemed to think that Maud Robinson could be slotted into this role of female victim. She was asked in court if she knew a criminal named Hope Johnson. Robinson responded that she had only heard that he was "a great dope fiend." Interestingly, the blackmailers, in planning their scheme, had taken advantage of such stereotypes, portraying Maud Robinson as the drugged victim of an Oriental. Charles Robinson was to say that his wife had been made drunk and then "certain things" were done to her. Hobbs pursued this scenario in court, claiming that a distraught Charles Robinson had cried, "You don't know what he [Singh] did to my wife."[25]

The Maud Robinson who appeared in court was not such a helpless creature; rather, she much more closely matched the 1920s image of the "gold
156   digger" or good-time girl. The press was fascinated by this adventurer, and
both condemned and admired her daring. A cartoon in *The People*, showing all the customers in a restaurant staring at one woman, was captioned:
"Which of all these people is the one who knew Mr. A?" Her looks and
clothes were described in detail. Maud Robinson, according to *The People*,
"a little, indiscriminate thing[,] is not pretty, but she looks as if she were
lively and likable at a party." The *New York Times* reporter noted apprecia-
tively that she wore "a coat of Kolinsky fur and a rope of pearls."[26]

Maud Robinson was presented on one level as the cool, calm "New
Woman" or flapper. She insisted that she was financially independent, having inherited in 1916 from her grandfather shares in the Grasshopper
Company, which produced Grasshopper remedies, ointments and pills.
Not averse to publicity, she actually was dressed as a grasshopper at the cos-
tume ball held November 11, 1919, at which she met Hari Singh; her picture had been in the press. She was a woman of the world; she lived apart
from her husband. In answer to a question about the many men she had
entertained in her home, she made the wonderfully modern observation
"It is possible to have dinner parties and be friendly with people without
sleeping with them."[27]

One paper claimed that in the court there were many of the "Mrs. Robinson type," women who were "smart, handsome, with that blank expression that veils extreme knowingness." This access to knowledge obviously
irritated many of the male observers. When the discussion of sexual practices was raised at the trial one barrister objected that such evidence should
not be heard as there were two women on the jury. Mr. Justice Darling, who
obviously did not want women on juries at all, riposted that women had
demanded to be on juries (their right to do so was only granted in 1918), so
they would just have to put up with it. The alternative was for the women to
step down and the trial proceed with ten members; this idea was not taken
up.[28]

The trial and the responses to it revealed both women's attempts at sexual emancipation and the backlash against it. The same newspapers that reported the Mr. A case carried accounts of Marie Stopes, the pioneering
birth control advocate, doing battle with Catholic opponents such as Dr.
Halliday Sutherland and Cardinal Francis Bourne.[29] Fittingly, a key medical

witness at the trial was Dr. Mary Scharlieb, who devoted a good deal of her career to warning girls of the danger of uncontrolled passion. Reproduction, according to some opponents of birth control, including Scharlieb, was at least to some degree a racial matter. In a collection of essays attacking contraception Scharlieb condemned "sensuous gratification" and predicted that "countries which practiced such self-abuse would rapidly degenerate, and would show a lack of physical vigour and of moral greatness." The same volume contained an essay by H. Rider Haggard, the man who in *King Solomon's Mines* (1885) had condemned racial mixing: "For the sun cannot mate with the darkness, nor the white with the black." Now he was bewailing the impact of contraception on the "White Man's Countries." Immigrants brought with them "watery blood . . . degeneration and effeminacy," he asserted, and the miscegenation that he saw in South Africa heralded the beginnings of "race suicide." "The best thing that we can do," concluded Haggard, "is to appeal to the women of the Empire to save the Empire, and to impress upon them the fact that great nations are not destroyed: they commit suicide."[30] The childless, self-employed, party-going Maud Robinson was obviously not doing her part.

Maud Robinson's apparent promiscuity was troubling. The court regarded her as doubly an adulteress in having crossed the racial line. Clearly, the court found it impossible to believe that any respectable white woman would consort with a black man, no matter how rich. The barristers claimed to be shocked by her explanation of how she responded, at the 1919 ball, to the potentate's servant's approach. "Was he a man of colour? . . . Was it the native secretary or some other native? . . . He asked whether he (this man of colour) could not drive you and Mrs. Bevan home, and you said, 'It is awfully nice of you'? . . . Had you ever accepted a lift from a man of colour before? . . . Are you a lady who would accept an invitation to go to a strange house to see persons, men of colour, even though they are splendid and wealthy, even though you do not know them?"[31]

The trial demonstrated the concern with which white males regarded the increasing restlessness of both women and men of color in the post–World War I world. This was particularly the case in the British colonies, where men suspected white women, because of their foolishness or moral laxity, of being at least partly responsible for causing trouble. People of mixed blood who resulted from such liaisons were always taken as a symptom of chaos.[32] Accordingly women, like natives, had to be kept under surveillance, though in the case of the women it was for their own good. A European man could consort with and perhaps even marry an Asian woman without necessarily losing rank; a European woman could not do the same with an Asian man. In European culture the West was usually read as "male" and the East as "female"; thus it was seen as "natural" for the white male to possess and control the nonwhite female. In the Mr. A case the roles were reversed. Into what existing cultural categories could it fit?

The difficulty of interracial relationships, the impossibility of mixed marriages, and the specter of the white woman in peril were all themes that by the 1920s had a long history in English fiction. Since the eighteenth century the theme of the white man attracted to the dusky Indian princess and the inevitable tragic consequences (she usually died) had proven popular. In the twentieth century only a few brave souls tackled the opposite scenario, of the white woman drawn to a black or Asian man. In Thomas Burke's comic short story "A Family Affair" a white girl's going out with a Chinese boy upsets the local community. "Connie Raymond, the accomplished little flirt, had walked out some evenings with a grave and courteous Chink, putting herself in the way of any little tricks he chose to work upon her. Asking for it, in fact." Her brothers are violent Cockney louts who think the Chinese boy will only stop seeing the girl if they pay his father "blackmail." To their amazement they discover that the father wants to bribe *them* "to remove this white woman of your low-born family from my son's neighbourhood and undertake that she shall at no time again seek him out and disgrace the honourable house of Quong by association with its upright son."[33] The humor of the story was predicated on the unexpected reversal of roles. Middle-class readers could contentedly chuckle at both the slow-wittedness of the working-class characters and the presumptuousness of the Chinese father.

Serious accounts of race crossing were inevitably condemnatory; it was thought shocking even to broach the subject. In Mrs. Frank Penny's *A Question of Love* (1926) the heroine is tempted, but realizes in time that "this way madness lies." In Mrs. E. W. Savi's cautionary tale *The Daughter in Law* (1913) the English heroine, who is so stupid as to marry an Indian, soon discovers that her princely husband is a brute. In England he had appeared civilized; in India he reverts to his true sensual, self-indulgent self. He spits, smokes his hookah, and demands his conjugal rights. "The leer upon his sensual face sent thrills of disgust and loathing through her . . . his dusky hand resting like a blot on the whiteness of her skin . . . [He was] a jealous and exacting male animal whose low instincts and suspicious nature were as apart from her as the East was from the West." "That an English girl should be mated with a man of Hurri Mohun's type," asserts the white male character who rescues her, "was an inconceivable degradation, the grossest outrage possible." Even liberal-minded English observers found it unthinkable that a white woman would find a soul mate in India— the land where females were subjected to arranged child marriages, polygamy, suttee, and infanticide.[34]

Western fictional portrayals of Oriental men commonly presented them as rapists; the opposite tack was to portray them as effeminate. A. E. W. Mason, a well-known author of imperial epics, produced a dreadful novel entitled *They Wouldn't Be Chessmen* (1935) based on the Mr. A affair. It told the story of the blue-eyed, blond-haired Elsie Marsh ensnaring the youthful heir of the Maharajah of Chitipur. Mason portrayed his prince as emasculated (he was described as having a "shrill, high laugh") and had his main female character complain that she was tired of "running round with a coloured boy." In the United States, Nathanael West's *A Cool Million* (1934), a Candide-like account of the Depression years in which a brothel provides the hero and a young woman for the pleasures of a lisping, perverted maharajah, also echoed the Mr. A affair.[35]

The press played its part in propagating fears of the degradation of white women by black men. "White Girls and Coloured Men in Raided Club" was the January 8, 1925, front-page story in the *Illustrated Police News*. In August *The People* ran an article entitled "White Brides Whose Hearts Are Broken in Paganland" claiming that the Colonial Office had sent out a circular warning women that if they married nonwhites they might well discover they were no more than paid mistresses or members of a polygamous household. In the same year the *News of the World* reported what it took to be the shocking story of an English woman in Hamilton, Ontario, who had married a "Chinaman." It noted that the marriage was apparently legal but applauded the local social services for launching an investigation into what they assumed was in effect an abduction. Such racial stereotyping had an impact. When a French woman shot and killed her Egyptian husband in London's Savoy hotel in 1923, British newspapers presented it as the case of a white woman who was defending herself against the eccentric sexual demands (by which anal intercourse was implied) of an oily Levantine. The jury agreed that the woman's fault lay not in shooting her husband three times, but in marrying an Oriental in the first place. She was found not guilty.[36]

160

The subject of racial mixing so preoccupied people at the time of the Mr. A trial because some Orientals had succeeded in "passing" as whites. The *Daily Mail* in 1921, for example, had carried the photograph of Mrs. Arthur Evelyn Ellis, who was to marry an Egyptian prince. "The prince is a bachelor of thirty-two and is very tall," reported the paper. "He has lived principally in England where he was educated. He is thoroughly European in appearance." Mrs. E. W. Savi, who likened European women's marriages to easterners to "white slavery," warned that visiting Indian princes appeared "grave, dark and reticent—surrounded by that halo of romance that all Orientals enjoy in England."[37] Male suspicions of such attractions were depicted in Lady Dorothy Mills's "The Arms of the Sun," a short story that appeared in first issue of *Woman* (April 1924), a magazine meant for the New Woman:

> "Ah, Madame, everywhere have I looked for you in this crowd. I had so hoped to see you before you went away, taking the brightness of London with you. I would like a few minutes' talk with you, if you can spare them to me." Caryll Rose had turned quickly at the sound of the foreign voice.
>
> "Delighted, Prince. Will you take me away and get me a glass of lemonade? I'm willing."
>
> Prince Ismar Mustapha offered her his arm with an old-fashioned formality that withal had nothing English about it. A good many people turned to watch the couple, so strangely contrasted as they went down the wide steps towards an alcove half screened by palms and trailing roses.
>
> "A confederate of Caryll's, or a tool?" murmured one man to another.
>
> "I don't like it anyway," answered the other; "They oughtn't to be allowed, these Orientals, mixing up with our women as if they were white."
>
> "East and West, what, or a grown-up version of Beauty and the Beast. Not much harm in Ismar, though, I imagine. He's pretty decent for a nigger."[38]

Blacks who sought to ape whites were viewed with suspicion at a time when the media applauded whites who passed as natives. The desire to vicariously live the life of the exotic "other" explained the enormous popularity of the real-life adventures of T. E. Lawrence as portrayed by Lowell

Thomas in *With Lawrence in Arabia* (1924) and the fictionalized escapades of the hero of Edith Hull's *The Sheik* (1919). Her novel, though a runaway success, going through fifty printings in a year, was attacked by prudes as 161 salacious and vicious. It was pornographic to the extent that its overheated dialogue dwelled on what the Arab might do with his captive, Lady Diana Mayo:

> "Lie still, you little fool!"
> "Why have you brought me here?"
> "Are you not woman enough to know?"

The novel's daring was the basis of its appeal to the flapper generation; to have read the book was a sign of a young woman's liberation. In fact, however, the book was quite conservative, appealing to the oldest forms of romanticism, and followed a familiar "taming of the shrew" theme. Diana (as her name implied) was the androgynous, tomboy type until she met the right man. She started out as a feminist in riding breeches and ended in a skirt. She was not quite raped. Ahmed Ben Hassan, with his huge phallic curved dagger at his waistband, turned out to be a disguised Scottish laird, the Earl of Glencarryl, who protected her from the real Arabs.[39] Once the problem of his ethnicity was removed, romance could ensue.

Rudolph Valentino's famous filmed version of *The Sheik* was released in October 1921. He starred in *The Young Rajah* the following year. A wave of similar films followed suit: *Arabian Love* (1922) with John Gilbert, *Song of Love* with Edmund Carewe (1923), and *Arab* with Ramon Novarro (1924). Ronald Colman and John Barrymore appeared as Arabs and Cossacks. The same papers that carried the story of the Hari Singh trial advertised Douglas Fairbanks starring in *The Thief of Bagdad* (1924). Such films allowed white women in America and England to "innocently" swoon over make-believe natives. An alluring man in 1920s America was referred to as a "sheik." Real miscegenation, of course, remained taboo. The writers and filmmakers who exploited the popularity of Orientalism and the exotic "other" were certainly not attempting to destabilize white power, but to profit from the release of a little sexual steam.[40]

Any hint of an actual crossing of the racial barrier by a white woman caused panic. Edwina Ashley, Lady Mountbatten, was suspected of making such dangerous liaisons. To scotch what it regarded as disgusting rumors Buckingham Palace forced her to sue *The People*, which had implied that

162

she was intimately involved with Paul Robeson, the African-American singer. Adopting the rhetoric of moral outrage, her lawyer called it "the most monstrous and most atrocious libel of which I have ever heard." How close they were is unclear, but she did have an affair with Jawaharlal Nehru in 1947 when her husband, Louis, Lord Mountbatten, Viceroy of India, was preparing that country for independence.[41]

The interwar public knew none of this, but had an insatiable appetite for fictionalized accounts that toyed with the explosive desires of race-crossing and then defused them. In the reports of the Mr. A blackmail trial observers were forced to make sense of real men and women who had acted out such fantasies. To explain the actions of Hari Singh, the press overlooked the facts and pressed into service the familiar image of the black man as racialized sexual villain. The media fitfully tried to slot Maud Robinson into the role of innocent white female in peril. At other times she was presented as a woman with no self-respect. The most convincing accounts portrayed her as a gold digger.

In America, because John R. Platt abandoned his case against Hannah Elias the public discussion of interracial passions and blackmail was not as extensive as it was in England, where the events of the Mr. A affair were dissected in two long trials. Yet both cases revealed that the interwar world was having problems in using old categories to explain the relations between the races and the sexes. Who was the victim? Who was villain? What was more disconcerting—racial difference or racial "passing?" How could the authorities protect men and women against their own desires?

A different set of racial questions surfaced in the 1930s. Under the headline "Paradise for Blackmailers of Tourists Seen in Law on Extramarital Relations," the New York Times noted in November 1935 that the Nazis' Nuremburg racial laws had had the unintended consequence of arming criminals. The laws stipulated that Jews could not have sex with Aryans, or newly employ any female German under forty-five or continue to employ any under the age of thirty-five. Even foreign diplomats and visitors could be compromised. Indeed the British government protested that Rudolph Selz, a British Jew, had been arrested in Munich for "racial disgrace." Selz, a fifty-nine-year-old German-born engineer, had become a naturalized British subject prior to World War I, in which he had fought as a British soldier. His arrest and eventual expulsion from Germany was taken by the press to mean that the Nuremberg laws for "the protection of German blood" would apply to both Germans and non-Germans. In another case a female member of the Nazi party picked up Lev Smechow, a stateless Jew, and then tried to use the racial law to blackmail him. The court found that he had not, as she claimed, made improper advances, but still sentenced him to six months in prison for having had "attempted race defilement" in mind. In noting that there were also reverse cases, in which non-Jews were imprisoned for having sex with Jewish women, the New York Times marveled that a such a repellent law, which naturally terrified tourists, should have been passed by a government attempting to attract visitors to the Berlin Olympics. By 1936 the paper reported that the Nuremburg racial laws had resulted in the jailing of thirty-two Jews for "race defilement" and the blackmailing of an undetermined number.[42]

Rightfully appalled by the Nazis' policy of Aryanization, both the American and the British press failed to recall that in their own countries the criminal and civil courts had also responded—if less virulently—to the perceived threat of race crossing. Though national and historical differences resulted in significantly different racialized cultural politics in England and the United States, reports of violations of the color bar enjoyed a similar fascination on both sides of the Atlantic. Blackmail stories were an inevitable product of societies that presumed to police sexual and racial relationships, a task made all the more difficult as women increasingly entered the public realm.

163

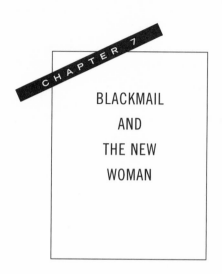

CHAPTER 7

BLACKMAIL

AND

THE NEW

WOMAN

Blackmail stories served to shore up the boundaries between races, classes, and sexes—boundaries that in the twentieth-century city were increasingly difficult to police. Just as members of the working class could "pass" as respectable and some blacks as white, so too women were moving from domestic to public spaces. The attention men gave to reports of their fellows falling prey to female blackmailers was due either to them finding these reports either amusing evidence of their peers' incompetence or sobering lessons: "There but for the grace of God go I." The real importance of the debate over the female blackmailer in America—and in England—is that it offered society a way of discussing the gender and economic divide that, despite the dislocations of World War I and then the Depression, continued to separate men and women.

At the beginning of the century antisuffragists, arguing that women had always been and would always be dependent on men, dismissed the issue of women's low wages. Feminists responded that a new day was dawning in which women were demanding economic and political independence. Indeed radical Olive Schreiner in *Women and Labour* (1911) attacked what she called the "sex-parasitism" of the "kept wife, kept mistress, or prostitute." Wielding the psychoanalytic insights embraced by progressives in the 1930s, Floyd Dell agreed that old notions of "purity" imbued women with a "prostitute psychology regarding marriage." He pessimistically concluded that rather than get a job as a modern woman should, most hoped to "capture" a husband. "To the extent, then, that 'purity' is still inculcated in girls to-day by well-meaning but mistaken parents, it trains them to be neurotic prostitutes, gold-diggers, or alimony hunters; but it unfits them to be happy wives." American feminist Charlotte Perkins Gilman went so far as to assert that in using sex to get ahead humans were lower than animals. The "gold digger" who wanted to be maintained by a male was, Gilman stated, seeking a life that was "utterly subhuman."[1]

These middle-class commentators were rejecting out of hand an option that the shrewd woman of modest means might envisage: the bargaining of her sexual favors. In larger American cities such as New York and Chicago young women had to be realistic. As one historian has noted, "Through dating, pickups, gold digging, temporary alliances and occasional prostitution, they sometimes found excitement, companionship, and not least, some relief from poverty." Investigators reported that waitresses and salesgirls who knew the rules of the game were represented by one who admitted, "All I've got to work with is my 'sex appeal.'"[2] In respectable Victorian circles such mercenary notions had been condemned; in the early decades of the twentieth century the idea that a smart young woman would know how to deal with admirers was expressed in popular songs such as "The Bonnet Shop."

> When a girl of common sense
> Wants to make a competence
> It's a theme for thought intense
> How she is to make it;
> If she happens to prefer
> Starting as a milliner
> There's a bonnet shop for her—
> She has but to take it.
> But what has she to do for it,
>   To do for it, to do for it?
> She has to snare a millionaire
> A Christian or a Jew for it,
> To smile and say, "Perhaps some day,"
> And then of course to stop—
> Oh, it takes a lot before you've got
>   Your little bonnet shop.[3]

Stage shows popularized the notion of the working-class chorus girl eagerly exploiting wealthy stage-door Johnnies, a notion given credence by Evelyn

Nesbit's marriage to New York millionaire Harry Thaw. Such a barter economy was not new, but the open defense of it was.[4]

166   Twentieth-century American sexual standards were based on an implicit belief in "individualism," meaning that each person was free to pursue his or her pleasure as each saw fit. The notion that women were joining in the chase was captured by singer Marion Harris's popularization of a tough, street-wise style with songs like "I'm Gonna Do It If I Like It." In reality, however, men were much freer to pursue pleasure than women. A certain liberal portion of the public acknowledged that the "sexual contract" was unfair to women and so could understand their recourse to subterfuge. But when did womanly wiles become falsehoods? When did pleas for consideration become threats? In men and women's sexual negotiations, where was the border between traditional responsibilities and illegal demands? Custom had previously determined such matters; in the twentieth century the courts were increasingly called on to do so. In the 1920s and 1930s, when women's legal, economic, political, and sexual relationships with men were rapidly changing, one of the functions of blackmail stories was to establish when women's escalating demands transgressed boundaries and crossed the line into the criminal.[5]

Such preoccupations were framed by the recognition that sexual mores were changing and the older world of separate male and female cultures was disappearing. The 1920s witnessed a sexual revolution in which Americans talked about such issues as birth control, venereal disease, and sex education with unprecedented candor. Premarital sex increasingly became part of courtship. One survey discovered that of women born between 1890 and 1900 74 percent were still virgins at marriage, as opposed to only 31.7 percent of those born after 1910.[6] The adventurous young woman was regarded as reacting against the nineteenth-century "cult of true womanhood" and the ideal of the passionless female. "The flapper is no longer naïve and charming; she goes to the altar of God with a learned and even cynical glitter in her eye," complained H. L. Mencken. The schoolgirl of today, he added, "knows as much as the midwife of 1885, and spends a good deal more time discharging and disseminating her information."[7] Some tabloids went so far as to claim that moral laxity was blurring the line between prostitution and courtship. In the modern business world men and women were thrown together as female secretaries displaced male clerks in offices. Some commentators told wives not to be suspicious. Yet the press

occasionally carried sensational stories about secretaries and typists purposely setting out to seduce and blackmail their bosses.[8]

Stories of the blackmailing woman were told in a variety of ways. The
press could hardly contain its amusement in reporting on a series of sensational trials in which prominent men who tried to prosecute women for extortion were humbled. In the interwar years, however, a movement—by
structuring an account of "heart balm" legislation to give the impression
that it armed the female blackmailer—succeeded in pushing through law
reforms in a number of states. To complicate matters further, Hollywood
produced dozens of "gold digger" movies in which the designing woman
was both glamorized and domesticated.

Judges often asserted that naïve men who had been dunned by wily females were usually reluctant to take the matter to court, because if a jury
had to decide between a man bringing suit and an obviously wronged
woman the man was likely to fare badly. Defense lawyers easily made such
men look foolish. For example, in 1922 the *New York Times* reported that
Angus Nicholson, a middle-aged, married stockbroker, charged that Mal-
vena Richman, a twenty-one-year-old actress, had imprisoned him for
three days and robbed him. His story was that on the night of March 24 he
met her and several other women, and had in the course of the evening become drunk and passed out. Richman took him to her apartment on Riverside Drive where he remained until March 27. He contended that he must
have been "doped" as during those three days he made out checks to her for
$4,000 and $5,000. In addition he lost a diamond tie pin, a walking stick,
and $300 in cash. The young woman was charged and released on $5,000
bail. Her version of the story was that Nicholson had given her a check simply because he wanted "to help me out for a while." She had passed the
$4,000 check on to a man named Joe Levy, to whom she owed money for
diamonds. Denying that Nicholson was a prisoner, she asked why he did
not simply use her telephone. His chauffeur, she further pointed out, had to
spend half the day sobering up Nicholson before he was fit to leave her
apartment. If this was indeed a case of blackmail it was successful. Nicholson said he was too ill to testify, and the case was abandoned.[9]

Well-off men obviously did not want their womanizing exposed to the
public gaze. Blackmail reports forced such activities into the open. The
March 16, 1923, chloroform death of Dorothy Keenan, a New York model,
was attributed by authorities to blackmailers seeking to obtain incriminat-

167

ing love letters sent to her by a married man. Though the district attorney initially attempted to protect the man's identity, he was soon revealed to be John K. Mitchell, son-in-law of E. T. Stotesburg of Philadelphia, a banker and an associate of financier J. P. Morgan. While Mitchell's wife was in Palm Beach, Mitchell had given Keenan gifts worth $10,000. Draper M. Daughtery, son of Harry M. Daughtery, the United States Attorney General, came forward and admitted that he too had been a friend of Keenan's, and that he had employed her brother, Francis Keenan. Daughtery was led to make this avowal by a man who had called him threatening that if he were not given a job in the Justice Department he would link Daughtery to the dead woman. Dorothy Keenan had kept Mitchell's letters in a safety deposit box, but according to the district attorney had opposed the idea of using them in a badger game. Evidence suggested that Albert Guimares, a business associate of Keenan's, might have been involved. He was sentenced in December 1923 to three years in prison on an unrelated charge. Keenan's murder was never solved, leaving the cynical to conclude that wealthy men aided by clever lawyers could always cover their tracks.[10] All the voyeuristic were left with was the hope that the mortified wives of the men involved would impose their own punishment. The 1931 Vivian Gordon murder case was remarkably similar to that of Dorothy Keenan. Gordon was found strangled after appearing at a vice enquiry. The press reported that she supplied "pretty women for gay parties" and kept in her diary the names of the hundreds of men who attended. The assumption was that her death was ordered by someone whom she had threatened to expose.[11]

Few men went to such extremes as murder, of course, but blackmail cases led the press to reveal how some routinely used private detectives and lawyers to deal with obstreperous mistresses. In 1926, for example, F. R. Hazard, a wealthy businessman, found himself blackmailed by his former stenographer. He turned first to a private detective and then to the police. The woman clearly was making demands. "I need $5,000 so that I can go to Europe to get a divorce," she wrote. When he balked she threatened, "If you don't give it to me I'll tell Arthur [her previous husband] and he will start the works." Hazard had known the woman for four years and had provided her with large amounts of money in the past. Given that she and her new husband offered to make restitution and that Hazard decided he did not want his wife and children to hear anymore about the case, in the end he refused to sign the complaint, and the couple was discharged.[12]

Out of such scandalous contests emerged a blackmail story that appealed to populist sentiment in America. Although American courts were not sympathetic to meretricious relationships, when a designing woman was pitted in court against a wealthy man, it was often the latter who came off the worse. A classic example of this occurred in 1929 when N. L. Amster, the ex-chairman of the board of directors of the Chicago, Rock Island, and Pacific Railroad, had Olga Edwards arraigned for extorting from him $170,000. When they had met in 1917 he was forty-eight and she was twenty-two. He paid for her acting lessons and for trips over the years to Madrid, Rome, and Paris, where they would meet "by accident." In 1922 she had a child. "He is a nice little chap," she wrote Amster and boldly threatened to mail the baby to him. Though Amster refused to accept paternity, he had his lawyer draw up a contract guaranteeing Edwards that, as long as she did not annoy him or his family, she would receive the interest drawn on a $100,000 trust fund—$6,000 a year—with the principal to go to the boy on her death. Amster asserted that Edwards had broken this contract. She made embarrassing scenes and coached her child into calling out "Daddy Amster" at his office. As a result of Amster's suit, Edwards faced losing both her liberty and the trust fund. In her criminal trial the judge's instructions to the jury were brutally precise. "The question is, do you believe that he told the truth or the defendant did. Under the law of the State there is no obligation on the father of an illegitimate child to support the mother, except during confinement." Though she was found guilty, both the jury and the public clearly wanted mercy shown. She was sentenced to five years' probation. Superior Court Justice Levy, who acted as the arbitrator of the trust fund, was even more supportive. Declaring that she was a good mother and "more sinned against than sinning," he assured her that her monthly payments would be reinstated.[13]

It is difficult to say how typical such cases were. The press was not interested in the everyday complaints of the new army of shop girls and typists who fought off the sexual overtures of their employers. What sold were accounts of designing women who exploited wealthy "sugar daddies." In these stories even the bright young gold digger charged with the crime of blackmail stood a good chance of escaping punishment. In their amorality these stories could be seen as fairy tales updated for modern times. Both women and men of modest means could enjoy such fantasies. Legal scholars complained, however, that the plundering of wealthy men was not a myth, that America had on its books laws that permitted "legal" blackmail. These were commonly referred to as the "heart balm" statutes.

170   In 1917 twenty-two-year-old Lillian Mendel began an affair with twenty-five-year-old Frederick Gimbel of the department store dynasty. He promised to marry her on the death of his father. When, fifteen years later, he failed to do so she launched a breach of promise of marriage suit against him, demanding $2 million in compensation. His lawyer's argument, that his client was a "simpleton" who had already foolishly spent $680,000 on the woman, failed to sway the jury. It awarded Mendel $250,000, later reduced on appeal to $125,000. The next year Gimbel settled out of court with a second woman who had threatened a million-dollar suit.[14] Through the 1920s and 1930s the American press played up the notion that many of the well-known actors, entertainers, businessmen, and sports personalities who found themselves embroiled in breach of promise and alienation of affection suits were in reality blackmail victims. The result was a nationwide campaign for the repeal of what were derogatorily called "heart balm" statutes.

    The breach of promise of marriage suit was the critics' chief target. The United States (Louisiana being the sole exception) inherited from English common law mechanisms by which a woman could be offered some legal remedy against "blackguardism." If, after a long courtship, a man jilted a woman, she found herself with her youth lost—in effect, she was defrauded. Some women might have lost their virginity in the process, making them now unmarriageable. Either way, a contract had been broken. The courts recognized that for middle-class women marriage had a real value; they accordingly allowed women to sue for loss of reputation and virtue, humiliation, and economic costs. If a child had resulted, the money a woman won could indirectly provide child support; there was almost no legal compulsion for a father to support an illegitimate child. The irony was that to be successful in such suits women had to present themselves as passive victims, whereas in reality it took enormous courage to expose oneself in such a public contest.[15]

    Criticism of these suits had begun in the late nineteenth century; a concerted campaign against them took off in the 1920s. Lawyers and academics first argued that the law could not deal with every misfortune, and certainly not with emotional loss. Such suits made unseemly secrets public. "Should so much festering corruption," asked a critic in 1921, "be yearly exposed to a jesting community, under the misnomer of blighted affection, and jealousy exact her blackmail?"[16] If *real* crimes had been perpetrated, commentators noted, the laws on rape and seduction could deal with them.

The critics' second complaint was that the existing law was inequitable. In practice, breach of promise suits were only used by women against men. In court the advantages all went to the woman. It was easier to advance evidence of a promise than to disprove it; sometimes a jury was even impressed by proof of a promise that was only implied or inferred. And what sort of woman would launch such an action? Real love, the critics argued, did not seek damages. The respectable and virtuous would nurse their wounds in silence, as women had done for centuries. Advancing the "unworthy plaintiff" argument, critics asserted that only the speculative and unchaste turned to dubious legal remedies. "It is left to the adventuress and the woman of shady character, who has no reputation to be lost, and whose actual needs (or better, wants) can be supplied by coin of the realm."[17] And not only were the vindictive rewarded, complained critics; the damages varied wildly, with some women awarded thousands of dollars, others a few cents. The rule of thumb, said cynics, was that the wealthier the man and the prettier the woman, the higher the award.

The sympathies of legal scholars, who were predominately male, went out to persecuted men. The author of a 1919 *Forum* article entitled "The High Cost of Loving" warned the male reader that the love letter he wrote to a woman was "a charge of high explosive beside which TNT is a spring zephyr." The compromised man faced scandal, disgrace, and social suicide. "Most men," claimed a 1921 text, "would rather pay hush-money than have the whole story of a love-folly trumpeted in the newspapers." Even innocent men were cowed. "The publicity of such a suit is terrifying, and this, plus the possibility of losing the suit to a consciousless and unscrupulous plaintiff who will make full use of her tremendous advantages with the jury, will induce almost any man of this type, who is so unfortunate as to be picked out as a subject for blackmail of this kind, to pay any sum demanded in order to have peace."[18] The assumption was that men were simply pursuing their rightful pleasures and should not be held responsible for giving way to a natural urge.

Central to the account crafted by the critics of the heart balm statutes was the notion that bad laws created a situation in which perjury and blackmail flourished. A contributor to a Virginia law journal stated in 1923 that breach of promise was more often "an instrument of oppression, blackmail, and fraud than for the righting of the wrongs of injured innocence." Lawyers were compromised in such dealings. Almost every case was pursued for mercenary reasons, claimed a 1929 commentator. "The result is that the suit is generally resorted to for the purpose of blackmail, the defendant knowing that if he does not pay up . . . the result will be a highly unpleasant court proceeding." A 1934 article carried the same message: "That this form of lawsuit is frequently a sub-legal basis for downright blackmailing, is a matter of general public knowledge."[19]

A good deal of obvious misogyny and mythmaking fueled the legal attacks. Critics portrayed the women who launched suits as lying parasites and gold diggers motivated by greed and revenge. Feminists joined in condemning the laws, and women legislators sponsored repeal legislation in a number of states. The leaders of the National Women's Party declared that "heart balm" suits should simply be laughed out of court. They took this position because they were opposed to the notion that women should be regarded as property. They wanted women to be economically independent, with marriage separated from commerce. Such feminists shared the optimistic view that in post–World War I America it was denigrating to believe that women could not fend for themselves—if given the opportunity. The belief that this should be as true in the private as in the public realm was the line taken by the advocates of the sexual revolution in the 1920s. Seduction was no longer thought to involve an active male and a passive female. In 1934 one commentator noted that now "seductions are largely mutual and they could be plausibly classified in that special division of the law of contracts known to lawyers as joint adventures."[20] Like most Americans, feminists also embraced the notion of companionate marriage. Such marriages could not be created by the threat of a lawsuit. Better to have a man back out of an engagement than to have two people yoked together in an unhappy relationship.

As no legal scholar has yet done a thorough investigation of breach of promise suits in twentieth-century America it is impossible to determine the accuracy of the bleak picture painted by the "heart balm" critics. What is clear is that the newspapers and law journals popularized the stereotype of the sexually active woman employing a crooked lawyer to successfully bilk wealthy men. The political campaign against this "sexual racketeering" took off in 1934. Indeed, reform statutes were pushed through so quickly that in some states their constitutionality was later questioned. The reform legislation was begun in Indiana under the leadership of the state's only female legislator, Roberta West Nicholson. The 1935 Indiana statute served as 173 a model for "anti–heart balm" legislation in other states. The term referred to four distinct torts: seduction, breach of promise, alienation of affection, and criminal conversation. Twenty-three states considered reform and seven of them acted in 1935—Indiana, New York, Michigan, Pennsylvania, New Jersey, Illinois, and Alabama. That same year the California legislature condemned the heart balm laws as "more the weapons of a blackmailer than the shield of an appealing victim."[21]

This preoccupation with blackmail framed every state campaign. In Illinois the statute was entitled "An Act in Relation to Certain Causes of Action Conducive to Extortion and Blackmail." In Michigan the passage of the statute was attributed to "the prevalence of blackmail peculiar to these actions." In New York state senator John J. McNaboe, author of that state's anti–heart balm bill, declared the enemy to be "a certain type of lawyer, who, working in cahoots with the modern female racketeer, seeks to become rich at the expense of reputation, embarrassment, and wide-spread publicity." The bill, he promised, would end "the tribute of $10,000,000 paid annually by New York men to gold-diggers and blackmailers. Nine out of ten . . . suits have been of the racketeer type." Governor Herbert H. Lehman concurred that the older laws had been "a fruitful source of coercion, extortion, and blackmail."[22] Under the proposed bill even threatening to launch such a suit could be regarded as a crime.[23]

Some legal scholars believed that the heart balm statutes had some merit. They noted that it was striking that such torts were abolished largely because of the purported fear that they could be used for blackmail. The threat of any lawsuit, they pointed out, could be used to extort money or services. Why then was there only a campaign against the filing of sexual suits? The answer is that in the 1920s and 1930s changing gender relationships had created uncertainty. As sexual activity became more liberated for both sexes and women became more willing to make their cases in public, well-off males became more defensive and complained that they required new means of protection. Lawyers and politicians used such concerns as the building blocks with which to construct the convincing story that antiquated laws placed innocent men at the mercy of ruthless women.[24] The fact that the states' late 1930s campaigns against "sex fiends" were aimed at protecting children rather than women was a further indicator that women were increasingly regarded as sexually savvy and potentially manipulative, 174 more likely to be perpetrators rather than victims of sexual aggression.[25]

Some commentators suggested that the "racket of alimony" was yet another way unscrupulous women and their lawyers blackmailed helpless men. Alimony was based on the prima facie common-law duty of the husband to support his wife even after divorce if he were responsible for the

Under the pressure of lobbyists Indiana took the lead in the United States in rescinding heart balm statutes, which purportedly armed the female blackmailer. ("A Valentine Day Sentiment," *Indianapolis Times,* Feb. 14, 1935, in M. B. W. Sinclair, "Seduction and the Myth of the Ideal Woman," *Law and Inequality: A Journal of Theory and Practice* 5, 1987: 83; by permission of *Law and Inequality.*)

breakup of the marriage. If the wife's immoral conduct came to the notice of the court, both her maintenance and custody of any children could be jeopardized. An article in a 1916 issue of *McLure's* magazine claimed that two-thirds of divorce was due to women's desire for alimony. In fact, however, support was granted to less than 10 percent of wives. Nevertheless as more women worked outside the home public support of alimony declined. A poll published by the *Ladies Home Journal* in 1938 revealed that 82 percent of respondents opposed support if there were no children and the wife could work. What had led the public to believe that alimony had become a social problem was the attention the press gave to unusually large divorce settlements, such as the $25 million purportedly paid out by dime-store baron Sebastien Kresge in 1924.[26] Alimony was portrayed in films as a form of female extortion carried out by the gold digger who had married only in order to entrap her prey. *For Alimony Only* (1926) presents the plight of a young couple trying to end the crushing payments demanded by the first wife. In *Alimony Madness* (1933) the second wife is portrayed as actually getting away with the murder of her predecessor when the court agrees that she was justified in protecting her husband from the "constant persecution of the alimony hunter." It was easier to blame the escalating divorce rate on criminal calculation than attempt to understand the social changes, such as urbanism and growing female economic independence, which led one in six marriages to end in divorce by the end of the 1920s. Under such titles as "Flaying the Alimony-Diggers" and "Plucking the Golden Gander" critics spun stories that presented alimony as just another type of female extortion. The economic consequences of divorce were in reality hardest on the woman, but by presenting her request for support as a form of blackmail commentators were able to deflect attention away from gross economic disparities and a divorce law based on the notion of a matrimonial "fault."[27]

In the 1930s the notion that single women should seek financial compensation for matrimonial promises or illicit sexual favors appalled legislators and legal scholars. In Hollywood films such stratagems were often sympathetically dissected. What are we to make of the fact that movie audiences cheered on the gold digger while in the courtroom judges decried her activities? The motion picture, perhaps better than any other medium, captured the complexities of the interwar public's reaction to the appearance of the modern woman. Film depictions of female blackmail provided the American public with an account of the interrelationships of gender, sexuality, and crime that was at times more nuanced than that offered by the statute book.

An extraordinary number of films in the first decades of the twentieth century addressed such sexual topics as adultery, divorce, prostitution, and promiscuity. Particularly in the early 1930s, Hollywood films presented women—in the form of sultry stars such as Greta Garbo, Marlene Dietrich, Jean Harlow, and Mae West—as sexual beings. In Alfred Hitchcock's *Blackmail* (1929) the flapper's adventurousness was hailed in the song "Young Miss of Today," which contains the line "They say you're wild, an awful child, Young Miss of Today." Female film stars were obliged to have sex appeal, or what writer Elinor Glyn called "It." Clara Bow was described by one admirer as "top-heavy with It." According to film historians, the sexual double standard was for a moment critiqued by this more active presentation of women.[28] The critique was made especially clear in the changing presentation of the woman who used her sexual powers to get ahead in the world.

One of the staple story lines of American films was what the *New York Times*'s film critic referred to as "that old theme, the shop girl's romance with her employer." The popular Clara Bow movie *It* (1927) glorified the woman who pursued and captured a man as a sort of modern-day Cinderella. Such sexy stories were thought to be wholesome enough as long as the young woman saved herself for marriage. If she did not, tragedy had to ensue. *Ladies of Leisure* (1930), starring Barbara Stanwyck, presented, according to one critic, "a searing portrayal of a type of metropolitan girl known as a 'gold-digger' who realizes how tawdry her life has become." The department store clerk (Constance Bennett) learns in *The Easiest Way* (1931) that becoming a wealthy man's mistress is a terrible mistake. The small-town factory girl (Joan Crawford) who is taken care of by a married lawyer reaches the same conclusion in *Possessed* (1931). *Back Street* (1932), based on Fannie Hurst's best-selling tearjerker, portrayed a faithful mistress (Irene Dunne) condemned to live her lonely life in the shadows.[29]

Filmmakers never stopped exploiting moralizing accounts of the bartering of sexual favors, but they struck a new note in the 1920s when they began to deal with the issue as the basis for comedy rather than melodrama. A more active female role emerged with the "gold digger" character, who used sex as a way of getting ahead in life by either taking advantage of men or actually blackmailing them. The term was first employed on the stage in a 1919 play about designing women entitled the *Gold Diggers*.[30] In the film *Manhandled* (1924) a shop girl (Gloria Swanson) tries to be good while her gold-digging friend is tempted by men with "smooth stories" offering "sable coats." In Anita Loos's best-selling novel *Gentlemen Prefer Blondes* (1925) the role usually played by the seduced shop girl is taken by the wisecracking chorus girl. Lorelei, the heroine, is the sort of young woman who can amaze "Dr. Froyd" with her lack of inhibitions and con a family out of $10,000 *not* to marry their young man. In the film version of 1928 enthusiastic audiences applauded the success of the "diamond diggers" at curing men of their parsimony. *That Certain Thing* (1928) likewise presented a gold digger seeking to trick a man into marriage. *Red Headed Woman* (1933), a film scripted by Anita Loos, starred Jean Harlow as a stenographer from the wrong side of the tracks who successfully seduces and abandons men.[31] Audiences sympathized with such a needy young woman who they felt deserved to do better.

177

Most of these films presented a lighthearted view of the sexual temptations of modern life. In *Classified* (1925) the telephone operator flirts with any male voice "with a smile." George Cukor's risqué *Girls About Town* (1931) has two "lilies of Broadway's fields" consoling lonely millionaires. *Convention City* (1933) boasts a cast of party girls, philandering salesman, and suspicious wives. In *The Greeks Had a Word for Them* (1932), as in so many of these movies, the story line is set so that the audience was from the start on the side of the "silk-stockinged musketeers."[32]

Mae West's character of Lady Lou in the smash success *She Done Him Wrong* (1933) came to epitomize the type. "I wasn't always so rich," she recalls. "I once was so poor I didn't know where my next husband was coming from." The virtual end of the sexual double standard appears to be sounded in her most memorable line, "When women go wrong, men go right after them." One English reviewer, though admiring West's toughness and sophistication, concluded that "the film is not a pleasant one—the reek of the underworld is in every foot of it." In contrast, the critic of the *New York Times* held that Lady Lou's only fault was that her heart was bigger than her sense of decorum. That the movies dared to show the gold digger apparently bargaining her sexual favors and actually succeeding reflected a changing moral climate, but there were limits.[33] In *I'm No Angel* (1933) Mae West declared, "When I'm good I'm very good, but when I'm bad I'm better." Yet in the end she was good. She tore up her successful breach of promise suit aimed at ensnaring Cary Grant. "So both the wages of sin and sentiment turn out to be equally gilt-edged," noted one reviewer. "And that, on reflection, may be the most cynical moral of all." Yet audiences in the 1930s were not overly worried by such moral dilemmas. Many no doubt left the theater musing if Lady Lou had been domesticated or was as usual only joking.[34]

Among the best known of these films was *The Gold Diggers of 1933* (1933) with Johnny Mercer's famous songs and the dance routines of Busby Berkeley. Mercer's song "We're in the Money" has added piquancy when it is recalled that it was originally entitled "The Gold Diggers' Song" and was as much about sexual as economic inequalities. The film begins with young women giving up their poorly paid jobs to join a chorus line and then portrays the most enterprising setting out to exploit well-heeled gentlemen. Trixie McMahon, the jaded veteran, leads the charge in the sex war, saying of men: "They've had their fun. Now let's have ours! Let's take them for a ride . . . we'll let those guys pay for their fun—right through the checkbook." In fact Trixie sets out to employ the old "badger game" by luring a wealthy lawyer to her apartment and having an accomplice, playing the role of her husband, catch them in the act. The filmmakers never forgot that they were making a comedy, however, so at the last minute Trixie is given a pang of conscience and calls the whole thing off; the lawyer nevertheless declares his love and the film ends with their happy marriage. Even reviewers in conservative papers found the ending contrived. "Miss McMahon is, like her partners in crime, Miss Joan Blondell, and Miss Ruby Keeler, a sheep in wolf's clothing, and all three end up in the bonds of respectable matrimony."[35] The intent was to allow the movie audience to cheer on the conniving vixen, safe in the knowledge that her virtuous side would be eventually revealed.

Other films went one step further and moved from the gold digger to the actual female blackmailer. A moralizing treatment of the subject was provided in *Party Girl* (1930), in which Jay (Douglas Fairbanks, Jr.) is made drunk by a party girl, who convinces him he has ruined her. He accordingly marries her. The police discover the ruse and the "sinful young creature" conveniently falls to her death, allowing Jay to return to his wholesome girlfriend. In *Good Sport* (1931), "party girls" discuss blackmail and decide they do not have to go that far. In *Bed of Roses* (1933) Lorry, a prostitute, declares after getting out of a reformatory: "I did a lot of thinking in that joint. I found out that the only difference between me and them women you see riding around in yachts is they use their heads. And believe me, I'm using mine from now on." She and a fellow bad girl set out in search of "umpchays with ashcay." In *Convention Girl* (1935) women are portrayed as attempting to entrap businessmen. The most sensational of such films was *Baby Face* (1933), in which Barbara Stanwyck plays the role of a "tramp" who, according to an overly imaginative scriptwriter, plunges into a career of vice and extortion after having heard Nietzsche's line "All life, no matter how we idealize it, is nothing more than exploitation." Working in a bank, she sleeps her way up the ladder of success and threatens to sell her secrets to the press. She ends up married to the bank's president.[36]

179

The economic dislocations caused by the Great Depression clearly played a part in the public's toleration of the representation of the liaisons of the smart set and kept women. Resentment toward the rich made audiences root for the working girl. Movies also reflected changing views on morality, implying that pre- or extramarital sex no longer always had to lead to a woman's fall.[37] Indeed the gold digger's success was represented by her acquisition of furs, apartments, and jewels; sex was equated symbolically with luxury. The interwar world was fixated on the glamorous woman (the term "glamour" originally referred to the sexual witchcraft women used to enslave men).

The optimistic, not to say amoral, view taken by the movies of the flapper, gold digger, and female blackmailer alarmed the censors. They argued that just as boys were attracted to gangster movies girls would be led astray by the glamour of the gold digger. The censors perceptively noted that the moralizing scenes usually tacked on to the end of such films—the gangster was inevitably killed and the gold digger married—did not compensate for youth's identification with the main characters' initially immoral struggle for success. The Catholic Legion of Decency insisted on an end to such lax portrayals. Father Daniel Lord wrote the 1930 Motion Picture Production Code, which banned the portrayal of nudity, excessive violence, white slavery, illicit drugs, miscegenation, lustful kissing, suggestive postures, and profanity. He called for movies that would focus on wholesome characters like Charles Lindbergh, Babe Ruth, and America's first

Catholic presidential candidate, Al Smith, Sr. *Baby Face* caused a major furor. Catholic officials insisted that the heroine be denounced for her "brazen method of using men" and that instead of her being trained by an advocate of Nietzsche she be seen reading a more uplifting text, like Samuel Smiles's *Self-Help*.[38] Hollywood feared that further attacks on "degenerate films" would result in the industry's losing its powers of self-policing. In response it revised the Motion Picture Production Code in 1934, which in effect terminated for a time the presentation of the woman who successfully exploited her sexual powers.

The fact remains that audiences clearly enjoyed the spectacle of the fast "party girl" entrapping and milking the slow-witted tycoon. Was this a sort of grass-roots feminism? One observer has suggested that, on the contrary, one reason such bright and attractive female characters were so popular was that they were presented as more interested in men than in politics. And a close examination of the films of the early 1930s reveals that they were neither as critical of sexual mores as the censors feared nor as liberating as some film historians have imagined. The censors were no doubt right in holding that the filmmakers' primary purpose in presenting the gold digger was to exploit the titillating opportunity of showing women's bodies. Moreover the films, in playing on the male fear that women would use their sexuality to compromise men, only appeared to be daring. In usually giving such scenarios a comedic treatment that concluded with a happy ending, moviemakers found a profitable way of exorcising the specter of "women on top." Yet, when all was said and done, these films also offered a way of discussing shifts in sexual behavior. The degree of tolerance shown to the good time girl's stratagems played an important part in dispelling the myth of female innocence and passivity.[39]

It is striking that the campaign against the heart balm statutes and the series of films portraying party girls peaked at roughly the same time. Trial cases and film portrayals seemed to be responding to a demand American society was making for stories that would make some sense of changing gender relations. If, despite all the talk about full citizenship, women were obviously not men's economic equals, did they have the right to use their sexuality as a resource? Were they ever justified in exploiting sexual secrets? The courtroom and the movie theater provided two contrasting responses. The courts responded negatively. Their pronouncements, given that they usually dealt with failed attempts at extortion which the judge was about to punish, necessarily had to be couched in tragic terms. The movies carried a more positive message. Filmmakers could adopt a comedic mode because they, unlike judges, portrayed "successful" attempts at blackmail, though they usually concluded them on a moralizing note. As old certainties concerning proper sex and gender roles eroded America increasingly tolerated such mixed messages.

Across the Atlantic moral standards changed more slowly. "The American 'gold digging' trick of marrying a rich man, goading him into infidelity, and then 'soaking' him," according to one account, "did not catch on in England." Yet British audiences flocked to the Hollywood films that portrayed such schemes. In the 1930s the United Kingdom had the highest per capita movie attendance in the world. Two-thirds of the population went to the cinema at least once a week, with women outnumbering men. Some American films were censored—*Party Girl* (1931) and *Good Sport* (1931) were banned, *Baby Face* (1933) was trimmed by twelve minutes, and *Red Headed Woman* (1933) was prevented from being shown in England until 1965— but the fact is that Hollywood films swamped the British market in the 1920s and 1930s.[40] In 1926 83.6 percent of the films shown in Britain were made in America; even after protective legislation was introduced in 1925 and 1927 the figure held at about 70 percent in the 1930s. American movies were what the public wanted to see, not the English "quota quickies."[41]

The fact that so many Hollywood gold digger films were shown on British screens is evidence of a cross-fertilization of blackmail stories across the Atlantic. To a degree these movies simply modernized the turn-of-the-century shop girl romances in which women angled for a wealthy husband. (In real life department store magnate George Selfridge married chorus girl Gaby Deslys.) But the British Board of Film Censors stated that it would not pass anything that would "demoralize an audience . . . bring the institution of marriage into contempt, or lower the sacredness of family ties." The board was especially concerned about the portrayal of women: "The betrayal of young women is a question which depends upon the treatment; when the subject is treated with restraint, it seems impossible to exclude it as a basis for a story. Objection, however, is taken when the treatment is such as to suggest that the girl is morally justified in succumbing to temptation in order to escape sordid surroundings or uncongenial work."[42] In other words, British censors did not object to the woman being portrayed as the passive victim of an aggressive man; what alarmed them was the woman being shown as an active sexual being, bargaining her favors for a monetary return. English courts made the same pronouncement. Just as America had its anti–heart balm movement, so too in England there was a legal backlash against designing women.

In 1930 a Mrs. Doris Jee threatened to publish her manuscript, "The Diary of a Discreet Woman." She was subsequently prosecuted for blackmail. At the trial it came out that her checkered past included bigamous marriages, breach of promise cases, and successful out-of-court slander suits. This "blackmailer of the worst type," as Scotland Yard characterized her, was found guilty and sentenced to eighteen months in prison.[43] In the eighteenth and early nineteenth centuries a threat to publish made by a woman like Mrs. Jee would not have been punished at all. For most of the Victorian period, too, English courts in effect refused to recognize the female blackmailer. A man menaced with the exposure of his misdeeds by the woman he seduced was expected to face up to his responsibilities. The courts did not condone the woman's demands, but they left it to the man to deal with them as he saw fit. By the end of the nineteenth century, however, as the image of the helpless, passive female was displaced by that of the politically and sexually aggressive and calculating woman, judicial attitudes hardened. Twentieth-century English judges made it known that they would not tolerate women's subjecting men to illegitimate demands. But that raised the question of what a "reasonable" demand might be. The trials of women accused of blackmailing men thus unexpectedly provided a forum in which the rights and wrongs of heterosexual relationships were debated.

Such discussions, of course, did not take place when the woman was clearly motivated simply by financial gain. Such women could be roughly divided into two groups—the professionals and the amateurs. Most of the women who acted on their own and asked for small sums were obviously amateurs. They included Emily Jeffrey, who in 1914 threatened to tell a hotel manager's fiancée of his goings-on with other women if he did not pay Jeffrey £5. Lillian Bristow, a cook who threatened to reveal a seventy-year-old architect's treatment of one of his maids, merely demanded her clothes and wages. The more ambitious Lillian Simmons threatened to cite the elderly Mr. A in divorce proceedings if not given £250. The Winchester Assizes heard that a woman threatened a Portsmouth businessman that if he did not pay she would make it known that he had impregnated her. Similarly a married woman claimed a Mr. X had impregnated her in his car. In 1922 a charwoman demanded money of a Windsor bank manager "to maintain your daughter."[44]

Such dreary accounts of relatively petty demands won little attention. The public was more interested in those who were portrayed as professional blackmailers. These included seasoned criminals who exploited middle-class males' increased sensitivity to having their sexual activities revealed to public view. At the top end of the interest scale was someone like Mrs. Robinson, who helped blackmail the nephew of the rajah of Kashmir. At the lower end were prostitutes who continued as they had in the past to extort money from clients. There were women in England as in America, the *Times* reported, who wrongfully used photos, letters, and breach of promise suits to extort money from male victims.[45] The author of *Blackmail and Co.* (1928) wrote of women who faked pregnancies. An investigator of the female "underworld" claimed to have observed a group of old women going through the newspapers looking for scandals to exploit. Servants purportedly provided them with details. Anyone well known could have his past scrutinized. Once hooked, the poor victim was bled for life. Professional female blackmailers included twenty-nine-year-old Dorothy Jenkins, who demanded money from three different men, claiming that each was the father of her nonexistent child. She meticulously researched the background of one victim in *Who's Who*, threatened the second that she would kill herself, and employed a solicitor to badger the third. (Curiously, one of the third man's sexual requests included asking her to obtain for him a copy of the banned lesbian classic *The Well of Loneliness*.)[46]

Detective-Inspector J. Kenneth Ferrier of Scotland Yard stated that in England most women involved in extortion began by primarily playing the role of bait; later they became "vamps." It is hardly surprising that in the vast majority of cases in which a woman was involved in extortion she acted as an accessory to a man. In most criminal activities women usually played secondary roles. In court, evidence that a woman had been assisted by a man in demanding money would usually be advanced by the prosecution as proof that a criminal conspiracy had taken place. Rose Jeffreys, prostitute, was shown to have worked with a bully who represented himself to her client as a police constable and demanded money. May Bass had 150 letters from the county councilor and solicitor with whom she had lived. Her male friend (the Cambridge-educated son of the Swedish consul) made the demands. In 1933 a man and woman extorted money from a lieutenant with the claim that she had had his baby. On occasion a trial revealed that a woman had unwittingly been used by men in a blackmail scheme. When a Mrs. R, a music hall performer, had an affair with an elderly man who set her up in a flat, two young male dancers who found out about the relationship decided to exploit it. One pretended to be a detective and the other Mrs. R's outraged husband, who threatened to cite the victim in a messy divorce suit if money was not forthcoming.[47]

Some of these blackmail schemes in which women were used as pawns were quite elaborate. May Levy, a twenty-year-old actress, was the bait used to compromise John Blake in 1920. While in her bedroom he heard a suspicious click. Sure enough, the noise was from a camera, the resulting photo later used by men who demanded £500. When Samuel James, a money-lender, was arrested for the indecent assault of Olive Walton, a nineteen-year-old secretary, she admitted that the charge had been orchestrated by his business rivals. In his defense Adolph Levy claimed he did not demand money; he only "advised" James to pay £1,000 so Walton would withdraw her charges.[48]

One of the more ruthless of such schemes resulted in two men and two women being found guilty at Leicester Assizes in 1925 for extorting money from an accountant, Mr. X. The thirty-eight-year-old victim in February 1922 met Harriet Worsley, a twenty-six-year-old typist. They had sex, and thereafter he gave her "a present of money" each time they met. In May a woman claiming to be Harriet's sister extorted from the victim £25. She asserted that the typist was in fact a married woman by the name of Mrs. Merritt, who was now pregnant. The money was presumably needed for an abortion. The next month Francis Merritt, a professional acrobat purporting to be the enraged husband, accosted the accountant. Merritt stated that he had learned of the affair and, if not given £100, would divorce his wife and cite the accountant as the correspondent. In fear of losing his family, the victim paid. In 1923 Merritt showed up again, claiming that he had contracted a venereal disease from his wife, which he said must have originated from the accountant. As this limited Merritt's acrobatic abilities he wanted a further £500 to set up a poultry business. By the time of the trial in 1925 Mr. X had been badgered more than thirty times by the gang in person or via letters and telegrams and had paid out close to £1,400. The judge sentenced the four "fiends and harpies" to long prison terms. Merritt, who had nineteen previous offenses and was indeed married, though not to Harriet Worsley, received five years.[49]

Married couples were occasionally charged with blackmail. In 1930 a husband and wife threatened another Mr. X with revealing the affair he had had with her five years previous. The same year a husband and wife were both given three years for menacing a seventy-three-year-old man who had been friendly with the woman. In 1932 a couple were imprisoned for blackmailing Mr. Y and Mr. Z. The marital status of the woman charged could have a bearing on such cases. In 1914 a woman threatened to tell the tabloid *John Bull* that the Reverend Arthur Wilde had followed her home. The judge agreed that Wilde may well have harassed her by following her to the top of an omnibus but concluded that her common-law partner did not have the right—which apparently a husband might have had—to demand compensation. But in another case, when Annie Williams was found guilty in 1925 of demanding money from a "young man," the court seemed to indicate that if she had been single her demand might have been justified, but the fact that she was married disqualified her from making a claim.[50]

Even though women were admitted to juries in the 1920s, courts remained very much a male institution. To ward off the notion that they were biased against women, judges made a point of treating them leniently. When a woman had been used as the bait in a blackmail scheme the man or men typically received a prison term and the woman a suspended sentence. The courts in this way attempted to maintain the notion of the responsible male and the dependent female. Some judges worried, however, that this notion of female dependency could lead one back into a justification of certain forms of extortion.

The most troubling revelation that emerged from the prosecution of women for extortion was that there were women who found themselves accused of blackmail when they sought to achieve what they regarded as justice. In terms of legal precedent the most important of these cases began on the night of December 27, 1919, in Great Torrington, Devon. We know that Thomas Luxton, the mayor of this small town, accompanied twenty-year-

185

old Emily Dymond to a local park. We do not know exactly what occurred that evening, but the following angry letter, which Dymond delivered to Luxton two days later, gives us an idea.

> I am sending you a notice I am going to Summons you for insulting Saturday night, 27 Dec., out reck park, for putting your hand in under my Clothes. I going to summons you for trying to take upper hand of me. What do you call yourself, a gentleman or no. I don't think that you are a gentleman for insulting me like you did. I will make you pay Dear enough for this. You call yourself the Mayor of the town. If you don't send Apologize to me I shall see further into tonight. I always pass you, and give you the time of the day in a reasonable manner. I leave this to you to think what you are going to do, paid or get summons; you can please yourself what to do. I expect a message this afternoon, you can send over a message by your boy over to the factory. Mrs. Rudd to me what you are going to do. You can't deny you dind to not ask me. I have not given any encouraged whatever, if you don't send to and apologise I shall let everybody knowed in the town it.
>
> from Emily Dymond
>
> If you like to paid for this I won't say anything, but if you don't I shall. I am not a hore for anybody. I will soon let the town knowed all about your going on. You wouldt like going up town hall to be cry down. I shall summons if it costs ten pound you got the money you will have to paid it you can send a message to me by four o'clock, then I can do what I want after I leave work. I like you men ought to be talk up a bit if I don't fine ant answer this afternoon I shall see further into it.[51]

For writing this letter Dymond was on March 8, 1920, charged, tried, and found guilty under the 1916 Larceny Act of employing menaces to extort money. Defense counsel held that Dymond, having been indecently assaulted, had a reasonable belief in her right to redress, but Mr. Justice Darling refused to allow the defense to provide evidence of the assault, pointing out that it was immaterial whether or not an assault had occurred. In law the crucial point was that menaces had been employed in an attempt to make an illegal gain. Many felt the process unfair, and in Parliament the government was questioned about the matter. Dymond appealed her conviction, but on March 17, 1920, the higher court concurred with Darling that in a case of blackmail the truth was immaterial. The prisoner had no right to the money she demanded. The courts were asserting that individuals could not invoke the notion of self-help in such a case. If her claim for redress had been made on her behalf by a solicitor through a civil suit Dymond would not have committed a crime. In a civil action cross-examination and evidence to prove reasonable and probable cause would have been allowed. Lay persons—particularly semiliterate ones like Dymond—were at a disadvantage when dealing with the fine line that separated legal and illegal threats.[52]

Having cautioned assaulted women not to take the law into their hands, English judges proceeded to tell dismissed mistresses that any demands that they might make could also be construed as blackmail. In 1920 Sir Herbert Cooke took out a summons against Helga Cookson of Mayfair, accusing her of threatening to publish "certain matters." At first glance it was hard to feel much sympathy for Mrs. Cookson, who appeared in the dock heavily veiled, wearing an expensive sealskin coat. Evidence was heard that she and Sir Herbert (a married man) had been "acquainted" since 1912 and that in 1914 he had settled on her the enormous sum of £10,000. She had subsequently married and borne two children. Now, six years later, she was threatening to write about her relationship with Sir Herbert unless he gave her a further £5,000 a year and a lump sum of £15,000 to purchase a new home. Was she simply the greedy vixen she appeared to be? Doubts crept in when it was reported that she actually sent her threatening letters to Sir Herbert's solicitor, who also served as her trustee. The fact that she demanded not only money but also assurances that her children would spend six months a year with her and that she would be recognized as their legal guardian also raised the unsettling question of their parentage. She was worried about the health of Sir Herbert and concluded one of her letters with the lament, "If Herbert Cooke was to die, where would I be? I can't bring an action against a dead man who is not there to defend himself, and I should hate to worry his family." What she wanted was "justice." "I repeat, I am not vindictive, but I can't face the fact that gradually everyone will die who knows about this affair, and then I shall stand alone with the children, with just enough to exist on and no one to help."[53] Mr. Justice Darling again found himself in the position of forcefully informing a woman that the threat to tell the "truth" about a liaison in an effort to extort money was a serious crime. Her well-paid counsel recognized that a dismissed mistress indeed by law could make no legitimate claim and had Cookson plead guilty. To diminish her culpability he described her letters as "extraordinary" if not "mad" and had a doctor testify that she was both neurotic and neurasthenic. Cookson adopted the appropriate female role of literally throwing herself on the mercy of the court: she fainted. Darling in turn took the part of the stern but chivalrous patriarch. After severely lecturing the accused on the long prison term she so richly deserved—and that she would serve if she resorted to such stratagems again—he released her on her own recognizance.

In the eighteenth and early nineteenth centuries mistresses successfully extracted money and gifts from their ex-lovers. The changes in the law pertaining to the definition of "threats" and "menaces" had the effect of preventing such raids being launched in the twentieth century. Accordingly women like Doris Fawcett found themselves in the dock. When Fawcett was twenty-four she had an affair with Mr. X while his wife was in an asylum. Five years later she wrote: "I do not pretend to be spiteful, but after the way you have treated me, if you do not send me some money by Wednesday I shall come to Sheffield and tell your wife. I have letters you have sent which will not be very nice for her to read. You have mentioned staying nights more than once in them. I only ask you to let me have 50s, and I am sure that would not hurt you."[54] This was a tiny sum, and the judge allowed the charges to be set aside on the understanding that Fawcett would cease her badgering.

Some women simply wanted what was rightfully theirs. In 1933 Lillian Simmons was tried on charges of blackmailing Mr. V. Their "intimacy" had begun in 1926 and ended in 1928. Mr. V testified that Simmons told him that her husband was launching a divorce and citing Mr. V but that she could stop it if he paid her £250. Though this sounded like a straightforward case of blackmail, it came out in court that Mr. V owed Simmons the money, which he had borrowed to finance a book he was writing on the Paris underworld, as well as a play entitled *The Guarded Woman*. She was acquitted; and as a way of punishing Mr. V, the prosecutor stripped him of his anonymity and revealed to the public that his name was Evelyn Charles Vivian.[55]

Revenge appeared to motivate women like Ellen Gordon. She had formerly been senior staff maternity nurse at St. George's Hospital and planned on going to work in India. Dr. X, to whom she was engaged, implored her not to go, to remain working where she was until they married. When he ultimately jilted her she successfully sued him for breach of promise. In 1930 she asked his solicitor for more money, which she considered fair considering "the way my life has been upset through my engagement to him." In threatening to give all the facts to the British Medical Association in order to make him do the honorable thing, she left herself open to being charged with extortion.[56]

Homilies on women simply having to accept being abandoned by men continued to be delivered by judges into the 1930s. In October 1936 Rosina Sharp found herself charged with blackmail after her affair with her employer came to an end. Her story was that she and Mr. A had been "imprudent" for the four years, but when the business had shut down he had dropped her. She denied demanding money from him, though she asserted that he had treated her badly and that she "did not want to see other women wronged by him." Sir Holman Gregory, the Recorder of the Criminal Central Court, in sentencing her to nine months' imprisonment, felt compelled to note: "I should like to take a very lenient course with you, but in the circumstances it is impossible. Women must know, and be made to understand, that, if, as you say happened in this case, a man is intimate with them, there is no reason why they should blackmail him in years to come. You have admitted visiting him with the intention of getting money from him. You had no right to the money. You were attempting to get it from him by threatening to let people know that which was a secret between the two of you."[57]

Two years later the *Times* noted that another judge made the same point in sentencing a Hungarian woman to nine months' imprisonment and deportation. But in this case a juryman protested that since Mr. A had, after the immoral relations ceased, promised the woman a monthly allowance and then reneged, one should accept that she honestly believed that the money she demanded was hers by right. The judge disagreed and "pointed out that no demand for money in consideration of past cohabitation could be enforced in law, the consideration being essentially an immoral consideration." The appeals court reversed the lower court's verdict, accepting the woman's argument that an agreement had been made, but stressing that the money she demanded was not for sex, as the affair was already ended.[58] This finding, and the relatively light punishments judges felt compelled to

189

dole out to women who were found guilty of blackmail in the 1930s, suggests that though the legal odds were still stacked against women, attitudes

toward sexual morality were shifting.

The fact that in the interwar period the English public became so interested in the figure of the female blackmailer was symptomatic of its uncertain sense of how modern men and women were supposed to relate both sexually and economically. As women's voices were increasingly heard, blackmail stories could no longer be presented without taking into account the relation of gender and power. During these years some legal reforms had chipped away at the old Victorian sexual double standard. The 1923 Matrimonial Causes Act finally made simple adultery by the male grounds for divorce; reforming legislation dealt with bastardy via acts on legitimacy (1923, 1925), and guardianship (1925). Women were legally freer than ever before—almost men's equals—which made the continued economic disparity between the sexes all the more apparent. Shifts in sexual theorizing and practices resulted in both a heightening of men's fears of the female blackmailer and the public's appreciation that economic disparity was what drove some women into activities that the courts declared to be crimes. Countering the reforming tendencies was a backlash of sorts and attempts to keep women in their place.[59] The courts, for example, lectured women on the fact that unless they were married to a man they could make no legitimate claims on him.

When, as was so often the case, a trial revealed that both the man and the woman had acted "immorally" the judge and jury could find themselves torn by conflicting concerns. Doris Semple had been maintained for three years in a St. John's Wood flat by a businessman. He had given her over £1,200 in loans. This, her counsel argued in 1933, gave her probable cause to demand help. Nevertheless Mr. Justice Wild condemned her as "an unscrupulous, dangerous, and heartless woman, essentially a blackmailer and vulgar thief who resorted to prostitution for fleecing men." The police stated that they had received many complaints about thefts at her home in St. John's Wood. "The woman was in the habit of plying men with drink and luring them to her flat, where she held pyjama parties. While the party was going on she would rob the men's clothes." The judge proceeded to castigate Mr. K, the blackmail victim, for his sexual indulgences: "A more poisonous human being I don't suppose anybody has seen in the witness box. That horrible person who has been allowed to call himself Mr. K; all decent people must revolt at even being near such a creature." The jury agreed with Mr. Justice Wild's view of Mr. K and, while accepting that the forty-year-old mother of four had broken the law, asked that Semple be shown mercy. Despite his earlier even-handedness the judge said leniency was not possible; he sentenced the woman to three years in prison.[60]

Such blackmail cases brought home to the English public the unsettling realization that though justice was blind and courts did not simply serve patriarchal power, something was not quite right when a particular type of crime almost invariably pitted an older, well-off man against a younger, poorer women. Why did judges have to lecture women, not men, on the rules of the sexual game? Were women inherently more irrational or more prone to criminality? Courts, wanting both to be just and to maintain gender difference, found themselves when dealing with blackmail cases in the embarrassing position of sustaining procedures that empowered one gender and victimized another. It was understood that the power enjoyed by men in the public sphere was balanced by the privileges women wielded in the private realm. But such comforting assertions were undercut when the woman's threat of making public what was supposed to remain private was declared to be a crime. Though many women charged were no doubt simple extortionists, there were also those whose trials made it all too apparent that the purpose of the courts was to see that the laws were enforced, not that justice was done. If Hollywood movies familiarized English audiences with the image of the daring, designing woman, English courts and culture successfully countered such subversive messages. Feminist historians have noted that as late as the 1940s the English, unlike the Americans, had difficulty in incorporating the concept of "pleasure-seeking, fun-loving, and sexually expressive women and girls." The fate met by those whom judges branded as blackmailers added to this chill and played its part in young English women internalizing the message to know their place and not be a gold-digger.[61]

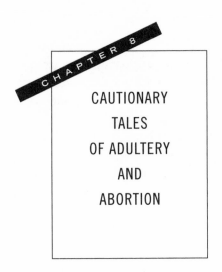

CHAPTER 8

CAUTIONARY
TALES
OF ADULTERY
AND
ABORTION

The fear of being labeled a gold digger or blackmailer kept some women in their place, but in the first half of the twentieth century stories of women being victimized by blackmailers were used more frequently to rein in female sexuality. The greater number of reports of men being entrapped than that of women was not thought worthy of comment, complementing as it did the notion that, as the aggressive sex, a certain proportion of males would naturally run the risk of unwise sexual entanglements and that they would just have to learn to take care of themselves. But accounts of women being victimized were used to warn them that more than ever they needed the protection of men. Sir James Marchant, president of the National Council of Public Morals, asserted in 1917 that the difficulty of safeguarding women from sexual exploitation was the "master problem" of the twentieth century. In his view of the world, the new regiments of shop girls were constantly at risk of being shanghaied into prostitution. He warned young working women that they should never talk to strangers ("either men or women"), loiter in the street, accept a ride, go with a stranger (even if she were dressed as a nurse or a nun), or accept sweets. It was a well-known fact, he claimed, that telephone operators had been "offered drugged chocolates in trains." He not only asserted that theatrical and music-hall agents might seek to take advantage of their clients; he went on to warn his female readers never to help a woman who fainted in the street but rather to call a policeman immediately. Behind such caution lay

Marchant's belief that the swooning invalid would all too likely be an agent of some brothel or massage parlor trolling for female victims. For men like Marchant the modern world was producing ever more snares that could   193 entrap the unwary and unsupervised woman. Sensational books and pictures aroused their passions, and anonymous post office boxes permitted them to carry on dangerous secret communications with men unknown to their families.[1]

Picking up on some of the same themes, a 1930s American journalist asserted that the blackmailer thrived on both men's and women's pursuit of forbidden fruit. "His staple is the oblique adventuring of men and women who cannot achieve what they think is romance without risk; but his net is spread to catch the guilty or timid in every human activity where men and women fear interference, hurt, or exposure."[2] Public reports suggested, however, that women, having less wealth than men, were for practical reasons far less likely to be the target of extortionists. Moreover many men ended up being blackmailed because of the active methods they adopted in pursuing sex. They risked being reported for rape, sexual assault, and violation of age-of-consent laws. Women did not. They were less free to pursue their passions. If not policed by as many laws as men, women found their interactions with the opposite sex subjected to formal and informal surveillance by their peers and the community at large. And most important in a pre-pill age, the risk of an out-of-wedlock pregnancy served as a major disincentive for female sexual adventuring. Nevertheless the courts and the press used blackmail accounts as cautionary tales to warn women that all sorts of conniving men lay in wait for gullible females. Simply by leaving the home and entering the twentieth-century public world of the workplace women were placing themselves in the company of dangerous strangers. They could be seduced and abandoned. And if they were so foolish as to find themselves with an undesired pregnancy they could be made vulnerable to both abortionists and extortionists.

Reports of women being waylaid served as a reminder that although the typical blackmail victim was the man with money, in the twentieth century the unwary female was also potential prey. As they were presented through newspaper reports of pre- and extramarital affairs and abortions, and film and literary treatments of promiscuity, the fate of women blackmail victims in England and America appeared to be remarkably similar. In each country the courts, the press, and the movies portrayed such women as having been taught a bitter lesson, a lesson that their sisters would be wise to heed.

194   Thanks to the moralizing narrative skills of Scotland Yard we know a good deal about one particular female blackmail victim.[3] In the 1930s Florence Ivy Browning was employed as a buyer for Selfridges, the London department store. As such she often had to be away from her home and husband. In July 1932 she met at Leicester and began an affair with Charles Gray, a married, thirty-five-year-old buyer for a Liverpool hosiery company. They first had sex at the Palace Hotel, Bloomsbury, London; thereafter their trysts took place at a series of provincial hotels. In 1932 Gray was doing well, earning £1,500 a year; unfortunately he soon lost his job. Florence, who drew £500 a year—a very good income for a woman—began to give him money. Apparently unsure of her feelings, she left her husband and moved in with a woman friend for a few weeks in October 1933. She returned home in November.

When Gray learned that she wanted to end the affair he was incensed and threatened to tell her husband and her employer about the relationship unless she gave him money to set up a dog track bookmaking business. Under duress she provided him with cash and continued to see him for another twelve months. In July 1934 he made a direct threat in a card he sent her: "Unless I receive £5 by the 7th and £30 by Monday 9th, I shall take action as I informed you." He in addition telephoned her at home nine or ten times between July and November. Angered by her refusal to pay, on November 19 Gray wrote directly to her husband. He shamelessly listed the hotels they had stayed in and the number of times they had been together. "We have also committed misconduct on countless occasions on Hampstead Heath, Hadley Woods, fields in Amersham, Wendover, Aylesbury, Wimbledon Common, Epson Downs, Banstead Downs, my old home 10 Hedge Lane, Palmers Green, once in 'Rinhemy' [the Browning home], at 37 South Park Rd. Wimbledon, and in railway trains. In brief your wife and I have committed misconduct continuously from Mar 1/33 to Nov. 5/34, (this was the last occasion in an entry in Wimbledon) on at least 300 occasions." He asserted that Florence only stayed with her husband because of his money. The aggrieved lover righteously concluded that she had destroyed other peoples' lives and now had to learn that she could not unthinkingly take that which she wanted.

Browning read the letter to his wife. Though insisting that Gray lied and exaggerated—she claimed that she had been with him only twice in 1934—she admitted her guilt. "I am so desperately sorry for what I have done and he has been making my life a hell for over a year by holding this over my head with the threat that he would advise you and your mother of my association with him unless I gave him money." 195

Fearing that Florence would destroy the letter before her husband read it, Gray also sent a copy to Browning's office at the London and Manchester Insurance Company. He wrote to Florence's mother and threatened to write to her neighbors. Mr. Browning phoned Gray, who at first apologized and promised to desist. Nevertheless in 1935, having lost another job in Glasgow, he again wrote to Florence to tell her that his wife was divorcing him and would cite her as the correspondent. Some times he claimed he was about to commit suicide; at other times he threatened to kill her ("If you don't live with me I will see no one else has you"). Having lost his job and family, Gray was intent on dragging his ex-mistress down with him. Apparently unbalanced, he began to pepper his letters with every compromising and sordid detail she had imprudently revealed about her husband, her mother-in-law, and her sister-in-law. For a week he stalked her. Florence tried everything to silence him. She ultimately gave him something like £300. She had a business acquaintance offer him a job on condition he stop hounding her. Gray refused. Finally, on November 15, 1935, concerned that Gray would badger her new employers, Marks and Spencer, Florence complained to the police. Fear of publicity had prevented her from acting sooner. "I would like to point out," she told the police, "that if a prosecution follows my complaint it is essential for business reasons that my name nor that of my husband is not made public." The chief inspector's cool comments on the file made it clear that though he would act, he felt little sympathy for the victim. "Mrs. Browning brought this trouble on herself, but the position that has now arisen [requires] that we must endeavour to protect her from this obvious blackguard."

On December 16, 1935, the police arrested Gray in Chalk Farm, London. The courts and the press did not accord Florence Browning the anonymity that almost every male blackmail victim was given. Under the heading "Married Woman Libeled" the *Times* reported that Charles Norman Gray, who in 1932 had become "friendly" with Florence Ivy Browning, had pleaded guilty to criminal libel and blackmail. He was sentenced to nine months in prison.[4]

196 The lesson that both the American and the English reading public was supposed to draw from such accounts was the same: a romantic affair could destroy a woman's life. If women crossed certain boundaries they faced danger. These reports of victimized women revealed that a woman's path to being blackmailed was quite different from that of a man. A man's pursuit of short-term sexual encounters might result in his being victimized by prostitutes or pimps or harassed employees. Women tended to engage in longer-term relationships. Such relationships were presumably more discreet and private, but ironically that meant that if women were blackmailed it was most likely to be by their ex-lovers.

After reading accounts of the unexpected risks an affair might entail, a single woman who contemplated a fling would likely think twice. Strangers could demand to be paid for their silence. In 1926 two men and a woman were found guilty of extorting £290 from Miss Violet Smith by making suggestions about her relationship with a married man. In another case, a private inquiry agent, working for a wife involved in divorce proceedings, threatened a domestic servant that, if not paid off, he would reveal her relationship with the wife's husband. More common, however, were cases of men blackmailing their ex-lovers. In 1915 a New York bride was blackmailed by her ex-suitor. In 1926 Mrs. J. J. Lowenthal received a threatening letter written "by a man she had known." In 1929 Frank Challoner, a married English actor, had a fling with an actress, identified as Miss A. He later told her that a third party had obtained a dictaphone of their tryst and was demanding £1,000 hush money from both of them. Miss A provided £300. When the truth came out that Challoner was in fact the villain, he was sentenced to four years in prison. In 1931 a married laborer was sentenced to seven years for having posed as a bachelor in order to woo a woman. When she was about to marry someone else he informed her that he had her letters and his diary. The same year the court heard the case of a married man who had had a long-term affair with a woman. When she tried to break it off he reminded her that they had stayed at hotels as man and wife and said he would publicize her past if he were not paid. "You cannot say it is slander, for I have all the proof and witnesses of where we have slept together . . . I smile when you mention the police for if they worry me they will worry you at the same time, and everything will come out then, and you will lose your job and relations."[5]

The boorishness of the men was matched by their rapaciousness. A musician proposed to Miss X, a fellow entertainer, and she accepted. He claimed not to have enough money to marry, though they spent a night in a hotel. She returned to Sheffield, but he then used the secret of their liaison to force her to continue the affair. Even after he went to India he sent demands by letter for more money. She finally told her father and the police. In 1933 a married man was tried in Rochdale for giving Miss X a venereal disease, and then adding insult to injury by threatening to publicize their affair if she did not pay. The same year in Warwick another married man demanded money from the woman who had left him, threatening to tell her parents. True pettiness was evident in a 1937 case of a twenty-two-year-old man who threatened his former fiancée with telling her father of the night they spent together and demanded his ring back and £1. In 1938 a thirty-one-year-old man, having been intimate with Miss X, sought money by threatening to tell the man with whom she was living. In 1937 actor George Lane was charged with having blackmailed actress Jessica Bevan. They had had an affair, and when she tried to end it Lane threatened to tell others. The Bow Street magistrate, in binding him over, lectured Lane on his cadishness: "There is no more contemptible creature than a man who tries to force a woman who has finished with him to come back to him against her will. When that is done by trying to blackmail her, or to threaten her with bodily harm, then it comes within the criminal law."[6]

Single women were exploited by blackmailers, but the press reported that the latter were even more ruthless in extorting money from married women who had engaged in adulterous affairs. A case of an English woman being caught in a badger game emerged in 1911. The victim's husband was in South Africa. The wife of a man with whom she was friendly claimed to have had a detective watching them and demanded £40. The police found that the two had been involved in similar setups before. In 1930 Hans Kuik, a Dutch artist, and his wife were tried for blackmailing Mr. and Mrs. Z. Mrs. Z had befriended the artist and sent him love letters, which he threatened to sell to the press. In 1932 a traveler told a woman that their relationship would be revealed to her husband. In 1934 James Conlin was sentenced to three years for threats to another Mrs. Z. He said that if he were not paid his wife would cite Mrs. Z in divorce proceedings and the names of her other male friends would be made public. Similarly in 1935 a married hairdresser told his ex-mistress who had come into some money that he would publish an account of their affair unless she paid him off. Then there was Kurt Frings, a classic gigolo. According to a police report in early 1936, this actor met and seduced Lady Keith Fraser in St. Moritz. He followed her to Paris, where he extorted £150 from her with the threat of telling her husband. Then he accompanied her to London. By the time Scotland Yard was alerted he had left the country. "We can do nothing regarding the alleged blackmail," someone wrote across the police report, "but it certainly looks as if Mr. Frings is undesirable."[7] A changing moral milieu, which accepted a greater sociability between the sexes but refused to view a woman's adultery as benignly as a man's, offered unscrupulous males many new opportunities to exploit.

Older women who consorted with younger men were also at risk. The *New York Times* reported in 1912 that "La Basse," the head of a French blackmail gang, had just been arrested. Posing as a U.S. banker two years previously, he had maneuvered a widow into a compromising position. She had been forced to pay the equivalent of $140,000. In 1925 another widow placed an advertisement in a newspaper and as a result met a man who stole her jewels and demanded money by insinuating that a "debauch" had taken place. In 1927 a twenty-eight-year-old man was sentenced to four years for extorting money from a widow with whom he had stayed. He threatened to release a letter of hers unless she provided him with £600 to finance a trip to Australia. Widows were also the target of two men tried in 1929. A Mrs. H, who was employed in some capacity by the royal family, testified that she had placed an advertisement in the paper and as a result met Arthur Hafner, who wooed and proposed to her. Then his partner appeared, representing himself as a private investigator and claiming to have caught them in a compromising position. Terrified of scandal, Mrs. H "lent" Hafner £200. When she found out that he was married she went to the police. Two other widows came forward to report that he had similarly fleeced them out of hundreds of pounds. In another case in 1936, Mrs. A and Mrs. B—both Scottish middle-aged women of "substance and social standing"—told the court that the man they had corresponded with soon used threats to demand money. At a 1938 trial participants heard that a sixty-year-old welfare worker had "misconducted herself" with a forty-two-year-old man she had befriended at the church of St. Martin's in the Field. When she tried to drop him he demanded money to go abroad.[8] These women had doubly compromised themselves: the men who exploited them were not just of a lower class than they were; they were also younger. It was assumed that a man would chase younger women; a woman who pursued younger men was regarded as ridiculous.

Stories of incautious women being compromised and robbed provided grist for the journalist's mill. Women with "more time and money than sense," the press reported, were the perfect victims of the dandified males of 1920s New York known as "tango pirates" and "lounge lizards." Given the importance of sexual respectability, a journalist wrote in an article entitled "America's Most Popular Crime" that blackmail had reached epidemic proportions. "The rich woman is now the best victim; the pocket-bulging man with sporting tastes, who formerly made game for the sharps, is now seldom used; he has learned to fight and no blackmailer is looking for trouble when rich women and eminently respectable men can be shaken down without an effort." The victim would first be approached at dances or tearooms by another woman who would introduce her to her "husband." An adventure would ensue involving the man and the wealthy dupe until she would be contacted by a lawyer, who would tell her that she was about to be cited in an alienation of affection suit. Just such a scenario was played out in 1921 when Mrs. Elizabeth Schill launched a $100,000 alienation of affection suit against Mrs. Aimée Crocker Gouraud. Gouraud's attorneys warned Mrs. Schill that they knew of her husband's checkered past. Her lawyer was subsequently charged with extortion. In 1913 Alice Watson was arrested for blackmailing Miss Laura van Liew. Detectives overheard Watson demand $2,500 in return for suppressing information regarding her husband's relationship with Miss van Liew. The latter, who had a New York residence and a summer home in New Jersey, had already paid out $1,200.[9]

Women were repeatedly cautioned that in entering the public world they made themselves a target for blackmailers. Female members of the social elite were prime candidates. In 1912 Percy L. Davis, a New York City alderman, and Eben J. Owen, an evangelist who rescued "fallen women," were arrested for extorting $5,000 from Mrs. Eva B. Carroll. Davis had Viola Dawson, a former servant of Carroll's, sign a forty-two-page affidavit claiming she had been raped by Mrs. Carroll's son. Davis told Mrs. Carroll that it would be easy to have the account published in the press, but if he were given money to support his congressional campaign he would hush it up. Mrs. Carroll informed the police that she would be meeting Davis and Owen at Pabst's Restaurant. All three returned to Carroll's home, where "Brother Eben" thanked the Lord for providing a way of protecting the reputation of "Sister Eva." Interrupting cries of "Praise the Lord" and "Hallelujah," the police made their arrests. The same year two agents demanded £1,000 from Anna, countess de Hamil de Manin, because of anonymous letters she had sent attempting to prevent a marriage. In 1914 Benjamin Brims attempted to extort money from Josephine, princess of Thurn and Taxis, who had visited the flat of an unmarried man in London. A man and a woman in 1932 pressured the daughter-in-law of a peer with the threat that they would tell him that she was living with her lover.[10]

The most "public" women were actresses, so it comes as no surprise that many extortion threats were reported against actresses. Youths seemed prone to choose them as victims, probably because such women were well-known and erotic figures on whom juvenile desires could be projected. In 1913 eighteen-year-old John Anderson sent letters to several London actresses demanding money. His letters threatened "murder, death, dishonor, dirtiness" and were signed "His Royal Highness, the Honourable John Anderson." In 1921 a nineteen-year-old engineering student blackmailed Mrs. Margaret Bannerman (Mrs. Margaret Home-Summer). He threatened that if he were not sent £25 he would inform the King's Proctor of what she had been up to between the time she left her husband and when she obtained her divorce. The defense's argument that the student's "mad act" was brought on by excessive study resulted in a short nine-month sentence. In 1937 Harold Armitage attempted to blackmail film actress Evelyn Laye, who was identified in court as Miss X. Her maid had given Armitage letters that Mr. Y had written to Laye. A seventeen-year-old young man, having read of the Laye case, tried in turn to extort money from Phyllis Robbins, another actress. In Hollywood Clara Bow, who in the popular film *It* (1927) had epitomized the free-spirited flapper, was blackmailed with papers taken by her secretary. "Hollywood Happy Hunting Grounds for Blackmailers" ran a headline in a 1933 edition of the *Los Angeles Times*. Meanwhile the *New York Times* reported that in Norway blackmailing—especially of theater people—was so rife that victims were promised anonymity in court. "A number of prominent men, actors and actresses with skeletons in their cupboards, are said to have been fleeced out of large sums."[11]

Perhaps the most bizarre case of a woman being blackmailed by someone who knew about her private life occurred in 1938 when an Englishman threatened a female colleague that he would reveal to the world that she was *married*. To twenty-first-century ears the disclosure of one's marriage hardly sounds menacing, but for some ambitious women in the 1930s it was. During the interwar years, in many professions—including teaching—a woman who married had to give up her job. A middle-class wife's place was in the home. In the 1938 trial the judge made the unusual request that the names of both the accused and the victim not be given out. "She was a married woman," the press explained, "and if that fact were known in her office she would be asked, in accordance with custom, to resign."[12] The moral of this story, like all the other blackmail stories in which women were victimized, was that women who ventured far from home placed themselves in jeopardy.

Affairs that led to marital breakups were also dangerous for women. Inequitable divorce legislation provided blackmailers with a way of terrorizing unfaithful wives. Even in the twentieth century, the general assumption still was that a woman's adultery was far more serious than a man's. A man who consorted with a prostitute was not considered an adulterer.[13] The husband himself might become a blackmailer of sorts in using the threat of exposing aspects of his spouse's sex life to avoid alimony or gain custody of their children. In 1918 William Jean Beauley, a well-known artist, went to elaborate lengths to compromise his wife in order to win a divorce suit. In May a man hired by Beauley prevailed upon Mrs. Beauley to come to his hotel room to discuss a mortgage. Just after she arrived detectives burst in. In order to disguise the fact that he was in cahoots with the "raiders" the man cried "Blackmail! Blackmail!" In August Beauley began divorce proceedings in which the detectives gave perjured evidence of breaking in on an "improper act." He won the judgment and subsequently remarried. But in 1921 the appeals court ruled that if adultery occurred it was by the procurement of the plaintiff and that therefore his divorce decree had been obtained by deceit. The divorce proceedings were reopened, and Harriet Beauley launched a $250,000 lawsuit against her ex-husband and seven other conspirators.[14]

When Rose Harper divorced Warren E. Murray she was awarded $100 a month. According to Harper, in November 1920 her ex-husband had a friend compromise her to modify the decree. Murray threatened that he would petition and publicize her improper conduct unless she agreed to end their alimony agreement. Out of fear of disgrace she accepted the modification of the decree but later successfully sought restitution. In 1932 a reporter living in England threatened to write to the husbands of two Hungarian sisters to have their alimony stopped. His extortion attempt was partly motivated by revenge, as he had left his own wife to live with one of the women, and had then been dropped.[15]

In 1921 Mrs. Wilhelmina Dougherty filed blackmail charges against W. Coleman Ally and his wife. While her husband, a wealthy Atlantan, had been in France with the YMCA during the war, she had become infatuated with a man to whom she gave her husband's automobile, his diamond ring, and the key to her safety deposit box. She claimed that she gave these presents to the man for "patriotic reasons." Her husband successfully filed for divorce, but the jury awarded her custody of their two children and financial support. Ally, who had testified to the "platonic" nature of Mrs. Dougherty's relationship with her male friend, then began to make financial demands, his threat being that if she were found unfit the children would go to the father.[16] Though such accounts of divorce blackmail had a moralizing intent, they had the unsettling effect of reminding twentieth-century women that a sexual double standard still existed.

The question of the parentage of a woman's children could also be exploited by the unscrupulous. Adoption was only beginning to be formalized in the early twentieth century. Adoptive middle-class parents feared that a "depraved" natural parent might someday appear and make demands. "At this time," warned one writer in 1914, "anyone adopting a child lays himself open to blackmail once he has become attached to it." In Britain the National Adoption Society believed poor mothers would even stoop to extortion. This worry was exploited in a 1930s short story entitled "A Lady Paramour" in which a wealthy woman whose own baby has died raises her maid's baby as her own. Eventually a villain shows up demanding to be paid for his silence. In America this concern was given a racist twist. The *Chicago Tribune* in 1916 ran a story about a childless woman who adopted a baby in the city and returned to her home town pretending that the child was hers. Somehow crooks discovered the subterfuge and one came to her house. "'Your child,' he said, 'is a Negro. You have a Negro coachman. My silence can be bought.'" She gave the man $500, but then had a detective track down the baby's biological parents. The story, according to the *Tribune*, had a happy ending: the parents "proved their untainted lineage."[17]

Lesbians were the sort of wayward women who rarely appeared in black-
mail stories, perhaps because the concept of lesbianism was not as yet recognized. This line of argument was taken by the defense counsel in a 1942 English case. The 1891 Slander of Women Act allowed a woman to sue for slander if unchastity had been imputed to her. Mrs. Innes Margaret Kerr accordingly sued Lady John Kennedy for having called her a lesbian. The latter's lawyers argued that the act did not apply in this case, as in 1891 the politicians who drafted it did not even imagine lesbianism. The judge disagreed: "As a phenomenon it [lesbianism] has existed for 2,500 years, and I should be much surprised if, under whatever name, the parliamentary draftsmen of the 1890s were ignorant of its existence. To assume this to be the case one must assume that they had little or no knowledge of the literature of the ancient world; an assumption which I make bold to repel."[18] He then proceeded to assert that imputation of "unnatural relations" was more wounding to a woman than imputation of adultery or fornication, assessed damages at £300, and awarded costs to the plaintiff.

In the 1920s and 1930s female same-sex relations came to be seen as qualitatively different from women's "romantic friendships" of the previous century. Yet the fact that lesbians were increasingly stigmatized—though not criminalized—was taken by contemporaries as explaining why lesbians did not show up in the press as blackmail victims. In 1921 attempts were made in the British Parliament to have the crime of "gross indecency" extended to women. A Scottish Member of Parliament reported that he had heard of husbands whose wives were seduced by women being unable to use the affair as grounds for divorce because lesbianism was not recognized in law. The successful opposition to the criminalization of lesbianism was led by Colonel Josiah Wedgwood, who argued that convictions would be impossible and, more important, that blackmailers would inevitably try to make use of such a law. Sex reformer George Ives agreed that the bill would have made "homosexual women prospective criminals and fresh prey for the blackmailer."[19]

Lesbianism was not criminalized, but with twentieth-century society's greater stress on heterosexual conformity, medical experts increasingly regarded the unattached woman as a problem. Dr. Mary Scharlieb warned her 1920s readers of the dangers of "absorbing" and "obsessive" female friendships.[20] One writer took up the notion that such seductions could lead to blackmail. Brian Tozer claimed that crooks exploiting Freud's popularity were drawing in women patients by advertising nursing homes for nerves, fatigue, exhaustion, and "nervous prostration." They demanded the confessions and confidences of their patients and then blackmailed them. Everyone knew how men were entrapped. "In the same way well-to-do women patients have been blackmailed when of a peculiar temperament and nursed by an exceptionally attractive nursing sister." The first important American play in which lesbianism was portrayed—Lillian Hellman's *The Children's Hour* (1934)—also exploited the blackmail theme. The play ended with the lesbian character committing suicide, which led critics to commend the author for her careful handling of a delicate subject.[21] Morality dictated that if the lesbian story were to be told, it had to be as tragedy.

The moralistic warnings the courts and press aimed at sexually adventurous women were duplicated in fiction and film. Much like nineteenth-century novels, many of the early movies that touched on blackmail eroticized female helplessness by arguing that if a woman gave in or was compromised sexually she placed herself at enormous risk. They thus perpetuated the melodramatic theme of the fallen woman, portraying sexual transgression as leading inevitably to disaster. The best known of such films today is probably Alfred Hitchcock's first talking picture, *Blackmail* (1929), in which a young woman incautiously visits a man's room. He tries to rape her, she accidentally kills him, and so falls into the clutches of an extortionist.[22]

There were many more movies of this ilk. The production of *Lilies of the Street* (1925) was sponsored by Mary E. Hamilton, who worked with the New York police for the rehabilitation of wayward girls. In this film a flapper, lured into a disreputable haunt, is mistaken as a prostitute by the police; the incident is used by the villain to blackmail her mother. In *House of Silence* (1918) a young woman is lured to a brothel, though the madam's attempts to blackmail her are foiled. A young woman is falsely arrested as a prostitute in *This Woman* (1924); having become a successful singer, she finds herself blackmailed by the man who knows her past. Judith (Mary Astor), a dance hall girl and "white slave," is reformed and pursued by a wealthy businessman in *Romance of the Underworld* (1928), but her old pimp shows up to make demands. A speakeasy called the "Sucker's Club" figures in *I Have Lived* (1933). The plot centers on an ex-prostitute whose hopes of marrying are threatened by a man who knows of her failings. "The young girl with a past which is continually casting shadows over her future," a jaded reviewer dryly noted, "is not an unfamiliar figure in the cinema."[23] Warning young women that any straying from the path of virtue would blight one's future was nothing new; what was distinctly modern was the assertion that punishment would take the form of blackmail.

Films also portrayed married women falling into the clutches of blackmailers. This theme was most successfully exploited in *Madame X* (1916, with American versions in 1920, 1929, 1937, and 1966), which portrays an unfaithful wife falling into a life of drink and prostitution, and only begin-

205

Blackmail (1929) was Alfred Hitchcock's first talking picture, but only one of many films exploiting the cautionary theme that the woman who was sexually adventurous would inevitably be compromised. In this scene the detective lover is attempting to protect the young woman from the blackmailer. (*Illustrated London News,* July 6, 1929.)

ning her recovery by murdering her blackmailing pimp. Crooks attempt to use compromising photos of a married woman in *The Lady Who Dared* (1931). In *Gambling With Souls* (1936) a doctor's wife, seduced and blackmailed by a gambler, is forced into prostitution. In all these films the same basic story line was followed: a woman's sexual laxity resulted not only in her degeneration but in her being placed at the mercy of a blackmailer; the only possible way her life could be salvaged was by repentance and male intervention. Hitchcock's *Blackmail* was subversive only to the extent that it raised the troubling idea of the policeman-boyfriend being responsible for the blackmailer's death, in effect replacing the villain with the hero as possessor of the woman's guilty secret.[24]

Writers of fiction harped on the same theme. In "Blackmailers Don't Shoot" (1933), Raymond Chandler's first piece of hard-boiled detective fiction, the detective aids a movie star threatened with the exposure of letters from an earlier love affair. In a 1937 thriller written by a retired Scotland Yard detective a society girl commits suicide after having been preyed on by a gang of "soul slayers." Prolific English novelist Michael Arlen dealt with the theme of blackmail in several of his works. In *These Charming People* (1923) the woman is saved from a blackguard by the patronizing hero. "'That,' he said harshly, 'will teach a lovely lady to love scum. You have sinned against yourself.'" In a similarly moralizing tale, "The Legend of the Crooked Coronet" (1937), Arlen presents an upper-class, Robin Hood type of thief who takes it upon himself to blackmail a wealthy woman who he knows indulges in "monkey business." He informs her that each time she does she will have to pay him £100. "It is on record, after all, that married men have paid much more than that for what is, I believe, known as 'fun' or 'nice change'—so why, in these days of equality for women, shouldn't you pay too?" Perhaps the most interesting of these tales was Stefan Zweig's "Fear" (which appeared in English in 1934) about yet another adulterous woman who is harassed by a blackmailer. To her horror she finds that the affair has to be paid for, first in danger and later in money. Only at the end do we learn that it is her husband who has sadistically orchestrated the blackmail threats. Having succeeded in driving his frightened wife into making the decision to end the affair, he calmly tells her that punishment can serve a useful function in restoring family harmony. Few went as far as Zweig in portraying so coldly and transparently a man's use of menace to ensure the surveillance and manipulation of a woman.[25]

The rash of cautionary films and stories in the 1920s and 1930s suggests that interwar Anglo-American culture clearly, if unconsciously, welcomed blackmail reports that demonstrated how wayward women could be disci-   plined. Women's entry into the public world was marked by tensions and contradictions. Stories of their being blackmailed provided society with a way of warning women of too casually throwing off the old moral restraints. It was assumed that a price the most daring would have to pay would be the risk of being blackmailed by gigolos and ex-lovers. It is difficult to say whether the frequency of such crimes increased. Knowing that the police and the courts found their increasing freedom difficult either to comprehend or sympathize with, women were probably less likely than men to report such demands.

The blackmail stories of the "Roaring Twenties" appeared to confirm the progressives' claim that the Victorian cult of sexual respectability was dead or dying. Family surveillance of women was difficult in a world in which sexual contacts could be initiated by car or telephone as well as the mail. Romantic women novelists like Elinor Glyn propounded the notion that affairs were more exciting than marriage. But young women had to decide for themselves how far they would go. The pessimistic drew from extortion stories the moral that women were paying the price for their newfound freedom. If the price were too high, went the prevailing thinking, they had been warned. But warned against what? Films and fiction held that bad men were the threat. The sexual double standard and inequitable divorce laws were only noted in passing. Commentators used the fear of blackmail to support, if not replace, older moral constraints on female behavior. In personalizing the blackmail threat they were able to pass over the social and legal structures that made many of its forms possible.

The majority of commentators implicitly assumed that what most held women's passions in check was their fear of pregnancy. Such a force for restraint, however, was undermined in the twentieth century, with the spread of information on how conception could be prevented and miscarriage induced. At a time when there was no foolproof form of contraception, abortion was relied on by many women as a backup method of birth control. "I have worked in a factory eleven years," wrote a correspondent of Margaret Sanger, America's pioneering advocate of birth control, "and the majority of women of my acquaintance procure abortion as their means of family limitation, regardless of the suffering and ill-health which it produces."[26] Women tried to abort themselves by taking all kinds of drugs. Some sought out backstreet abortions. A woman who sought to induce a miscarriage was, as the result of laws passed only in the latter half of the nineteenth century, committing a crime. In using the threat of such laws to extort money from desperate women and those who sought to aid them, blackmailers forced on the public the uncomfortable knowledge that thousands of wives and mothers were running enormous risks to control their fertility. The challenge that faced the courts and the press was to produce an abortion blackmail story that condemned extortionists without critiquing the law that the criminal exploited.

The biggest blackmail attempt in history took place as a result of the criminalization of abortion. Beginning in 1896 three brothers, named Chrimes, advertised in cheap English newspapers and sold by mail a variety of pills and potions that promised to remove "obstructions." After two years they had on file the names of approximately ten thousand women who had sent for these abortifacients. In September 1898 the brothers decided to extort a few pounds from each victim by threatening to reveal that she had attempted to induce a miscarriage. The Chrimeses rented an office, purchased twenty-five reams of paper and a cyclostyle, and ordered 12,000 letterheads and addressed envelopes. The letter they concocted asserted that an official had proof of the woman's attempt to abort and that, unless she returned £2 2s and swore never again to abort, legal proceedings would commence.[27]

Although the Chrimeses failed in their scheme and were sentenced to prison terms of seven to twelve years, this could not cloak the enormity of the blackmail attempt. Approximately 8,100 women were sent threatening letters and close to 3,000 responded. A servant girl sent her money along with the following plea: "I should not like my missus to know, else I shall lose my situation. Hoping you will send the paper by return of post and stick to your promise not to bother me any more about it." Observers were scandalized that a crime on such a scale should have been attempted. They were equally shocked by the women's attempts at abortion, though the word was not mentioned. One paper only reported that the blackmailers had obtained a list of purchasers of "a remedy of a character which need not be further specified." The fact that the police uncovered the scheme, the press lamented, was a "discreditable commentary on the extensiveness of such cases." Women in almost every large town had been involved, "many of them in good positions." Some had even received their information from religious newspapers. Nurses also spread such information; even the wife of a clergyman was reported to have encouraged "improper proceedings." The respectable press attacked cheap newspapers—such as the *Family Reader, Illustrated Bits,* and the *Weekly Times and Echo*—that had carried advertisements for the abortifacients for contributing to "pruriency and crime."[28]

Some wanted to believe that the women acted in ignorance in purchasing what they might have construed to be a harmless tonic. A medical correspondent in the *Lancet* soberly retorted that there could be no doubt that thousands knew that they were committing a criminal act: "Certainly in cases of blackmail innocent, or comparatively innocent, people who have placed themselves in compromising circumstances pay to avoid publicity or some charge not obviously easy to refute; but no one can believe that the most ignorant woman suffering from amenorrhoea, neither pregnant nor having incurred the risk of pregnancy, would submit to extortion because she had taken an emmenagogue [menstrual purgative] mixture or would believe that to take such a mixture was a criminal act." These women paid, the writer argued, because they had "guilty consciences." At least one London newspaper called for the women to be prosecuted.[29]

The legal establishment had no intention of broaching the abortion debate. They restricted themselves simply to proving that the Chrimes brothers had employed menaces to make an illegal gain. Summing up a case in which thousands of *women* had been blackmailed, Mr. Justice Hawkins bizarrely expressed his concern for the blackmailers' victimization of *men:* "To trade upon another man's weakness, to make him the victim of extortion, to compel him to pay money to stop proceedings to escape from the meshes of the law was in the last degree antagonistic to the interests of justice and to the interests and safety of the public."[30] Of course, in legal discourse "man" meant either man or woman, but Hawkins certainly had no intention of pondering the consequences of the criminalization of abortion. The all-male jury abetted him in calling attention to the culpability of the "religious and secular press" in carrying advertisements for abortifacients. They, like every other commentator, refused to recognize that so many women could be made victims of an extortion attempt only because, on the one hand, pressure to limit family size was increasing and, on the other, abortion had recently been declared a statutory offense. If anyone were motivated by a "guilty conscience" it was the press and the courts, who

210   sought to trivialize the physical and legal dangers women faced in seeking to control their fertility.

Despite attempts to bury the topic, such court cases and newspaper reports inspired a number of writers to broach the taboo subject of abortion. Harley Granville Barker's play *Waste* (1907), though it deals with abortion in a moralistic fashion (the woman and the baby die and the lover commits suicide), was denied a license and was only performed privately until 1936. Elizabeth Robins's play *Votes for Women* (1907), by contrast, presents the feminist heroine as using her own abortion to advantage. Ten years earlier she had been seduced and abandoned by a Tory Member of Parliament who is now about to marry. She threatens to reveal the secret of their affair as well as her earlier abortion in order to blackmail him into supporting the suffrage cause. In his best-selling succès de scandale *The Green Hat* (1924) Michael Arlen explicitly referred to divorcées resorting to abortion clinics. Sophisticated viewers of the 1928 film version, *A Woman of Affairs*, knew just why the character played by Greta Garbo was ill. Nathanael West peppered *Miss Lonelyhearts* (1933) with references to the Depression forcing women to contemplate abortion. Women desperately seeking aid was portrayed by Rosalind Lehman and Jean Rhys, while the indignation felt by some doctors that they were being "used" by demanding female patients was captured in A. J. Cronin's autobiographical *Adventures in Two Worlds* (1935). In an important 1938 test case of the English law Dr. Aleck Bourne informed the authorities that he had performed an abortion on a fourteen-year-old-girl who had been brutally raped by a gang of soldiers. In *Between the Acts* (1941) Virginia Woolf alluded to this case, which was being publicized by the Abortion Law Reform Association to demonstrate the need for changes in the law. Poor, young women were at greatest risk. A character in Vita Sackville West's *The Easter Party* (1953) who "had a fright" tells her friend that money made all the difference. It is "quite easy," she said, "if you know how, and if you can afford to pay. It costs about fifty pounds."[31] These fictionalized accounts of abortion presented women's experiences in ways glaringly missing in the court accounts of abortion blackmail.

The authorities wrestled with the problem of how to punish those who preyed on women without appearing at the same time to countenance the inducement of miscarriage. In England the typical abortion blackmail scheme that came to light involved only a few people. Women were, of course, always either the direct or indirect victims of such crimes, but only in a small number of cases did the courts focus on their needs. In the 1936 Devon assizes Mrs. A, a lady's companion living apart from her husband, was described in court as being in September 1935 pregnant "and she desired to rid herself of that condition." The term "abortion" was never employed. What the court was told was that Mrs. A met a palmist and "thought reader" who said she would help her. Mrs. A went to a nursing home and miscarried. The psychic and her husband then proceeded to blackmail Mrs. A for both her abortion and her affair with Mr. B. In sentencing the couple to five years the judge described the case as "one of the most wicked blackmails it has ever been my ill-fortune to try. It is a shocking case."[32]

In 1937 at the Birmingham assizes a fifty-three-year-old man was sentenced to ten years in prison for extorting money from Mrs. A and Mrs. B, apparently because they sought his help to miscarry. He had also preyed on other women, who refused to testify. The press reported that the man "had posed as a doctor so that he might be able to talk to them [women] on sexual matters and had pretended to assist them when they got into trouble." "You have not been found out," said the judge, "but you have been living on wretched women whom you induced to treat you as though you were a doctor. Your conduct in regard to those two women has been terrible."[33] Many women would not give evidence in such cases, the police reported, because they were afraid of publicity.

It saved the authorities embarrassment to turn the public's attention to the wretches who provided or promised to provide illegal services and away from the desperate women who sought them. In April 1933 two men were found guilty of seeking to extort money from Susan Wilson, a Port Glasgow maternity nurse. The girlfriend of one of the accused had asked Wilson for an illegal operation. Wilson claimed that she refused to help, but one of the men demanded money, writing, "Don't try any tricks. If you do you will go to jail along with us. Your term of imprisonment will be longer than ours."[34] Because the rumor of Wilson's providing abortions had spread, the judge wanted her name published so her reputation could be cleared.

George Snowball was not as pure as his name suggested. He was found guilty at London's Central Criminal Courts in 1936 of demanding £300 from Dr. X. If the "loan" were not given he threatened to accuse the doctor—whom he admitted not even knowing—of providing abortions. Such cases brought to the attention of the public the knowledge that doctors as well as amateurs were providing abortion services. In 1929 a man threatened David Constantine (whose name was given), a London doctor with a practice in Mecklenburgh Square, that his abortion activities would be revealed. In sentencing the accused to three years the judge upbraided the doctor for initially paying the extortionist. The jury, he added, "must assume that the accusation that the doctor had performed an illegal operation on a woman was without foundation."[35] But why should it have? It was easier to assume that the court wished to cover up the issue.

In some cases the doctor's involvement was too obvious to deny. In 1934 a man was charged with threatening to accuse a gynecologist of "a certain crime." Entered in evidence was a letter written December 28, 1933, by the man's wife, who had been operated on, saying that she was ill and wanted her money back. If not, she would go to the police. She added, "The local doctors are very inquisitive as to who was the performer of the illegal operation." The doctor ignored her request, so she wrote again January 12, 1934, threatening to expose him: "Such men as you, who make a business of a poor girl's misfortune, deserve all you are likely to get, and thank God the laws of the country cater very heavily for crimes such as yours." The doctor admitted examining the woman but denied operating on her and insisted he had been paid nothing. The woman claimed that the doctor had used instruments on her and that she paid him £25, which he promised to return if the operation were unsuccessful. When he refused to return the money, the husband turned to threats to "put the wind up him." The chemist whom the couple alleged had originally recommended that they see the gynecologist confirmed their account that he gave a drug to the woman and sent her on to the doctor.

> The Recorder—What for?
> Birth control treatment.
> Did you know she was pregnant?
> Not at the time.

The chemist also stated that he sent £10 in an envelope to the doctor.

> The Recorder—Anything to do with abortion?
> Oh, no.

Summing up with the observation that blackmailers had to be tried even when their allegations were true, the Recorder—one of the judges of the

Central Criminal Court—made it clear that he regarded the doctor as an abortionist; but the couple should have gone to the authorities if they had a grievance. The jury returned a guilty verdict, but recommended mercy.[36]   213

A 1947 English observer noted that abortion was "nasty and dangerous, for not only does the criminal play about with human life and health, but he dabbles with fraud and blackmail as a sideline." When such blackmailers went on trial they forced the public to acknowledge that women were desperate to control their fertility, thus piercing the shroud of silence which hung over the issue. An investigating committee estimated that in the 1930s up to 150,000 abortions took place annually in Britain, though on average only 116 were known to the police, with 57 persons being committed to trial and 45 convicted. While the police frequently complained that the woman was usually not cooperative, the authorities did their best to ignore the issue.[37]

In America as in England the public usually only heard about abortion when a death resulted. In September 1916 the *Chicago Tribune* ran the headline "Abortion Mill List of 1,500." A Mrs. Ella Kulken had died, and the police were looking for James Wade. He had left three books containing the names of 1,500 patients he had serviced and letters from them asking about what medicines they should take.[38] In America as in England blackmail cases also revealed how the criminalization of badly needed medical services poisoned physician-patient relationships.

Doctors sometimes turned on each other. In 1914 a New York court heard that Charles S. Andrews had libeled Dr. Asa Bird Gardiner—who in 1911 had helped convict a third physician, a Dr. Conrad, of abortion—as a blackmailing scoundrel. Gardiner, who worked for the New York Medical Society in tracking down abortionists, was himself charged with extortion and got off on a technicality. Doctors also blackmailed each other. On December 26, 1912, a young couple called at Dr. Bertschinger's office in Portland, Oregon, to see if the woman were pregnant. The doctor later claimed in court that he carried out an examination, but refused to provide the abortion that they requested. In early January 1913 he received a letter from Dr. R. H. Campbell of Little Falls, Washington. "A young lady lays dying from septic condition and incomplete abortion. She has made a full confession. You are charged with the crime. The confession is in my possession. In the event of her death it will be turned over to the police. Confession is witnessed." Bertschinger, taking this to be a blackmail threat, went immediately by train to Little Falls. Campbell would not allow the unconscious woman to be seen and, explaining that he was the local health officer who would sign her death certificate, told Bertschinger to pay up. The nurse was to receive $25 and Campbell $1,000. Bertschinger borrowed the money and paid Campbell with twenty-dollar gold coins. The lower court felt Bertschinger's suit for the return of his money was tainted, but the appeals court found in his favor, turning back the defense argument that one had a right in good faith to threaten a wrongdoer with either a civil suit or criminal prosecution. According to section 2610 of the Washington Criminal code the threat "to expose or impute disgrace" was punishable by up to a five-year prison term.[39]

Women with an unwanted pregnancy found that doctors regarded them with suspicion. The doctors' concern was that if they were to provide abortions women might eventually turn them in to the police. In fact most female patients, even those dying as a result of botched operations, were unusually loyal. Some physicians, however, extorted both money and sexual favors from desperate women. One historian has found that some doctors "equated abortion with sexual availability and tried to turn their patients into prostitutes."[40]

Reputable doctors worried that if they were the last individual attending a woman who had aborted they could be arrested by the police. They also feared being hounded by extortionists. In 1910 New York attorney Almuth C. Vandiver warned physicians that "unscrupulous women and their accomplices have it within their power . . . to successfully blackmail the respectable practitioner, who omits the essential precaution [notifying colleagues] for his protection." In some blackmail reports it is difficult to determine if a doctor did indeed turn away a patient or, for self-protection, only claimed to have done so. Dr. Henry Dawson Furnis asserted that because he refused to help a woman she maliciously blamed him for her abortion. A clear example of a doctor's claiming to be blackmailed as a way of covering up his abortion practice came to light in 1943. Dr. Anthony Renda complained to the police that he was being blackmailed, but wound up being arrested for abortion and homicide. The charge was based on the February 1943 death of James Cardito's wife. Renda stated that Cardito and his brother claimed that Renda had killed the wife and demanded that he pay the hospital bill, the funeral expenses, and $2,500. The police witnessed Renda give Cardito $1,000, but rather than seeing this as extortion the court decided that the doctor was attempting to avoid responsibility for Mrs. Cardito's death. Renda was sentenced to three-and-a-half to seven years in prison.[41]

Despite the medical profession's suspicion of women patients, American doctors involved in abortion were far more likely to be subjected to shakedowns by criminals, colleagues, or the police. In 1904 two men tried to blackmail a Williamsburgh, Pennsylvania, doctor by saying that he was responsible for the death of a woman whom he had refused to attend. In 1913 New York detectives arrested a man for threatening to tell the district attorney about another doctor's malpractice. In 1916, when Don Collins's nefarious activities were in the news, the press reported that his gang, in addition to exploiting the Mann Act, blackmailed New York physicians implicated in abortion. In 1926 a "colored physician" was forced to pay $300 to two Brooklyn detectives to have them stop the investigation of a female patient's death. In 1931 Louis Bernstine, a lawyer, was indicted in Pennsylvania for threatening to lay an abortion charge against a Mrs. Sidney Garrod, who in August 1929 was alleged to have performed an abortion on his client, Mrs. Florence Casey. The lawyer kept $1,500 of the $2,500 that Garrod paid. One month later a go-between brought to Bernstine a woman named Doris Davis, who had similarly incriminating information regarding a Dr. Shriner. The doctor paid $1,000 to have Davis drop her suit. Bernstine, though claiming that the money received was for damages and not for dropping criminal charges, was convicted of extortion.[42]

The onset of the Depression in the 1930s dramatically increased poor women's need to limit family size. In 1936 the authorities discovered an "abortion club" in New Jersey with eight hundred dues-paying patients. In major cities such as New York and Los Angeles the demand led to the emergence of abortion syndicates. In October 1936 Reginald Rankin and ten others were found guilty in Los Angeles of being members of a West Coast abortion ring. It was revealed in court that this group had provided abortions to women for years and bought off the police in cash or services.[43]

Blackmailers were not slow to realize how they could take advantage of such operations. In 1930 in Philadelphia nine men were arrested, including attorneys, a naturopath, and lawyers' runners, who had been active nationwide in preying on doctors accused of "having committed illegal operations." The gang members were indicted for extorting over $15,000 from four doctors; Dr. Frederick W. Faltermeyer stated that he alone had paid out $11,500. The scam had originated in Chicago, where gangsters, aided by doctors, manufactured fraudulent evidence.[44]

216   The same year Dr. Maurice A. Sturm was charged with the February 1929 first-degree manslaughter death of Mrs. Ruth Weir of East Orange, New Jersey. Mrs. Weir had been operated on by Sturm and was sent to the home of a Mrs. Sanger on West 149th Street to recuperate. Before her death—due to septicemia—in Orange Memorial Hospital, she told police of the operation and Sturm's involvement. Four doctors testified against Sturm; the press noted that this breaking of professional ranks was unusual. Sturm, in response, claimed that an assistant prosecutor tried to extort $10,000 from him via a Hoboken judge by saying he could quash the case. Sturm's assertion led to a reorganization of the Homicide Bureau of the district attorney's office, and Assistant District Attorney Thomas J. Ryan subsequently resigned. When Sturm's trial finally took place he admitted carrying out the operation on Weir but insisted it was not illegal. The jury could not reach a verdict, and Sturm was acquitted.[45]

    The most sensational New York scandal concerning police and judges demanding protection money from abortionists came to light in 1937. The case led Special Assistant Attorney General John Harlan Amen, the chief investigator, to assert that "the abortion racket is the most corrupt and vicious racket yet uncovered in connection with public officials." The story began in 1935 when Dr. Louis Duke, ex-president of the Brooklyn Civic Club, was indicted for carrying out abortions. Judge George W. Martin swiftly dismissed the indictment. In 1937 the same Dr. Duke was the victim of an extortion attempt. A twenty-four-year-old chauffeur of the State Asylum at Central Islip pleaded guilty in May to threatening "a well-known physician to pay $15,000 or suffer violence." The FBI had participated in the case. That July the police again arrested Duke for abortion and took into custody the two nurses, an attendant, and four patients found at Duke's Bedford Avenue address. Once more, thanks to the help of Judge Martin, who found the evidence insufficient, the indictment was quashed. The authorities believed that Duke had bribed Martin, however, and in April 1939 Martin was indicted for corruption. Duke told the court that since the Depression he had "specialized in both legal and illegal abortions." He had purchased his abortion practice for $2,500 and provided about six to ten abortions a week at $60 to $75 each. He relied on a network of approximately two hundred physicians and druggists who for a fee referred clients to him. He also had to pay 10 percent of his annual salary of $30,000 as hush money to public officials. The police were aware of the extent of such practices. When Duke was interviewed one officer was quoted 217 as saying, "any doctor who says he is not doing abortions is a goddam liar."[46] As he had been arrested in December 1938 on an abortion-manslaughter charge, which was still pending against him, Duke had good reason to be cooperative in the 1939 Martin case.

Duke's story was that he paid off Judge Martin, who accordingly dismissed the doctor's indictment in October 1937. The judge, who was deeply in debt and had had his salary garnished for the previous ten years, insisted on calling the $1,000 a "loan." In return for his testimony the prosecutor promised Duke immunity. Despite the evidence Martin was acquitted in June 1939 and survived a senate attempt to have him removed from the bench. Undeterred, in July Amen prosecuted Dr. Abraham Ditchik, who had acted as Duke's go-between with the authorities and was described in the press as the alleged collector of "fabulous sums" in the abortion racket. Ditchik was charged with having extorted over $65,000 from ten Brooklyn physicians between 1933 and 1939 with the threat of revealing their unethical activities. Duke had paid Ditchik over $6,000, Dr. Henry L. Blank $8,500, Dr. Maxwell Ornstein $4,000, and Dr. Herman Elster $13,500. Such was the importance of the trial that a blue-ribbon panel of 150 jurors was drawn. Amen ultimately indicted thirty-seven officials, but faced the hostility of Brooklyn judges. His crusade did have the support of New York mayor Fiorello La Guardia and Manhattan District Attorney Thomas Dewey. Dewey in fact took over the prosecution of Ditchik, who had promised Dr. George Rothenberg, a Manhattan physician, that in return for $40,000 he would "take care" of the State Board of Medical Examiner's investigation into his performing a criminal abortion.[47]

The Brooklyn Superior Court heard that Ditchik approached doctors who were known for "helping out women," promising them that he could "fix" any problems they might have with the medical grievance bureau, as he was on good terms with the assistant district attorney who sat on it. Several of the doctors who were called to testify refused to admit that they provided abortions and insisted that they simply paid to prevent "unpleasant publicity" or to avoid a frame-up. After twelve hours of deliberation the jury found Ditchik, a forty-three-year-old father of seven, guilty on seven of the eleven counts. He was sentenced to four-and-a-half years in Sing

Sing. William Lurie, Duke's lawyer, testified to having bribed Judge Martin and having paid $5,000 to prosecutor Francis A. Madden "to be reasonable with Dr. Duke." Both Lurie and Madden were disbarred.[48]

Abortion was first and foremost a woman's issue. Yet strangely enough, in reviewing newspaper accounts of the authorities' prosecution of "abortion racketeers," one is surprised to find that the women have disappeared. This was not an accident. In the 1898 Chrimes trial, which involved thousands of women, women were ignored. Forty years later American authorities took the same tack. The casting of abortion-related blackmail so that it appeared as simply a contest between criminals and the police could be attributed in part to officials' gallantly seeking to spare women witnesses unnecessary embarrassment. This erasing of women from the record, however, had more to do with the way in which the abortion issue was framed in the interwar period. The courts and the press used blackmail cases to direct the public's attention to the issues of male criminality and corruption; neither the woman's circumstances nor her right to choose nor the question of the viability of fetal life was ever mentioned. The authorities sought to ignore, but could never obliterate, the evidence that supported a more worrying and embarrassing story: that thousands of women were breaking the law against abortion and there was no way of stopping them.

The Depression forced the abortion rate up to new heights. In the United States Frederick J. Taussig reported that around one-fifth of all pregnancies ended in abortion. Dorothy Dunbar Bromley argued in 1934 that America could avoid 8,000 maternal deaths a year by legalizing abortion—at least until adequate contraceptives were made available. The idea that the woman less than three months pregnant who sought to "put herself right" was committing a crime was clearly not accepted by a large section of the female population. This should have been made clear by the papers' uncovering of "abortion clubs" and "abortion syndicates." An American survey of college students found that for female students, who prided themselves on their poise, abortion was more of an embarrassment than anything else. Havelock Ellis, the English sexologist, stated that women felt no regret and could not understand the legal and medical opposition to abortion. In Britain the Birkett Committee, after hearing evidence in 1937, conceded that "although the crime [of abortion] is very frequently resorted to with dislike and reluctance, the increasing frequency of the practice, in spite of all efforts to combat it, indicates a growing tendency to accept termination of pregnancy as a legitimate method of family limitation, and as a right to be exercised without scruple."[49] By the 1930s many knew that in the first trimester medical abortion was as safe as delivery at term. The old argument in defense of the law based on risk to the mother was thereby undermined. What the courts and the press refused to acknowledge was that criminalizing a medical procedure had driven thousands of women into the arms of backstreet abortionists and blackmailers. Regardless of the authorities' intent, blackmail trials demonstrated that just as the law had made homosexuals into criminals, so too it had made desperate women into outlaws.

Judging from the press coverage, all forms of sexual blackmail appeared to peak just as the Depression bottomed out in the mid-1930s. Economic misery presumably drove some to contemplate crimes that they would have otherwise spurned. But what drove the telling of blackmail stories in the interwar decades was not just a concern for the yawning gulf between rich and poor. These stories had been constructed both to rationalize and to resist the changes in the relationships of men and women that heralded the making of modern sexuality. Such stories were particularly needed in the 1920s and 1930s. Whether they would they have a role to play in wartime remained to be seen.

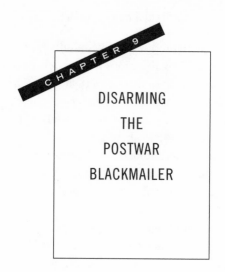

DISARMING
THE
POSTWAR
BLACKMAILER

By inflicting on America and England massive social disruption that undermined sexual restraints, World War II should have provided potential blackmailers with fresh stores of ammunition. Affairs were common during the war; rates of venereal disease and illegitimacy, and likely abortion too, climbed. Immediately after the war many marriages made in haste broke down, and divorce petitions doubled. Moreover, wartime governments in both Britain and America were more sensitive than ever to the idea of criminals and enemy agents seeking to exploit secrets. In 1941 J. Edgar Hoover sought an extension of wiretaps in the United States to combat espionage, sabotage, kidnapping, and extortion. (At that time, however, the FBI did not claim that sexual blackmail posed a major security risk. It would only make such assertions in the postwar years as part of its campaign against homosexuals in government service.)[1]

Yet during World War II, sexual blackmail ceased to exist—or so it appeared from the newspapers. In 1939 the index to the *Times* of London listed seventeen references to blackmail; in 1940 it listed two; in 1941, one; and in 1942, none at all. The *New York Times* had always contained fewer blackmail reports, but its readers detected a similar decline, with a drop in references to extortion from six in 1941 to none in 1944. What caused such a change? Had the actual incidence of blackmail fallen? Criminologists have noted that during the war some forms of crime plateaued or even declined. In the case of sexual blackmail, perhaps being under attack from outside enemies made civil society less judgmental of minor sexual failings, especially those of young men who entered the military. Some women in the ranks, and others allowed entry into new forms of work, also found the 221 war emancipating. In this less moralistic climate, potential blackmailers might have been disarmed. Observers in the 1940s agreed that the war had led to a general relaxing of moral restraints at home. "It was wartime," recalled one West Coast American, "and all bets were off. Everybody who had any money was spending it. There was an attitude that was partly desperation and partly the feeling that life had better be enjoyed right now."[2]

The number of all forms of blackmail reported to the English police fell from one hundred a year in the early 1930s to about fifty a year during World War II; the number of sexual blackmail attempts may also have fallen.[3] More striking, however, was the fact that in the United States and in England stories of blackmail virtually disappeared. Not only did the English and American press virtually stop reporting cases of blackmail; writers and filmmakers also abandoned it as a plot device. These stories lost favor because the sorts of lessons they customarily taught were for the moment regarded as inappropriate. The stories had warned women of the dangers of venturing outside the home; now governments were pleading with them to engage in war work. They had warned men to stick to their own class and in particular to avoid handsome youths; now the armed services were forcing thousands of young men, strangers to each other, to live together in barracks and camps. In the 1920s and 1930s the media had exploited accounts of those caught in compromising sexual situations. The reports were at times moralizing and at other times comedic. Once the war broke out the Allies sought to present themselves as nations in which all their citizens—no matter what their sex or race, creed or color—were united against the enemy. Sexual blackmail stories—exposing as they did such disruptive issues as adultery, abortion, and homosexuality—had no place in the armory of propagandists trumpeting their country's moral superiority. This was too serious a time to waste on light comedies depicting gold-digging women or promiscuous playboys. The focus shifted to virtuous "war wives and waiting women." If a book or film did note female unfaithfulness, it was to roundly condemn it. And though it was estimated that 80 percent of American soldiers who were abroad for more than two years had at least one sexual encounter, the infidelity of men at war was simply too sensitive a subject to be discussed.[4]

True, in American film noir—in, for example, *The Maltese Falcon* (1941), *Murder My Sweet* (1944), and *The Big Sleep* (1946)—hard-boiled detectives continued to battle femmes fatales and homosexual villains. Nevertheless, Hollywood did play its part in "cultural mobilization." In *Casablanca* (1943)—the most successful of the pro-war propaganda films—Rick sacrifices his personal happiness to fight the Nazis. With their country under siege, English filmmakers were even more careful than their American counterparts to avoid compromising scenarios. They now stigmatized the glamorous woman. The best British wartime films that dealt with sexual entanglements—*Perfect Strangers* (1945), *Piccadilly Incident* (1945), and *Brief Encounter* (1945)—raised the specter of a third party threatening a marriage only to assert more effectively the rewards of virtue. In the interwar period a host of commentators had found the sexual blackmail story the perfect vehicle by which a range of sex, class, and race issues could be discussed. Its sudden disappearance during World War II dramatically demonstrated that an examination of such problems—even if carried out for the purposes of sustaining the status quo—was, at least for the duration, not wanted.[5]

In both England and America after the war, concerted efforts were made to revive domesticity and sexual "normalcy." Although blackmail stories reemerged in the 1950s and played a role in the policing of sexuality, they never regained the power they had wielded in the interwar years. Ironically the cultural importance of blackmail stories in the latter half of the twentieth century increasingly resided in activists' using them to support law reform campaigns. Blackmail stories had in the 1920s and 1930s been employed to preach cautionary messages, and conservatives would continue to employ them in this way. But a real change occurred when reformers in the 1950s and 1960s used these tales in calling for the decriminalization of homosexuality and abortion.

The blackmailing of homosexuals was clearly facilitated by repressive laws in both England and the United States. The two countries' concerns fed off each other. In the 1950s the American notion that homosexuals' susceptibility to blackmail posed a security threat helped fuel the British police's crackdown on sexual deviance. In the 1960s Parliament's discussion of homosexual law reform inspired American law activists to advance a similar

agenda in their own country. In the 1970s the emergence of the gay liberation movement in America popularized on both sides of the Atlantic the
notion that blackmail—the most dramatic demonstration of the victimiza-   223
tion of homosexuals—could only be defeated by "coming out." This chapter and the next tell the story of the changes in the laws as they affected homosexuals, with this chapter devoted to an examination of events in
England and the following chapter those in America.

In England blackmail stories based on newspaper and court reports
played a key role in the 1950s and 1960s in convincing both the public and
politicians of the need for homosexual law reform. Journalists, novelists,
playwrights, and moviemakers provided the reformers additional ammunition in dramatizing and popularizing the notion that homosexuals were
victimized by extortionists. The "blackmail card" was crucial for the reformers' eventual success. In playing it they could in effect finesse homophobic counterarguments by insisting that the campaign for law reform
was aimed not so much at defending homosexuality—which some reformers actually hoped would decline in significance—as at ending the extortionate activities of criminals who threatened not just a sexual minority but
brought the entire legal system into disrepute. The role that blackmail
played in the reform campaign helped the drive for decriminalization to
succeed—and also caused homosexuals to be disappointed with the results.

The decriminalization campaign in England began as a backlash against
the ham-handed excesses of the police in its early 1950s' crackdown on homosexual activity in London. Though it was generally accepted that World
War II had loosened morals, Sir Theobald Matthews, a dedicated Roman
Catholic and Director of Public Prosecutions, and Sir David Maxwell-Fyfe,
the Conservative Home Secretary, nevertheless set out to purge England of
vice. Chiefly due to police zeal the annual number of prosecutions of male
homosexual offenses rose from 800 in 1945 to 2,500 in 1955. The press coverage of the trials of homosexuals similarly peaked in the mid-1950s because, to the embarrassment of the government, the victims of the police
clampdown included a number of well-known personalities. On October
21, 1953, Sir John Gielgud, one of England's most eminent Shakespearean
actors, was arrested for "importuning." The same year Labour MP William
Field was forced to resign after having been caught in a West End lavatory
by agents provocateurs. The most sensational trials were those of novelist
Rupert Croft-Cooke, journalist Peter Wildeblood, Michael Pitt-Rivers

(great-grandson of the famous archaeologist Augustus Pitt-Rivers), and Lord Montagu of Beaulieu. It was unprecedented for such socially impor-
tant individuals to fall victim to a morals charge. In addition, while the police had previously been content to employ the law to target public indecency, it came out in court that they now were employing informers to ferret out information on private acts.[6]

The ensuing public debate over the relationship of homosexuality to blackmail made it clear that the English were as preoccupied as ever by questions of class. Croft-Cooke indignantly complained that prison authorities treated homosexuals—many from higher ranks in business and the armed forces—more severely than thugs and "shifty little clerks." Yet if he, Montagu, Pitt-Rivers, and Wildeblood were not the egalitarian martyrs they at times claimed to be, their tactic of pointing out that the law led to the arrest and blackmailing of the wrong sorts of people worked. Earlier lobbying had not. The public had ignored The Invert (1948), an anonymously authored work which charged that in the House of Commons, Hitler's Germany, and Huey Long's New Orleans the charge of homosexuality was used for political purposes. A similar stony silence met the 1949 request of a committee of the British Medical Association and the Magistrates Association for the government to bring English law on homosexuality into line with that of Europe. Similarly futile was a 1952 letter to the Times in which H. J. Blackham, Lord Chorley, Marcus Lipton, Herbert Read, Lord Russell, and Glanville Williams pointed out that the existing law on adult consensual sex was hard to enforce and offered "undesirable opportunity for blackmail."[7] Only the sensational trials of 1953 and 1954 finally forced Whitehall to act.

Though the Conservative government did not wish to appear lax, with the wrong sorts of people being harassed it was obvious that existing policing arrangements were not working. As a result it set up the Wolfenden Committee, which had as its mandate an examination of the laws pertaining to homosexuality and prostitution. From the very start reformers pointed to blackmail as a symptom of a bad law. In the House of Lords, Lord Jowitt, former Lord Chancellor, made his famous (though inaccurate) statement that when he was Attorney General he had discovered that 95 percent of blackmail cases involved homosexuals. The Times concurred with the need for reform and affirmed that the existing law helped "create conditions in which blackmail and provocation flourish."[8]

The committee, chaired by John Wolfenden, vice-chancellor of Reading University, began its work in August 1954. At its very first meeting a member noted that everyone assumed that the existing law was an incentive to 225 blackmail. This view was hammered home by a parade of witnesses. In his testimony Peter Wildeblood noted the irony that though the government purportedly favored social stability, the existing law made it more likely that a homosexual would be blackmailed as a result of a long-term relationship than by a mere pickup. He knew of two such victims. One of the committee's internal memos similarly mused that the homosexual man's fear of extortion might lead him to try to seduce boys since they would be less likely than adults to resort to blackmail. Two anonymous witnesses debated the blackmail issue before the committee, one saying the rate was high and the other that it was low. A third anonymous witness argued that suicide and entrapment were serious problems, but that blackmail was the "most common social abuse due to the existing law." The case of A. B., who had been blackmailed five times between 1944 and 1953, was introduced. The committee perused an actual blackmail letter from yet another case in which a sailor threatened his victim: "Now if I were suddenly to remember when, where and with whom, it might be very embarasing [*sic*] for you."[9]

Various national organizations also testified to the ways in which the law led to the blackmail of homosexuals. A representative of the Howard League stated that some victims were naturally afraid to go to the police and that only law reform could diminish blackmail's role. "An easy weapon is placed in the hands of the blackmailer for all kinds of purposes—financial, personal, and ideological," stated a spokesperson of the British Medical Association. "Such experiences of blackmail may produce in homosexual persons an exaggerated degree of nervous tension and strain." Dr. Kreamer, of the Davidson Clinic, Edinburgh, asserted that the law helped criminals and reported that he had heard patients joke about turning "King's evidence." Representatives of the General Council of the Bar agreed that though most extortion went undetected, the law was a blackmailers' charter. Delinquency experts concurred that only with law reform could the legal climate be improved. Even those who felt homosexuals were "ill" and deserved "treatment" pointed out that the existing legislation was cruel and unworkable.[10]

Not everyone on the committee took this view of blackmail. James Adair, a Scottish attorney, insisted that there was no proof of the direct linkage of the existing law to blackmail. In his view the stigma of homosexuality was as important as the law in placing homosexuals at the mercy of the extortionist. The Home Office also insisted that the law alone did not create conditions that encouraged threats. Dr. Joseph Whitby, in his testimony, agreed with Adair that blackmail was based more on the victim's fear of social exposure than of criminal proceedings. But a committee member tartly replied that a victim probably did not draw such nice distinctions, and Whitby conceded that no matter what the Home Office claimed, the public *believed* that the existing law on homosexuality led to blackmail. Moreover the committee heard how the police themselves used the law as a "latent" form of blackmail to threaten or terrorize those they did not like. One London policeman later recalled that some of his colleagues "looked on homosexuals as a source of extra income." Evidence was heard that homosexuals who complained to the police of being blackmailed could find themselves arrested for indecent acts: "There was also ample opportunity for blackmail," John Wolfenden recalled, "compounded by the danger that if a man who was being blackmailed revealed the fact to the police he might be charged and sentenced for homosexual offenses."[11]

The report of the Wolfenden Committee on Homosexuality and Prostitution was published in September 1957. The report did not so much call for the acceptance of homosexuality as argue that private consensual, nonviolent acts should not concern the police. Wolfenden's key argument was that homosexuality was a medical rather than a criminal problem. Some of the tabloids attacked the report and argued that any relaxation of the law would result in an increase in homosexuality. Sir W. Norwood East had earlier made the curious assertion that many homosexuals were chaste and a less repressive law would make their self-control more difficult. Despite such warnings, surveys indicated that the majority of the public agreed with the committee's findings.[12]

As far as blackmail was concerned the report concluded that the 1885 Labouchère Amendment was not the primary cause of extortion, as it had been preceded by laws against buggery, attempted buggery, and indecent assault. It did note that of the seventy-one cases of blackmail reported to the police in England and Wales between 1950 and 1953, thirty-two involved homosexuals. The report put an optimistic spin on these findings: "These figures [for homosexual blackmail cases] represent an average of eight cases a year, and even allowing for the reluctance of the victim to approach the police, they suggest that the amount of blackmail which takes place had been considerably exaggerated in the popular mind." The figures made it obvious, however, that among those who were blackmailed, homosexuals were overrepresented. Asserting that social stigma and the current law were both at fault, the report conceded that at the very least the law expanded the blackmailer's opportunities. The committee also publicized the shocking fact that victims who went to the police were sometimes charged with crimes themselves. It gave the example of A, who had had a long affair with B. When A complained to the police of B's blackmail threat both A and B were charged with buggery and sentenced to nine months in jail.[13]

Despite the public's generally sympathetic response to the report, the Conservative government was not prepared to respond positively to the Wolfenden Committee's recommendations. Another decade of campaigning was required to bring about the partial decriminalization of homosexuality. Blackmail stories figured centrally in the arguments of those calling for reform of the law. First came those who had been victimized by the existing statutes. Wildeblood's trial and incarceration led him to write *Against the Law* (1955), which began with the famous line "I am a homosexual." The first English writer to declare that he was not ashamed of being a homosexual proceeded to provide an eloquent argument in favor of tolerance and legal reform. Wildeblood presented himself as a victim of a witch-hunt, "a political manoeuvre, designed to allay American fears that people susceptible to blackmail were occupying high positions in Britain."[14] The blackmail theme was picked up by Rupert Croft-Cooke, arrested in 1953 after a young male friend informed on him. Croft-Cooke described in his poignant account of his life in prison, *The Verdict of You All* (1955), the blackmailers he had met. All six had preyed on homosexuals, some by impersonating police officers and others by threatening to inform the authorities. As one of his informants explained, a homosexual could be blackmailed whereas a thief (or "screwsman") could not.

It's the sort of man. You can't put the blacks on a screwsman even if you knew the lot. He wouldn't stand for it. But a "queer" can't do anything else. He's usually got a position to keep up, for one thing. There's his family for another. Besides, the information's easier to get. See, if you knew about a screwsman it could only be from someone who had had a tickle [helped in a theft] with him. He'd be done, too, if the Law got to know. But with "queers" it's usually a young one with an older one and the young one knows the police will only be too glad to protect him. He may put the blacks on himself or he may give his information for a share in the profs., but anyway, he's safe. I tell you, "queers" ask for it.[15]

228

Croft-Cooke, like Wildeblood, appealed to the British middle classes' latent anti-Americanism. If the law were not reformed, he warned, McCarthyite witch-hunts, with their prudery and hypocrisy, would proceed in Britain. His dire prediction was that "since blackmailers continue to enjoy their charter and quiet and useful lives are perpetually threatened, England will return to a Cromwellian state and this beastly form of McCarthyism will make life impossible for anyone who does not actively support it."[16]

The press was naturally attracted to blackmail stories. Most papers would say little about homosexuality, but they did report on blackmail cases. The tabloids were only too ready to play up sensational stories about the "vice" of members of the decadent, effeminate upper classes, such as homosexual spies Guy Burgess and Donald MacLean, whose activities had been revealed in 1951. In 1952 the *Daily Mirror* ran a series on such "evil men." In 1956 the *Sunday People* produced a similar series of stories on the way in which blackmail had been purportedly employed by Burgess to worm out secrets from upper-class degenerates. In 1955 a retired police detective provided the *Empire News* with an account in several installments of the career of Harry Raymond, whose last bout of blackmailing wealthy homosexuals had only ended in 1948.[17]

The quality press lamented such disclosures and the fact that the wrong sorts of people—that is, wealthy people—were being charged as homosexuals and victimized by blackmailers. In 1959 the *Times* carried only three reports of blackmail trials. In every one the victim was a homosexual. In January a story headlined "£8,800 By 'Slow Torture'" informed the public that a retired army captain had paid off a twenty-six-year-old Trinidadian over two and a half years because of a single incident in which they had "behaved improperly together." Painting a picture of a pathetic victim who had been reduced to fearing every mail delivery, every phone call, every turn on a street corner, the irate judge sentenced the accused to a seven-year prison term. In August the same paper provided an account of how a servant had blackmailed his ex-employer, a middle aged clergyman, out of £1,500 over the course of three years. Of the fifty-six badgering letters the accused had sent, one clearly demonstrated that he felt that he had less to fear from the police than the victim: "I should like to see you in court as a homosexual or as Mr. X . . . I have nothing to lose so make it worth my while."[18]

The most brazen example of such extortion emerged from the trial of Joseph Coleman, who forty years earlier had been the batman, or servant, of a young officer. Coleman, who claimed to have been "corrupted" by the officer, successfully made demands for money from 1922 to 1929 and then again from 1953 to 1958. "I can get the quite magnificent sum of £1,500 from a sensational section of the Press by supplying your name," wrote Coleman in his final letter. "In either case they get the scoop and I get the money. You can please yourself. Accept this as a threat if you will." The court heard that the accused had spent twenty-two of the past forty-two years in prison whereas Mr. X, the victim, was a peer of the realm. Not surprisingly, the judge sympathized wholeheartedly with the latter. "Things happen in most men's lives which are mercifully covered up by the years, and the law does not allow the past to be dug up, or the skeletons and bones of past misdeeds rattled in front of a man in order to frighten him into paying up."[19]

Such trials provided damning evidence that the law against homosexuality was indeed a "blackmailer's charter." While there is no hard evidence that a conservative newspaper such as the *Times* consciously set out to use blackmail trials as a way of supporting calls for the decriminalization of homosexuality, merely reporting how a black man, a servant, and an ex-convict had used the threat of the law to extort money from a clergyman, a retired army officer, and a lord dramatically demonstrated to the propertied the need for reform. In so doing the *Times* added its considerable weight to the Wolfenden Committee's recommendations. So too did the leading London weeklies. In the *Spectator* Desmond Donnelly, MP, described the existing law in the title of his article, "The Blackmailer's Charter." In the *New Statesman* C. H. Rolph declared that "the present law can be effectively operated only by the blackmailer."[20]

By the late 1950s most medical experts declared themselves on the side of reform. In 1958 François Lafitte (son of Havelock Ellis's partner) argued that the law led to blackmail. Eustace Chesser, in *Odd Man Out: Homosexuality in Men and Women* (1959), went further and asserted that a liberalizing of mores would deglamorize homosexuality and reduce its number to a "hard core." Present laws, which forced homosexual men (unlike lesbians) to "live in dread of discovery and possible imprisonment or blackmail," prevented them from returning to the "mainstream." Psychiatrist Clifford Allen made the astounding claim that homosexuals were "often" driven to murder their blackmailers. "It must not be thought that all homosexuals are weaklings or spineless, flabby creatures. Some are determined, strong-willed men—I have met fighter pilots who admitted to homosexuality but who had performed acts of calculated bravery. It is little wonder that when a blackmailer meets a man of this type he is ruthlessly exterminated and a large number of unexplained murders must be of this kind, since the motive is often concealed, and difficult to detect." Doctors and psychoanalysts produced accounts that could easily be interpreted as self-serving. They presented homosexuality as a potentially curable "disorder" that the existing repressive laws only aggravated. Medical experts claimed that they could deal with an issue that had frustrated the best efforts of lawmen.[21]

Law reform was also pushed by artists and academics. Novelist Angus Wilson—a blackmail victim himself in the early 1950s when deputy superintendent of the British Museum's Reading Room—joined the executive of the Homosexual Law Reform Society in 1958. But many were naturally reluctant to go public. Only a small coterie knew of the sexual orientation of Somerset Maugham, England's best-known novelist. Indeed in 1966 *Time* magazine was so much in the dark that it cited him as a great writer who could be taken as an authority on the artistic limitations of homosexuals. E. M. Forster was also cautious. Even Antony Grey, the secretary of the Homosexual Law Reform Society, who so much appreciated Forster's support, was unaware that Forster was gay. *Maurice,* Forster's classic homosexual novel, which referred in passing to blackmail, was only published after his death in 1970.[22]

A number of writers disguised their defense of homosexuality. Somerset Maugham's nephew Robin Maugham based *The Servant* (1948) on his own experience with his butler, who brought a boy back to the flat and offered him to Maugham. "At that moment," Maugham later recalled, "I saw the portals of blackmail and the gates of prison yawning open before my gaze. I pretended I hadn't heard."[23] In his novella Maugham changed the sex of the bait. "He" became "she": a girl who reveals that she is underage. A homosexual blackmail scenario was thus presented in a heterosexual guise.

Similar discretion was demonstrated by Terrance Rattigan. His play *Table Number Seven* (1954) was inspired by John Gielgud's 1953 arrest, but Rattigan, though he referred to blackmail, made the persecuted character a   231 heterosexual, a retired major bound over for an offense against a woman in a cinema. When attempts are made to have the major ejected from his hotel a younger male guest comes to his defense with a moving speech: "The Major presumably understands my form of lovemaking. I *should* therefore understand his. But I don't. So I am plainly in a state of prejudice against him, and must be very wary of any moral judgment I may pass in this matter."[24] Rattigan no doubt hoped that the playgoers who applauded such generous sentiments would be led to sympathize if only unconsciously with the sexual minority to which Rattigan belonged.

In his novel *Thin Ice* (1956) Compton Mackenzie provided a sympathetic fictional account of how a brilliant politician's homosexuality made him susceptible to blackmail. The story is told in the first person by a stuffy heterosexual who discovers how the threat of public revelation blights the careers of some public servants and drives others to suicide. A few scenes in the book were clearly based on the life of Labour MP Tom Driberg. Readers were made to sympathize with the main character and the narrator's fight to rescue his old friend from the ruthless youths seeking to "rent" him. The novel was well received, its fans including a number of homosexuals who wrote to Mackenzie to say that he had presented a fair view of their world.[25]

In addition to Rattigan's work the theater produced a number of plays that exploited the blackmail theme. Kenneth Halliwell, who was to become Joe Orton's partner, wrote an unpublished play entitled *The Protagonist* (1949) in which the actor Edmund Kean, when faced with a sexual blackmail threat, "comes out." Noël Coward, England's best known living playwright, was carefully closeted for most of his life. In 1955 he confided to his diary his distaste for the laws that continued to criminalize homosexuality in England. Not until the 1960s did he finally write a play about homosexual blackmail. *A Song at Twilight,* first performed in 1966, involves a famous playwright who is blackmailed by a woman who has in her possession his letters to his dead male lover. Coward was still cautious; he insisted that the main character was based not on his own life but on that of Somerset Maugham. John Osborne, one of England's "Angry Young Men," used the blackmail theme several times. In *Inadmissible Evidence* (1964) he had a character who was arrested for importuning and then blackmailed by a bobby into providing sexual favors. Osborne based *A Patriot for Me* (1965) on the famous Colonel Alfred Redl affair, which involved a homosexual officer in the pre–World War I Austrian army. The first time Redl goes to bed with a private he is attacked and robbed by the private's accomplices. Osborne presents the private as shocked by Redl's indignation at being blackmailed: "Don't be too upset, love. You'll get used to it." All these plays presented their audience, both homosexual and heterosexual, with the question of whether or not they should continue in the mid-twentieth century to maintain laws that allowed blackmailers to use the knowledge of a man's past to victimize him.[26]

It says something about English society's preoccupation with homosexuality at the time that in the early 1960s a number of films focused on the issue. *Oscar Wilde* (1959) was a maudlin account of the fall of a literary master. *The Trials of Oscar Wilde* (1960), starring Peter Finch, cautiously noted the blackmail theme but timidly attempted to present Wilde as strangely fascinated by, rather than sexually attracted to, Lord Alfred Douglas. A far more important film was *Victim* (1961), in which Dirk Bogarde courageously risked his reputation as a "star" leading man by playing the role of a homosexual barrister victimized by blackmailers. This Basil Dearden film, later criticized for being too cautious, was both a plea for law reform and an account of the supposed special nature of gays. Bogarde's character was portrayed as a "victim" of both blackmailers and his own passions. The film had a clear heterosexual bias in that it ended with Bogarde tempted but still married and the real villain proving to be a spinster whose failure to have a normal sex life underlay her hatred of homosexuals. The film thus captured the tenor of the times; the moral was that gays need to be pitied, not persecuted. As the *Times* reviewer put it, the film invited a "compassionate consideration of this peculiar form of human bondage." But if homosexual men were represented for the most part as being fearful and passive, it has to be remembered that this was the first film in which they began to be heard. At the very least the gay community was portrayed and so normalized to a degree. In addition, the fact that matinee idol Dirk Bogarde took the leading role (the public did not then know that he himself was homosexual) undermined the old notion that "one can always tell." And the filmmaker's belief in the need for decriminalization was driven home by a policeman ponderously informing a colleague that homosexuals were the victims in 90 percent of blackmail cases, crimes made possible by an antiquated law. The reviews made clear how successful this "problem film" was in winning the sympathy of middlebrow audiences to the notion that evil blackmailers posed a far more serious threat than harassed homosexuals.[27]   233

While playwrights and filmmakers were familiarizing the public with the plight of the homosexual, English academics were producing the first sex surveys that demonstrated that attempts at curing and/or punishing homosexuals did not work. The stigmatization of homosexuality, asserted Michael Schofield (who wrote under the name Gordon Westwood), led to an epidemic of antisocial acts including lying, promiscuity, alcoholism, suicide, police corruption, and blackmail. Schofield's was the first Kinsey-style survey of British homosexual men. In his sample of 127 informants, 13 percent said they had been blackmailed. Of those asked what they would do if they were blackmailed, less than a quarter (31) said they would go to police, 10 said they would assault the extortionist, 7 said they would commit suicide, and 7 would pay up. Schofield, like Kinsey in the United States, concluded that the "containment" of homosexuality could be best accomplished by dismantling the laws that isolated it.[28] Increasing numbers of medical and legal experts in the 1960s argued that to take into account changing realities, to protect health, and to prevent the law from falling into disrepute it had to be reformed in areas pertaining to prostitution, abortion, and contraception. The same argument was employed for those insisting on the decriminalization of homosexuality.

Reformers still faced challenges in the long march toward decriminalization. Toward the end of World War I a Conservative MP had made the astounding claim that the Germans were trying to incite homosexuality in England as "fear and exposure entraps and makes slaves of men whom money could not buy." In the 1950s the traitorous behavior of Burgess and MacLean had renewed the notion that homosexuals posed security risks, and the claim resurfaced in 1962 with the arrest of John Vassall. An Admiralty clerk assigned to naval intelligence in Moscow, Vassall had provided photographs of naval weaponry to the Soviets. In his defense he tried to present himself as a martyred homosexual whom the Russians had caught in a compromising position and then blackmailed. The extent to which the climate had changed since the 1950s was demonstrated when Labour MP Neil MacDermott turned the event to the purposes of the reform campaign: "It is not that homosexuals are more likely to be traitors," declared

MacDermott. "The point is that homosexuals in this country are peculiarly vulnerable to blackmail . . . It seems to me that we are paying the price as a country for our attitude to homosexuality." Others argued that homosexuality had nothing to do with it; they believed Vassal had been motivated simply by greed and desperately hoped the current discussions of homosexual blackmail might offer him some cover.[29]

In March 1963 the Profumo scandal erupted, which revealed that a Conservative cabinet minister was sharing the favors of a London call girl with a Soviet diplomat. Despite the fact that this was a heterosexual affair the official inquiry raised once again the specter of homosexual extortion. Lord Denning concluded that immorality only posed a security risk if it "might expose the person concerned to blackmail or to undue pressures which might lead him to give away secret information. For instance, I would normally regard homosexual behaviour, or perverted practices with a prostitute as creating a security risk."[30] Denning's attempt to shift the focus towards gays demonstrated the extent to which homosexuality and blackmail were still linked in the public mind.

The victory of the Labour Party in 1964 led the police to reduce the number of arrests of homosexuals, especially in cases that came to light as the result of blackmail. John Wolfenden had finally achieved his goal of relieving "from the threat of prosecution the victim of blackmail who revealed homosexual behavior." In Parliament reformers played up the idea of blackmail and the poor wretches who needed protection. "Blackmail," notes one historian, "was the key used by the reformers to enlist the sympathy of their colleagues." Careful lobbying of politicians had been carried out from 1958 on by the Homosexual Law Reform Society led by Antony Grey. The society's propaganda included illustrations showing a door marked "Blackmailers Welcome," pointing out that the law made some men "fair game for blackmailers." Lord Arran pushed the decriminalization bill in the House of Lords. Leo Abse did the same in the Commons, arguing that homosexuality would decline as a result of reform.[31] Fear of blackmail clearly helped lead public opinion to support decriminalization. The Labour Party achieved a comfortable majority in 1966 and passed the Sexual Offenses Act (1967), which put into place the reforms called for by Wolfenden a decade earlier. As a way of making amends for his ancestor's persecution of Oscar Wilde, the Marquis of Queensbury gave the bill his full support.

234

As explained in this Homosexual Law Reform Society flyer, a key argument of the English law reformers who supported the Wolfenden Committee's recommendations was that the laws against homosexuality inevitably resulted in blackmail. (By permission of Antony Grey.)

The goal of the British legislation was improved social management and discipline, not sexual liberation. Criminalizing consenting forms of adult sexual behavior had kept up the pretense of moral protection but incurred the heavy costs of police corruption and blackmail.[32] Many in positions of authority now recognized that the old methods of repression had been counterproductive. The partial decriminalization of homosexuality between consenting adults in private was regarded by most public commentators as a revolution; in fact it was only a modest step. The act did not cover Scotland or Northern Ireland, members of the armed forces, or the merchant marine. The age of consent for males was set at twenty-one whereas for females it was sixteen.

The Gay Liberation Front, which emerged in Britain in 1970, was angered by the limited nature of the 1967 reforms. A 1969 Dutch report showed that young men had no need for special protection; nevertheless in England arrests for gross indecency with males between sixteen and twenty-one actually increased after 1967, and pandering and public indecency continued to be prosecuted. Young scholars later disparaged the Wolfenden Committee's report as simply an attempt to employ more sophisticated means to repress homosexuality. Homosexual men, such as Antony Grey, who had participated in the Committee's work insisted that the courage of those who fought for even half-measures should be recognized.[33] The disappointment felt by radicals was due in part to their not understanding that it was antisocial behavior, and in particular blackmail, that Parliament really wanted to end, not the stigma from which homosexuals suffered. Homosexuals and their friends succeeded to an extent in employing blackmail stories to advance the cause of reform, but the same stories continued as always to play a central role in moralists' cautionary tales portraying the bleak existence of the homosexual.

In the 1960s England's leading poet (W. H. Auden), composer (Benjamin Britten), choreographer (Frederick Ashton), and painter (Francis Bacon) were all known to be gay, but the press still viewed homosexuality with distaste. In reforming the law Parliament gave only grudging acceptance to gays' right to privacy and accordingly warned them not to "flaunt" themselves. The Wolfenden reforms were aimed at ending blackmail and public scandal, not intolerance. A contributor to the *Evening Standard* was quite explicit on this score: "Of course, a desire to end the blackmail racket implies no kind of approval for the homosexuality the

blackmailer preys upon." Much of the stigma of homosexuality remained.
Much of the public continued to assume that only homosexuals could
blackmail other homosexuals and therefore all were to be regarded with   237
suspicion. Even Ian Harvey, a junior minister in Harold Macmillan's Conservative government who was forced to resign in 1958 after being arrested
with a guardsman in St. James' Park, took this view. He wrote of the
Wolfenden Committee's work: "A highly satisfactory result of the new legislation has been the removal of blackmail, as an instrument in the hands
of homosexual prostitutes. Blackmail is rightly regarded as one of the most
evil of all crimes. Used by the homosexual it undoubtedly increased his activities and lowered his moral character, such as it was. It also increased homosexual practices in general because men who were not normally addicted to any extent found it a lucrative pursuit." Here, Harvey was
returning to the central notion of many of the reformers that the old law
made blackmail possible and blackmail in turn actually increased homosexuality.[34]

Did the decriminalization of homosexuality lead to a decline in blackmail as the reformers promised? According to one homophobic observer,
retired police officer Robert Fabian, it did not. "The pervert usually hasn't
the guts to achieve a successful career; he is often short of money," wrote
Fabian; such a man would turn to blackmail knowing—even after the law
reforms—how threatening exposure remained. Fabian wrote with the obvious purpose of frightening men away from giving in to the "cancer" of
same-sex attraction. Once dragged into a life of degradation the final consequences were, he claimed with obvious satisfaction, inevitably horrific.
"Be under no delusions: it is the pervert, the sadist, the dabbler in fetishes,
who finds his habits taking control of his actions. He is the kind of man
who one day suddenly discovers himself in an alley, or in a country ditch or
rain swept wood, with the throat of a dead child between his hands." Less
bloodcurdling accounts reporting a drop in homosexual blackmail gave
some comfort to reformers. Whereas Schofield in 1960 had found that 13
percent of his sample had been victims of blackmail, studies carried out in
the 1980s show a marked decline in such activity.[35]

The law on homosexuality in England was reformed for a variety of reasons, not simply because of the fear of blackmail. Indeed a recent chroni-

cler of the work of the Wolfenden Committee, while noting its many references to homosexual blackmail, dismisses their importance. His view is that the reality of extortion "will always remain hidden from the historian however ingeniously he tries to expose it."[36] The point, however, is that the actual extent of blackmail was never the key issue. It was the importance of blackmail stories, as propounded in newspaper and court reports, in novels, plays, films, and academic treatises, that played a key role in the 1950s and 1960s in convincing both the English public and their politicians of the need for homosexual law reform.

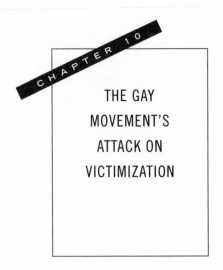

CHAPTER 10

THE GAY
MOVEMENT'S
ATTACK ON
VICTIMIZATION

"I have been sentencing people for twenty-seven years and it has been a long time since I have come upon a case that was so revolting as your case. I think you are so steeped in filth that as I read the report I cringed, and my flesh crept as I read the depth of iniquity to which you have allowed yourself to sink."[1] With these words Judge Irving Ben Cooper sentenced the first of the accused in an enormous homosexual blackmail ring, which in 1966 forced itself on the American public's attention. This and subsequent trials, coming as they did at the very time that the British Parliament was finally carrying out the Wolfenden Committee's recommendation for the decriminalization of homosexuality, played a key role in demonstrating to North Americans how laws aimed at victimless crimes armed blackmailers.

On February 18, 1966, the *New York Times* reported that nine extortionists had been arrested and eight others were being sought. Frank S. Hogan, the New York City District Attorney heading the investigation, stated that the gang, employing "chickens" (including college students) and fake police officers (ex-convicts and at least one retired policeman), had been active since 1961 and operated nationwide. In one instance, for example, gang members entrapped and beat up a New York businessman in Chicago and then had fake police officers shake him down in New York City.[2] Because conspiring to use interstate facilities to extort money was a federal crime, the FBI had been actively involved in the case.

Three gang leaders—Sherman Kaminsky of Baltimore, Maryland, John Fellenbaum of Monroeville, Pennsylvania, and Elwood Lee Hammock of

Durham, North Carolina—were indicted in June 1966. They had primarily worked in New York City, patrolling conventions and looking for victims. The court heard that Fellenbaum, a twenty-seven-year-old weight lifter, would pick up likely candidates at bars or hotel lobbies and return to their hotel rooms for sex. There he would beat and rob the victim of his credit cards and ID. Fellenbaum would then send the stolen identification to Hammock and Kaminsky. Posing as policemen, they would begin the shakedown by telling the victim that they would have to summon him to testify at the trial of the male prostitute whom they had recently arrested. The panicked prey would offer hush money, which they would reluctantly agree to accept. For his part in the operation Fellenbaum was in August 1966 sentenced to five years in prison and a $10,000 fine.[3]

John J. Pyne, a retired Chicago policeman, was identified as a ringleader of the gang. At his home the FBI found police badges, identification papers for almost every state, arrest warrants, and extradition forms. Indicted in Chicago and New York, Pyne in July 1966 forfeited $50,000 bail but was convicted in Chicago in December 1967 of conspiring with Fellenbaum to extort over $2 million from thirty or more victims, including a congressman, a general, an admiral, and a British film producer.[4]

At the 1967 trial in which Christopher Hughes was sentenced to five years for conspiracy to blackmail, the press reported that the gang was by then known to have included up to seventy members. The assistant district attorney stated that over a two-year period at least 700 victims had been preyed on in New York, Illinois, and Pennsylvania. Forty-five members of the gang had either pleaded guilty or been convicted. The courts tried to protect the identity of the victims. Judge Cooper castigated Hughes as "doubly vicious" for having first robbed his victims and then insisting on his full constitutional rights, including the cross-examination of witnesses. Hughes, said the judge, "demanded that we [the court] parade [the victim] in here with all the embarrassment that would entail [for the victim] for the rest of his life, perhaps." At Hughes's retrial (he successfully appealed his conviction on the grounds that the judge's statement was prejudicial), the court heard a detailed account of how the scam worked. In November 1965 Hughes, playing the role of "chicken," had picked up in the Taft Hotel in New York City Charles Schwarz (a pseudonym), the director of a North Carolina state-sponsored antipoverty program and a married man, the father of four children. Hughes returned with Schwarz to his hotel room at the Hilton, where Hughes beat and robbed him. He passed on Schwarz's wallet and identification—the "poke"—to Thomas S. Rochford and Sherman Kaminsky. They called Hammock about shaking down the victim in Schwarz's hometown of Durham, North Carolina. Hammock excitedly reported back that Schwarz looked "like he might be a $10,000 man. He is certainly worth playing for." On a New York City municipal printed form Kaminsky, Hammock, and Rochford made up a phony warrant for Schwarz's arrest for "oral copulation" and a "confession" signed by Hughes linking him to Schwarz. Not knowing that he was out of the country, the three sought to track down Schwarz in Durham. Then, moving on to Florida, where they were attempting another sting operation, their suitcase full of badges and phony warrants fell into the hands of the police, who promptly arrested them. Under grilling, Hammock turned state's evidence. Rochford cooperated with the FBI and received a two-year sentence. Hughes was given a five-year sentence, which was confirmed on appeal. Kaminsky pleaded guilty to sixty-four counts of extortion, but fled New York City to avoid a two-year prison sentence. Eleven years later the FBI arrested him in Seattle.[5]

The FBI employed the Travel Act—a federal antiracketeering law passed to fight organized crime—against a number of the gang members. The Hughes case, for example, was based on the argument that a threat made in North Carolina to reveal sodomy carried out in New York involved interstate commerce. In another case the defendants were indicted for shakedowns of victims in New Jersey, Illinois, and Pennsylvania. They appealed on the grounds that they had been charged in Pennsylvania for "blackmail," but the Travel Act only specified "extortion." A Pennsylvania district court agreed to dismiss the indictments, but the United States Supreme Court led by Chief Justice Earl Warren unanimously confirmed the original judgment.[6]

Fortuitous discoveries, as the suitcase in the Hughes case, were crucial to the police's discovery of the gang's activity. Few of the victims had complained to the authorities, in part because some did not even know they were dealing with criminals. Although the press did not pursue the embarrassing implications, the fact that many victims assumed that they were simply being subjected to a routine police shakedown was in itself a damning indictment of the law. In England it was accepted that laws against homosexuality armed blackmailers. A similar conclusion was beginning to be drawn in the United States. Many were shocked to read that a blackmail ring had extorted millions of dollars from more than a thousand victims. Furthermore, the victims were not lowlife deviants. They included two deans of eastern universities, an assistant principal, professors, army officers, theatrical personalities, TV stars, jazz musicians, actors, and art gallery owners. Two gang members posing as police officers had actually walked into the Pentagon and "arrested" a high-ranking army officer. The night before he was scheduled to testify before a grand jury he committed suicide. A successful businessman who refused to pay lost his wife and family when the gang told her of his activities. A wealthy teacher from the Midwest was milked out of $120,000 over four years.[7] Reading that the lives of successful and productive members of society had been blighted while criminals—though occasionally inconvenienced by being arrested and sent to jail—could always return to their lucrative activities, many came to appreciate the need for law reform.

The 1966 and 1967 trials were both a cause and an effect of a change in the social and sexual climate. The fact that the FBI, which in the 1950s was tracking down homosexuals, was in the late 1960s targeting the blackmailers of homosexuals was perhaps the best evidence of the enormous cultural shift that was occurring in America in the late 1960s. A decade earlier the FBI had assumed that the purported danger homosexuals posed in being susceptible to blackmail meant that one of the agency's key roles should be to track down and eliminate them from government service. Peter Wildeblood and Rupert Croft-Cooke had attributed the crackdown on homosexuals in England to an aping by the British government of the McCarthyism that swept the United States in the 1950s. The notion of homosexuals posing a threat to the United States' national security had first been trotted out by the anxious as an explanation for the "loss" of China in the 1950s.

For many American homosexuals who enlisted, World War II had led to a welcomed relaxation of moral restraints. Eventually, however, the screening process tightened, and by the war's end thousands had been given a "blue discharge"—that is, discharged without honor. Between 1947 and 1950 the American military discharged a further four thousand recruits. In the civil service the government long downplayed the issue of homosexuals. Even when their systematic exclusion began in the mid-1940s, they were not then scapegoated as politically dangerous. Anticommunism was

rife, but it was only wedded to homophobia when Senator Joseph McCarthy turned on the civil service and led the Republicans in accusing President Harry Truman of sheltering "perverts." In 1950 the Senate authorized   243
the formal investigation of those whose "degraded" and "immoral" activities made them "unreliable." "The pervert," McCarthy's committee asserted, "is an easy prey to the blackmailer." The public accepted what seemed to be a commonsense claim, but to back it up the committee could do no better than cite the case of Colonel Redl, the World War I Austrian traitor. It was also conveniently overlooked that Guy Burgess and Donald MacLean, the famous British secret agents who delivered secrets to the Russians, had been moved by their political loyalties, not by a fear of having their homosexuality revealed.[8]

In 1953 a presidential executive order made male homosexuality an absolute bar to security clearance. The Department of Defense stated that not only were homosexuals emotional and unreliable; their susceptibility to blackmail also made them security risks. The premise was that they posed a danger of both seducing others and being blackmailed. The FBI concurred, though like the defense department it offered no hard evidence to support such a contention. Interestingly, the best-known account of such a blackmail attempt showed that it did not work. While on a 1957 trip to the USSR, American journalist Kenneth Alsop was approached by a young man. KGB agents photographed them in bed together and later tried to force Alsop into providing information. He refused and followed the ambassador's advice to inform the CIA, who passed on the information to the FBI.

Despite the lack of evidence that homosexuals were security risks, under the Eisenhower administration more than sixty suspect civil servants were fired each month. Congressman Wilbur Mills claimed that the Russians were training gay agents, while the tabloids played up the notion of a dangerous homosexual colony in Washington, D.C., and the immense security risks it posed. Both major political parties agreed on the threat posed by subversives and the need for surveillance; both regarded homosexuals as sexually and politically unreliable. The film *The Manchurian Candidate* (1962) owed its enormous popularity to exploiting the chilling idea of the communists' ability to employ "brainwashing" to infiltrate the country with sexual and political saboteurs. Laurence Harvey played the role of a man first victimized by his smothering mother and then by the communists. Blackmail stories provided the homophobic with one more reason why homosexuals could not be trusted.[9]

244   A few voices were raised in protest. Max Lerner, a Brandeis University political science professor and *New York Post* columnist, derisively noted in July 1950 that he could not find "one verified case of a government worker having been blackmailed by a foreign agent because of his sexual orientation." Claiming that homosexuals were blackmailable, psychotherapist Benjamin Karpman observed, could become a self-fulfilling prophecy.

> The crux of the argument [that homosexuals posed security risks] revolves around the "particular susceptibility of homosexuals to blackmail." The proponents of this argument do not seem to realize that they are placing a premium on blackmail—the most despicable of activities—and are deliberately inviting every unscrupulous policeman (and there are many such, I understand) and every vindictive and sadistic individual with a grudge, to engage in the very activity they are claiming as the basis of their discrimination against homosexuality. The easiest way to prevent the blackmailing of homosexuals is to recognize homosexuality as a fact and to remove the unreasonable laws which discriminate against it—laws which have created far more mischief than they started out to eradicate.

Karpman went on to assert that the notion of communism and homosexuality being necessarily related made no psychological sense. "The silly shallow homosexual is not interested in politics; the serious intelligent homosexual, if interested in politics, is more likely to be conservative to compensate for his sexual unconventionality. The linking of communism with homosexuality is absurd."[10]

Not surprisingly the nascent homosexual rights movement took a similar line. The April 1958 issue of *One Magazine* quoted Gerald Albritten, who had been recently forced out of the State Department. "If some homos are sensitive to blackmail," he said, "it's society that forces them into secrecy. The best foreign service men are single, and usually gay. The man who puts his family first is the real security risk." Few knew of such underground publications, however, while millions read Allen Drury's novel *Advise and Consent* (1959), which enjoyed an enormous success, remaining ninety-three weeks on the *New York Times*'s best-seller list and winning its author the Pulitzer Prize. The film version appeared in 1962. Apparently based on Franklin Delano Roosevelt's desire to have Sumner Welles as his secretary of state, the book has as one of its key story lines the account of a crusading young senator who, because of a brief homosexual affair, is blackmailed by those who want to control his vote. Seeing no way out, he commits suicide. For many the cautionary tale with the mandatory suicide of the gay protagonist underlined the danger of giving way to homosexual temptation; for a homosexual publication like the *Mattachine Review*— which both advertised and praised the novel—the book demonstrated the need for law reform that would do away with blackmail.[11] The story easily lent itself to a variety of interpretations.

By 1958 the McCarthyite witch-hunt was over, but government hostility towards homosexuals remained constant. In the army, when asked at their preinduction physical examination if they had "homosexual tendencies," some men felt "boxed in." To answer truthfully meant disqualification; to lie meant committing a federal crime. A 1962 study noted that many homosexuals were turned in by their chaplain. The army not only discharged them; it also often notified the local police. The military and civil service purge of "security risks" coincided with police crackdowns in major American cities. Even outside Washington the danger of homosexual blackmail was clear. Sodomy in private between consenting adults was still a crime in most states, though it was rare to prosecute heterosexual anal intercourse unless it involved rape. Sodomy was moreover a designated offense against which police were allowed—until the 1980s—to use wiretaps.[12] If a case went to trial the homosexual person's past was dug up, and judges frequently allowed the discrediting of witnesses. Once convicted, homosexuals became "marked men" in fear of both police and blackmailers.

In the 1950s homosexual blackmail and shakedowns were largely ignored in the respectable U.S. press, but gay publications constantly referred to their existence and used such accounts as evidence of the need for law reform. In November 1955 *One Magazine* noted the shakedowns carried out by phony cops in a Kansas City rest room. In a January 1956 open letter to the Senate Subcommittee on Constitutional Rights the magazine's editor protested the various forms of shakedowns to which homosexuals were subjected. In the following month the magazine reported extortion practices in Indiana and New York. In its June–July issue it cited the Church of England's submission to the Wolfenden Committee, which stated that bad laws led to blackmail. In July 1956 the *Mattachine Review* reported that a Honolulu vice squad policeman was involved in shakedowns. It too hailed the Wolfenden Committee's report and noted the attention the committee had paid to the blackmail issue. In April 1958 *One Magazine* referred to shakedowns in Miami and Cleveland. In the latter city the crime only came to public attention because the extortionist made the mistake of attempting to victimize a policeman. In July 1959 the magazine reported that the Chicago police had gunned down "Uncle Harry" Fiegel, "the head of a ring of fifteen to twenty youths who extorted as high as $1,000 a day from homosexuals." In November 1959 the magazine reported that a San Diego man had been blackmailed by two marines. When he went to the police, the district attorney had the victim arrested. "A defense by *ONE*'s attorney, Eric Jubler, and testimony by a Catholic priest whom the same marines had tried to blackmail, won the victim's acquittal. The opposite result seems more common—often making heroes of hustlers who murder homosexuals."[13]

In August 1959 *One Magazine* spelled out in detail what was now a common concern:

> For many homosexuals, even those who have refrained from overt, illegal acts, what-to-do-when-the-blackmailer-comes poses quite a problem. There's little point in paying, since like postmen, blackmailers always ring at least twice. They'll bleed you for years, and probably expose you eventually anyhow. Still it takes guts for a homosexual to go to the cops, who often turn on him instead of helping him. Many police do the right thing—they are sworn to defend victims against blackmail. But *often* the victim gets locked up and the blackmailer goes free . . . You take a calculated risk however you handle it. You might take a worse drubbing from the cops (some of whom believe gays have no rights) than from [the] blackmailer, but going to them is [the] only course that makes sense, and until homosexuals are willing to take risks to defend their rights and security they'll have neither rights nor security.

The *Mattachine Review* took the same line. A 1960 article entitled "Never Pay Blackmailers" cited a talk given by Donal E. L. MacNamara, dean of the New York Institute of Criminology, who stressed the need to report threats to the police. The following year the magazine reprinted a glowing account of the film *Victim* starring Dirk Bogarde. The Production Code Administration refused the film a seal of approval, and *Time* magazine's review of the film protested that what began as an attack on blackmail ended up as a defense of homosexuality, a "sick-silly self-delusion." Most other reviewers were far more positive, and almost all echoed the film script's assertion that 90 percent of Britain's blackmail stemmed from the law on homosexuality. The American gay press took the line that in Europe the police now defended the homosexual while in America they were more likely to entrap him.[14]

247

At the very time that the government was beginning to claim that homosexuals posed a security threat, Alfred C. Kinsey was reporting in *Sexual*

While they reported many shakedowns carried out by police officers, American homosexual publications like the *Mattachine Review* nevertheless called on homosexuals to face down blackmailers and report all attempts to the authorities. (By permission of the Institute for the Study of Human Resources.)

Behavior in the Human Male (1948) that a large percentage of male population had had homosexual experiences. Kinsey asked his male subjects if
248   they had by any means ever climaxed with another male. Thirty-seven percent stated that they had. Kinsey, though initially surprised, concluded that
this was probably an underestimation. He was not asserting that over a
third of the population was "homosexual"; what he advanced was the notion of a sexual continuum along a scale, from 0 for the individual who
never had a homosexual experience (about 50 percent of the male population) to 6 for men who throughout their whole life had only had same-sex
relationships (about 4 percent). The remaining 45 percent had experienced
both forms of sexual release at least once in their lives. Many of America's
best-adjusted men—if their sex lives were revealed—would, Kinsey declared, be categorized under existing laws, moral codes, and psychiatric
teachings as perverts. To those alarmed by such news, he offered one faint
ray of hope. If society ceased to ostracize and persecute the sexually experi-
mental, the number driven to homosexuality exclusively might be lessened.
At the moment America's restrictive moral code, in labeling some men as
deviant, limited them to "perverse" forms of behavior. Some found
Kinsey's findings enlightening and liberating; for others they raised the
frightening prospect of America being engulfed by deviants.[15]

Fears of homosexuality underlay Americans' postwar panic over sexual
psychopaths. In 1955 the national press raised the alarm that a ring of gay
men was preying on the high school boys of Boise, Idaho. Only years later
did it come out that a number of the youths involved were juvenile delin-
quents who prostituted themselves and then blackmailed their clients. The
specter of perverts was played up by J. Edgar Hoover, head of the FBI. Between 1947 and 1955 twenty-one states passed laws targeting "deviants,"
the purported purpose being to better protect women and children. A
sense of this mind-set was provided by J. Paul de River in his book *The Sexual Criminal: A Psychoanalytic Study* (1949). In the introduction Eugene D.
Williams, a former Los Angeles district attorney, noted that sex perversions
could be likened to "pimples" that revealed the illness of the community.
Some might regard the "queer individual" as innocuous, but he was not.
"All too often we lose sight of the fact that the homosexual is an inveterate
seducer of the young of both sexes, and that he presents a social problem
because he is not content with being degenerate himself; he must have degenerate companions, and is ever seeking for younger victims." De River,

who created the Sex Offense Bureau of Los Angeles, then proceeded to enumerate (and illustrate with horrific photographs) the rapes and murders committed by the "anally sadistic." Crimes among homosexuals, he complained, were hard to solve, as these people had an "ironclad rule" not to talk of the misdeeds of the "contra-sexual group."[16]   249

Doctors pondered the "problem" of homosexuality. In 1952 the American Psychiatric Association developed the *Diagnostic and Statistical Manual of Mental Disorders* (DSM-1), which declared homosexuality a sociopathic personality disorder.[17] The postwar medical consensus was that the self-destructive actions of the homosexual proved that homosexuality was not a crime but a disease. This implied that a cure was possible. But general practitioners were ill qualified to deal with the issue; many continued to confuse homosexuality with pedophilia. The "sex experts" had equally blinkered views. Endocrinologists employed dangerous hormonal treatments. While they could blunt the homosexual's sex drive, they could not eliminate the direction of the passion. Psychoanalysts, convinced that homosexuality was to the result of the neurotic patient's having a weak father and an aggressive mother, subjected clients to countless sessions in which they inculcated such views.

Edmund Bergler, an avowed enemy of Kinsey, saw it as his task to strip away the glamour of homosexuality. For Bergler the homosexual, though he might claim he did not want to be mistreated, was in fact a masochist. Bergler provided in a 1959 study the case of one patient, Mr. L, who in Rome had once been accosted by a boy. The patient recalled, "Then I noticed that there were two suspicious-looking men; they were watching me very closely. I concluded that these two unsavory-looking characters were blackmailers, and that the boy was the bait they used for trapping wealthy Americans. I was frightened; I got an immediate picture of a scare headline: WEALTHY AMERICAN ARRESTED."[18] The patient—a twenty-four-year-old man who was about to inherit a $50 million fortune—now used this scene in his masturbation fantasies. As a young boy he had witnessed the police beat a man who had tried to pick him up. According to Bergler this had turned him into a masochist. His patient was moved to relive how the man must have felt while being beaten and was attracted to danger. Once he freed himself of his masochism, asserted Bergler, he would be freed of his homosexuality. In other words, Bergler was arguing that homosexuals must *like* being blackmailed or being beaten up by the police; otherwise they would stop being homosexuals. According to such twisted logic, there could only be bad individuals, not bad laws.

250   The fact that Tennessee Williams had emerged as America's finest playwright and Gore Vidal as one of its better novelists might explain Bergler's reference to the "glamour" that homosexuality purportedly enjoyed in the late 1950s. Hollywood movie stars such as Rock Hudson were protected from media exposés by the major studios. The critical acclaim won by Williams's *Suddenly Last Summer* (1957) demonstrated that homosexuality could now be openly dealt with on the American stage. One of the writers of the British film *The Trials of Oscar Wilde* (1960) asserted, "We couldn't have made this picture ten years ago, but now, after *Suddenly Last Summer* the subject is tolerated." By the 1960s the press was claiming that members of the "homintern" controlled the film and fashion worlds. *Life* magazine protested in June 1964 that though the "gay world" was actually a "sad and often sordid world," gays were no longer "furtive." Many were now "flaunting their deviation." At the same time the magazine acknowledged that the nine-tenths of gay men who were not obviously homosexual feared exposure. It reported that the Los Angeles police used decoys to entrap risk takers, in 1963 arresting 3,069 men for soliciting. In Washington, D.C., Walter Jenkins, President Lyndon B. Johnson's chief of staff, was arrested in a YMCA rest room. The White House let it be known that Jenkins, a married man with children, was not "biologically" a homosexual and attributed his behavior to exhaustion. Arthur Krock, a leading columnist of the *New York Times,* agreed that it was a tragedy, but added that "it would be irresponsible if the American people felt no anxiety over the fact . . . that a Government official to whom the most secret operations of national security were accessible . . . is among those unfortunates who are most readily subject to the blackmail by which security secrets are often obtained by enemy agents." There was no place for homosexuals in sensitive positions. In its January 21, 1966, issue *Time* magazine noted with some concern that growing toleration was leading to a growth in homosexuality. Those who fell victim to such a "pernicious sickness" were reminded that their activities could lead to more than legal problems. "There is also a constant opportunity for blackmail and for shakedowns by real or phony cops, a practice known as 'gayola.'" Little did *Time* writers know that the next month was to see the breaking of the story of America's biggest homosexual blackmail ring with the arrest of Fellenbaum, Kaminsky, and Hammock.[19]

In reporting the 1966 trial of Fellenbaum, *Time* magazine fell back on the blame the victim trope. "Apparently the victims were so racked by feelings of guilt," it stated, "that few of them had enough self-possession to 251 challenge the blackmailers." Those calling for law reform asserted that decriminalization of homosexuality would reduce just such a sense of guilt. In reply, a contributor to *America,* a Jesuit publication, claimed that homosexuals did not fear the law; rather, they feared exposure, since "the common American moral sense cannot stomach inversion." The author went on to ask, "In the matter of extortioners and homosexuals, who are the truly evil ones, who are the real disgrace even to fallen nature, who are the vicious enemies of society?" The adult homosexual was not attractive, but at least he was not a criminal. Rather like the alcoholic the "deviationist suffers from a crippling weakness." The homosexual was weak, the black-mailer was strong. "It is the old, old story. Sin is sin, vice is not virtue. Evil cannot be good. But there is the sin of weakness and there is the sin of malice. The first cries out to be medicined [*sic*] and may be cured. The second must be punished: always in due proportion, but promptly, inflexibly, and to the limit of the law." The authors of such moralizing accounts clearly regarded themselves as being courageous in simply asking for the law to be enforced.[20]

Law reformers and gay activists sought to rescue the victims of blackmail from the disdain of popular commentators by telling the truth about extortion and shakedowns. Criminologists referred to the "blocked victim," meaning one who suffered from a self-imposed helplessness and who accordingly was the ideal fall guy. But, argued reformers, the victimization of homosexuals was hardly self-imposed. Police shakedowns were common. In addition, the law put gays at risk of psychopaths. As early as 1954 psychotherapist Benjamin Karpman provided a portrait of one such black-mailer, who was "bent completely on bleeding his homosexual partners. It would seem that he is less interested in the actual sex relationship than in the amount of money he can squeeze out of his partner. To achieve his ends, he resorts to all sorts of tricks, including threats of blackmail. He gets an almost orgiastic satisfaction from having cheated a partner out of his money." Delinquency expert Gerhard Mueller, in calling for a relaxation of repressive sex laws, used the blackmail argument as an example of the laws' pernicious, if unintended, consequences. "Cases are not at all infrequent in which one partner to a homosexual relation will blackmail the other for years, threatening him with public prosecution unless he makes one payment after another to the blackmailer." Wainwright Churchill's pioneering 1967 cross-cultural study pointed out that laws against homosexuality permitted extortion, blackmail, bribery, entrapment, and shakedowns. They allowed youths, engaged in vicious "queer-baiting," to see themselves as self-righteously ridding the community of degenerates. In targeting gays, laws created a fertile ground for corruption as police, lawyers, and bondsmen all had to be paid off.[21]

Sociologist Laud Humphreys made the important point that homosexuals were the "only known group who are discriminated against for being prone to blackmail." In his classic 1970 study of the "tearoom trade" in a St. Louis rest room, Humphreys reported that every homosexual he interviewed over the age of thirty had a story of paying off the police at one time or another. He found that,

> in regard to the blackmailing of tearoom participants: (1) most blackmailing is done by law enforcement personnel and as a result of decoy operations; (2) some blackmailing is practiced by those who pose as police officers; (3) a small amount is attempted (seldom with success) by close friends of the victim . . . Every respondent over the age of thirty whom I interviewed extensively had at least one story of police payoffs amounting to blackmail. With some, the police were paid off by sexual services rendered. In two instances, "donations" were made to a "charity fund" in return for release. One man alone—a prosperous married salesman who travels a great deal—has provided me with detailed accounts of eight instances in which he has "bought off" decoys for amounts ranging from sixty to three hundred dollars. In each of these encounters with the law, the respondent had been "led on" by the decoy.

Moreover, by threatening to arrest young men for petty crimes, the police in effect blackmailed them into acting as decoys. Because homosexuals were used to being victimized by the police they were conditioned to be exploited by those pretending to be the police. Lacking a supportive culture, married gay men were most at risk. Being covert about their sexuality increased rather than decreased the dangers they ran. Humphreys' first conclusion was that a bad law was responsible for blackmail. His second was that openness offered the homosexual protection; at the very least the already discredited could not be further marginalized.[22]

These arguments were taken up by the gay liberation movement. The members of Harry Hay's Mattachine Society, organized in Los Angeles to respond to Senator McCarthy's exploitation of homophobia, fought for years for the "acceptance" of homosexuals and a simple end to discrimination. The group avoided publicity, hoping that a low profile and the slow education of the public would bring understanding. But just as the women's liberation movement eventually broke with old-style liberal feminists, so too in the late 1960s the gay rights movement broke with older homosexual lobbying groups and adopted a more radical, assertive notion of "gay liberation." In so doing its members were inspired by the civil rights and anti–Vietnam war movements in which many had participated.

The four-day Stonewall riots enjoy a legendary status of having launched the gay liberation movement. They began in June 1969 with a police raid on a Greenwich Village gay bar. The story goes that there for the first time patrons refused to put up with police harassment and fought back. In fact San Francisco had been the site of similar confrontations since the mid-1960s. Nevertheless the Stonewall riots—because of where and when they occurred—detonated an explosion of gay self-assertiveness. Gay men's consciousness was raised. Liberation groups sprang up across America and then around the world. Thousands of men across the country "came out of the closet." As opposed to the quiet lobbying of earlier homosexual groups, newly "out" gays stressed action and employed sit-ins and demonstrations to demand change.[23]

The gay movement seized on blackmail as a dramatic demonstration of the importance of openness, of "coming out." "Gay Pride" marches quickly became an annual ritual. Whereas discretion had once been lauded, by the 1970s gays held that secrecy was dangerous. To substantiate such claims they could point to inquiries on gay life in Germany and America that revealed the therapeutic importance of coming out. Statistics suggested that candor cut the suicide rate in half. The hope was that blackmail would also be reduced. "Spokesmen for the gay liberation movement have asserted," one academic study of sex crimes noted, "that the man who openly proclaims his homosexual activity is almost immune to blackmail."[24]

Gays' success in forging alliances with liberal lawyers and clergy led fifteen states by 1976 to dismantle their anti-sodomy laws. Larger cities and university towns passed civil rights codes. Citing the Wolfenden Committee report as evidence, one author noted that "almost every expert body passing upon the question has recommended that consensual acts between adults in private should not be criminal at all." Yet the extent of change should not be exaggerated. Unlike European nations, each American state had its own set of laws, and many that remained on the books—pertaining to age of consent, sodomy, indecency, and fornication—could be used to police homosexual activity and levy blackmail. John H. Gagnon and William Simon found in 1973 that 10 to 15 percent of the gays in their sample had been blackmailed. Alan P. Bell and Martin S. Weinberg in 1978 reported that 25 percent of white lesbians reported being threatened with exposure, but these were not classic blackmail threats. Usually a lover was trying to prevent a breakup. For example, one respondent related, "She said she'd call my job and get me fired. She wanted me to stay with her, not leave her." The same study found that 10 percent of gay men were subjected to shakedowns and about 14 percent paid blackmail to someone other than the police. Demands were made for money and for sex. Joseph Harry reported that 16 percent of his sample had been victimized, but he added that the notion of the professional blackmailer was a myth. The typical blackmail scenario was a "one shot" payment to someone whom the victim knew.[25]

Nevertheless the 1970s witnessed a new confidence in gays' seeking the assistance of the authorities. On June 17, 1970, officer Maurice Homan arrested a Manhattan businessman in the men's toilet at the 51st Street stop of the Lexington Avenue IRT. Homan told the victim to go to Donald F. Gilbert for advice, but the victim went instead to the district attorney's office. Homan and Gilbert, who had demanded $1,500, were charged with conspiracy and criminal solicitation. In another case, in 1977 the owner of the Renaissance Spa, a massage parlor that catered to gays, tape-recorded an extortionist's demand for protection money and presented it to the police. He did this despite his previous difficulties with the authorities over prostitution and obscenity charges.[26]

Blackmail stories played a central role in the discussion of homosexuality in post–World War II America. In the 1950s the notion that homosexuals might be blackmailed by Soviet agents was seized upon by the homophobic as a reason why gays should be expelled from the military and civil service. But the very irrationality and unfairness of the argument helped goad into existence an American homosexual emancipation movement. In the late 1960s gay activists turned the argument around and asserted that the fact that law-abiding citizens could, simply because they were homosexuals, be subjected to extortion provided the most dramatic and compelling demonstration of the need for law reform that would allow them to enjoy all the rights of citizenship. 255

In the case of *Webster v. Doe* the United States Supreme Court ruled in June 1988 that the CIA could not dismiss an employee simply because of his sexual orientation. "John Doe" had argued that his "homosexuality was not a problem because he was open about it and thus not a candidate for blackmail." Civil libertarians hailed the decision as a signal to government agencies that they could no longer advance homosexuals' purported susceptibility to being blackmailed as a valid reason for regarding them as security risks. The press recalled that at earlier 1985 Senate hearings the FBI could not produce any evidence of gay state employees being blackmailed. Of fifty espionage convictions since World War II only two concerned homosexuals, and in neither did blackmail play a part.[27] Homosexuals, according to the optimistic, could now look forward to a time when public accounts of their lives would no longer be framed by blackmail stories. Some believed that heterosexuals had already freed themselves of such fears.

FROM
BLACKMAIL
TO TABLOID
EXPOSÉ

Under the byline "Kiss, Tape, and Tell," *Newsweek* magazine reported in its issue of October 7, 1963, a story that might have been penned by John Updike. In the upscale community of North Bellmore, Long Island, the police had charged Joseph I. Heneghan, assistant district attorney of Nassau County, and his wife, Constance, with blackmailing a thirty-one-year-old widow out of $25,738. Heneghan, described by U.S. Supreme Court Chief Justice Earl Warren as a young, "brilliant" lawyer, had represented Mrs. Margaret Mirabella the previous year in the settlement of her husband's estate. They had had an affair. Mirabella claimed that to stop her from terminating the relationship Heneghan recorded two of their conversations and threatened to give the tapes to his wife. Mirabella called his bluff, and Heneghan gave his wife the tapes. His story was that he only handed them to her to prove that the affair was over. In any event her angry response was to say they should use them to get "all her [Mirabella's] money." Faced with the indignity of having to pay off her lover's wife, Mirabella turned the tables by having the police tape her in a subsequent incriminating telephone conversation with Heneghan. He and his wife were arrested and indicted on felony charges. They were ultimately allowed to plead guilty to misdemeanors—Constance Heneghan to coercion and Joseph Heneghan to receiving stolen property—and received suspended one-year sentences. Heneghan was disbarred for what the presiding judge called "a terrible and stupid mistake." "Adultery may be old hat in the suburbs," *Newsweek* breezily concluded, "and blackmail has been known to catch the commuter's train too. But put them together and lay them at the door of a law enforcement official, and eyebrows go up even in the bedroom communities around New York."[1]

What makes the Heneghan case worthy of note is that it was one of the few heterosexual blackmail trials of the 1960s that won the public's attention. While homosexual blackmail stories retained their importance in the 1950s and 1960s, heterosexual blackmail stories lost much of their vigor. Following World War II, writers and filmmakers once again churned out hackneyed accounts of risk takers being entrapped by extortionists, but few of these creations had much bite. In England, the old theme of a woman who is blackmailed for bigamy by her caddish first husband whom she thought dead was trotted out in the feeble film *Cage of Gold* (1950). Slightly more interesting was Joseph Losey's *Intimate Stranger* (1956), which portrays a film producer badgered by a woman who claims to have been his mistress. In America critics were kind to Fritz Lang's *Woman in the Window* (1944), in which Edward G. Robinson plays a professor who befriends a young woman and in so doing compromises himself. In ending the film on a comedic note, Lang gutted the story of any significance. Max Ophuls' *The Reckless Moment* (1949) failed to convince viewers they should sympathize with Joan Bennett, a woman whose rash disposal of the man whom she thinks her daughter has murdered leaves her open to extortion. *Portrait in Black* (1960), with Anthony Quinn as the doctor-lover and Lana Turner as the adulterous wife who find themselves blackmailed for the murder of her husband, fared no better. Critics laughed that it was a "nearly complete record of cinematic clichés." Fiction writers also failed to bring new life to the old theme. In *The Little Sister* (1949) Raymond Chandler tried to match the success of *The Big Sleep* and failed. Less accomplished writers did no better.[2]

Real blackmail cases were apparently no more interesting than the fictional. In the latter half of the twentieth century both the *Times* of London and the *New York Times* provided fewer and fewer accounts of sexual blackmail. Yet the actual number of cases of blackmail known to the police after the war continued to rise.[3] The statistics, however, were deceptive. In a more liberal sexual climate people would be more likely to report being blackmailed than they had in the past; so the actual rate of extortion might have been going down while the number known to the police increased.

But the question remains: Why did heterosexual blackmail stories cease to attract the sort of attention that they once had? One possible explanation is
258 that with the emergence of a more sexually permissive culture—what some dubbed a "sexual revolution"—the public took a less moralistic view of sexual foibles. In such a healthier, more rational sexual climate those caught in incriminating situations were viewed not as bad, but as stupid. Another, less simple interpretation is that moralizing was far from dead, but was increasingly countered by those who accepted the emergence of a new age of sexual pluralism. The best example was, of course, that of the gay liberation movement, which battled older forms of moral regulation.

What seemed to underlie the decline in interest in blackmail stories was the withering on both sides of the Atlantic of the notion of "public morals." The Mann Act's inability to end prostitution and, more important, the failure of Prohibition to end drinking substantiated Americans' distrust of the state policing of morality. The dislocations caused by the war led to a further relaxing of restraints. Most adults unconsciously abandoned the concept of public morals, and a new deregulated moral market took its place. Conservatives certainly made attempts in the 1950s and again in the 1980s to turn the clock back, but enjoyed only limited success.

Central to the new moral climate were the propagandistic activities of Alfred C. Kinsey. His *Sexual Behavior in the Human Male* (1948), a report based on the largest sex survey in history, was a cultural bombshell. Though posing as an objective scientist, Kinsey had the avowed intent of inculcating a moral rationality and set out to naturalize a variety of sexual practices. Generations of self-important but innumerate observers, he complained, not only fell back on such meaningless terms as "normal" and "abnormal"; they had terrorized the public with loaded words like "infantile, frigid, sexually under-developed, under-active, excessively active, over-developed, over-sexed, hypersexual, or sexually over-active." What such experts called "abnormal" behavior was, Kinsey wryly noted, displayed by 60 to 75 percent of the population. Kinsey's most sensational findings pertained to the extent of male homosexual practices, but he praised all forms of virility, claiming that men who had the earliest sexual experiences went on to become the most "alert, energetic, vivacious, spontaneous, physically active, socially extrovert, and/or aggressive individuals in the population." Kinsey's 1953 report *Sexual Behavior in the Human Female* created another sensation. Fifteen years previously Dorothy Dunbar Bromley and F. H.

Britten had revealed that 25 percent of American women had intercourse at least once before marriage. Kinsey's data indicated that now only about 50 percent of brides were virgins.[4]

Kinsey asserted that extramarital sex was also common. His figures revealed that 50 percent of married men had been unfaithful. Such affairs were in theory still taken very seriously in the 1950s. Though laws against adultery were rarely enforced, the ten northeastern states continued to treat them as crimes punishable by prison terms. Psychologists attacked adultery as a sign of immaturity. In Kinsey's view such liaisons could primarily be understood as simple searches for pleasure. He found that the working-class male tended to have extramarital affairs early in life, while the upper classes had them later, in middle age. Working-class women "expected" their men to "step out." An English researcher reported that unhappily married women also frequently wanted an extramarital fling.[5] Those who suffered as a result of affairs, Kinsey claimed, did so because society put such an exaggeratedly high value on fidelity and social conformity.

Most commentators insisted that the danger of adultery was that it led to divorce. In the United States the divorce rate doubled immediately after World War II, and in England, where it had been much lower, the rate increased fivefold. Kinsey was one of the few to argue that adultery did not inevitably harm marriage. He found that only about a fifth of those women who had affairs and later divorced reported that adultery was the prime motivating factor.[6] Men, however, were twice as likely as women to blame divorce on a wife's affair. Whatever the moralists might say, Kinsey was convinced that the general public regarded such escapades with a high degree of tolerance, if not envy.

Skirting the complex questions posed by pornography, rape, voyeurism, and gay public sex, Kinsey made it seem that the only sex that existed was private sex. He attempted to split the ideal from the real, morality from science. A large portion of the American public embraced his convincing picture of private acts. His approach had apparently demystified sexuality: as one scholar recently noted, "the matter-of-factness and neutrality of scientific discourse—its apparent lack of a moral agenda—contributed to its triumph and endurance." The popularizers of Kinsey's message heralded a new age of "bachelor girls," college "panty raids," sexually savvy wives, and birth control in which a degree of polygamous behavior was condoned. Enlightenment, it was believed, would solve every problem. More important, in providing statistical evidence demonstrating that premarital sex, adultery, and homosexuality were common, Kinsey's writings helped form the basis for campaigns for the decriminalization of a variety of sexual practices.[7]

In the mass media, Hugh Hefner's *Playboy* magazine, which first appeared in 1953, represented yet another assertion that what adult heterosexuals did in private was nobody's business but their own. Older men's magazines, such as *Argosy* and *True,* had provided men an escape in the great outdoors. Hefner, carrying on *Esquire's* notion of male sophistication and exploiting the idea of the Vargas girl pinup popularized during the war, offered his bachelor readership an escape at home or in a penthouse via a fantasy of sexual consumerism. Critics regarded him as simply the producer of masturbatory pornography who was seeking, by a compulsive harping on the female form, to reassure his readers that though they had shucked off many of the accoutrements of old-fashioned forms of rugged masculinity they were no less virile. With a peculiar American earnestness Hefner produced a "philosophy" to dignify his undertaking. *Playboy* preached a form of libertinism with the avowed goal of freeing men from the clutches of women who sought to tie them down. Its attack on moral hypocrisy heralded not the dawning of an age of equality, but one of sexual "hard bargains." Women were warned that if they were seduced, that was their problem; men were told not to feel guilty. Linda R. Hischman and Jane E. Larson note: "The first issue contained an article titled 'Miss Gold Digger of 1953' attacking the extortionate female ethic that required marriage for sex. 'All woman wants [*sic*] is security,' *Playboy* accused, '[a]nd she's perfectly willing to crush man's adventurous, freedom-loving spirit to get it.'"[8] The magazine went on to condemn alimony as a vicious weapon wielded by vengeful ex-wives. Blackmail would presumably have no place in *Playboy's* world, a sexual marketplace where every man and woman entered every relationship knowing the rules of the game.

Related to the new crop of pornographic magazines like *Playboy* and yet another cause for the decline in the cultural significance of sexual blackmail in its classic form was the rise of the tabloid press. In the 1920s the *New York Graphic* and *John Bull* in London owed much of their popularity to their occasional lurid exposés. In the 1930s and 1940s Walter Winchell used his "Broadway Hearsay" column in the *New York Post* to retail rumors and innuendoes that could make or break the careers of entertainers and politicians. Given Winchell's success, almost every American newspaper was forced to follow suit with its own gossip column. The 1950s tabloids, which consisted of nothing but gossip, pushed the sexual exposé up to, and sometimes beyond, the legal limits. Jimmie Tarantino, editor of *Hollywood Life*, was tried for extortion in 1955. In a March 1957 article entitled "Gutterdammerung," *Time* noted that the California state senate had launched an investigation of Robert Harrison, "the king of leer." During the war Harrison had been successful with cheesecake publications like *Wink, Titter*, and *Flirt*. In 1952 he created *Confidential*, a gossip rag that was sufficiently homophobic and reactionary to win the support of Walter Winchell, who brought it to national attention. Howard Rushmore, who served as editor of *Confidential* in 1954–55, was a veteran smut peddler, having started on the *New York Graphic* in the 1920s. Film critic for the communist *Daily Worker* during the Depression, he later flip-flopped to become a red-baiter for the *Journal-American*. He left that paper when not allowed to do an unflattering story on Eleanor Roosevelt. *Confidential's* sole purpose was to publish lurid accounts of the secret lives of rich and famous entertainers. At its peak the bimonthly's circulation was an astounding four million. The competitors that sprang up—such as *Hush Hush, The Lowdown, Exposed, On the Q.T., Uncensored, Top Secret, Inside Story*, and *Suppressed*—were far less popular, with circulations in the 100,000 range. This "gutter journalism" lived on smut and scandal. As early as 1955 it was reported that confidence men claiming to represent *Confidential* were also indulging in outright blackmail.[9]

Confidential's investigative procedures were made public at the 1957 Los Angeles trial of Mrs. Marjory Mead, niece of Robert Harrison and director of Hollywood Research, Inc., the magazine's West Coast office. She was accused of telling a theatrical producer that an embarrassing story could be "killed" for $800 to $1,000. Howard Rushmore admitted to the court that the tabloid hired prostitutes to seduce movie stars and paid detectives to provide incriminating material. The magazine counterattacked by threatening to prove the truth of its stories and subpoenaed a host of leading actors, including Van Johnson, Marilyn Monroe, Deanna Durbin, Rory Calhoun, Dorothy Dandridge, Mae West, Dick Powell, and Robert Mitchum.[10]

The establishment press paraded its distaste for such muckraking, while the Hearst newspapers and British tabloids like the *Mirror* retold *Confi-*

261

dential's exposés. Hollywood responded by portraying the tabloids' editors as vermin. The film *Slander* (1956), for example, focuses on a magazine editor who is ultimately shot to death by the mother of the television actor he has blackmailed. "It makes scandal-mongering," dryly noted the *New York Times* critic, "the menace of free enterprise, parental love, and the Ameri-

In the 1950s a crop of lurid American tabloids emerged, promising to deliver the sort of exposure of sexual indiscretions that blackmail trial reports had previously provided. (From "The Curious Craze for 'Confidential' Magazines," *Newsweek*, July 11, 1955.)

can home." In the English comedy *The Naked Truth* (1957), shown in the United States as *Your Past is Showing* (1958), the victims decide to eliminate a gutter press baron. The best of the genre was *The Sweet Smell of Success* (1957) in which Burt Lancaster played a vicious Walter Winchell–style gossip columnist and Tony Curtis his blackmailing lackey.[11]

Having survived its criminal prosecution because of legal technicalities, *Confidential* nevertheless disappeared in a blaze of lawsuits in 1958. Despite its demise, the enterprising recognized that *Confidential* had opened up a huge market, and a number of similar if slightly more cautious publications soon took its place. They tended to work with, rather than against, the Hollywood studios. Yet like *Confidential* they had the effect of at times marketing the sort of information that had previously appeared in blackmail trials. Blackmailers had always threatened to take their information to the press. The unprecedented upsurge in tabloids specializing in smut gave them far more options. "Checkbook journalism" in effect provided a growing and, more important, legal outlet for the sale of secrets. Stories of the infidelities of celebrities that had previously emerged from blackmail trials would increasingly appear as tabloid exposés.[12]

Whereas the tabloids continued to prosper by servicing the public's appetite for salacious revelations, the proponents of the so-called sexual revolution of the 1960s and 1970s sought to create a more honest culture in which the gap between morality and behavior, which resulted in scandals, would be closed. Though they saw themselves as radicals, a number of their concerns were shared by the authorities. For example, in 1970 Robert K. Ruskin, the New York Commissioner of Investigations, in noting the case of two police officers who attempted to extort money from a couple they found having sex in a car, called for the repeal of laws that fostered corruption. Ruskin recognized that antiquated laws on victimless crimes were dangerous not just to the public, but also to the police. Many politicians agreed with the reformers that the law had lagged behind social change and thus armed extortionists. Among the extortionists—though few knew it at the time—was J. Edgar Hoover, head of the FBI, who had a passion for collecting compromising sexual material on public figures. He assembled wiretap information on Martin Luther King Jr.'s extramarital affairs in the hopes of discrediting or neutralizing the black civil rights leader and is said to have used evidence of John F. Kennedy's womanizing to force him to accept Lyndon Johnson as his vice-presidential running mate.[13]

Despite the opposition of figures like Hoover, law reforms in the 1960s began to catch up with social change, and the decriminalization of sexual practices began. The campaigners for the decriminalization of homosexuality played up the notion that bad laws led to blackmail. In a similar fashion the reporting of abortion-related blackmail directed the public's attention to the need for reform of the laws on abortion. The plight of women seeking to terminate a pregnancy was embodied by the case of a Los Angeles woman identified as Anne who, having missed two periods, was in October 1946 taken by a young woman to May Ramsey's house. They entered through the back door, and Anne gave Winifred Howard $150. In return she received one yellow pill and two green pills, which made her groggy. Howard took her to lie down in a room where another woman was resting. She was then taken to the kitchen and put on a table that was equipped with stirrups. She had her legs up when May Ramsey entered the room. Anne reported that she felt herself being touched and "she heard a 'vacuumy' sound" and felt a "kind of suction" for about twenty minutes. She was then taken back to the bedroom to rest. Howard gave her a penicillin shot and some pills. Anne was still in bed when the police arrived. In Ramsey's well-stocked residence they found—in addition to her notebook with Anne's scheduled visit written in—syringes, rubber tubing, stirrups, pills, bark, cotton, rubber gloves, forceps, and penicillin. Asked why she gave abortions Ramsey (who had been previously convicted in 1941) said she had meant to stop two weeks before her arrest and went on to protest, "I have certainly been shaken down in this blackmail," meaning that she had had to pay off the authorities. She was convicted on one of four charges; Winifred Howard was convicted on one of two.[14]

Millions of women like Anne had to take their chances when turning to trained and untrained practitioners. The American police had for most of the 1940s turned a blind eye to such activities, but from the 1950s on began a crackdown. In such an age of hypocrisy and legal ambiguity, corruption flourished. In 1951 a onetime police hero was charged with four other men in blackmailing a Bronx physician for $3,600 to cover up a supposed abortion. In 1962 the New York police employed wiretaps to track down extortionists and abortionists. As a result four persons were charged with conspiracy, though one claimed that she had been the victim of an extortion attempt by the others. In 1965 three Harlem policemen (all previously cited for honor) were dismissed from the force for having demanded $50,000 from an unlicensed Cuban doctor. Dr. Luis Barquet had been arrested for abortion in Florida in 1961 and was indicted again in New York in February 1965. The three officers carried out a "police raid" on his North Bergen, New Jersey, home on June 30, catching him with three women. He promised to pay off his captors at Kennedy Airport, but was able to alert the police, who arrested the rogue officers; Barquet managed to slip away.[15]

Police corruption was not as evident in England, but similar stories surfaced there. In 1954 a flight lieutenant demanded £6,000 from a Miss X, threatening to accuse her of performing illegal operations. In December 1963 two men and a woman sought to blackmail three doctors out of £7,000 with the threat that they would tell the tabloid *News of the World* and the British Medical Association of their abortion practice. Detectives listened in on the telephone and foiled the attempt. In December 1967 two men were charged at the Marlborough Police Court with "demanding money with menaces" from Dr. X, a Harley Street consultant gynecologist who provided abortion services. The pair had obtained sixty to eighty case histories that had been stolen from Dr. X's office. Their plan was to blackmail the doctor, his female patients, and their relatives. Two weeks after the files were taken they sent the doctor one case history and a demand for £20,000 for the return of all the files. He was told that if he did not pay his practice would be destroyed. Fearing the authorities as much as the criminals, the doctor reported neither the break-in nor the extortion threat. The police only heard of the affair because the criminals also threatened Mr. A, a Knightsbridge company director, that if he did not pay £5,000 they would make public the file that revealed that his stepdaughter had had three abortions, the last one shortly before her recent marriage. Alerted by Mr. A, the police arrested the two gang members when they showed up to collect their money. Each received a seven-year sentence.[16]

Such reports added to the groundswell of support in favor of reform of the abortion law in both England and the United States. Lawyers complained that the vast number of criminal operations made a mockery of the law. The 1960 American Medical Association convention heard a report that a million criminal abortions were carried out each year in the United States alone. Feminist grassroots abortion systems, including one operating in Chicago known as "Jane," provided approximately 12,000 abortions between 1961 and 1973. In California another network helped women travel to Mexico for abortions. Some American women had to go as far afield as

Cuba, Haiti, and England. Doctors expressed their concern that although the number of abortion-related deaths was far lower than they had been in the 1930s, women continued to die as a result of backstreet operations. Many others found themselves sexually and financially exploited.[17]

As was the case with homosexuals, abortion law reformers saw a need to end the silence that perpetuated women's victimization. In France public awareness of the issue was dramatically raised when on April 5, 1971, 343 prominent French women proclaimed in a *Nouvel Observateur* article that they had had abortions. This tactic of "coming out" was taken up in the United States. Gloria Steinem later recalled her feelings on testifying on the liberalization of New York State's abortion law. "Suddenly, I was no longer learning intellectually what was wrong. I knew. I had an abortion when I was newly out of college, and had told no one. If one in three or four women shares this experience, why should each of us be made to feel criminal and alone?"[18] When she launched in July 1972 the premiere issue of *Ms.* magazine it published a list of fifty-two public figures—including Billie Jean King, Lillian Hellman, Lee Grant, Barbara Tuchman, and Judy Collins—who had had abortions when the operation was still illegal. The year 1973 saw the landmark *Roe v. Wade* decision, in which the U.S. Supreme Court finally held that a woman's "right of privacy" overrode existing state laws against abortion.

Based on the premise that immorality and illegality should no longer be linked, that a sin was not a crime, a host of similar reforms were passed on both sides of the Atlantic. English governments carried out changes in the laws on prostitution in 1959, obscene publications in 1964, homosexuality, contraception, and abortion in 1967, and divorce in 1969. The U.S. Supreme Court ruled in *Griswold v. Connecticut* (1965) that that state's birth control law was unconstitutional. It was unthinkable, asserted Justice William O. Douglas, that police should have the right to search for contraceptives in the bedrooms of married couples. The 1972 case of *Eisenstadt v. Baird* extended the right of privacy to those engaging in unmarried sex. Across the board states shifted away from using the power of the courts to determine what was "normal" behavior with regard to fertility, marriage, and sexual preference.[19]

The decriminalization of a wide variety of sexual practices presumably disarmed many blackmailers. So too did a new openness, which reformers hoped would remove feelings of guilt and shame. The contraceptive pill purportedly "freed" women. The advice now was "If you can't be good, be careful." Helen Gurley Brown asserted in *Sex and the Single Girl* (1962) and in the pages of *Cosmopolitan* (where she was editor from 1964) that "nice   267 girls" had sex. Shotgun weddings declined, and out-of-wedlock births and abortions climbed. Couples in the 1970s and 1980s lived in a new age of sexual negotiation. Sex and marriage manuals popularized experimentation and condemned guilt. Whereas in the 1950s Kinsey had written that a quarter of American women would have a least one extramarital affair, a 1973 survey put the figure at 40 percent. Polls revealed that the public was increasingly tolerant of such adventures. The media played up reports of "open marriages," "swinging couples," and "group sex."[20]

The notion of "no fault" divorce best captured the spirit of the time. In England a "matrimonial fault" continued to be required until divorce reform came in 1969. Divorce was to be finally emptied of moral blame; the issue of consent was now central. Such reforms, which finally brought English law into line with that of most American states, on the one hand gave heightened importance to the quality of the marital relationship and on the other recognized that though sex was supposed to be restricted to marriage, "love" permitted exceptions. In the 1970s several states, including Texas, Georgia, and New Mexico, at last struck down laws that allowed cuckolded husbands to carry out vengeance killings. Adultery in a society where divorce was easily available had lost much of its meaning. The adulterer's fear of blackmail similarly declined.

While reformers hailed the gains made as a result of the "sexual revolution," conservatives condemned them as aspects of a culture of permissiveness. A new balance was struck between the forces of change and those of order. Enlightened authorities recognized that liberalization could provide better, reconfigured means of control. They could accept a reappraisal of the sexual aspects of social conduct because it appeared to mirror a free-market mentality that valorized privacy. Capitalism, once puritanical, was now sensual; it once stressed saving, but now it pushed spending. The radical reformers could only be said to have won a series of ambiguous victories. The modern sexual morality was more personalized, but the 1960s and 1970s witnessed not so much "sexual libertinism" as the "deregulation of personal life."[21]

The media optimistically embraced the notion that with the emergence of feminism and women's enjoyment of greater economic independence, men and women were now close to being equal. Occasional blackmail cases indicated, however, that the sexual double standard was far from being obliterated. In 1970, when a London prostitute was blackmailed by a solicitor the press published her name and address. But in 1974, when Janie Jones, a London madam, was charged with extorting £12,000 from a wealthy man, he was identified only as Mr. Y. She had threatened to reveal his penchant for viewing black men pretending to rape white women—prostitutes dressed as schoolgirls complete with teddy bears—whom he "rescued" before ravishing them himself. Crusading journalist Paul Foot, in an article entitled "Y, oh Lord, oh why . . ." that appeared in the *Socialist Worker*, protested the anonymity given the victim. "Now Mr. Y is not Mr. Y at all. He is Lord Y, or to be specific, Lord Belper, brother-in-law of the Duke of Norfolk." Foot pointed out that women who were the victims of rapists were not given anonymity. Why men like Mr. Y should receive the protection of the court, Foot caustically noted, "is not immediately clear." The argument that blackmail victims in England would only come forward if promised that their names would not be made public Foot dismissed as nonsense. Mr. Y had not come to the police; they had stumbled upon the prostitution racket and required him to testify. Foot concluded that what underlay the courts' policy were concerns for the sensitivities of the powerful and propertied. For his pains he was found guilty of contempt of court.[22]

Just how much had changed and how much had remained the same regarding public attitudes toward sexuality in the United States was revealed in an extraordinary trial involving Playboy "bunnies." The case came to light on March 15, 1978, when the police arrested Jack Zarzatian and Jack Witte for assaulting a woman. The trunk of their car contained $30,000 of hashish. On raiding the assailants' home, officers discovered shotguns and handguns, seventy obscene photos, fifty pornographic videotapes, and a list of the women who had been forced to perform in them. The police had chanced upon a seven-man gang of pornographer-blackmailers, which had been in operation for at least six months. It used the prospect of a television promotion to lure fifteen or more women to a mountaintop chalet in rural Sussex, New Jersey, where they were drugged at gunpoint and videotaped performing sex acts. At least six worked as Playboy bunnies at the Great Gorge Resort Hotel, part of the Playboy empire. The men then threatened to distribute the tapes and photos in order to force the women to hand over cash and cars, and to help them distribute drugs. The police located ten of the victims; three came forward to testify. One had alerted her superiors at the Playboy club. Ultimately four men pleaded guilty to charges of rape, kidnapping, sodomy, extortion, and narcotics distribution. Witte was sentenced to twelve years in prison; three others received seven-year sentences.[23] It was ironic that women working for Hugh Hefner, the man who proclaimed the dawning of a new, sexually liberated age, should be so victimized.

269

Feminists disappointed with the continuation of more mundane types of exploitative sexual relationships coined the terms "sexual harassment" in the 1970s and "date rape" in the 1980s. These notions allowed a range of troubling sexual relationships to be problematized and discussed. Decades earlier a woman who had been sexually victimized but could provide no evidence of physical violence had no option other than to remain silent. If she made demands for compensation she ran the risk of being charged with blackmail. With the establishment in government and industry of harassment committees a new option was made available. Films such as *Fatal Attraction* (1987) and *Disclosure* (1995) warned the late-twentieth-century womanizer that a sexual fling could end not in blackmail, but in being pursued by either a vindictive psychopath or the politically correct members of a sexual harassment tribunal. Some blackmailers exploited the new vocabulary. A typist who had lured her boss into bed and had her sister take photos of them threatened to show the photos to the members of his synagogue if he did not pay up. In her defense she claimed that she only sought to "teach him a lesson for sexually harassing her at work."[24]

By the 1980s innovative extortionists were employing tape recorders and video cameras, but sexual blackmail cases were rarely reported by the establishment press. Under the heading "blackmail," the 1987 index of the *Times* of London listed the ransoming of a dog and four kidnapped owls from the London Zoo. Threats were made—if money were not paid—to poison prison staff, to decapitate a businessman, to contaminate chicken pies with AIDS blood, to tamper with Cadbury's chocolates, to retain stolen nineteenth-century paintings, and to put glass in a supermarket's food. Whatever happened to the classic accounts of sexual blackmail? The answer must be that, for the reasons examined earlier, they no longer held the interest they once had. But sexual blackmail stories had not disappeared altogether. Through the 1980s and 1990s the public continued to relish the occasional blackmail story—such as the Bill Cosby saga—that appeared to expose moral hypocrisy.

270   Most of these cases involved the supporters of Prime Minister Margaret Thatcher and President Ronald Reagan, successful right-wing politicians who paraded their attachment to conservative moral standards and their distaste for the "permissiveness" of the 1960s. The most infamous case involved Maryland congressman Robert E. Bauman, who in 1980 admitted to the FBI that he was being blackmailed. The subsequent investigation led the police to charge Bauman, a leading congressional conservative and de facto floor leader of the Republican Party, with soliciting sex from a sixteen-year-old boy. Bauman's colleagues were stunned that the president of the 200,000-strong Conservative Union should have met such a fate. After all, he had led the charge for moral reform, originating the legislation that allowed states to ban Medicaid abortions. He had been a leading sponsor of the Family Protection Act, which would allow employers to discriminate against gay employees. He had pushed a bill to deny benefits to gays discharged from the military. With a photogenic wife and four children, he was a potential Senate contender.[25]

"I have confessed my wrongs to God," was all Bauman would say at first. He later blamed his "homosexual tendencies" on his alcoholism. The U.S. Attorneys Office's willingness to agree to drop the soliciting charge if he completed an alcoholism rehabilitation program led some to protest that people like Bauman were giving booze a bad name. He was defeated the following November, his political career ended. In an article entitled "Has Duplicity Become the Gravest of Politicians' Sins?" *New York Times* columnist John Herbers pointed out that public officials hypocritically preaching one thing and practicing the other was what enraged the public. The press was certainly much less interested in the trial of the twenty-four-year-old niece of Democratic senator Thomas F. Eagleton. She and her lawyer were convicted of extortion for attempting to force the senator to pay her $220,000 for stock in a pipe-fitting company by threatening to claim that he had once had a homosexual affair. The relative lack of attention paid to Eagleton suggested that sexual attitudes were more flexible than they had been in the past. Divorce and heavy drinking were once cause for censure, but were now accepted. Even the adulterer, if contrite, could make a comeback. Acceptance of homosexuality was in the offing. Herbers reported that at least one southerner was willing to assert that he preferred a "queer conservative to a macho liberal."[26]

Other well-known conservatives who were purported victims of black-
mailers included Jeffrey Archer, who in 1986 was forced to resign as deputy chairman of the Tory Party after a tabloid, irritated by the moral posturing of Margaret Thatcher's government, revealed that he had made a payment to a prostitute. Archer, who had written a best-selling novel in which a rising politician faced down a blackmailing prostitute, successfully sued the newspaper that had claimed he had been with the woman. In July 2001, however, he was found guilty of having perjured himself in the earlier trial and sentenced to four years in prison. In a 1987 scandal referred to as "Pearlygate," Jessica Hahn claimed that seven years earlier she had been raped by the Reverend Jim Bakker, head of the PTL Ministries, one of America's more active arms of the Christian Right. Bakker in turn claimed that for years he had paid Hahn hush money to protect his ministry and his family.[27]

In 1992 Sol Wachtler, chief judge of the New York State Court of Appeals and a possible Republican gubernatorial candidate, was charged with trying to extort money from socialite and Republican Party fund-raiser Joy Silverman. They had had an affair. When she ended it he began to send her letters written under a pseudonym threatening her daughter and demanding money in exchange for photographs and tapes. His apparent intent was to scare her back to him. Alan Dershowitz, the well-known defense attorney, noted that never before had such a high-ranking judge been tried for such a serious offense. He warned Wachtler's fellow judges that if they did not sentence him to the customary amount of prison time set by federal guidelines for such a crime—fifty-seven to seventy-two months—they could be accused of cronyism. In the end Wachtler resigned from the bar and served thirteen months. He later wrote a book on the need for prison reform, which led to the joke: "What is the definition of a liberal? A conservative who has been arrested."[28]

If blackmail cases involving Republicans received so much attention, it was not necessarily because they engaged in more risky behavior than Democrats. What the public enjoyed was the irony of seeing conservatives who had sought to exploit the notion of "dangerous sexual secrets" being hoisted on their own petard. When the Republicans sought to impeach

President Bill Clinton on the basis of his extramarital affairs, pornographer-publisher Larry Flynt retaliated by threatening to "out" Republican adulterers who posed as defenders of family values. In the October 4, 1998, edition of the *Washington Post* he offered $1 million to anyone who could offer proof of a congressman or senator who had had illicit sexual relations. One result was the resignation two months later of House Speaker Robert Livingston. In addition, the web-based magazine *Salon* revealed that Henry Hyde, chair of the House Judiciary Committee, which was to consider the Starr report and decide on impeachment proceedings, had also had an adulterous affair. Right-wing publications like the *National Review* were outraged by such "gutter journalism." Flynt protested that he was only telling the truth. Flynt was certainly not a blackmailer; he was paying money in order to have secrets exposed rather than covered up.[29]

A history of sexual blackmail would be incomplete if it failed to note the emergence of its counterpart, "outing." Outing was a logical extension of the "coming out" story that gays had embraced from the 1960s onward. The difference was that in outing, the activist was forcing others from the closet rather than oneself. In 1992 gays outed John Schlafly as a homosexual. His mother, Phyllis Schlafly—a leading defender of family values and a vocal opponent of abortion, feminism, and homosexuality—personified for many Americans the religious right's backlash against the sexual revolution. She had campaigned against AIDS education as teaching "safe sodomy." Her supporters were indignant to hear that her family's privacy had been violated. Outing, protested a conservative commentator, "is what used to be known as blackmail. And thanks to the 'silent approval' of good liberals, blackmail now hangs over one side in the debate on gay rights. It's an attempt to intimidate opposition, with the tacit support of the news media." In other words, the author was arguing that it was unfair to reveal that strident opponents of homosexuality were themselves homosexuals or were, as in Schlafly's case, intimately linked with them. What the writer failed to note was that conservatives like Schlafly, in focusing on private values, prepared the way for exposés and scandals, which were guaranteed to entertain a public always eager to see hypocrisy unmasked.[30]

The ethics of outing were discussed by members of the gay community as early as 1987. As a beleaguered minority, they naturally enough wanted it known that their ranks included esteemed entertainers, businessmen, and sports stars. After the death of Malcolm Forbes in 1990, even the mainstream media noted that the multimillionaire had had gay affairs. In June 1989, after Republicans falsely suggested that the Democratic House Speaker was gay, Representative Barney Frank—an open homosexual— threatened to expose closeted Republicans who really were gay. Outing was moreover a symptom of anger that gays felt in the 1990s when, at a time when many gay men were dying of AIDS, others were hypocritically posing as heterosexuals and even supporting antigay legislation. In England the radical organization OutRage! targeted religious hypocrites, raising placards on the steps of Church House in 1994 that named ten Church of England bishops as gay. In 1995 Sir James A. Kilfedder, an Ulster Unionist Member of Parliament, died of a heart attack after being informed by Out-Rage! that he was about to be outed.[31]

The issue of outing split the gay community. Opponents argued that such an invasion of privacy was a new form of McCarthyism and the last thing homosexuals should support. The threat of outing one's partner, it was said, could even be used by gays as a form of "homophobic control." Forced disclosure harmed the individual targeted and reinforced the public perception that homosexuality was a shameful secret.[32] Defenders of outing responded that the idea of a "victim" was fraudulent. They pointed out that justice would have been better served if some of the most ferocious gay bashers of the past, such as Senator McCarthy's henchman Roy Cohn and FBI chief J. Edgar Hoover, had been exposed as homosexuals. In the United States most gay publications adopted what came to be known as the "Barney Frank rule," which held that outing was only justified to expose the gross hypocrisy of a public official who condemned gay people while being one himself.

The 1990s radical gay movement's tactic of outing powerful closeted gays was a sort of reverse blackmail: it revealed secrets in order to end, rather than to perpetuate, sexual duplicity. The activist who employed outing was protesting against hypocrisy for social benefit, whereas the blackmailer usually wished the hypocrisy to continue and hoped to benefit from it monetarily. Outing revealed relations of power and sexuality and broke one of the century's last taboos—the discussion of the sexual orientation of public personalities. Outing emerged just as interest in sexual blackmail waned, thus marking the end of one era and the beginning of another.

As Larry Flynt demonstrated, heterosexuals could also be outed. The most sensational case occurred in 1991 during confirmation hearings held to determine if Clarence Thomas was qualified to become a U.S. Supreme Court Justice. Anita Hill, a law professor at the University of Oklahoma, charged that Thomas had sexually harassed her. Though Thomas was confirmed, Hill's disclosures heightened the public's awareness of harassment. Philosopher Nancy Fraser's insightful interpretation of the Thomas-Hill affair echoes one of this book's key findings: "these events . . . show that publicity as a political weapon cannot be understood simply in terms of making public what was previously private. They demonstrate that merely publicizing some action or practice is not always sufficient to discredit it; that is only the case where the view that the practice is wrong is already widely held and uncontroversial. Where, in contrast, the practice is widely approved and contested, publicity means staging a discursive struggle over its interpretation."[33]

The various stories the public told about sexual blackmail were just such attempts to tease out its evolving views of a range of sexual practices. Extortion was particularly preoccupying in societies emerging from an age of sexual repression. At the beginning of the twentieth century the knowledge that a woman had had an abortion or an out-of-wedlock child or that a man was a homosexual or had had an adulterous affair could have disastrous consequences. By the 1990s a distinct shift had obviously occurred. The majority of the population had come to accept the notion that adults' private, consensual sexual acts should be left alone. Only those exposés that revealed rank hypocrisy received much attention. Failing to appreciate the mood of the populace, the Republican Party's futile attempt to have President Clinton impeached turned into a fiasco.

Well before Clinton entered the White House, conservatives had thrown themselves into the "culture wars" with the intention of turning the clock back. The battle peaked in the late 1990s. Robert H. Bork, President Reagan's unsuccessful 1987 nominee to the Supreme Court, condemned what he saw as the current age of "radical egalitarianism" in which women could have access to abortion and homosexuals be protected from discrimination. William Bennett, a former Secretary of Education, decried in the *Death of Outrage* (1998) the American public's continued support for President Clinton, an avowed adulterer and womanizer, as merely the most blatant evidence of the decline of common decency in modern culture. The Clinton–Monica Lewinsky affair Bennett viewed as "an assault on American ideals." Sex, Bennett insisted, was "the most value-laden of any human activity." Some suggested Americans should become more sophisticated or European in their attitudes toward sex. If that happened, Bennett warned, "moral disarmament" or "moral bankruptcy" would occur. The country 275 needed a society that "judged" as opposed to one influenced by the laxity of the sexual revolution.[34]

Attacks on the new morality were not restricted to politicians. Academics also pointed to the parading of sexual practices and preferences as symptoms of the loss of sexual respectability. According to historian Gertrude Himmelfarb, author of *The De-Moralization of Society* (1995), we were living in a world that ignored crime and vice. The effect was "to normalize and legitimize what was once regarded as abnormal and illegitimate, and, conversely, to stigmatize and discredit what was once normal and respectable." "When I was growing up in the 1950s," concurred James Twitchell in *For Shame* (1997), "public drunkenness, filing for bankruptcy, having an abortion or a child out of wedlock, drug addiction, hitting a woman, looting stores, using vulgar language in public, being on the public dole (what there was of it), or getting a divorce was enough to make you hang your head." Those were good times, but now, he stated, we lived in "shameless times." Sometime around 1960 shame had disappeared. The modern Hester Prynne sold her story to the tabloids. Many others jumped on the nostalgia bandwagon, bewailing the fact that we had all sold out for commercial gain and were only now beginning to look back longingly at the Victorians, who had nicely balanced sexual repression and sexual liberation.[35]

The Right as ever treasured the notion that there once existed an age of innocence.[36] Conservative authors, however, failed to note that the nineteenth century's purported sanctity of marriage and privacy cloaked a sexual double standard. They lamented the passing of an age in which a variety of widely practiced sex acts were stigmatized and criminalized and ignored the fact that it was just such a culture that spawned sexual blackmail. A review of the history of blackmail leads one inevitably to wonder how the policing of private morality could ever be done without replicating the unreasonable standards of sexual respectability that first armed extortionists.

Sexual blackmail stories declined in importance in the latter half of the twentieth century because from the 1950s onward sexual standards changed and the notion of "public morals" ebbed. There seemed to be no turning back. One result of this shift was the decriminalizaton of a number

of common sexual practices. If potential blackmailers were thereby disarmed, their potential victims were emboldened. Homosexuals "came out,"
276   and so did women who had had abortions or been sexually harassed. In the
1950s sexual nonconformists had sought to hide their stigmatized status
from snooping journalists. Beginning in the 1960s they increasingly made
themselves heard on talk radio shows and TV tabloid programs.[37] The cultural purchase once enjoyed by sexual blackmail stories accordingly waned.
Their importance in the interwar period had resided in their providing a
legitimate way of discussing a variety of illegitimate sexual practices. When
the time came that such sensitive sexual issues could be openly broached,
blackmail narratives, though they did not disappear, ceased to fulfill the
crucial role that they had long played.

We will never know the full extent of sexual blackmail. What the reports of blackmail trials from the late eighteenth century onward offer us are not so much trustworthy accounts of particular crimes as unique opportunities for listening in on English and American conversations about a range of illicit sexual practices and their relationship to issues of class, race, gender, and sexual identity. A tracing of the history of sexual blackmail in effect reveals a series of flash points in the discussion of modern sexuality. Sexual behavior changed over time, but far more important were the changes in the ways in which people discussed sexuality.

We began our account in the eighteenth and nineteenth centuries, when in both England and America the middle class made vigorous attempts to create rigid boundaries between the public and private, normal and abnormal, healthy and perverse, and masculine and feminine worlds. A wide range of sexual practices was hedged about by taboos, stigmas, and criminal sanctions. An unintended consequence of the assertion that character was to be equated with sexual respectability was the creation of a climate in which sexual blackmail emerged. As the importance of sexual respectability became inflated, the public became ever more fixated on the possession by the malicious of dangerous, potentially deflating, secrets.

The repressive nineteenth-century sexual morality, which cloaked an institutionalized double standard, was created by and served the interests of a white, male elite. Accordingly, sexual blackmail stories had as their primary ideological task that of supporting this dominant cultural order.[1] All-male institutions, including the courts, the churches, the press, and the professions, used such accounts for their own purposes of protecting masculine sexual prerogatives. But if blackmail stories were employed at times to support the moral and social status quo, at the same time they served the purpose of subverting it. These stories were not just about sex. They revealed the intimate—and what some regarded as the unnatural—interactions of men and women, the rich and the poor, the powerful and the weak. Blatant evidence that the influential used their authority to extort sexual favors made even conservative judges and juries uneasy.

In blackmail trials the authorities sought to ensure social conformity, shore up morality, and if possible rationalize away the guilt of the respectable victim by giving the events a certain framing.[2] To do so the courts and the press constructed a sexual problem and advanced a story—the "blackmail plot"—that provided a narrative through which key sexual and social tensions were revealed and their conflicts hopefully negotiated. Though blackmail trials often led to embarrassing revelations, the court's intent was to defuse or manage these revelations and attain some resolution. For example, an effort was often made to suggest that well-off men caught in homosexual extortion plots were not sodomites, but "innocent" victims.

An analysis of blackmail trials reveals that the intention of the authorities was not merely to punish evildoers but also to define sexuality in a way that reflected the dominant cultural expression. Such presentations were not easy to make when the public suspected that both the victim and the villain were each in his or her own way guilty of something. Unavoidable contradictions at times emerged. Though privacy was treasured by the middle class, blackmail cases demonstrated that the notion of privacy could be contested.[3] Did the woman who sought an abortion or the man who engaged in same-sex relations or the individual who hid his or her true racial identity have a right to privacy? The respectable assumed that only the virtuous deserved to have their privacy respected, while the deviant warranted regulatory scrutiny. For the middle class, and particularly middle-class men, privacy was in effect a proprietary concept, something that should only be truly enjoyed by those who had the power to defend it. They were accordingly all the more outraged when their secrets were penetrated by blackmailers. The newspapers helped create and managed the menace posed by the exposure of sexual secrets. Yet the general reading public appeared not to be shocked by sex scandals and as often as not treated extortion tales as sources of entertainment and instruction. When sexual respectability was so overvalued, it was little wonder that as many 279 would be exhilarated as were horrified by its threatened destruction.

The cultural preoccupation with blackmail as reflected in the press and popular fiction peaked in the 1920s and 1930s, when the gap between actual sexual behavior and ideal deportment had become a chasm. In an age of transition blackmail stories helped articulate concerns regarding the relationship of sexual rights to responsibilities, the private life to the public life, the individual to the community. Newspapers gave their readers a way of thinking about the intersection of sex with class, gender, and race. National differences stood out in the telling of blackmail stories. British law and culture were obsessed with issues of class and homosexuality. In contrast Americans were presented with more attempts at repressing sexual license and at the same time more defenses of sexual experimentation. The victimization of American men was framed by warnings of the corrosive power of sexuality. Trial and movie accounts of gold diggers permitted the public to discuss the rights and wrongs of the semi-liberated female. Several sensational trials in the 1920s and 1930s implicitly justified women's attempts at private justice when public remedies proved inadequate, whereas the portrayal of the woman as blackmail victim was employed to rein in female sexuality. Some of the stories that emerged from these legal confrontations were turned to political purposes, as in demands for reform of the laws pertaining to breach of promise of marriage. An account of interwar blackmail stories in effect provides a revealing reconstruction of a complex world of sexual bartering. They serve as a dramatic reminder that thanks to criminal cases stories about abortion, homosexuality, and sexual harassment were being publicly aired in the 1920s and 1930s, though the issues were not framed in the ways in which they would be after the 1960s sexual revolution.

World War II witnessed a striking and in some ways unexpected decline in the telling of blackmail stories. Sexual practices did not so much change as did the social world in which they occurred. In the decades following the war the old preoccupation with sexual reputation as a key indicator of social standing was undermined by a number of important social developments. With postwar prosperity, mass secondary education, and the possibility of college entry for working-class youths, class barriers were seriously eroded. The change was especially dramatic in England, where it was exemplified by the breakthrough of the Labour Party. Gender relations also

changed. Although women who had engaged in war work in the main responded to the call to return to the home, the tensions of the 1950s revealed that the old domestic norms of the interwar period could not be easily reestablished.

Fear of blackmail flourished when those who dared to challenge traditional standards of sexual behavior risked social ostracism, if not imprisonment. The dislocations of World War II began the undermining of this culture of deference. A different world came into being in which people thought differently about sex. A new skepticism regarding authority was particularly spurred on in the turbulent 1960s. Homosexuality at last had a public face, emerging first as "camp" as personified by personalities like Liberace and then finally as the serious "coming out" of gay activists. Women who announced that they had had an abortion and gay men who left the closet declared that sexual secrets were dangerous. Did the "sexual revolution" of the 1960s and 1970s contribute to a decline in traditional forms of sexual blackmail? Such an outcome was certainly campaigned for by those inspired by earlier writers such as Alfred C. Kinsey, who had exposed the duplicitous lives many men and women were forced to lead. The feminist and gay movements recognized how blackmail stories could be turned to publicize the need for law reforms. For most of the twentieth century the middle class accepted restrictions on individual rights when it came to abortion and homosexuality. The breakthrough came in the 1960s when a heightened individualism emerged, which was attacked by some as self-indulgent but which won the support of elements of the political left and right.

In order to be blackmailed one had to fear the loss of a reputation for respectability. Determining the meaning of sexual respectability became increasingly difficult in the 1960s as young people embraced a new secular morality and lost their sense of obligation to an antiquated Christian code of conduct that had long been propounded by church and state. A decade or two earlier premarital sex would have been a distinctly risky form of sexual behavior for members of the middle class. By the 1960s that was no longer the case. A new sexual persona, that of the sexually "liberated" individual, had emerged. In the 1920s the limited liberalization of sexual beliefs and practices had been accompanied by a surge of blackmail cases. That a similar eruption of extortion stories did not take place in the 1960s must be attributed to the far more liberal social climate, which in turn gave rise to law reforms pertaining to divorce, abortion and contraception, and the 281 emergence of the gay and feminist movements. Moreover in the last decades of the century the availability of a new range of public stories—told by lesbians, gay men, bisexuals, and transsexuals, and by "survivors" of incest, rape, child abuse, divorce, and wife battering—allowed a wide range of issues once held secret to be publicly exposed. The public, fascinated as ever by unfamiliar sexual practices, no longer had to turn to that venerable narrative device that first allowed so many of them to be discussed—stories of sexual blackmail.

The very fact that that there was a conservative backlash in the 1980s was evidence that the general public, whether it liked it or not, had been made familiar with a series of new sexual stories about sexual harassment, premarital sex, out-of-wedlock birth, and homosexual "coming out." Every social survey revealed increasing rates of abortion, divorce, and cohabitation. Despite these enormous and apparently irreversible changes, however, life went on. To the dismay of conservative commentators, western societies by the end of the twentieth century had calmly accepted the fact that contraception, abortion, common-law marriage, premarital sex, and homosexuality were here to stay. Definitions of marriage and the family were hotly debated, but most people were not overly alarmed by the lack of a moral consensus.[4] They increasingly accepted sexual diversity and the availability of more options.

What resonance do blackmail stories have today? Sexual blackmail did not simply disappear. New forms emerged. In 1992, for example, a lawyer threatened his male lover that if the lawyer were not given $10,000 a month for life he would reveal that his victim was a homosexual and had a lover who had AIDS. When the payments were stopped in 1995 the lawyer filed a $20 million breach of contract lawsuit. The court dismissed the suit as extortionate and fined the lawyer for frivolous litigation. The New York Bar's disciplinary committee subsequently disbarred him.[5] One could argue that the leveling of such a cruel threat is proof that not that much had really changed. But the point is that the lawyer actually felt that he had a chance of succeeding in a breach of contract suit against a homosexual companion. Moreover, it was the menace of revealing the lover's disease rather than his sexual orientation that was the basis of the lawyer's threat. There is still a

good deal of hostility to homosexuality, but inasmuch as it is not institutionalized to the degree that it once was, the potency of sexual blackmail
282 has declined.

To take a less optimistic view of the decline of traditional blackmail fears,
while public tolerance of sexual minorities may have grown, many sexual
acts are still stigmatized. Public voyeurism appears to be more rampant
than ever. But with the flourishing of "checkbook journalism," those seeking to peddle information on sexual indiscretions do not have to proffer
blackmail threats; they can sell their sordid story to tabloid newspapers or
TV shows, which have mushroomed since the 1990s. Ironically, in the age
of the "post–sexual revolution" the public's appetite for sex scandals seems
only to grow. Financial payments are now made for disclosure rather than
to prevent it. It might be argued that this results in just another sort of
blackmail, with the celebrity victim paying, if not in cash, then in a marriage breakup or in a forced resignation from office.

Nevertheless, if sex scandals are still newsworthy the evidence suggests
that they are not as destructive of one's public reputation as they once were.
In the United States, for example, President Bill Clinton was battered by the
fallout from the Monica Lewinsky affair, but nevertheless emerged trium-
phant. Similarly, in England Robin Cook, the Foreign Minister, was embar-
rassed by the tabloids revealing that he had a mistress, but he did not lose
his cabinet post as a result. The most serious damage to public personalities
results when proof is unearthed of their hypocrisy or abuse of power. Despite the conservative complaints that we now live in an age of "political
correctness" and "new puritanism," there has been a distinct decline in the
old anxiety that a career could be destroyed simply by the sudden revelation of one's adultery, homosexuality, or abortion. Evidence of consensual,
private sexual acts is no longer taken (except by the most prudish) as an in-
delible sign of an individual's basic immorality or dishonesty. Our culture
continues to regard a number of sexual practices as transgressive, but it has
seriously downplayed the significance of sex as the final social arbiter of
one's character.

The history of sexual blackmail serves as a reminder of the great gap that
for many decades separated sexual beliefs and practices. Though it would
be nonsense to suggest that we now live in a world of complete candor, one
can at the very least assert that many topics that we now face unblinkingly
were once declared unmentionable. The corresponding decline in the

significance of sexual blackmail can be taken as one symptom of this liberalization of sexual mores. If we still owe anything to the blackmailers of the past it is perhaps our thanks. Their activities forced us to direct our attention to the ways in which over many generations the law, morality, and prejudice on the one hand and social inequality on the other created conditions that heightened the dangers of sexuality and limited its pleasures.

NOTES

INTRODUCTION

1. *New York Times*, Jan. 21, 1997, sec. 2, p. 3, col. 6 (hereafter, for example, p. 3:6); July 10, sec. 2, p. 1:2; July 11, sec. 2, p. 3:5; July 16, sec. 2, p. 1:2.

2. *New York Times*, July 12, 1997, p. 24:1; July 15, sec. 2, p. 3:1.

3. Commentators pointed out that if Jackson had begun by hiring a good lawyer and had acted discreetly she could have gone after Cosby for back child support. *New York Times*, July 18, 1997, p. 29:1; July 21, p. 16:6; July 28, sec. 2, p. 3:1; *United States v. Jackson*, 986 F. Supp. 829 (S.D.N.Y. 1997).

4. *New York Times*, June 10, 1999, sec. B, p. 1:5; Nov. 16, sec. B, p. 4:1; *United States v. Jackson*, 180 F.3d 55 (2d Cir. 1999); *United States v. Jackson*, 196 F.3d 383 (2d Cir. 1999).

5. Michel Foucault, *The History of Sexuality* (New York: Pantheon, 1978); Jeffrey Weeks, *Sex, Politics, and Society: The Regulation of Sexuality since 1800* (London: Longman, 1989); John d'Emilio and Estelle B. Freedman, *Intimate Matters: A History of Sexuality in America* (Chicago: University of Chicago Press, 1988); Angus McLaren, *Twentieth-Century Sexuality* (Oxford: Blackwell, 1999).

6. Mike Hepburn, *Blackmail: Publicity and Secrecy in Everyday Life* (London: Routledge and Kegan Paul, 1975); Alexander Welsh, *George Eliot and Blackmail* (Cambridge, Mass.: Harvard University Press, 1985); on narratives, see Ken Plummer, *Telling Sexual Stories: Power, Change, and Social Worlds* (London: Routledge, 1995).

7. Leo Katz, *Ill-Gotten Gains: Evasion, Blackmail, Fraud, and Kindred Puzzles of the Law* (Chicago: University of Chicago Press, 1997).

8. Kurt H. Wolff, ed., *The Sociology of George Simmel* (Glencoe, Ill.: Free Press, 1950), p. 331; Michael Mason, *The Making of Victorian Sexuality* (New York: Oxford Uni-

versity Press, 1994); William A. Cohen, *Sex Scandal: The Private Parts of Victorian Fiction* (Durham, N.C.: Duke University Press, 1996); Jonathan Ned Katz, *The Invention of Heterosexuality* (New York: Dutton, 1995).

9. H. L. A. Hart, *Law, Liberty, and Morality* (Stanford: Stanford University Press, 1963), p. 16; Richard A. Posner, *Sex and Reason* (Cambridge, Mass.: Harvard University Press, 1992).

10. Karen Halttunen, *Confidence Men and Painted Women: A Study of Middle-Class Culture in America, 1830–1870* (New Haven: Yale University Press, 1982); Martin J. Wiener, *Reconstructing the Criminal: Culture, Law, and Policy in England, 1830–1914* (Cambridge: Cambridge University Press, 1990).

11. On ways in which the press stages scandals, see Lee Edelman, *Homographesis: Essays in Gay Literary and Cultural Theory* (New York: Routledge, 1994), pp. 148–172.

12. David Ray Papke, *Framing the Criminal: Crime, Cultural Work, and the Loss of Critical Perspective, 1830–1900* (New York: Archon Books, 1987).

13. For a similar chronicling of the concept of consent and how at key moments it marked changes in attitudes towards sexuality, see Pamela Haag, *Consent: Sexual Rights and the Transformation of American Liberalism* (Ithaca: Cornell University Press, 1999).

1. SODOMY AND THE INVENTION OF BLACKMAIL

1. John Richardson, *Recollections, Political, Literary, Dramatic, and Miscellaneous, of the Last Half Century* (1855), cited in Chris White, ed., *Nineteenth-Century Writings on Homosexuality* (London: Routledge, 1999), pp. 31–32; see also H. Montgomery Hyde, *The Strange Death of Lord Castlereagh* (London: Heinemann, 1959), pp. 182–190; Louis Crompton, *Byron and Greek Love* (Berkeley: University of California Press, 1985), pp. 302–305.

2. Laura Gowing, *Domestic Dangers: Women, Words, and Sex in Early Modern London* (Cambridge: Cambridge University Press, 1996); Mary Beth Norton, "Gender and Defamation in Seventeenth-Century Maryland," *William and Mary Quarterly* 44 (1987): 3–39; S. M. Waddams, *Sexual Slander in Nineteenth-Century England: Defamation in the Ecclesiastical Courts, 1815–1855* (Toronto: University of Toronto Press, 2000).

3. Leon Radzinowicz, *A History of the English Criminal Law* (Oxford: Clarendon, 1948), vol. 1, p. 641; Sir Walter Scott, *Waverley* (Oxford: Clarendon Press, 1981), pp. 70–71; Frederic Hill, *Crime: Its Amount, Causes, and Remedies* (London: John Murray, 1853), p. 6.

4. E. P. Thompson, "The Crime of Anonymity," in Douglas Hay, ed., *Albion's Fatal Tree* (Harmondsworth: Penguin, 1975), p. 257.

5. Radzinowicz, *Criminal Law*, vol. 1, pp. 73–74, 308, 641; E. P. Thompson, *Whigs and Hunters: The Origins of the Black Act* (London: Allen Lane, 1975), p. 271.

6. Sir William Blackstone, *Commentaries on the Laws of England*, 15th ed. (London: Strahan, 1809), vol. 4, p. 215; Anthony E. Simpson, "Masculinity and Control: The

Prosecution of Sex Offenses in Eighteenth-Century London," (Ph.D. diss., New York University, 1984), p. 431.

7. Anthony Simpson, "The 'Blackmail Myth' and the Prosecution of Rape and Its Attempt in Eighteenth-Century London: The Creation of a Legal Tradition," *Journal of Criminal Law and Criminology* 77 (1986): 123; Randolph Trumbach, *Sex and the Gender Revolution: Heterosexuality and the Third Gender in Enlightenment London* (Chicago: University of Chicago Press, 1998); Tim Hitchcock, *English Sexualities, 1700–1800* (New York: St. Martin's Press, 1997).

8. *Lady's Magazine* cited in Gordon Rattray Taylor, *The Angel-Makers: A Study in the Psychological Origins of Historical Change, 1750–1850* (London: Heinemann, 1958), p. 277.

9. Simpson, "Masculinity and Control," pp. 509–584; Rictor Norton, *Mother Clapp's Molly House: The Gay Subculture in England, 1700–1830* (London: GMP Publishers, 1992), pp. 134–145; Randolph Trumbach, ed., *Sodomy Trials: Seven Documents* (New York: Garland, 1986). See also Trumbach, *Sex and the Gender Revolution*, pp. 55–59; *Dictionary of National Biography* (London: Smith Elder, 1889), vol. 19, pp. 370–375.

10. *King against Thomas Jones* (1776) 1 Leach 139.

11. *King against Donnally* (1779) 1 Leach 193–194, 197, 198.

12. *King against Daniel Hickman* (1783); 1 Leach 278, 280. See also *Reane's Case* (1794) 2 Leach 616; *Rex v. Thomas Cannon and James Coddington* (1809), Crown Cases Reserved 146; R and R 146; *Rex v. Egerton* (1819) Crown Cases Reserved 375; R and R 375; *Rex v. Edward* 1 M & Rob. 257, 174 English Reports 88 (hereafter Eng. Rep.).

13. Louis Crompton, "Jeremy Bentham's Essay on 'Paederasty': An Introduction," *Journal of Homosexuality* 4 (1978): 100.

14. Robert Holloway, *The Phoenix of Sodom, or the Vere Street Coterie* (London: Holloway, 1813), pp. 46, 53–54.

15. *Times* (London), July 30, 1829, p. 3f; Feb. 11, 1833, p. 3e; *Regina v. James Norton* (1838) 8 Car. & P. 671, 173 Eng. Rep. 667; *Times* (London), Dec. 21, 1838, p. 6c; see also Jan 10, 1826, p. 3c; July 19, p. 3d; Oct. 9, p. 3b.

16. *Times* (London), Dec. 11, 1867, p. 11e; Nov. 26, 1869, p. 9e; Feb. 10, 1871, p. 11f; July 17, 1871, p. 6d.

17. Symonds cited in Richard Davenport-Hines, *Sex, Death, and Punishment: Attitudes to Sex and Sexuality in Britain since the Renaissance* (London: Fontana, 1990), p. 131; Xavier Mayne [Edward Irenaeus Prime Stevenson], *The Intersexes: A History of Similisexualism as a Problem in Social Life* (New York: Arno Press, 1975 [first ed. 1908]), p. 508; see also Jeffrey Weeks, *Coming Out: Homosexual Politics in Britain, from the Nineteenth Century to the Present* (London: Quartet, 1977), pp. 11–14.

18. Robert Louis Stevenson, *Strange Case of Dr. Jekyll and Mr. Hyde* (London: Folio Society, 1948), p. 30, see also p. 53; Oscar Wilde, *A Picture of Dorian Gray* (Oxford: Oxford University Press, 1974), p. 171; Oscar Wilde et al., *Teleny*, ed. John McRae (London: GMP Publishers, 1986), p. 134. On *The Blackmailers*, which dealt with the blackmailing of a woman by a former lover but had a homosexual subtext, see

Laurence Senelick, *Lovesick: Modernist Plays of Same-Sex Love 1894–1925* (New York: Routledge, 1999), pp. 15–60. *Times* (London), June 8, 1894, p. 8b; June 9, p. 14f.

19. PRO HO 144/8/21080; HO 144/73/A43930; *Times* (London), Aug. 6, 1886, p. 7d; May 6, 1892, p. 14d; May 14, p. 18f.

20. *Times* (London), Nov. 28, 1889, p. 10d; Dec. 16, 1895, 6d; *Leeds Daily News,* Dec. 14, 1895, p. 4; Dec. 16, 1895, p. 3.

21. Louise Jackson, "The Child's Word in Court: Cases of Sexual Abuse in London, 1870–1914," in Margaret L. Arnot and Cornelie Usborne, eds., *Gender and Crime in Modern Europe* (London: University College Press, 1999), pp. 222–237; *Times* (London), Aug. 1, 1889, p. 11f; Feb. 26, 1887, p. 12e. On Gray and Markham see *Times* (London), May 11, 1887, p. 5a; May 18, p. 5a; June 1, p. 13a; July 4, p. 10f.

22. *Times* (London), June 20, 1895, p. 3g.

23. Sir Melville MacNaghten, *Days of My Years* (London: Edward Arnold, 1914), p. 131; *Times* (London), Dec. 5, 1898, p. 10e; July 14, 1899, p. 7c. On the authorities' attempts to minimize the reportage of same-sex practices, see Mayne, *The Intersexes,* p. 482.

24. Richard Ellman, *Oscar Wilde* (London: Penguin, 1988), p. 363.

25. Ibid., p. 419.

26. I. Playfair [Alfred Douglas], *Gentle Criticism on British Justice* (n.p., 1895), pp. 3, 7, 14; Ellman, *Oscar Wilde,* p. 447; H. Montgomery Hyde, ed., *The Trials of Oscar Wilde* (London: William Hodge, 1948), pp. 207–210, 300; see also pp. 195, 276, 303; H. Montgomery Hyde, *Oscar Wilde* (London: Eyre Methuen, 1976), pp. 247–252.

27. Ellman, *Oscar Wilde,* p. 427; Hugh Stevens, *Henry James and Sexuality* (Cambridge: Cambridge University Press, 1998), pp. 126, 130; Jonathan Freedman, *Professions of Taste: Henry James, British Aestheticism, and Commodity Culture* (Stanford: Stanford University Press, 1990), pp. 168–171; Vernon A. Rosario, *The Erotic Imagination: French Histories of Perversity* (Oxford: Oxford University Press, 1997), p. 103.

28. David S. Reynolds, *Walt Whitman's America: A Cultural Biography* (New York: Knopf, 1995), pp. 394–395; *National Police Gazette,* Dec. 31, 18821, p. 10; Mary Warner Blanchard, *Oscar Wilde's America: Counterculture in the Gilded Age* (New Haven: Yale University Press, 1998), pp. 4–12.

29. C. S. Clark, *Of Toronto the Good: A Social Study, the Queen City of Canada as It Is* (Montreal: Toronto Publishing Co., 1898), p. 90; see also James Gifford, *Daynesford's Library: American Homosexual Writing, 1900–1913* (Amherst: University of Massachusetts Press, 1995), p. 119.

30. *People v. Hall,* 49 N.Y.S. 158 (Sup. Ct. 1898); *People v Hall,* 51 A.D. 57, 64 N.Y.S. 433 (Sup. Ct. 1900).

31. Senelick, *Lovesick,* pp. 67–75.

32. Mayne, *The Intersexes,* pp. 455, 457.

33. Ibid., pp. 466, 472, 490–491.

34. Ibid., p. 480.

35. Ibid., pp. 469, 484.

36. *Times* (London), June 14, 1870, p. 11e; June 20, p. 13e; May 8, 1895, p. 4f; 20 June 20, 1895, p. 3g.

37. "Urning" was Ulrichs's term for a male body inhabited by a female mind. See Hubert Kennedy, *Ulrichs: The Life and Works of Karl Heinrich Ulrichs, Pioneer of the Modern Gay Movement* (Boston: Alyson, 1988), p. 28; see also pp. 243, 157–159, 172–173; Edward Carpenter, *The Intermediate Sex* (London: Swan Sonnenschein, 1909), p. 79; Ellman, *Oscar Wilde*, p. 343.

38. Havelock Ellis, *Studies in the Psychology of Sex* (New York: Random House, 1936), vol. 1, part 4, p. 853; Carpenter, *The Intermediate Sex*, p. 79; Morris B. Kaplan, "Did 'My Lord Gomorrah' Smile? Homosexuality, Class, and Prostitution in the Cleveland Street Affair," in George Robb and Nancy Erber, eds., *Disorder in the Court: Trials and Sexual Conflict at the Turn of the Century* (New York: New York University Press, 1999), p. 83.

2. THE MODERN MANIA FOR MORALITY

1. "Observations on Certain Documents Contained in Nos. V and VI of *The History of the United States for the Year 1796*, in which the Charge of Speculation against Alexander Hamilton, late Secretary of the Treasury, is fully refuted" (Philadelphia: John Fen, 1797) in *Early American Imprints*, no. 32222 (Worcester: American Antiquarian Society, 1964), pp. xx, 9, 17.

2. Robert A. Hendrickson, *The Rise and Fall of Alexander Hamilton* (New York: Van Nostrand Reinhold Co., 1981), p. 481. See also Julian P. Boyd, ed., *The Papers of Thomas Jefferson* (Princeton: Princeton University Press, 1971), vol. 18, pp. 613–688; Mary-Jo Kline, *Alexander Hamilton: A Biography in His Own Words* (New York: Harper and Row, 1973), pp. 250–251, 262–263, 352–356; Arnold A. Rogon, *A Fatal Friendship: Alexander Hamilton and Aaron Burr* (New York: Hill and Wang, 1998), pp. 152–156.

3. Lawrence Stone, *Uncertain Unions and Broken Lives: Marriage and Divorce in England, 1660–1857* (New York: Oxford University Press, 1995), pp. 265, 267.

4. Ian McCalman, *Radical Underworld: Prophets, Revolutionaries, and Pornographers in London, 1795–1840* (Cambridge: Cambridge University Press, 1988), pp. 41, 223–224; Kenneth Bourne, *The Blackmailing of the Chancellor* (London: Tree Press, 1975); Elizabeth Longford, *Wellington* (London: Weidenfeld and Nicolson, 1972), p. 108.

5. McCalman, *Radical Underworld*, p. 41.

6. *The Queen v. Nathalie Miard* (1844), 1 Cox's Criminal Cases 22; see also *Times* (London), Mar. 9, 1844 , p. 7e.

7. *Hansard Parliamentary Debates*, 3d ser., vol. 71 (1843), col. 893.

8. Pat Thane, "Women and the Poor Law in Victorian and Edwardian England," *History Workshop Journal* 5 (1978): 32; Anthony E. Simpson, "The 'Blackmail Myth' and the Prosecution of Rape and Its Attempt in Eighteenth-Century London: The Creation of a Legal Tradition," *Journal of Criminal Law and Criminology* 77 (1986): 101–150.

9. House of Commons, "Report of the Royal Commission on Divorce and Matrimonial Causes," *Parliamentary Papers,* vol. 34 (1912–13): 865–866; Gail L. Savage, "The Divorce Court and the Queen's/King's Proctor: Legal Patriarchy and the Sanctity of Marriage in England, 1861–1937," *Historical Papers* (1989): 210–227.

10. Judith Walkowitz, *Prostitution and Victorian Society: Women, Class, and the State* (Cambridge: Cambridge University Press, 1980), pp. 78–79.

11. Ginger S. Frost, *Promises Broken: Courtship, Class, and Gender in Victorian England* (Charlottesville: University Press of Virginia, 1995), pp. 107–114.

12. *Hansard Parliamentary Debates,* 3d ser., vol. 71 (1843), cols. 881, 886, 894.

13. W. H. D. Winder, "The Development of Blackmail," *Modern Law Review* 5 (1941): 24; Glanville L. Williams, "Blackmail," *Criminal Law Review* (1954): 80; Peter Alldridge, "'Attempted Murder of the Soul': Blackmail, Privacy, and Secrets," *Oxford Journal of Legal Studies* 13 (1993): 372.

14. *Times* (London), June 16, 1853, p. 7d; June 17, p. 7c.

15. *R. v. Hamilton* (1843) I Car. & K 212, 174 Eng. Rep. 779; *Times* (London), Aug. 26, 1843, p. 6d.

16. *R. v. Chalmers* 10 Cox's Criminal Cases 450 (CCR 1867); *Times* (London), Mar. 9, 1861, p. 12c.

17. *Queen v. Tomlinson* (1895), 1 Q.B.D. 706 at 708; see also Winder, "The Development of Blackmail," 37–39; J. W. Cecil Turner, *Russell on Crime* (London: Stevens and Sons, 1964), vol. 2, p. 870.

18. See Mr. Justice Hawkins in *Allen v. Flood* (1897) 1 Law Reports Appeal Cases 1 at 17–18.

19. Oscar Wilde, *An Ideal Husband,* in H. Montgomery Hyde, ed., *Three Plays* (London: Eyre Methuen, 1981), p. 128.

20. William A. Cohen, *Sex Scandal: The Private Parts of Victorian Fiction* (Durham: Duke University Press, 1996), p. 9.

21. Giles St. Aubyn, *Edward VII: Prince and King* (New York: Atheneum, 1979), pp. 151–154; Margaret Blunden, *The Countess of Warwick* (London: Cassell, 1967), pp. 236–243.

22. Frost, *Promises Broken,* pp. 107–114.

23. Edward W. Cox, *The Principles of Punishment* (London: Law Times Office, 1877), p. 112; A. S. Taylor, *A Manual of Medical Jurisprudence* (New York: Lea, 1897), p. 670; *Truth,* May 17, 1885, pp. 758–759; Lawson Tait, "An Analysis of the Evidence in Seventy Consecutive Cases of Charges Made under the New Criminal Law Amendment Act," *Provincial Medical Journal* (May 1, 1896): 227.

24. Lynda Nead, *Myths of Sexuality: Representations of Women in Victorian Britain* (Oxford: Blackwell, 1988); Arthur W. Pinero, *The Second Mrs. Tanqueray* (London: Heinemann, 1895), p. 14.

25. *Times* (London), Feb. 5, 1895, p. 10b; May 13, 1888, p. 12a.

26. *Times* (London), Apr. 29, 1895, p. 11c; July 31, 1885, p. 5c; Aug. 10, p. 3f; Nov. 13, 1897, p. 15a; Nov. 25, p. 13f; Dec. 14, 1886, p. 4f; Dec. 22, p. 13d; Jan. 15 1887, p. 10b; Feb. 16, 1892, p. 12b; Feb. 24, p. 12c; Mar. 2, p. 3e; Mar. 12, p. 20e; *New York Times,* Mar. 2, 1892, p. 1:3; Mar. 12, p. 1:4.

27. *Times* (London), Dec. 21, 1885, p. 11f; Dec. 22, p. 11e; July 23, 1890, p. 4b; Oscar Wilde, *The Picture of Dorian Gray* (Oxford: Oxford University Press, 1974), p. 124.

28. *Times* (London), Sept. 14, 1895, p. 12a; May 4, 1898, p. 3f; Dec. 10, p. 8d.

29. *Times* (London), May 7, 1886, p. 10e.

30. See Ann-Louise Shapiro, *Breaking the Codes: Female Criminality in Fin-de-Siècle France* (Stanford: Stanford University Press, 1996), p. 219; "Quacks and Abortion: A Critical and Analytical Inquiry," *Lancet*, Dec. 31, 1898, p. 1807; Feb. 16, 1901, p. 493. In the United States Anthony Comstock claimed that sellers of cures for masturbation became blackmailers; see Comstock, *Frauds Exposed* (Montclair, N.J.: Patterson Smith, 1969 [first ed. 1880]), p. 291.

31. *Times* (London), Aug., 7, 1891, p. 8e; Aug. 8, 1891, p. 6a.

32. J. Edgar Foster, *The Fallen Woman and Other Sermons* (London: Digby and Long, n.d.), p. 4; Michael Rubinstein, *Wicked, Wicked Libels* (London: Routledge and Kegan Paul, 1972).

33. *New York World*, July 15, 1874, cited in Paula S. Fass, *Kidnapped: Child Abduction in America* (New York: Oxford University Press, 1997), p. 29; *New York Times*, Sept. 25, 1874, p. 1:2; Oct. 3, p. 7:4.

34. *People v. Gillian*, 2 N.Y.S. 476 (Sup. Ct. 1888); *People v. Gillian*, 115 N.Y. 643 (Ct. App. 1889).

35. *Motsinger v. State*, 123 Ind. 498, 24 N.E. 342 (Sup. Ct. 1890).

36. Karen Halttunen, *Confidence Men and Painted Women: A Study of Middle-Class Culture in America, 1830–1870* (New Haven: Yale University Press, 1982), pp. 1–32; Richard Wightman Fox, *Trials of Intimacy: Love and Loss in the Beecher-Tilton Scandal* (Chicago: University of Chicago Press, 1999), p. 155; see also pp. 156–157, 298, 305; Nicola Beisel, *Imperiled Innocents: Anthony Comstock and Family Reproduction in Victorian America* (Princeton: Princeton University Press, 1997), pp. 77–80.

37. *Oregon State Journal*, Aug. 3, 1867, p. 3; *New York Times*, Feb. 4, 1874, p. 2:6; Nov. 20, 1874, p. 20:5.

38. *New York Times*, Feb. 6, 1872, p. 1:6; Mar. 24, p. 3:6; Nov. 24, p. 5:4.

39. *New York Times*, Nov. 27, 1875, p. 3:1; *National Police Gazette*, Aug. 25, 1883, p. 10; Oct. 6, pp. 7, 9.

40. "Love Is Not Enough," *Harper's Monthly Magazine* 7 (1884): 560–567; *New York Times*, Mar. 13, 1872, p. 4:4; Mar. 15, p. 2:7; Mar. 26, p. 8:5.

41. *New York Times*, Mar. 14, 1872, p. 5:5; Apr. 15, 1877, p. 5:3; *People v. Wightman*, 104 N.Y. 598; 11 N.E. 135 (Ct. App. 1887); *In re Hart*, 116 N.Y.S. 193 (Sup. Ct. 1909).

42. *National Police Gazette*, Oct. 22, 1881, p. 10; see also Jan. 25, 1879, p. 6; Robert C. Allen, *Horrible Prettiness: Burlesque and American Culture* (Chapel Hill: University of North Carolina Press, 1991), pp. 201–221.

43. *National Police Gazette*, Sept. 12, 1896, p. 6; Oct. 22, 1881, p. 10; Feb. 3, 1883, p. 7.

44. *People v. Williams*, 127 Cal. 212, 59 P. 581, 582 (Sup. Ct. 1899); May Churchill Sharpe, *Chicago May: Her Story* (London: Sampson Low, Marston and Co., 1929), pp. 25, 256. See also Charles Hamilton, ed., *Men of the Underworld: The Professional Criminal's Own Story* (London: Gollancz, 1953), p. 15.

45. *New York Times,* Aug. 6, 1874, p. 2:4; Aug. 10, p. 8:4; Feb. 9, 1875, p. 6:5. See also Norma Basch, *Framing American Divorce: From the Revolutionary Generation to the Victorians* (Berkeley: University of California Press, 1999), p. 165; *New York Times,* Nov. 18, 1897, p. 12:5; Nov. 23, p. 7:4.

46. *National Police Gazette,* Nov. 22, 1894, p. 6; Jan. 14, 1882, p. 14; May 13, p. 6; Sept. 22, 1894, p. 7.

47. *In re Estate of Baldwin,* 162 Cal. 471, 123 P. 267 (Sup. Ct. 1912). The family of financial baron Jay Gould similarly portrayed as a blackmailer the woman who claimed to be his first wife. *New York Times,* Nov. 30, 1898, p. 1:4; Dec. 2, p. 3:2; Dec. 6, p. 3:2; Mar. 12, 1899, p. 18:3.

48. *New York Times,* Nov. 6, 1877, p. 2:2; July 4, 1877, p. 5:4; *Austine v. People,* 110 Ill. 248 (Sup. Ct. 1884); *Utterbach v. State,* 153 Ind. 545, 55 N.E. 420 (Sup. Ct. 1899); *National Police Gazette,* Jan. 11, 1879, p. 10. But a district attorney argued that the fact that a woman did not blackmail her employer was proof that he had not raped her as she had claimed: Pamela Haag, *Consent: Sexual Rights and the Transformation of American Liberalism* (Ithaca: Cornell University Press, 1999), p. 30.

49. *National Police Gazette,* May 11, 1878, p. 3; *Beadleston v. Beadleston,* 2 N.Y.S. 809 (Super. Ct. 1888); *National Police Gazette,* Nov. 25, 1882, p. 7. See also Robert L. Griswold, *Family and Divorce in California, 1850–1890* (Albany: State University of New York Press, 1982), pp. 76–77; Laura Hanft Korobkin, *Criminal Conversations, Sentimentality, and Nineteenth-Century Legal Stories of Adultery* (New York: Columbia University Press, 1998), p. 122.

50. *New York Times,* Feb. 25, 1873, p. 8:3.

51. *New York Times,* Jan. 5, 1877, p. 7:7; *National Police Gazette,* Jan. 14, 1882, p. 12; Nov. 4, pp. 7–8.

52. Karl Miller, *Doubles: Studies in Literary History* (Oxford: Oxford University Press, 1985); Barbara Leckie, *Culture and Adultery: The Novel, the Newspaper, and the Law, 1857–1914* (Philadelphia: University of Pennsylvania Press, 1999).

53. Edgar Allan Poe, *The Gold Bug, the Purloined Letter, and Other Tales* (New York: Houghton Mifflin, 1898), p. 55; Nathaniel Hawthorne, *The Scarlet Letter* (New York: Norton, 1978), p. 92; Charles Dickens, *Bleak House* (Oxford: Oxford University Press, 1996), pp. 758–759.

54. Mary Elizabeth Braddon, *Aurora Floyd* (Oxford: Oxford University Press, 1996), p. 283; Wilkie Collins, *No Name* (Leipzig: Tauchnitz, 1863), vol. 1, p. 35; see also Jeanne Fahnestock, "Bigamy: The Rise and Fall of a Convention," *Nineteenth-Century Fiction* 36 (1981): 47–71.

55. Donald Thomas, *Swinburne: The Poet in the World* (London: Weidenfeld and Nicolson, 1979), pp. 87–88, 116.

56. Anthony Trollope, *Castle Richmond* (London: Trollope Society, 1994), p. 229; *John Caldigate* (London: Trollope Society, 1995), p. 180; George Eliot, *Middlemarch* (London: J. M. Dent, 1977), pp. 475, 545–547, 558–559, 634–637.

57. *File No. 113* (London: Routledge, 1887), *The Blackmailers,* tr. Ernest Tristan (London: Lotus Library, 1907); Fortuné du Boisgobey, *The Red Lottery Ticket* (London: Vitzelly, 1887), pp. 43, 47; Henrick Ibsen, *Hedda Gabler,* tr. Kenneth McLeish

(London: Nick Hern Books, 1995); Olga Meier, *The Daughters of Karl Marx: Family Correspondence, 1866–1898*, tr. Faith Evans (New York: Harcourt Brace Jovanovitch, 1982), pp. 297–299; Arthur Conan Doyle, "Charles Augustus Milverton" (1899) in *The Penguin Complete Sherlock Holmes* (Harmondsworth: Penguin, 1981), p. 581.

293

58. Edith Wharton, *House of Mirth* (1905) in *Edith Wharton's New York Novels* (New York: Modern Library, 1998), p. 103; see also *Age of Innocence* (1920), p. 873. Wharton moved in a world where blackmail was practiced. Morton Fullerton, her bisexual lover, was apparently a victim of an earlier mistress who threatened to expose his homosexual past. Marion Mainwaring, *Mysteries of Paris: The Quest for Morton Fullerton* (Boston: University Press of New England, 2001).

59. Alexander Welsh provides a penetrating analysis of the relationship of secrecy, the "information culture," and the "knowledge industry" in the context of George Eliot's novels, but he curiously slights the significance of sexual deviancy. Accordingly he finds the cause of secrets "puzzling." Alexander Welsh, *George Eliot and Blackmail* (Cambridge, Mass.: Harvard University Press, 1985).

60. Or at least there was no male equivalent in England. The erring (and inevitably forgiven) husband was a stock figure in French bedroom farces. Stuart E. Baker, *Georges Feydau and the Aesthetics of Farce* (Ann Arbor: UMI Research Press, 1981), pp. 26–41.

61. *Times* (London), Jan. 10, 1826, p. 3c.

62. Some legal historians state that Warren was prompted by the news coverage his wife had received at the time of their wedding; they had, however, married years before, in 1883. Others, as mentioned, claim that his daughter's marriage preoccupied him; but as she was only six in 1890, this is unlikely. The appeal of the story that the first legal defense of privacy was sparked by a gentleman's concern for a lady is that it complements the stereotyped notion of the active male and the passive female. See Alpheus Thomas Mason, *Brandeis: A Free Man's Life* (New York: Viking Press, 1946), p. 70; William L. Prosser, "Privacy," *California Law Review* 48 (1960): 383–423; Lewis J. Paper, *Brandeis* (Englewood Cliffs, N.J.: Prentice-Hall, 1980), pp. 34–35.

63. Samuel D. Warren and Louis D. Brandeis, "The Right to Privacy," *Harvard Law Journal* 4 (1890): 196.

3. WOMANIZING ACROSS CLASS LINES

1. See Annette Lawson, *Adultery: An Analysis of Love and Betrayal* (New York: Basic Books, 1988).

2. G. K. Chesterton, *A Miscellany* (1912), cited in Karl E. Scheibe, *Mirrors, Masks, Lies, and Secrets: The Limits of Human Predictability* (New York: Praeger, 1979), p. 87; Henry James, *In the Cage* (London: Martin Secker, 1919), p. 67; John Galsworthy, "Blackmail," in *Captures* (London: Heinemann, 1923), pp. 131, 144; George Bernard Shaw, *Pygmalion*, in *The Bodley Head Bernard Shaw* (London: Bodley Head, 1972), p. 710.

294

3. Saki [H. H. Munro], "The Treasure Ship," (1914), in *The Short Stories of Saki* (London: Bodley Head, 1930), p. 301; E. F. Benson, "The Countess of Lowndes Square," in *The Countess of Lowndes Square and Other Stories* (London: Cassell, 1920), p. 8.

4. William Le Queux, *The Man About Town: A Story of Society and Blackmail* (London: John Long, 1916); see also his *Blackmailed* (London: Evelyn Nash and Grayson, 1927). L. G. Redmond-Howard, *Radio Blackmail* (London: Mellifont Press, 1936). See also Arthur Applin, *Blackmailed* (London: Everett and Co., 1915); F. M. White, *Blackmail!* (London: Ward, Lock and Co., 1918); Edgar Wallace, *Blackmail and the Iron Grip* (London: Readers' Library, 1940).

5. Herbert Jay, "Into the Enemy's Camp," in Lady Asquith et al., *My Grimmest Nightmare* (London: George Allen and Unwin, 1935), p. 113.

6. "Sapper" [H. C. McNeile], "Blackmail," in *Word of Honour* (London: Hodder and Stoughton, 1926), pp. 139, 143.

7. Eden Phillpotts, "Grey Lady Drive," in *Peacock House and Other Mysteries* (London: Hutchinson, 1926), p. 156; see also W. W. Jacobs's short stories "The Well" and "Captain Rogers" in *The Lady of the Barge* (New York: Harper, 1903).

8. A Veteran Diplomat, "Men Who Trade in the Secrets of Others," *New York Times,* Dec. 13, 1908, sec. 6, p. 6:1.

9. *Times* (London), Mar. 11, 1925, p. 9e; *Parliamentary Debates,* Commons, 5th ser., vol. 181 (1924–25), cols. 1239–40, 1249, 1260–1261; see also vol. 180 (1924–25), col. 27.

10. *Times* (London), May 13, 1927, p. 18f; Feb. 23, 1937, p. 5d; "Crimes Known to the Police (Annual Averages)" in Home Office, *Criminal Statistics: England and Wales* (London: HMSO, 1939); Herman Mannheim, *Social Aspects of Crime in England between the Wars* (London: George Allen and Unwin, 1940), p. 65.

11. *Times* (London), Nov. 30, 1933, p. 4f; Dec. 5, p. 8d; Dec. 13, p. 4e; Jan. 12, 1934, p. 9d; Robert Skidelsky, *Interests and Obsessions: Selected Essays* (London: Macmillan, 1993), pp. 156–157; *Times* (London), July 14, 1911, p. 3c; July 19, 1911, p. 4c.

12. *Times* (London), Mar. 22, 1929, p. 13e; June 13, p. 5g; see also *New York Times,* Mar. 22, 1929, p. 18:6; Sept. 22, p. 12:2.

13. *Daily Rand* (Johannesburg), June 12, 1930, p. 10; June 13, p. 11; June 14, p. 11; June 17, p. 13; June 21, p. 9.

14. *Times* (London), Apr. 18, 1914, p. 5d.

15. *Times* (London), Nov. 17, 1902, p. 10d; Aug. 13, 1930, p. 7e; May 25, 1931, p. 7e; Jan. 28, 1933, p. 12b.

16. *Times* (London), Apr. 15, 1914, p. 3a; Apr. 22, p. 6f; Nov. 3, 1930, p. 20c; Jan. 15, 1931, p. 9b; Mar. 3, p. 5c.

17. "A Vile Conspiracy," *Lancet,* Dec. 17, 1904, pp. 1733–34; *Times* (London), 23 Aug., 1913, p. 8b; see also Mar. 14, 1924, p. 9e; July 25, 1932, p. 14c; Sept. 22, p. 7a.

18. *Times* (London), Oct. 4, 1911, p. 3b; May 14, 1928, p. 9d; May 15, 9d; *New York Times,* Mar. 11, 1928, p. 6:2.

19. *Times* (London), Mar. 1, 1928, p. 11g; Dec. 3, 1935, p. 5b; Nov. 25, 1937, p. 4e, Jan. 20, 1931, p. 9b.

20. *Times* (London), Dec. 15, 1930, p. 9d; Feb. 9, 1931, p. 9f; Feb. 23, p. 9f; Mar. 6, p. 11c; Nov. 5, 1936, p. 9b; "Recent Judicial Decisions," *Police Journal* 4 (1931): 629.

21. Victor Bailey and Sheila Blackburn, "The Punishment of Incest Act 1908: A Case Study of Law Creation," *Criminal Law Review* (1979): 715; *Times* (London), Feb. 28, 1917, p. 10c.

22. *Times* (London), Apr. 23, 1912, p. 6d; Aug. 26, 1925, p. 7b; Nov. 3, p. 13e.

23. *Times* (London), May 31, 1926, p. 11f; June 5, p. 11d; June 30, p. 10e; Feb. 21, 1931, p. 6e; *Glasgow Herald*, Apr. 22, 1936, p. 9e; *Times* (London), Jan. 5, 1937, p. 9g; Jan. 20, p. 9g; *Glasgow Herald*, July 23, 1937, p. 9a.

24. Pigeons were reportedly used for the same purpose in Belgium and Argentina. *Times* (London), July 28, 1931, p. 13d; *New York Times*, Apr. 3, 1935, p. 4:3.

25. Martin J. Wiener, *Reconstructing the Criminal: Culture, Law, and Policy in England, 1830–1914* (Cambridge: Cambridge University Press, 1990), p. 245.

26. *Times* (London), Mar. 10, 1938, p. 11c; Jan. 2, 1931, p. 12a; Feb. 14, p. 14c; June 13, 1939, p. 13b.

27. *Times* (London), Mar. 1, 1919, p. 7b; Sept. 8, 1921, p. 5f; Oct. 22, p. 5c; May 18, 1927, p. 18f; July 26, 1932, p. 14d; June 22, 1940, p. 3d; R. I. McDonald, "Blackmail," *Police Journal* 11 (1938): 315.

28. *Times* (London), Sept. 8, 1932, p. 4b; PRO CRIM 1/313; *Times* (London), May 26, 1925, p. 13c; June 2, p. 9e; June 19, p. 13c.

29. *Times* (London), Mar. 21, 1914, p. 5d; Dec. 21, 1920, p. 4f; Sept. 3, 1921, p. 5c; Sept. 20, p. 12c; Nov. 16, 1923, p. 11d; Mar. 18, 1930, p. 18d; Aug. 17, 1932, p. 12f; Mar. 19, 1934, p. 11d; Oct. 12, 1938, p. 8d.

30. *Times* (London), Aug. 27, 1921, p. 5b; Aug. 20, 1931, p. 7e; Aug. 1, 1933, p. 9d; *Illustrated Police News*, Sept. 21, 1933, p. 4.

31. *Times* (London), Mar. 13, 1937, p. 4c; *Report of the Royal Commission on Divorce and Matrimonial Causes* (London: Eyre and Spottiswoode, 1912), vol. 37, pp. 558–570, 817–840.

32. *Times* (London), Aug. 26, 1937, p. 9e; Sept. 2, p. 6d; Sept. 9, p. 9e; Sept. 23, p. 6a; Dec. 15, p. 13c. On the scandalous reports that to advance his career Denniston had also welcomed his first wife's affair with a superior officer, see *New York Times*, Mar. 21, 1925, p. 4:2; Mar. 24, 1925, p. 1:2.

33. *Times* (London), Apr. 28, 1923, p. 7e; Sept. 20, 1933, p. 15d; Feb. 19, 1931, p. 17f; Oct. 20, p. 11d; Nov. 5, 1936, p. 9b.

34. *Times* (London), May 9, 1931, p. 9e, Nov. 16, 1923, p. 11d; see also Glanville L. Williams, "Blackmail," *Criminal Law Review* (1954): 79–92, 162–172, 240–246.

35. *Times* (London), Dec. 16, 1930, p. 16g; Aug. 13, p. 7e.

36. *Glasgow Herald*, Apr. 8, 1933, p. 7a; *Times* (London), Apr. 28, 1923, p. 7e.

4. ENTRAPPING THE JAZZ-AGE AMERICAN MALE

1. Nan Britton, *The President's Daughter* (New York: Elizabeth Ann Guild, 1927), pp. 40, 49, 77, 78, 173, 311, 357; Carl Sferrazza Anthony, *Florence Harding: The First Lady, The Jazz Age, and the Death of America's Most Scandalous President* (New York:

William Morrow, 1998), pp. 180–186, 201–204, 254–257, 297–299, 361; Robert H. Farrell, *The Strange Death of President Harding* (Columbia: University of Missouri Press, 1996), pp. 50–84.

2. On the demise of the older self-controlled and disciplined model of masculinity, see Kevin White, *The First Sexual Revolution: The Emergence of Male Heterosexuality in Modern America* (New York: New York University Press, 1993); Howard P. Chudacoff, *The Age of the Bachelor: Creating an American Subculture* (Princeton: Princeton University Press, 1999); Tom Pendergast, *Creating the Modern Man: American Magazines and Consumer Culture, 1900–1950* (Columbia: University of Missouri Press, 2000).

3. Richard A. Posner and Katharine B. Silbaugh, *A Guide to America's Sex Laws* (Chicago: University of Chicago Press, 1996), p. 106.

4. *Town Topics Pub. Co. v. Collier,* 99 N.Y.S. 575 (Sup. Ct. 1906); *New York Times,* Apr. 7, 1922, p. 19:2; Andy Logan, *The Man Who Robbed the Robber Barons* (London: Gollancz, 1966), pp. 24, 51, 161.

5. *New York Times,* June 14, 1905, p. 1:3; Mar. 27, 1918, p. 9:3; Sept. 13, 1925, p. 12:4; Sept. 17, p. 11:1; Sept. 22, p. 2:1; Apr. 13, 1929, p. 36:5.

6. *New York Times,* Oct. 20, 1907, sec. 2, p. 1:5; Sept. 3, 1909, p. 7:7; Mar. 4, 1916, p. 7:5; Mar. 17, 1917, p. 1:5; Mar. 18, p. 5:5; Mar. 17, 1918, p. 16:1; Apr. 3, p. 19:2; Feb. 28, p. 3:8.

7. *New York Times,* Aug. 15 1922, p. 29:1; Dec. 21, 1921, p. 14:3; Feb. 11, 1922, p. 14:3. On the "badger game" in Pullman cars and ocean liners, see Edward H. Sutherland, *The Professional Thief* (Chicago: University of Chicago Press, 1937), p. 81.

8. *Barrett v. People,* 77 N.E. 224 (Ill. Sup. Ct. 1906); *People v. Preston,* 127 P. 660, 679 (Calif. Ct. App. 1912).

9. *New York Times,* Feb. 26, 1914, p. 1:4; Dec. 6, 1914, sec. 2, p. 1:3; *San Francisco Examiner,* May 24, 1921, p. 1. See also David J. Langum, *Crossing over the Line: Legislating Morality and the Mann Act* (Chicago: University of Chicago Press, 1994).

10. *New York Times,* Feb. 4, 1915, p. 8:3; Sept. 20, 1916, p. 8:3; Sept. 24, sec. 7, p. 2:2; Jan. 17, 1917, p. 20:3; Feb. 16, p. 20:2.

11. *New York Times,* Jan. 13, 1916, p. 1:5.

12. *New York Times,* Jan. 14, 1916, p. 8:4; Nov. 4, p. 10:6. On Winpenny see *New York Times,* Jan. 15, 1916, p. 6:6; Apr. 28, p. 22:3.

13. *New York Times,* May 16, 1921, p. 1:2; May 17, p. 1:4. On Warner, see also *Dunn v. Warner,* 200 A.D. 895 (N.Y. Sup. Ct. 1922).

14. *New York Times,* May 18, 1921, p. 21:1; May 19, p. 7:1; May 20, p. 17:7; May 21, p. 17:1; May 22, p. 16:2; May 25, p. 19:7; May 27, p. 36:2; June 17, p. 5:2; Dec. 18, p. 21:2.

15. *New York Times,* Feb. 8, 1922, p. 6:5; Mar. 2, 1922, p. 12:1; Mar. 15, p. 9:4; May 18, 1924, sec. 8, p. 14:1; June 8, p. 17:1; June 10, p. 16:3; John B. Kennedy, "Millions for Tribute," *Collier's,* Mar. 25, 1933, p. 21.

16. *Chicago Tribune,* Sept. 21, 1916, p. 5:3; Sept. 22, p. 1:1; Sept. 29, p. 1:2; *New York Times,* Sept. 29, 1916, p. 9:5; Oct. 1, p. 21:2; *San Francisco Examiner,* Sept. 21, 1916, p. 11:5; Sept. 30, p. 6:4.

17. *Chicago Tribune*, Sept. 20, 1916, p. 1:3; *New York Times*, Jan. 30, 1916, p. 18:7; Sept. 18, p. 8:1; Sept. 22, p. 11:1; Oct. 15, sec. 7, p. 3:3; *San Francisco Examiner*, Sept. 22, 1916, p. 5:5.

18. *New York Times*, Sept. 19, 1916, p. 5:2; Sept. 21, p. 24:3; Sept. 25, p. 7:1; Sept. 27, p. 7:4; Oct. 7, p. 5:5; *San Francisco Examiner*, Sept. 25, 1916, p. 5:1; *Chicago Tribune*, Sept. 25, 1916, p. 1:1; Sept. 26, p. 1:1; Oct. 1, 1916, p. A1:1.

19. *Chicago Tribune*, Sept. 20, 1916, p. 7: Sept. 21, p. 5:4; *New York Times*, Oct. 24, 1916, p. 8:1; Nov. 4, p. 11:3; Nov. 8, p. 8:7; Nov. 23, p. 8:4.

20. *New York Times*, Aug. 23, 1921, p. 32:2; Aug. 25, 1928, p. 9:7; Aug. 1, 1937, p. 18:1; Aug. 2, p. 34:4; Dec. 31, p. 3:3; Jan. 18, 1938, p. 2:2; Jan. 15, p. 32:4.

21. "'White-Slave' Law and Blackmail," *Literary Digest*, Jan. 27, 1917, p. 178. For the argument that the Mann Act did not encourage blackmail, see William Seagle, "The Twilight of the Mann Act," *American Bar Association Journal* 55 (1969): 641–647.

22. *State v. Astin*, 106 Wash. 336, 337–338, 180 P. 394 (Sup. Ct. 1919); and see C. Samuel Campbell, *Sex and Blackmail Rackets Exposed* (Girard, Kans.: Haldeman-Julius Publications, n.d.).

23. J. Herbie Difonzo, *Beneath the Fault Line: The Popular and Legal Culture of Divorce in Twentieth-Century America* (Charlottesville: University of Virginia Press, 1997), pp. 54, 89.

24. *New York Times*, Jan. 29, 1919, p. 11:1; Jan. 30, p. 4:3; Jan. 31, p. 11:4; Mar. 13, p. 4:4; Mar. 14, p. 3:5; Mar. 18, p. 24:3; Mar. 19, p. 9:5; Jan. 21, 1921, p. 4:3; Jan. 26, p. 1:4; Mar. 15, p. 8:1; Apr. 28, p. 8:2; Sept. 20, p. 7:1.

25. *Eacock v. State*, 169 Ind. 488, 496, 82 N.E. 1039 (Sup. Ct. 1907). For a similar case see *People v. Marks*, 257 P. 92 (Calif. Ct. App. 1927).

26. *New York Times*, Feb. 20, 1918, p. 7:2; Nov. 9, 1918, p. 13:2, Nov. 15, p. 20:2; Dec. 20, 1927, p. 6:2; *People v. Kastel*, 222 N.Y.S. 744 (Sup. Ct. 1927).

27. *Attorney General v. Tufts*, 132 N.E. 322 (Mass. Super. Judicial Ct. 1921); *New York Times*, Oct. 21, 1922, p. 17:2; July 26, 1923, p. 17:4; July 31, p. 4:4; Dec. 19, p. 11:1; Jan. 27, 1924; p. 20:2; Feb. 6, p. 7:1; July 4, p. 14:4; Dec. 19, p. 2:4.

28. *New York Times*, June 4, 1927, p. 8:1; Apr. 16, 1930, p. 25:3; Apr. 20, 1933, p. 10:4; *King v. Barton*, 263 N.Y.S. 913 (Sup. Ct. 1933); *New York Times*, Aug. 1, 1933, p. 38:5; Aug. 2, p. 34:5; Aug. 3, p. 36:2; Aug. 5, p. 26:5.

29. *In re Pollack*, 246 A.D. 211, 213, 285 N.Y.S. 344 (Sup. Ct. 1936). On Pollack's efforts in the 1960s to reopen the case, see *New York Times*, Jan. 13, 1961, p. 37:1; Feb. 13, p. 24:5; *Pollack v. Barton*, 17 A.D. 2d 609 (N.Y. Sup. Ct. 1962); *Pollack v. Barton*, 191 N.E. 2d 467 (N.Y. Ct. App. 1963).

30. *New York Times*, Mar. 15, 1912, p. 5:2; Mar. 16, p. 1:2; May 5, 1915, p. 22:3; May 6, p. 1:1.

31. *New York Times*, July 22, 1925, p. 21:8; see also *Fontaine v. Whitney*, 213 N.Y.S. 802 (Sup. Ct. 1926); *Fontaine v. Whitney*, 220 N.Y.S. 854, Supreme Court of New York, 1926; *Fontaine v. Whitney*, 214 N.Y.S. 838 (Sup. Ct. 1927); *New York Times*, May 22, 1929, p. 11:1; May 23, p. 21:1; May 25, p. 4:1; June 25, p. 12:2. Another boxer, Max Baer (heavyweight champion 1934–1935), was the target of a suit launched in 1933 by Bee Star, a circus performer. *New York Times*, Dec. 30, 1933, p. 9:2.

297

32. *Literary Digest,* Apr. 18, 1936, p. 11.
33. *New York Times,* Sept. 29, 1932, p. 16:2; May 17, 1936, p. 3:4; *Time,* May 25, 1936, p. 62.
34. *New York Times,* May 15, 1936, p. 7:6; May 16, p. 3:1; May 28, p. 12:2; May 30, p. 32:6.
35. *New York Times,* Oct. 19, 1935, p. 5:2.
36. *New York Times,* May 19, 1936, p. 4:3; May 20, p. 4:4; May 21, p. 4:4; May 23, p. 3:5; May 24, p. 9:2.
37. *New York Times,* May 27, 1936, p. 12:4; Dec. 9, p. 2:2; Dec. 11, p. 2:2.
38. *New York Times,* May 26, 1936, p. 5:1; June 3, 1936, p. 46:3; June 10, p. 2:7; June 23, 1936, p. 48:3; July 12, p. 15:1; July 15, p. 20:4.
39. *New York Times,* Nov. 25, 1936, p. 3:5; Nov. 29, p. 3:3.
40. *New York Times,* June 13, 1936, p. 3:2.
41. *New York Times,* Jan. 4, 1935, p. 26:6; Oct. 29, 1937, p. 10:3; *Time,* Jan. 25, 1937, p. 52.
42. Although Rogers's behavior was suspicious, a grand jury eventually decided that Evelyn Hoey had committed suicide. *New York Times,* Sept. 13, 1935, p. 3:5; Sept. 17, p. 2:4; Oct. 15, p. 3:1; Oct. 29, p. 23:5; Nov. 19, p. 46:2.
43. *New York Times,* Aug. 4, 1936, p. 20:2; Aug. 7, p. 16:5; Aug. 11, p. 14:3; Aug. 12, p. 7:1; Aug. 13, p. 19:5, Aug. 14, p. 4:5; Aug. 15, p. 2:3; Aug. 18, p. 14:4; Oct. 8, p. 48:4.
44. *New York Times,* Dec. 16, 1936, p. 9:5; Jan. 19, 1937, p. 26:4; Jan. 20, p. 5:1; Jan. 21, p. 3:3.
45. *New York Times,* Aug. 18, 1936, p. 12:2; Aug. 23, sec. 2, p. 7:1; Sept. 1, p. 6:6; Oct. 7, p. 56:6.
46. Samuel Taylor Moore, "Those Terrible Tabloids," *The Independent,* Mar. 6, 1926, pp. 264–266; Oswald Garrison Villard, "Sex, Art, Truth, and Magazines," *Atlantic Monthly,* March 1926, pp. 388–398.
47. *New York Times,* Feb. 6, 1937, p. 36:2.
48. On the emergence of the theme of sophisticated male sexuality, see Kenon Breazeale, "In Spite of Women: *Esquire Magazine* and the Construction of the Male Consumer," *Signs* 20 (1994): 1–23.
49. *New York Times,* Jan. 28, 1939, p. 32:5; Feb. 3, p. 36:3; Mar. 3, p. 44:6; Apr. 13, p. 48:5.
50. *New York Times,* Feb. 28, 1918, p. 3:8; Nov. 13, 1920, p. 10:4; Kennedy, "Millions for Tribute," p. 21.

5. THE HOMOSEXUAL TARGET BETWEEN THE WARS

1. Angus McLaren, *Twentieth-Century Sexuality: A History* (Oxford: Blackwell, 1999), pp. 33, 36, 99.
2. *Parliamentary Debates,* Commons, 5th ser., vol. 181 (1924–1925), col. 1262; *Times* (London), Mar. 11, 1925, p. 9e.
3. *Parliamentary Debates,* Commons, 5th ser., vol. 181 (1924–1925), cols. 1270–1271.
4. R. I. McDonald, "Blackmail," *Police Journal* 11 (1938): 313; M. Fordstan, "Male Persons Soliciting or Importuning for Immoral Purposes," *Police Journal* 22 (1949):

57–64, 133–146; for Jowitt see J. Tudor Rees and Harley V. Usill, eds., *They Stand Apart: A Critical Survey of Homosexuality* (London: Heinemann, 1955), pp. 23, 198–99, 206–207.

5. *Times* (London), Oct. 23, 1937, p. 9d; Oct. 28, p. 10f; Nov. 4, p. 16a; Dec. 1, p. 13b; Dec. 2, p. 16c; Dec. 4, p. 4f; *News of the World,* Dec. 5, 1937, p. 10.

6. June 8, 1937, PRO MEPO 3/923.

7. Statement of Edward Seago, Sept. 23, 1937, PRO MEPO 3/923, 13; PRO MEPO 3/923, 17. Edward Seago (b. 1910) later became a highly successful society portrait painter, his sitters including Noël Coward, Raymond Massey, Prince Philip, and Queen Elizabeth. His biographer discreetly states that "when he was emotionally involved with a man physical satisfaction with a woman was unappealing" and that his intense relations with young male assistants were "something more than normal." Jean Goodman, *Edward Seago: The Other Side of the Canvas* (London: Collins, 1978), pp. 70, 192.

8. Letter dated Apr. 1, 1937, PRO MEPO 3/923; Apr. 26, 1937, PRO MEPO, 3/923; May 26, 1937, PRO MEPO 3/923.

9. June 2, 1937, PRO MEPO 3/923; Aug. 21, 1937 PRO MEPO 3/923.

10. Harold Vernon statements, PRO MEPO 3/923; January 1938, PRO MEPO 3/923.

11. *Times* (London), May 21, 1927, p. 11c; May, 24, p. 13c; May 25, p. 13a; *New York Times,* May 29, 1927, sec. 2, p. 2:5; Robert Jackson, *The Chief: The Biography of Gordon Hewart, Lord Chief Justice of England, 1922–40* (London: Harrup, 1959), pp. 176–177.

12. PRO MEPO 3/923, 24.

13. Statements of Francis Lawrence Walsh, PRO MEPO 3/923, 14; Sept. 13, 1937, 3/923, 22.

14. Statement of Francis Berkeley Hyde Villiers, PRO MEPO 3/923, 15.

15. Statement of Captain Harold Godwin, PRO MEPO 3/393, 11.

16. Statements of Ashley Pearce, PRO MEPO 3/923, 13; 3/923, 19.

17. Statement of Ashley Pearce, PRO MEPO 3/923, 14.

18. Statements of Ian B. Fraser, PRO MEPO 3/923, 7–9.

19. Statement of Leslie Townley, October 1937, PRO MEPO 3/923, 10. The homosexual sadist in question was purportedly Roger Keyes, naval hero and Conservative MP.

20. Raymond was an extra in Israel Zangwill's *The King of Schnorrers* (1925); a "soldier" in *The Firebrand* (1926), which starred Ivor Novello; and "Benny" in *The Ringer* (1926), Edgar Wallace's first stage success. Wallace, famed for his thrillers, had shocked the theatrical world in 1926 by writing an article in the *Daily Mail* entitled "The Canker in Our Midst," alleging that some actors indulged in sexual perversions. J. P. Wearing, *The London Stage: 1920–1929* (London: Scarecrow Press, 1984); Margaret Lane, *Edgar Wallace: The Biography of a Phenomenon* (London: Heinemann, 1939), pp. 313, 319–322.

21. Leslie Townley statement, PRO MEPO 3/923, 10; *Times* (London), Jan. 25, 1933, p. 4f.

22. *Illustrated Police News,* Feb. 2, 1933, p. 2.

23. Alan Sinfield, *The Wilde Century: Effeminacy, Oscar Wilde, and the Queer Moment* (New York: Columbia University Press, 1994), p. 3.

24. *Illustrated Police News,* March 13, 1930, p. 3.

25. Bryan Connon, *Somerset Maugham and the Maugham Dynasty* (London: Sinclair-Stevenson, 1997), p. 101; Anthony Masters, *Nancy Astor: A Life* (London: Weidenfeld and Nicolson, 1981), pp. 165–167; Christopher Sykes, *Nancy: The Life of Lady Astor* (London: Collins, 1972), pp. 326–327. See also Noel Annan, *Our Age: Portrait of a Generation* (London: Weidenfeld and Nicolson, 1990), pp. 101–119; E. M. Forster, *Maurice* (Toronto: Macmillan, 1971), p. 191; Bevis Hillier, *Young Betjeman* (Edinburgh: John Murray, 1988), pp. 177–178; and Richard Davenport-Hines, *Auden* (London: Heinemann, 1995), p. 108, who notes that Auden's lawyer prevented the anecdote from appearing in the United Kingdom edition of Charles Osborne's *W. H. Auden*. Michael Thornton, *Royal Feud: The Queen Mother and the Duchess of Windsor* (London: Pan, 1985), pp. 127, 402n101; Hillier, *Young Betjeman,* p. 181.

26. *Worcester Daily Times,* Oct. 24, 1921 (n.p.).

27. *Worcester Daily Times,* Sept. 6–25, 1921; *Times* (London), Aug. 30, 1921, p. 5b; Sept. 7, p. 5e; Sept. 14, p. 5a; Oct. 8, p. 4e.

28. *Times* (London), Feb. 12, 1927, p. 9d; Feb. 19, p. 4d; Mar. 16, p. 18d. To the annoyance of the judge the cleric's name was published in the *Eastern Daily Press,* Feb. 12, 1927, p. 3; Feb. 19, p. 10; Arthur R. L. Gardner, *The Art of Crime* (London: Philip Allan, 1931), pp. 108–110.

29. *Times* (London), Sept. 27, 1934, p. 7b; see also Sept. 18, 1931, p. 9b; Oct. 20, p. 11d.

30. *Times* (London), Sept. 24, 1934, p. 18b; Oct. 1, p. 9b; Oct. 30, p. 7c; *Police Journal* 8 (1935): 3.

31. *Times* (London), Jan. 7, 1939, p. 7d; Jan. 14, p. 9f; Feb. 15, p. 9c.

32. *Times* (London), Sept. 3, 1902, p. 9e; Sept. 17, p. 10e.

33. *Times* (London), July 2, 1919, p. 9d; *Glasgow Herald,* June 11, 1937, p. 11a; Sir Charles Biron, *Without Prejudice: Impressions of Life and Law* (London: Faber and Faber, 1936), pp. 327–328.

34. *Times* (London), Jan. 1, 1931, p. 9d; Jan. 20, p. 9e; Jan. 21, p. 11c; Feb. 18, p. 11f; Feb. 19, p. 17f; July 26, 1937, p. 3g; July 30, p. 11c; Sept. 28, p. 9b; Sept. 29, p. 5f.

35. *Times* (London), May 26, 1911, p. 4b; see also June 1, p. 3b.

36. *Times* (London), July 1, 1911, p. 4c.

37. Marek Kohn, *Dope Girls: The Birth of the British Drug Underground* (London: Lawrence and Wishart, 1992), pp. 91–95; *Illustrated Police News,* Feb. 6, 1919, p. 4; Feb. 27, pp. 2, 4.

38. *Times* (London), Aug. 13, 1913, p. 2f; Aug. 20, p. 2e; Sept. 4, p. 3b; Sept. 5, p. 2f; Feb. 9, 1928, p. 11b; Feb. 20, p. 7d; Mar. 27, p. 18b.

39. *Times* (London), Oct. 17, 1935, p. 4b; Jan. 7, 1914, p. 3b; Feb. 12, 1924, p. 9e; *Illustrated Police News,* Feb. 21, 1924, p. 7; Jackson, *The Chief,* pp. 175–176; *Illustrated Police News,* Dec. 18, 1924, p. 3.

40. *Times* (London), Aug. 25, 1921, p. 5e; Apr. 24, 1926, p. 8e; Dec. 7, p. 13e; Nov. 14, 1933, p. 16a; Nov. 22, p. 8d; Dec. 7, p. 11b; *Illustrated Police News,* Dec. 14, 1933, p. 7;

Times (London), Jan. 16, 1934, p. 4d; Jan. 17, 1938, p. 9d; Jan. 24, p. 4c; Feb. 9, p. 9b; Feb. 10, p. 11c.

41. *Times* (London), Feb. 12, 1924, p. 5g; Feb. 20, p. 9f; Mar. 19, p. 11b; Mar. 29, p. 9d; Apr. 2, p. 9e. PRO MEPO 3/369.

42. *Times* (London), Mar. 8, 1932, p. 4g; Mar. 15, p. 5d; Mar. 17, p. 8f; Mar. 31, p. 6d; Apr. 15, p. 7g.

43. *Times* (London), Sept. 24, 1932, p. 7d; Nov. 4, 1932, p. 16d.

44. Gardner, *The Art of Crime*, p. 104; *Times* (London), Jan. 16, 1930, p. 5d; Jan. 20, p. 9b; Jan. 24, p. 7e; Feb. 25, p. 5d.

45. PRO MEPO 3/362; *John Bull*, Nov. 16, 1929.

46. Gardner, *The Art of Crime*, p. 107; *Times* (London), Aug. 23, 1938, p. 7c; Oct. 5, p. 8d.

47. Mark Benney [Henry Ernest Degras], *Low Company: Describing the Evolution of a Burglar* (London: Peter Davies, 1936), p. 259.

48. Ibid., p. 261.

49. Kevin Porter and Jeffrey Weeks, *Between the Acts: Lives of Homosexual Men, 1885–1967* (London: Routledge, 1991), p. 63; E. S. P. Haynes, *The Decline of Liberty in England* (London: Grant Richards, 1916), pp. 61–63; George Ives, *A History of Penal Methods* (London: Stanley Paul, 1914), pp. 353–356; Jeffrey Weeks, *Coming Out: Homosexual Politics in Britain from the Nineteenth Century to the Present* (London: Quartet, 1977), pp. 118–124.

50. *New York Times*, June 12, 1908, p. 16:1.

51. *New York Times*, June 12, 1908, p. 16:1; June 13, p. 4:2; June 16, p. 5:3; June 17, p. 5:5; June 18, p. 16:4; *New York Herald*, June 12, 1908, p. 6; June 13, p. 7.

52. Jonathan Ned Katz, *Gay/Lesbian Almanac: A New Documentary* (New York: Harper and Row, 1983), pp. 325–326. Katz does not trace the events that followed in 1909. *New York Times*, Feb. 17, 1909, p. 16:5; Feb. 18, p. 5:1; Feb. 19, p. 6:2; Feb. 20, p. 4:5; Feb. 24, p. 3:4; Feb. 25, p. 1:5; Feb. 26, p. 4:1.

53. *Times* (London), Feb. 13, 1909, p. 13d; *New York Times*, Feb. 12, 1909, p. 1:3; Feb. 13, p. 6:7.

54. On polygraph testing in such cases, see John A. Larion, *Lying and Its Detection* (Chicago: University of Chicago Press, 1932), p. 322.

55. Richard A. Posner and Katherine B. Silbaugh, *A Guide to America's Sex Laws* (Chicago: University of Chicago Press, 1996), p. 70; see also Massachusetts General Laws ch. 272 sec. 34 (1784) and California penal code 286 (1872) and 288a (1921); *People v. Hall*, 16 N.Y.S. 2d 328, 330 (Jefferson County Ct. 1939).

56. Vice Commission of Chicago, *The Social Evil in Chicago* (Chicago: Vice Commission of Chicago, 1911), p. 298; *Town Topics* quoted in Andy Logan, *The Man Who Robbed the Robber Barons* (London: Victor Gollancz, 1966), p. 136. See also James Brough, *Princess Alice: A Biography of Alice Roosevelt Longworth* (Boston: Little, Brown, 1975), pp. 131–132.

57. *New York Times*, Oct. 29, 1915, p. 9:5.

58. *New York Times*, Jan. 3, 1923; Jan. 4, p. 18:5; Jan. 24, p. 14:1; Sept. 22, p. 1:3; Sept. 28, 1:3; Sept. 29, p. 1:8. On the Ward family's attempts to limit publicity see also *Ward v.*

Morschauser, 195 N.Y.S. 63 (Sup. Ct. 1922); *Ward Baking Co. v. Western Union Telegraph Co.* 200 N.Y.S. (Sup. Ct. 1923); John Loughery, *The Other Side of Silence: Men's Lives and Gay Identities, a Twentieth-Century History* (New York: Henry Holt, 1998), pp. 94–95.

59. *New York Times,* June 12, 1931, p. 2:4; July 11, p. 3:7; July 12, sec. 2, p. 2:7; Feb. 2, 1945, p. 21:4.

60. Thomas Doherty, *Pre-Code Hollywood: Sex, Immorality, and Insurrection in American Cinema, 1930–1934* (New York: Columbia University Press, 1999), p. 121; Floyd Dell, *The Briary Bush* (New York: Knopf, 1921), p. 31; see also Ernest Hemingway, "Mother of a Queen," in *The Short Stories of Ernest Hemingway* (New York: Scribners, 1938), pp. 415–420. James M. Cain, *Serenade* (New York: Knopf, 1937), p. 209; John Dos Passos, *The Big Money* (New York: Harcourt Brace and Co., 1933), p. 517.

61. Raymond Chandler, *The Big Sleep* (Harmondsworth: Penguin, 1948), pp. 50, 63, 95, 98–99, 107. See also Michael Mason, "Marlowe, Men and Women," in Miriam Gross, ed., *The World of Raymond Chandler* (London: Weidenfeld and Nicolson, 1977), pp. 89–102.

62. Raymond Chandler, *The High Window* (London: Hamish Hamilton, 1943), p. 23.

63. George Chauncey, *Gay New York: Gender, Urban Culture, and the Making of the Gay Male World, 1890–1940* (New York: Basic Books, 1994), pp. 265–266; Loughery, *The Other Side of Silence,* pp. 50–51.

64. Blair Niles, *Strange Brother* (New York: Liveright, 1931), p. 316; for a less stilted account of homosexuality between the wars, see Charles Henri Ford and Parker Tyler, *The Young and Evil* (Paris: Obelisk Press, 1933); Chauncey, *Gay New York,* p. 324.

65. Samuel Kahn, *Mentality and Homosexuality* (Boston: Meador Publishing, 1937), p. 135; Joseph Collins, *The Doctor Looks at Love and Life* (New York: Dorn, 1926), p. 68; Aaron J. Rosanoff, *Manual of Psychiatry* (New York: Wiley, 1920), pp. 304–305.

66. Edward H. Sutherland, *The Professional Thief* (Chicago: University of Chicago Press, 1937), pp. 79, 80.

67. *New York Times,* July 8, 1922, p. 2:4; July 9, p. 5:2; Dec. 14, p. 22:6; Feb. 8, 1923, p. 16:4.

68. *New York Times,* July 7, 1927, p. 3:3. The 1937 Cabany threat was recorded on a dictaphone: see *People v. Jones,* 25 Cal. App. 2d 517, 519, 77 P. 2d 897 (Ct. App. 1938); *New York Times,* Apr. 25, 1930, p. 17:4; *Times* (London), Apr. 25, 1930, p. 9c; May 26, p. 21b; May 27, p. 8d.

69. *New York Times,* Jan. 22, 1939, p. 25:5.

70. *New York Times,* Dec. 18, 1939, p. 44:1.

71. William R. Peer, "One Story the Tabloids Couldn't Touch," *American Mercury,* September 1953, p. 122.

72. *New York Times,* Dec. 21, 1939, p. 17:3; Dec. 23, p. 32:4; *Forcier v. Andenocci,* 20 N.Y.S. 2d 495 (Sup. Ct. 1940); *In re Application of Forcier,* 20 N.Y.S. 2d 984 (Sup. Ct. 1940).

73. *New York Times,* Nov. 5, 1941, p. 25:2; Nov. 11, p. 18:2; Mar. 26, 1942, p. 18:4.

74. *New York Times,* Oct. 23, 1942, p. 23:4; Nov. 17, p. 27:6; Feb. 19, 1943, p. 38:2.

75. *New York Herald Tribune,* Dec. 21, 1939, p. 21.

76. Peer, "One Story," pp. 121–125.

77. Allan Berubé, "The History of Gay Bathhouses," in Dangerous Bedfellows, eds., *Policing Public Sex: Queer Politics and the Future of AIDS Activism* (Boston: South End Press, 1996), pp. 190–192.

6. EXPLOITING RACIAL ANXIETIES

1. Williams was declared mad and sent to an asylum. A Central Park memorial bench honors Green, hailed in the press as the "father of Greater New York." *New York Times,* June 1, 1904, p. 1:1; June 2, p. 1:1; *New York Herald,* June 1, 1904, p. 3.

2. *New York Times,* June 3, 1904, p. 1:1; June 6, p. 14:5; June 7, p. 5:1; June 8, p. 1:7.

3. *New York Times,* June 9, 1904, p. 1:3; June 11, p. 1:7.

4. *New York Times,* June 28, 1904, p. 16:3; Sept. 11, p. 12:4; Sept. 25, p. 3:4; Jan. 19, 1905, p. 16:3; Feb. 22, p. 3:2. See also *Platt v. Elias,* 91 N.Y.S. 1079 (Sup. Ct. 1905); *Platt v. Elias,* 79 N.E. 1 (N.Y. Ct. App. 1906).

5. Kevin J. Mumford, *Interzones: Black/White Sex Districts in Chicago and New York in the Early Twentieth Century* (New York: Columbia University Press, 1997), pp. 138, 163–164.

6. Peggy Pascoe, "Miscegenation Law, Court Cases, and Ideologies of 'Race' in Twentieth-Century America," *Journal of American History* 83 (1996): 56–57; David H. Fowler, *Northern Attitudes towards Interracial Marriage* (New York: Garland, 1987), pp. 247, 299; *New York Times,* Dec. 3, 1925, p. 3:1. See also Mark J. Madigan, "Miscegenation and the 'Dicta of Race and Class': The Rhinelander Case and Nella Larsen's *Passing," Modern Fiction Studies* 36 (1990): 523–528.

7. David J. Langum, *Crossing over the Line: Legislating Morality and the Mann Act* (Chicago: University of Chicago Press, 1994), pp. 181–186; Gail Bederman, *Manliness and Civilization: A Cultural History of Gender and Race in the United States, 1880–1917* (Chicago: University of Chicago Press, 1995), pp. 1–10.

8. Stewart E. Tolnay and E. M. Beck, *A Festival of Violence: An Analysis of Southern Lynchings, 1882–1930* (Urbana: University of Illinois Press, 1995), pp. 77–78; Mumford, *Interzones,* p. 163; Arthur F. Raper, *The Tragedy of Lynching* (Chapel Hill: University of North Carolina Press, 1933).

9. *Times* (London), Feb. 11, 1925, p. 7b; C. E. Bechhofer Roberts, ed., *The Mr. A Case* (London: Jarrolds, 1950), p. 102.

10. *Times* (London), Dec. 3, 1924, p. 5a.

11. C. E. Bechhofer Roberts, *Sir Travers Humphreys* (London: Bodley Head, 1936), p. 204; *Times* (London), Mar. 10, 1925, p. 6c; Douglas G. Browne, *Sir Travers Humphreys: A Biography* (London: Harrup, 1960), p. 240.

12. *The People,* Dec. 7, 1924, p. 1.

13. Roberts, *The Mr. A Case,* p. 299; *The People,* Dec. 7, 1924, p. 1.

14. Roberts, *The Mr. A Case,* pp. 10, 87, 92; Roberts, *Sir Travers Humphreys,* pp. 195, 196.

304

15. Roberts, *The Mr. A Case*, p. 97; Roberts, *Sir Travers Humphreys*, p. 201.
16. Roberts, *The Mr. A Case*, p. 74; *New York Times*, Nov. 27, 1924, p. 1:3; Roberts, *The Mr. A Case*, pp. 28, 112; *Times* (London), Mar. 7, 1925, p. 9a; *Nottingham Evening Post*, Mar. 12, 1925, p. 5.
17. Frances G. Hutchins, *The Illusion of Permanence: British Imperialism in India* (Princeton: Princeton University Press, 1967), pp. 65–69; Robert J. C. Young, *Colonial Desire: Hybridity in Theory, Culture, and Race* (New York: Routledge, 1995), p. 93; Paul B. Rich, *Race and Empire in British Politics* (Cambridge: Cambridge University Press, 1986), pp. 120–131; *Illustrated Police News*, Jan. 16, 1919, p. 2; Peter Fryer, *Staying Power: The History of Black People in Britain* (London: Pluto Press, 1984), p. 299; *Illustrated Police News*, Apr. 24, 1919, p. 5; May 8, p. 8.
18. *Liverpool Courier* and *Manchester Guardian* quoted in Fryer, *Staying Power*, pp. 302, 311; *Times* (London), June 14, 1919, p. 8b.
19. *Illustrated Police News*, Sept. 4, 1919, p. 5; Mar. 24, 1921, p. 5; E. D. Morel, *The Horror on the Rhine* (London: Union of Democratic Control, 1920), pp. 9–10.
20. *Report of the Committee Appointed by the Government of India to Investigate the Disturbances in the Punjab, Parliamentary Papers*, Cmd 681 (1920); *Illustrated Police News*, Dec. 18, 1919, p. 4; Helen Fein, *Imperial Crime and Punishment: The Massacre at Jallianwalla and British Judgment, 1919–1920* (Honolulu: University of Hawaii Press, 1977).
21. Madison Grant, *The Passing of the Great Race, or, The Racial Basis of European History* (New York: Scribner's, 1916); Lothrop Stoddard, *The Rising Tide of Color against White World-Supremacy* (New York: Scribner's, 1920); "Eugenics and Race Development," *Eugenics Review*, 11 (1919–20): 126.
22. Martin Waters deposition, *Rex v. Hobbs*, PRO CRIM 1/301; *Evening News*, Dec. 13, 1924, in PRO HO 144 21492/474 398/6.
23. *Times* (London), Dec. 12, 1911, 3c; Dec. 22, 3f; *New York Times*, Dec. 4, 1924, p. 6:2–3; Fatesinghrao Gaekwad, *Sayajirao of Baroda: The Prince and the Man* (Bombay: Popular Prakashan, 1989), pp. 231, 248; Anton Gill, *Ruling Passions: Sex, Race, and Empire* (London: BBC Books, 1995), pp. 96–97.
24. For a fictional account of a rajah victimized by a woman, see Melville Davisson Post, "The Blackmailer," in *The Bradmoor Murder* (New York: J. H. Sears, 1929), pp. 83–108.
25. *Illustrated Police News*, Jan. 2, 1919, p. 2; Jan. 23, p. 4, Jan. 30, p. 4; Apr. 17, p. 5; "Black and White: The Problem of Coloured Men and English Girls," *Illustrated Police News*, Mar. 4, 1920, p. 4. See also DeWitt Mackenzie, *Hell's Kitchen: The Story of London's Underworld as Related by the Notorious Ex-Burglar George Ingram* (London: Herbert Jenkins, 1930), pp. 65–69; Roberts, *The Mr. A Case*, p. 203. See also Marek Kohn, *Dope Girls: The Birth of the British Drug Underground* (London: Lawrence and Wishart, 1992); *The People*, Mar. 8, 1925, p. 3.
26. *The People*, Nov. 30, 1924, p. 9; Nov. 23, p. 1; *New York Times*, Nov. 22, 1924, p. 17:2.
27. *Daily Chronicle*, November 22, 1924, pp. 3, 4, 7; Roberts, *The Mr. A Case*, pp. 176, 186.
28. *The People*, Nov. 30, 1924, p. 5; Roberts, *The Mr. A Case*, pp. 196–197.

29. *Daily Herald*, Nov. 21, 1924, p. 5; *The People*, Nov. 23, 1924, p. 2.

30. Mary Scharlieb, "Social and Religious Aspects," in James Marchant, ed., *The Control of Parenthood* (London: Putnam, 1920), pp. 95, 99; H. Rider Haggard, *King Solomon's Mines* (London: Cassel, 1933 [first ed. 1885]), p. 260; H. Rider Haggard, "Imperial and Racial Aspects," in Marchant, *The Control of Parenthood*, pp. 172, 188.

31. Roberts, *The Mr. A Case*, pp. 176–177.

32. Gina Marchetti, *Romance and the "Yellow Peril": Race, Sex, and Discursive Strategies in Hollywood Fiction* (Berkeley: University of California Press, 1993), pp. 4–37; Ann Laura Stoler, *Race and the Education of Desire: Foucault's History of Sexuality and the Colonial Order of Things* (Durham: Duke University Press, 1995), p. 46.

33. Thomas Burke, *More Limehouse Nights* (New York: George H. Doran, 1921), pp. 123, 127, 128–129. See also "The Chink and the Child," in his *Limehouse Nights* (London: Grant Richards, 1921), pp. 15–37, the basis of D. W. Griffith's silent film classic *Broken Blossoms* (1919).

34. Mrs. Frank [Fanny] Penny, *A Question of Love* (London: Hodder and Stoughton, 1926); see also her *Mixed Marriage* (London: Methuen, 1903); Mrs. E. W. Savi, *The Daughter in Law* (London: Hurst and Blackett, 1913), pp. 65, 66, 67; Shamsul Islam, *Chronicles of the Raj: A Study of Literary Reactions to the Imperial Idea towards the End of the Raj* (London: Macmillan, 1979).

35. A. E. W. Mason, *They Wouldn't Be Chessmen* (London: Hodder and Stoughton, 1935), pp. 27, 28, 34; Nathanael West, *Novels and Other Writings* (New York: Library of America, 1997), pp. 191–193.

36. *Illustrated Police News*, Jan. 8, 1925, p. 1; *The People*, Aug. 2, 1925, p. 5; *News of the World*, Feb. 15, 1925, p. 1; Andrew Rose, *Scandal at the Savoy: The Infamous 1920s Murder Case* (London: Bloomsbury, 1991).

37. *Daily Mail*, Sept. 23, 1921, p. 7; Savi, *The Daughter in Law*, p. 157.

38. Cited in Derek Thompson, "Courtship and Marriage in Preston between the Wars," *Oral History* 3 (1975): 43–44.

39. Lowell Thomas, *With Lawrence in Arabia* (London: Hutchinson, 1924); T. E. Lawrence, *Revolt in the Desert* (New York: Doran, 1927); Edith Hull, *The Sheik* (Boston: Small, Maynard and Co., 1921), pp. 54, 57. For an incredibly popular account of a British officer who disguises himself as an Arab to free his comrades see A. E. W. Mason, *The Four Feathers* (London: Smith, Selder, 1902), with film versions in 1915, 1921, 1924, 1939, 1955 (entitled *Storm over the Nile*), and 1977.

40. Gaylin Studlar, "Discourses of Gender and Ethnicity: The Construction and De(con)struction of Rudolph Valentino as Other," *Film Criticism* 13 (1989): 18–30; Alexander Walker, *Rudolph Valentino* (London: Hamish Hamilton, 1976), p. 50; Marjorie Garber, "The Chic of Araby: Transvestism and the Erotics of Cultural Appropriation," in *Vested Interests: Cross-Dressing and Cultural Anxiety* (New York: Routledge, 1992), pp. 304–309; Billie Melman, *Women and the Popular Imagination in the Twenties: Flappers and Nymphs* (London: St. Martin's, 1988), pp. 89–106. For a comparison of the Sheik with Edgar Rice Burroughs's Tarzan (alias Lord Greystoke), see Bederman, *Manliness and Civilization*, pp. 219–334.

41. Richard Hough, *Edwina* (London: Weidenfeld and Nicolson, 1983), pp. 125–127; Philip Ziegler, *Mountbatten: The Official Biography* (London: Collins: 1985), pp. 214, 360, 345; David Hooper, *Public Scandal, Odium, and Contempt* (London: Secker and Warburg, 1989), p. 137.

42. *New York Times*, Nov. 17, 1935, p. 1:6; *Times* (London), Oct. 26, 1935, p. 11b; Dec. 18, p. 11b; *New York Times*, Dec. 18, 1935, p. 20:6; May 20, 1936, p. 11:3.

7. BLACKMAIL AND THE NEW WOMAN

1. Olive Schreiner, *Women and Labour* (London: Virago, 1978 [first ed. 1911]), p. 82; Floyd Dell, *Love in the Machine Age: A Psychological Study of the Transition from Patriarchal Society* (New York: Farrar and Rinehart, 1930), pp. 65–66; Charlotte Perkins Gilman, "Parasitism and Civilized Vice," in Samuel D. Schmalhausen and V. F. Calverton, eds., *Woman's Coming of Age: A Symposium* (New York: Liveright, 1931), pp. 110–127; see also Emma Goldman, *Anarchism and Other Essays* (New York: Dover, 1969 [first ed. 1910]), p. 235.

2. Kathy Peiss, *Cheap Amusements: Working Women and Leisure in Turn of the Century New York* (Philadelphia: Temple University Press, 1986), pp. 107–114; Paul G. Cressy, *The Taxi Dancer: A Sociological Study in Commercialized Recreation and City Life* (Chicago: University of Chicago Press, 1932), pp. 47, 48, 100–101; Walter C. Reckless, *Vice in Chicago* (Chicago: Chicago University Press, 1933), pp. 146, 162.

3. Peter Bailey, "'Naughty but Nice': Musical Comedy and the Rhetoric of the Girl, 1892–1914," in Michael R. Booth and Joel H. Kaplan, eds., *The Edwardian Theatre: Essays on Performance and the Stage* (Cambridge: Cambridge University Press, 1996), p. 50.

4. Agnes Repplier, "The Repeal of Reticence," *Atlantic Monthly*, March 1914, pp. 297–304; Albert Auster, *Actresses and Suffragists: Women in the American Theater* (New York: Praeger, 1989), pp. 39, 59–60.

5. William Howland Kenny, *Recorded Music in American Life* (New York: Oxford University Press, 1999), p. 104; see also Pamela Haag, *Consent: Sexual Rights and the Transformation of American Liberalism* (Ithaca: Cornell University Press, 1999), pp. 172–174; Linda R. Hirshman and Jane E. Larson, *Hard Bargains: The Politics of Sex* (New York: Oxford University Press, 1998), pp. 126–129, 130–140, 165–166.

6. Leslie Fishbein, *Rebels in Bohemia: The Radicals of "The Masses"* (Chapel Hill: University of North Carolina Press, 1982), pp. 74–112; Christine Stansell, *American Moderns: Bohemian New York and the Creation of a New Century* (New York: Henry Holt, 2000), pp. 250–288; Katharine Bement Davis, *Factors in the Sex Life of Twenty-Four Hundred Women* (New York: Harper and Brothers, 1929); Phyllis Blanchard, "Sex and the Adolescent Girl," in V. F. Calverton and S. D. Schmalhausen, eds., *Sex in Civilization* (London: Allen and Unwin, 1929), pp. 538–546; Lewis M. Terman, *Psychological Factors in Marital Happiness* (New York: McGraw Hill, 1938), p. 321.

7. H. L. Mencken, "The Blushful Mystery," in *Prejudices: First Series* (New York: Knopf, 1919), p. 199.

23. From the 1930s on women demanded diamond engagement rings as a new type of "collateral." See Rebecca Tushnet, "The Rules of Engagement," *Yale Law Journal* 107 (1998): 2583–2618; Margaret F. Brinig, *From Contract to Covenant: Beyond the Law and Economics of the Family* (Cambridge, Mass.: Harvard University Press, 2000), pp. 40–41.

24. Sinclair, "Seduction," 85; for an English defender of such suits, see Viscount Birkenhead, *Law, Life and Letters* (London: Hodder and Stoughton, 1927), p. 128.

25. Jennifer Terry, *An American Obsession: Science, Medicine, and Homosexuality in Modern Society* (Chicago: University of Chicago Press, 1999), p. 274.

26. Carleton Simon, "Divorce and Its Relations to Crime," *Vital Speeches* 1 (Dec. 3, 1934): 143; *McLure's* cited in William O'Neill, *Divorce in the Progressive Era* (New Haven: Yale University Press, 1967), pp. 79–80; *Ladies Home Journal* cited in Paul Bohannan, ed., *Divorce and After* (New York: Anchor Books, 1971), p. 301n3; for Kresge see Willard Waller, *The Old Love and the New: Divorce and Readjustment* (New York: Liveright, 1930), pp. 239–240.

27. *New York Times*, Sept. 21, 1926, p. 33:1; May 5, 1933, p. 18:1; see also the later film *Alimony* (1949), reviewed in the *New York Times*, July 22, 1949, p. 16:3; "Flaying the Alimony-Diggers," *Literary Digest* 100 (Mar. 16, 1929): 26; "Plucking the Golden Gander," *North American Review* 225 (April 1928): 461–464.

28. Robert J. Corber, *In the Name of National Security: Hitchcock, Homophobia, and the Political Construction of Gender in Postwar America* (Durham, N.C.: Duke University Press, 1993), p. 126; *New York Times*, Feb. 13, 1927, sec. 7, p. 7:3; Molly Haskell, *From Reverence to Rape: The Treatment of Women in the Movies* (Chicago: University of Chicago Press, 1987), pp. 90–102.

29. *New York Times*, Feb. 13, 1927, sec. 7, p. 7:3. On the Cinderella myth in the 1930s being the female equivalent of the self-made man myth, see Lois Banner, *American Beauty* (New York: Knopf, 1983), pp. 180–182. *New York Times*, May 24, 1930, p. 21:3; Feb. 28, 1931, p. 156:2; Nov. 28, p. 20:4; Aug. 29, 1932, p. 9:2.

30. On the 1930s portrayal of the conniving woman, see Lori Landay, *Madcaps, Screwballs, Con Women: The Female Trickster in American Culture* (Philadelphia: University of Pennsylvania Press, 1998), pp. 53–61, 75–85; Thomas Doherty, *Pre-Code Hollywood: Sex, Immorality, and Insurrection in American Cinema, 1930–1934* (New York: Columbia University Press, 1999), pp. 131–136.

31. *New York Times*, July 29, 1924, p. 9:2; Aug. 3, sec. 7, p. 2:7; Anita Loos, *Gentlemen Prefer Blondes* (London: Penguin, 1992), pp. 118, 121; for the "much- married" showgirl who inspired Loos, see Constance Rosenblum, *Gold Digger: The Outrageous Life and Times of Peggy Hopkins Joyce* (New York: Holt/Metropolitan, 2000); *New York Times*, Jan. 16, 1928, p. 24; July 1, 1932, p. 19:3.

32. *New York Times*, Nov. 2, 1925, p. 20:1; Nov. 8, 1931, p. 27:1; Dec. 25, 1933, p. 28:2; Feb. 4, 1932, p. 25:2.

33. James Robert Parrish, *Prostitution in Hollywood Films* (Jefferson, N.C.: McFarland, 1992), p. 399; *New York Times*, Feb. 10, 1933, p. 12–3; *Times* (London), April 3,

8. *Chicago Tribune,* Sept. 21, 1916, p. 5:4; see also Peter N. Stearns, *Jealousy: The Evolution of an Emotion in America's History* (New York: New York University Press, 1989).   307

9. *New York Times,* Apr. 13, 1922, p. 1:4; Apr. 16, p. 16:5; Apr. 19, p. 23:1.

10. *New York Times,* Mar. 16, 1923, p. 3:3; Mar. 24, p. 1:4; Mar. 26, p. 1:8; Mar. 29, p. 1:6; Mar. 31, p. 4:2; Apr. 2, p. 7:1; Apr. 3, p. 25:3; Oct. 21, sec. 2, p. 4:2; Dec. 19, p. 11:1.

11. *New York Times,* Feb. 28, 1931, p, 1:1; Mar. 3, p. 1:8; Mar. 25, p. 1:1; Mar. 26, p. 2:5; July 1, p. 4:2.

12. *New York Times,* July 1, 1926, p. 25:4; July 2, p. 16:1; July 7, p. 14:4; July 8, p. 11:2.

13. *New York Times,* Nov. 14, 1929, p. 1:2; Mar. 21, 1930, p. 30:1; Apr. 8, p. 19:3; Apr. 9, p. 15:1; Apr. 17, p. 29:2; see also Apr. 11, p. 17:1; May 8, p. 29:4; May 23, p. 7:7.

14. *New York Times,* Apr. 2, 1936, p. 26:3; Apr. 16, p. 5:6, Apr. 28, p. 4:8; Mar. 10, 1937, p. 4:6.

15. Michael Grossberg, *Governing the Hearth: Law and Family in Nineteenth-Century America* (Chapel Hill: University of North Carolina Press, 1985), pp. 30–63; Great Britain Law Commission, *Breach of Promise of Marriage* (London: HMSO, 1969).

16. James Schouler, *A Treatise on the Law of Marriage, Divorce and Separation, and Domestic Relations* (Albany, N.Y.: Matthew Bender and Co., 1921), vol. 2, p. 1546; see also Haag, *Consent,* pp. 53, 199n88.

17. Robert C. Brown, "Breach of Promise Suits," *University of Pennsylvania Law Review* 77 (1929): 494; see also Jane E. Larson, "'Women Understand So Little, They Call My Good Nature Deceit': A Feminist Rethinking of Seduction," *Columbia Law Review* 93 (1993): 392–396.

18. Delancey Cox, "The High Cost of Loving," *Forum,* June 1919, p. 739; A Barrister-at-Law, "Blackmail within the Law," *Living Age,* May 16, 1925, p. 362; Schouler, *Law of Marriage,* vol. 2, p. 1547; Robert C. Brown, "Breach of Promise Suits," *University of Pennsylvania Law Review* 77 (1929): 494.

19. Harter F. Wright, "Action for Breach of the Marriage Promise," *Virginia Law Review* 10 (1923–24): 361; Brown, "Breach of Promise Suits," 492; Anthony M. Turano, "Breach of Promise: Still a Racket," *American Mercury,* May 1934, p. 46.

20. Mary Coombs, "Agency and Partnership: A Study of Breach of Promise Plaintiffs," *Yale Journal of Law and Feminism* 2 (1989–90): 1–23; *New York Times,* June 24, 1935, p. 1:2; Turano, "Breach of Promise," pp. 43–44.

21. H. S., "Anti-'Heart-Balm' Legislation," *Temple Law Quarterly* 11 (1936–37): 396–397; M. B. W. Sinclair, "Seduction and the Myth of the Ideal Woman," *Law and Inequality Journal* 5 (1987): 82; *Fearon v. Treanor,* 5 N.E. 2d 815 (N.Y. Ct. App. 1936); "The Work of the 1939 California Legislature," *Southern California Law Review* 13 (1939): 37; Cal. Stats. (1939), c. 128, sec. 2. Though the majority of states retained laws on seduction and alienation of affection, they fell into disuse.

22. Illinois Revised Statutes (1943), ch. 38, par. 246.1 and 246.2; Nathaniel Feinsinger, "Legislative Attack on Heart Balm," *Michigan Law Review* 33 (1935): 979; *New York Times,* Mar. 30, 1935, p. 3:1; "The Outlawry of Heart-Balm Suits," *Literary Digest,* Apr. 13, 1935, p. 22.

1933, p. 12c; *New York Times*, Feb. 10, 1933, p. 12–3. On the bargaining of sexual favors see Joanna Meyerowitz, *Women Adrift: Independent Wage Earners in Chicago, 1880–1930* (Chicago: University of Chicago Press, 1988), p. 144.

34. *Times* (London), Nov. 30, 1933, p. 12e; see also *New York Times*, Oct. 14, 1933, p. 18:2.

35. Arthur Hove, ed., *Gold Diggers of 1933* (Madison: University of Wisconsin Press, 1980), pp. 117, 159–161; *Times* (London), Oct. 16, 1933, p. 10b; *New York Times*, June 8, 1933, p. 22:3.

36. *New York Times*, Jan. 2, 1930, p. 29:2; Dec. 12, 1931, p. 23:4; Parrish, *Prostitution*, p. 41; *New York Times*, June 30, 1933, p. 20:3; Lea Jacobs, *The Wages of Sin: Censorship and the Fallen Woman Film, 1928–1942* (Madison: University of Wisconsin Press, 1991), pp. 70–71, 76; *New York Times*, June 24, 1933, p. 16:2.

37. Lea Jacobs, "Censorship and the Fallen Woman Cycle," in Christine Gledhill, ed., *Home Is Where the Heart Is: Studies in Melodrama and the Woman's Film* (London: British Film Institute, 1987), pp. 100–113.

38. Herbert Blumer and Philip M. Hauser, *Movies, Delinquency, and Crime* (New York; Macmillan, 1933), pp. 80–100; Jacobs, *The Wages of Sin*, pp. 11–17; Gregory D. Black, *Hollywood Censored: Morality Codes, Catholics, and the Movies* (Cambridge: Cambridge University Press, 1994), p. 63; Richard Maltby, "'Baby Face,' or How Joe Breen Made Barbara Stanwyck Atone for Causing the Wall Street Crash," *Screen* 27, 2 (1986): 41–42.

39. Angela J. Latham, "The Right to Bare: Containing and Encoding American Women in Popular Entertainments of the 1920s," *Theatre Journal* 49 (1997): 455–474.

40. Robert Graves and Alan Hodge, *The Long Weekend: A Social History of Great Britain, 1918–1939* (London: Cardinal, 1991 [first ed. 1940]), p. 110; Annette Kuhn, "Cinema, Culture, and Femininity in the 1930s," in Christine Gledhill and Gillian Swanson, eds., *Nationalising Femininity: Culture, Sexuality, and British Cinema in the Second World War* (Manchester: Manchester University Press, 1996), pp. 178, 181; James C. Robertson, *The British Board of Film Censors: Film Censorship in Britain, 1896–1950* (London: Croom Helm, 1985), p. 187.

41. Kristin Thompson, *Exporting Entertainment: America in the World Film Market, 1907–34* (London: British Film Institute, 1985), p. 125; Ian Jarvie, *Hollywood's Overseas Campaign: The North Atlantic Movie Trade, 1920–1950* (Cambridge: Cambridge University Press, 1992), pp. 111, 135; Jeffrey Richards and Dorothy Sheridan, *Mass Observation at the Movies* (London: Routledge and Kegan Paul, 1987), pp. 45, 82, 100–102; Stephen C. Shafer, *British Popular Films 1929–1939: The Cinema of Reassurance* (London: Routledge, 1997), pp. 143–144.

42. Rachel Law, *The History of the British Film, 1918–1929* (London: Routledge, 1997), p. 59.

43. *Times* (London), Apr. 19, 1930, p. 7d.

44. *Times* (London), July 25, 1914, p. 4b; Oct. 23, 1931, p. 14c; Dec. 22, 1932, p. 3d; Mar. 9, 1933, p. 9b; *Illustrated Police News*, Mar. 16, 1933, p. 2; *Times* (London), Apr. 12, 1933, p. 9f; July 7, p. 4d; Oct. 17, 1922, p. 9c.

45. On prostitutes acting with bullies in badger games see the trial reports of *Times* (London), Sept. 8, 1921, p. 5f; Oct. 22, p. 5c; Nov. 18, 1925, p. 11g; May 13, 1927, p. 18f. On women threatening to cite men in divorce proceedings see the *Times* (London), Jan. 7, 1922, p. 7b; Jan. 14, p. 4d; Jan. 21, p. 7e; Nov. 16, 1923, p. 11d; July 15, 1927, p. 5e; Sept. 21, p. 7d. On the use of photos see the *Times* (London), Sept. 3, 1921, p. 5c, Sept. 20, p. 12c.

46. J. C. Ellis, *Blackmail and Co.* (London: Selwyn and Blount, 1928), p. 18; Mrs. Cecil Chesterton, *Women of the Underworld* (London: Stanley Paul, 1928); *Times* (London), Dec. 9, 1931, p. 6g.

47. J. Kenneth Ferrier, *Crooks and Crime* (London: Seeley, Servine and Co., 1928), pp. 172–173; Kathleen Daly, "Gender, Crime, and Criminology," in Michael Tonry, ed., *The Handbook of Crime and Punishment* (New York: Oxford University Press, 1998), p. 91; *Times* (London), Sept. 8, 1921, p. 5f; Oct. 22, p. 5c; Jan. 7, 1922, p. 7b; Jan. 14, p. 4d; Jan. 21, p. 7e; Feb. 10, p. 4f; June 5, 1933, p. 7b; July 15, 1927, p. 5e; Aug. 4, p. 12e; Sept. 21, p. 7d.

48. *Times* (London), Sept. 3, 1921, p. 5c; Sept. 20, p. 12c ; May 19, 1926, p. 6d; May 22, p. 5f; May 29, p. 7e; June 18, p. 11c; July 13, p. 5g; July 14, p. 11f; Aug. 20, p. 4g.

49. *Leicester Mail,* Jan. 28, 1925, pp. 1, 8; Jan. 29, pp. 1, 2, 8; Jan. 30, pp. 1, 8; *Times* (London), Jan. 31, 1925, p. 14e.

50. *Times* (London), June 11, 1930, p. 11f; July 2, p. 11c; Nov. 20, p. 5c; July 26, 1932, p. 14d; Apr. 15, 1914, p. 3a; Apr. 22, p. 6f; Apr. 27, p. 3d; Apr. 28, p. 3f; Nov. 18, 1925, p. 11g.

51. *R v. Dymond* (1920) 2 K.B. 260, 260–261; *Times* (London), Feb. 3, 1920, p. 9c; Mar. 9, p. 5c.

52. *Parliamentary Debates,* Commons, 5th ser., vol. 129 (1920), col. 81; 15 Criminal Appeal Reports (1920–21) 1; Glanville L. Williams, "Blackmail," *Criminal Law Review* (1954): 166.

53. *Times* (London), Nov. 2, 1920, p. 9e; Nov. 18, p. 5f. On Lieutenant-General Sir Herbert Fothergill Cooke (1871–1936), see *Who Was Who,* vol. 3, 1929–1940 (London: Adam and Black, 1947), p. 284.

54. *Times* (London), Jan. 14, 1932, p. 14c. For a similar case see Sept. 23, 1936, p. 9f; Sept. 24, p. 7d.

55. *Times* (London), Jan. 14, 1933, p. 7f; Jan. 18, p. 3c.

56. *Times* (London), Apr. 2, 1930, p. 8g. Though the *Times* index states that an account of Gordon's acquittal appears in its issue of June 27, 1930, p. 8d, the microfilm version of the paper does not carry the story.

57. *Times* (London), Oct. 22, 1936, p. 4g.

58. *Times* (London), Feb. 3, 1938, p. 9b; Feb. 12, p. 17e; Feb. 15, p. 11c; Mar. 23, p. 4a; *R v. Bernhard* (1938) 1 K.B. 264.

59. Billie Melman, *Women and the Popular Imagination in the Twenties: Flappers and Nymphs* (London: St. Martin's, 1988), p. 6; Susan Kingsley Kent, *Making Peace: The Reconstruction of Gender in Interwar Britain* (Princeton: Princeton University Press, 1993), pp. 99–105.

60. *Times* (London), Oct. 7, 1933, p. 9e; Nov. 23, p. 4g; *Illustrated Police News*, Nov. 30, 1933, p. 3.

61. Sonya O. Rose, "Sex, Citizenship, and Nation in World War II Britain," *American Historical Review* 103 (1998): 1164; Judy Giles, "Playing Hard to Get: Working-Class Women, Sexuality, and Respectability in Britain, 1918–40," *Women's History Review* 1 (1992): 247.

8. CAUTIONARY TALES OF ADULTERY AND ABORTION

1. James Marchant, *The Master Problem* (London: Stanley Paul, 1917), pp. 174–196, 264–268, 316–317; see also G. K. Chesterton, "The Emancipation of Domesticity," in *What's Wrong with the World* (New York: Dodd Mead and Co., 1927), pp. 159–167.

2. John B. Kennedy, "Millions for Tribute," *Collier's*, Mar. 25, 1933, p. 21.

3. PRO MEPO 3/927/11.

4. *Times* (London), Jan. 14, 1936, p. 11b.

5. *Times* (London), Dec. 7, 1926, p. 18d; Oct. 21, 1931, p. 11d; *New York Times*, June 8, 1915, p. 22:6; June 20, sec. 2, p. 5:5; June 13, 1926, p. 20:4; *Times* (London), Mar. 6, 1930, p. 11c; Mar. 13, p. 5d; Mar. 20, p. 5f; Apr. 4, p. 5f; Jan. 15, 1931, p. 14c; Feb. 21, p. 3g.

6. *Times* (London), July 15, 1939, p. 6f; *Illustrated Police News*, Oct. 5, 1933, p. 2; Dec. 7, pp. 2–3; *Times* (London), Feb. 13, 1937, p. 9e; Feb. 11, 1938, p. 11d; May 17, 1937, p. 7f.

7. *Times* (London), Sept. 12, 1911, 2d; May 13, 1930, p. 13c; Aug. 19, 1932, p. 15c; Nov. 5, p. 7g; Jan. 19, 1934, p. 4c; Feb. 1, p. 16g; May 11, 1935, p. 9b; PRO MEPO 3/921.

8. *New York Times*, Aug. 5, 1912, p. 6:2; *Times* (London), Feb. 4, 1925, p. 19e; Dec. 8, 1927, p. 5g; Nov. 1, 1929, p. 18f; Nov. 15, p. 11f; Nov. 22, p. 5b; Jan. 25, 1930, p. 14e; Jan. 28, p. 11e; *Glasgow Herald*, June 6, 1936, p. 19f; *Times* (London), Feb. 9, 1938, p. 4f.

9. "America's Most Popular Crime," *Literary Digest*, Oct. 14, 1916, p. 977; see also Lewis A. Ehrenberg, *Steppin' Out: New York Nightlife and the Transformation of American Culture, 1890–1930* (Westport, Conn.: Greenwood Press, 1983), p. 84; *New York Times*, Dec. 16, 1921, p. 18:2; Feb. 17, 1922, p. 19:1; Sept. 8, 1913, p. 16:4.

10. *New York Times*, Sept. 5, 1912, p. 1:1; Sept. 7, p. 22:5; Dec. 22, p. 13:1; Dec. 24, p. 4:6; Jan. 7, 1913, p. 3:2; *People v. Davis*, 141 N.Y.S. 83 (Sup. Ct. 1913); *Times* (London), May 4, 1912, p. 4a; May 8, p. 4a; Feb. 12, 1914, p. 5a; Feb. 20, p. 4e; Feb. 21, p. 4c; Apr. 1, p. 4c; Apr. 8, p. 4d; Apr. 15, p. 3b; Apr. 29, p. 3f; May 22, p. 5b; May 23, p. 5d; Sept. 30, 1932, p. 9g; Dec. 1, p. 9b.

11. *Times* (London), Mar. 3, 1913, p. 3c; Mar. 8, p. 3e; Apr. 10, p. 2f; May 26, 1921, p. 7e; June 4, p. 7a; Mar. 30 1937, p. 12d; Apr. 10, p. 7f; Evelyn Laye, *Boo, to My Friends* (London: Hurst and Blackett, 1958); *Times* (London), July 3, 1937, p. 4e; July 14, p. 11a; *Los Angeles Times*, Apr. 25, 1931, sec. 2, p. 2:3; *New York Times*, Jan. 15, 1931,

p. 20:6; Apr. 23, p. 4:2; June 13, p. 2:6; *Los Angeles Times,* Mar. 26, 1933, sec. 2, p. 1:7; *New York Times,* June 8, 1934, p. 12:1.

12. *Times* (London), Jan. 12, 1938, p. 7d.

13. In Minnesota, for example, a married man who had sex with an unmarried woman was not committing adultery, but a married woman who had sex with an unmarried man was. Richard A. Posner and Katharine B. Silbaugh, *A Guide to America's Sex Laws* (Chicago: University of Chicago Press, 1996), p. 106.

14. *Beauley v. Beauley,* 190 N.Y.S. 129 (Sup. Ct. Special Term 1921); *New York Times,* Aug. 13, 1921, p. 18:2. For a similar case, see *National Police Gazette,* Sept. 29, 1894, p. 7.

15. *Harper v. Murray,* 193 P. 576 (Calif. Sup. Ct. 1920); *Times* (London), Feb. 25, 1932, p. 7b; Apr. 14, p. 9b.

16. *New York Times,* Apr. 20, 1921, p. 3:2.

17. J. H. MacNair, "The Case for Adoption," *Contemporary Review* 105 (May 1914): 707; George K. Behlmer, *Friends of the Family: The English Home and Its Guardians, 1850–1940* (Stanford: Stanford University Press, 1998), p. 310; E. Wayne Carp, *Family Matters: Secrecy and Disclosure in the History of Adoption* (Cambridge, Mass.: Harvard University Press, 1998), pp. 106–107; William J. Locke, "A Lady Paramour," in *The Town of Tombarel* (London: John Lane, 1930), pp. 104–138; *Chicago Tribune,* Sept. 21, 1916, p. 5:4. For the case of a couple who threatened to tell a young woman's father that they were raising her child, see *Times* (London), Dec. 19, 1931, p. 5g.

18. *Kerr v. Kennedy,* 1 K.B. 410 (1942).

19. *Parliamentary Debates,* Commons, 5th ser., vol. 1245 (1921), cols. 1799–1801; Lords, 5th ser., vol. 46 (1921), cols. 568–574; George Ives, *The Continued Extension of the Criminal Law* (London: J. E. Francis, 1922), p. 14.

20. Dr. Mary Scharlieb, *The Bachelor Woman and Her Problems* (London: Williams and Norgate, 1929), pp. 49–50. For the more progressive views that emerged in the 1930s, see Laura Hutton, *The Single Woman and Her Emotional Problems* (London: Bailliere, Tindale and Cox, 1935), pp. 89–114; Robert Latou Dickinson and Lura Beam, *The Single Woman: A Study in Sexual Education* (London: Williams and Norgate, 1934), pp. 203–212.

21. Basil Tozer, *Confidence Crooks and Blackmailers: Their Ways and Methods* (London: Werner Laurie, 1929), pp. 207–209, 227; Martha Vicinus, ed., *Lesbian Subjects: A Feminist Studies Reader* (Bloomington: Indiana University Press, 1996), pp. 33–34; Kaier Kurtin, *"We Can Always Call Them Bulgarians": The Emergence of Lesbians and Gay Men on the American Stage* (Boston: Alyson Publications, 1987), p. 199.

22. Hitchcock based his film on the successful 1928 play of the same name. See Charles Bennett, *Blackmail: A Play in Three Acts* (London: Rich and Cowan, 1928); Tom Ryall, *Blackmail* (London: British Film Institute, 1993).

23. Kevin Brownlow, *Behind the Mask of Innocence* (New York: Knopf, 1990), pp. 32, 36, 89, 516n113; James Robert Parrish, *Prostitution in Hollywood Films* (Jefferson, N.C.: McFarland, 1992), p. 160; *New York Times,* Oct. 21, 1924, p. 21:3; Jan. 7, 1929,

p. 36:2; *Times* (London), Sept. 4, 1933, p. 8b; see also *New York Times*, Sept. 6, 1933, p. 24:4.

24. *New York Times*, Apr. 25, 1929, p. 32:3; June 6, 1931, p. 15:6; Parrish, *Prostitution*, pp. 163–164; Donald Spoto, *The Art of Hitchcock* (London: W. H. Allen, 1977), pp. 19–24.

25. Raymond Chandler, "Blackmailers Don't Shoot," in William F. Nolan, ed., *The Black Mask Boys: Masters in the Hard-Boiled School of Detective Fiction* (New York: Morrow, 1985), pp. 231–264; Cecil Bishop, *The Blackmail Gang* (London: Mellifont Press, 1937); Michael Arlen, *These Charming People* (New York: Collins, 1923), p. 143; Michael Arlen, "The Legend of the Crooked Coronet," in *The Crooked Coronet* (London: Heinemann, 1937), p. 12; Stefan Zweig, "Fear," in *The Royal Game and Other Stories* (London: Cape, 1981), pp. 160–215. See also Gilbert Frankau, *Experiments in Crime* (London: Hutchinson, 1937); G. D. H. Cole and Margaret Cole, *Double Blackmail* (London Collins, 1939).

26. Margaret Sanger, *Motherhood in Bondage* (New York: Brentano, 1928), p. 410; see also John Keown, *Abortion, Doctors, and the Law: Some Aspects of the Legal Regulation of Abortion in England from 1803 to 1982* (Cambridge: Cambridge University Press, 1988); James Mohr, *Abortion in America: The Origins and Evolution of National Policy* (New York: Oxford University Press, 1978).

27. *Times* (London), Dec. 17, 1898, p. 14e; Dec. 19, p. 14b; Dec. 20, p. 9d.

28. *London Star*, Dec. 21, 1898, p. 3; *Birmingham Daily Mail*, Oct. 11, 1898 [n.p.]; *Times* (London), Oct. 12, 1898, p. 4d; *Birmingham Daily Mail*, Oct. 12, 1898; Nov. 28; Dec. 2; see also Angus McLaren, *Birth Control in Nineteenth-Century England* (London: Croom-Helm, 1978), pp. 231–253.

29. "Quacks and Abortion: A Critical and Analytical Inquiry," *Lancet*, Dec. 31, 1898, p. 1807; *East London Advertiser*, Dec. 24, 1898.

30. *Times* (London), Dec. 21, 1898, p. 12c.

31. Richard Findlater, *Banned! A Review of Theatrical Censorship in Britain* (London: McGibbon and Kee, 1967), pp. 97–98; Elizabeth Robins, *Votes for Women* (Chicago: Dramatic Publishing Co., 1907), pp. 110, 118–132; Michael Arlen, *The Green Hat* (London: Grosset and Dunlap, 1924), pp. 161–168; Nathanael West, *Novels and Other Writings* (New York: Library of America, 1997), pp. 60, 90, 123; Jean Rhys, *Voyage in the Dark* (New York: Norton, 1968 [first ed. 1934]), pp. 176–188; Rosamond Lehman, *The Weather in the Streets* (London: Virago, 1981 [first ed. 1936]), pp. 236–239; A. J. Cronin, *Adventures in Two Worlds* (New York: McGraw-Hill, 1935), pp. 230–235; Sackville West cited in Barbara Brookes, *Abortion in England, 1900–1967* (London: Croom Helm, 1988), pp. 65–66; Judith Wilt, *Abortion, Choice, and Contemporary Fiction: The Armageddon of the Maternal Instinct* (Chicago: University of Chicago Press, 1990), pp. 21–23.

32. *Times* (London), Nov. 7, 1936, p. 4d.

33. *Times* (London), Mar. 12, 1937, p. 18e.

34. *Glasgow Herald*, Apr. 25, 1933, p. 7c.

35. *Times* (London), Nov. 11, 1936, p. 18e; Jan. 15, 1929, p. 14d; Mar. 2, p. 9b.

36. *Times* (London), Feb. 6, 1934, p. 11b.

37. A. E. Rowsell, "Abortions—Search Warrants," *Police Journal* 20 (1947): 111; Brookes, *Abortion*, p. 159n68.

38. *Chicago Tribune*, Sept. 26, 1916, p. 1:6.

39. *Andrews v. Gardiner*, 150 N.Y.S. 891 (Sup. Ct. 1914); *Andrews v. Gardiner*, 154 N.Y.S. 486 (Sup. Ct. 1915). Bertschinger sued to recover the $1,025 that had been extorted from him by Campbell. *Bertschinger v. Campbell*, 168 P. 977, 977 (Wash. Sup. Ct. 1917); see also J. J. Taylor, "Blackmail in Its Relation to Journalism," *Proceedings of American Medical Editors* 41 (1910): 125–129.

40. Leslie J. Reagan, *When Abortion Was a Crime: Women, Medicine, and Law in the United States, 1867–1973* (Berkeley: University of California Press, 1997), p. 199; see also pp. 200, 225.

41. Vandiver quoted in ibid., p. 123; *New York Times*, Apr. 1, 1943, p. 25:1; Apr. 21, p. 21:7; Apr. 22, 21:3; May 12, 1944, p. 21:3; *People v. Renda*, 269 A.D. 736 (N.Y. Sup. Ct. 1945).

42. *New York Times*, Sept. 3, 1904, p. 3:5; Nov. 5, 1913, p. 18:3; Jan. 14, 1916, 20:8; Jan. 15, p. 6:6; Oct. 2, 1926, p. 2:7; *Commonwealth v. Bernstine*, 157 A. 698 (Penn. Sup. Ct. 1931); *Commonwealth v. Bernstine*, 162 A. 297 (Penn. Sup. Ct. 1932).

43. Reagan, *When Abortion Was a Crime*, p. 134; Rickie Solinger, *The Abortionist: A Woman against the Law* (New York: Free Press, 1994), pp. 15, 36, 118–119, 182.

44. *New York Times*, Mar. 30, 1930, p. 3:2, Apr. 8, p. 7:6.

45. *New York Times*, Mar. 19, 1930, p. 26:6; Mar. 21, p. 24:2; Mar. 22, p. 40:6; Mar. 26, p. 5:1; Mar. 27, p. 22:4; Mar. 28, p. 14:2; Apr. 10, p. 29:7.

46. *People v. Duke*, 280 N.Y.S. 1015 (Sup. Ct. 1935); *New York Times*, May 4, 1937, p. 14:6; July 12, p. 4:2; *In re Martin*, 11 N.Y.S. 2d 607 (King's County Ct. 1939); *New York Times*, May 28, 1939, p. 17:1.

47. *New York Times*, May 26, 1939, p. 15:3; May 27, p. 1:2; May 28, 1–3; June 1, p. 1–6; June 4, p. 1:6; July 15, p. 32:5; Aug. 8, p. 2:2; Sept. 13, p. 26:3; Sept. 19, p. 16:6; Nov. 17, p. 1:8; Jan. 13, 1940, p. 6:6; Feb. 1, p. 14:2; Feb. 6, p. 8:1; Mar. 22, p. 42:3; *People ex rel. Ditchik v. Sheriff of King's County*, 12 N.Y.S. 2d 341 (Sup. Ct. Special Term 1939).

48. Dr. Irving P. Weinstein, whose medical license had been suspended, testified that his 1937 indictment for committing abortion was dropped after he paid Ditchik. Weinstein had his medical license suspended again in 1943, but the suspension was annulled when evidence of his involvement in a 1941 abortion conspiracy was deemed to have resulted from entrapment. See *People v. Weinstein*, 18 N.Y.S 2d 707 (Kings County Ct. 1940); *Weinstein v. Board of Regents*, 44 N.Y.S. 2d 917 (Sup. Ct. 1943). On Ditchik's trial see *New York Times*, Feb. 10, 1940, p. 32:1; Mar. 6, p. 1:4; Mar. 22, p. 42:3; Apr. 17, p. 24:4; on his appeal see May 28, p. 11:3; Apr. 22, 1941, p. 23:7; see also May 18, 1940, p. 34:2; June 20, p. 11:5. On Madden and Lurie see *In re Madden*, 20 N.Y.S. 2d 169 (Sup. Ct. 1940); *In re Madden*, 24 N.Y.S. 2d 127 (Sup. Ct. 1940); *In the Matter of William Lurie*, 34 N.Y.S. 2d 247, 249 (Sup. Ct. 1942).

49. Frederick J. Taussig, *Abortion, Spontaneous and Induced: Medical and Social Aspects* (St. Louis, Mo.: Mosby, 1936), p. 368; Dorothy Dunbar Bromley, *Birth Control: Its Use and Misuse* (New York: Harper, 1934), pp. 3–4; Dorothy Dunbar Bromley and

Florence Haxton Britten, *Youth and Sex: A Study of 1,300 College Students* (New York: Harper, 1938), pp. 260–261; Havelock Ellis, *Studies in the Psychology of Sex* (New York: Random House, 1936), vol. 4, pp. 601–610; Ministry of Health, Home Office, *Report of the Inter-Departmental Committee on Abortion* (London: HMSO, 1939), p. 105; see also Madeleine Simms, "Midwives and Abortion in the 1930s," *Midwife and Health Visitor* 10 (1974): 114–116; Nicky Leap and Billie Hunter, *The Midwife's Tale: An Oral History from Handywoman to Professional Midwife* (London: Scarlett Press, 1993), pp. 92–98.

315

9. DISARMING THE POSTWAR BLACKMAILER

1. John Costello, *Love, Sex, and War: Changing Values, 1939–1945* (London: Collins, 1985), pp. 259–260, 273–274; *New York Times*, Feb. 28, 1941, p. 12:2; Feb. 26, p. 1:4; see also May 21, 1942, p. 6:1; May 22, p. 10:6; Oct. 10, p. 16:5. John Loughery, *The Other Side of Silence: Men's Lives and Gay Identities, a Twentieth-Century History* (New York: Henry Holt, 1998), p. 152.
2. Quoted in Donald Spoto, *The Kindness of Strangers: The Life of Tennessee Williams* (Boston: Little, Brown and Co., 1985), p. 98.
3. Herman Mannheim, *Social Aspects of Crime in England between the Wars* (London: George Allen and Unwin, 1940), p. 65; "Extortion by Threats Other Than Threats of Violence—Annual Averages," in Home Office, *Criminal Statistics: England and Wales* (London: HMSO, 1950); see also Edward Smithies, *Crime in Wartime: A Social History of Crime in World War II* (London: George Allen and Unwin, 1982).
4. Molly Haskell, *From Reverence to Rape: The Treatment of Women in the Movies* (New York: Holt, Rinehart and Winston, 1973), p. 192; Costello, *Love, Sex, and War*, p. 147; Lucy Noakes, *War and the British: Gender, Memory, and National Identity* (London: I. B. Tauris, 1998), p. 72; David Reynolds, *Rich Relations: The American Occupation of Britain, 1942–1945* (New York: Random House, 1995), pp. 201–208, 262–279.
5. Antonio Lant, *Blackout: Reinventing Women for Wartime British Cinema* (Princeton: Princeton University Press, 1991), pp. 117–126, 135–136, 153–196.
6. Matt Houlbrook, "The Private World of Public Urinals: London 1918–57," *London Journal* 25 (2000): 52–70; Antony Grey, *Quest for Justice: Towards Homosexual Emancipation* (London: Sinclair/Stevenson, 1992), p. 21; Richard Davenport-Hines, *Sex, Death, and Punishment: Attitudes to Sex and Sexuality in Britain since the Reformation* (London: Fontana, 1992), p. 297; *Glasgow Herald*, Oct. 22, 1953, p. 5c; *News of the World*, Oct. 25, 1953, p. 3; Chris Waters, "Disorders of the Mind, Disorders of the Body Social: Peter Wildeblood and the Making of the Modern Homosexual," in Becky Conekin, Frank Mort, and Chris Waters, eds., *Moments of Modernity: Reconstructing Britain, 1945–1964* (London: Rivers Oram Press, 1999), pp. 137–140; Patrick Higgins, *Heterosexual Dictatorship: Male Homosexuality in Postwar Britain* (London: Fourth Estate, 1996), p. 267.
7. Rupert Croft-Cooke, *The Verdict of You All* (London: Secker and Warburg, 1955), p. 149; Higgins, *Heterosexual Dictatorship*, pp. 244–245; Anomaly, *The Invert* (Lon-

don: Thouless, 1948), pp. 233–234; *Times* (London), May 3, 1952, p. 3b; see also Nov. 25, p. 9d.

8. J. Tudor Rees and Harley V. Usill, eds., *They Stand Apart: A Critical Survey of Homosexuality* (London: Heinemann, 1955), pp. 23, 198–199, 206–207; Peter Wildeblood, *Against the Law* (New York: Julian Messner, 1955), p. 142.

9. Frank Mort, "Mapping Sexual London: The Wolfenden Committee on Homosexual Offences and Prostitution, 1954–57," *New Formations* 37 (1999): 92–113; Leslie J. Moran, *The Homosexual(ity) of Law* (London: Routledge, 1996), p. 52; PRO HO 345/13; 345/4; 345/14; 345/8.

10. PRO HO 345/9; 345/16; *Memorandum of Evidence from the Ethical Union to the Department Committee on Homosexuality and Offences Related to Prostitution and Solicitation, April 1955* (London: Ethical Union, 1955); Edward Glover, *The Problem of Homosexuality* (London: Institute for the Study and Treatment of Delinquency, 1954).

11. Higgins, *Heterosexual Dictatorship*, pp. 99–101; PRO HO 345/12; Harry Daley, *This Small Cloud: A Personal Memoir* (London: Weidenfeld and Nicolson, 1986), p. 112; Moran, *The Homosexual(ity) of Law*, pp. 53–54; John Wolfenden, *Turning Points: The Memoirs of Lord Wolfenden* (London: Bodley Head, 1976), p. 131.

12. Sir W. Norwood East, *Society and the Criminal* (Springfield, Ill.: Charles C. Thomas, 1949), p. 150; Eustace Chesser, *Live and Let Live: The Moral of the Wolfenden Report* (London: Heinemann, 1958).

13. "Report of the Committee on Homosexual Offences and Prostitution, 1957," *Parliamentary Papers*, Commons, vol. 14 (1956–57), p. 40.

14. Wildeblood, *Against the Law*, pp. 1, 45–46; see also Hugh David, *On Queer Street: A Social History of British Homosexuality, 1895–1995* (London: Harper Collins, 1997), pp. 170–176.

15. Croft-Cooke, *The Verdict of You All*, p. 145; see also pp. 146–148.

16. Ibid., p. 151.

17. Stephen Jeffrey-Poulter, *Peers, Queers, and Commons: The Struggle for Gay Law Reform from 1950 to the Present* (London: Routledge, 1991), p. 11; *Sunday People*, Feb. 11, 1956, pp. 1,7; Mar. 11, pp. 1, 3; Mar. 18, p. 3; Mar. 25, p. 3; Apr. 1, p. 3; Apr. 8, p. 8; *Times* (London), Dec. 14, 1948, p. 2d; *Empire News*, July 3, 1955, p. 2; July 10, p. 6; July 17, p. 6.

18. Waters, "Disorders of the Mind," pp. 137–140; *Times* (London), Jan. 10, 1959, p. 4f; Aug. 22, p. 10d.

19. *Times* (London), May 26, 1959, p. 5a; June 3, p. 8f; July 3, p. 4g.

20. Desmond Donnelly, "The Blackmailer's Charter," *Spectator*, Feb. 23, 1962, p. 232; C. H. Rolph, "Homosexuality: Reform at Last?" *New Statesman*, Feb. 4, 1966, p. 152.

21. François Lafitte, "Homosexuality and the Law: The Wolfenden Report in Historical Perspective," *British Journal of Delinquency* 9 (1958): 8–19; Eustace Chesser, *Odd Man Out: Homosexuality in Men and Women* (London: Gollancz, 1959), pp. 175, 191; Clifford Allen, *A Textbook of Psychosexual Disorders* (Oxford: Oxford University Press, 1962), p. 186.

22. Margaret Drabble, *Angus Wilson: A Biography* (London: Secker and Warburg, 1995), pp. 133, 243, 613; Bryan Connon, *Somerset Maugham and the Maugham Dynasty* (London: Sinclair-Stevenson, 1997), pp. 100–101; "The Homosexual in America," *Time*, Jan 21, 1966, pp. 42–43; Grey, *Quest for Justice*, pp. 177–178.

23. Connon, *Somerset Maugham*, p. 204.

24. Terrance Rattigan, "Table Number Seven," in *Separate Tables: Two Plays* (London: Samuel French, 1955), p. 67; see also Alan Sinfield, *Out on Stage: Lesbian and Gay Theater in the Twentieth Century* (New Haven: Yale University Press, 1999), p. 165.

25. Compton Mackenzie, *Thin Ice* (London: Chatto and Windus, 1956), pp. 183–185; see also his afterword to Wilfred Macartney, *Walls Have Mouths: A Record of Ten Years' Penal Servitude* (London: Gollancz, 1936); Compton Mackenzie, *My Life and the Times, Octave Ten, 1953–1963* (London: Chatto and Windus, 1971), p. 91. On Driberg's brushes with the law, see Francis Wheen, *Tom Driberg: His Life and Indiscretions* (London: Chatto and Windus, 1990), pp. 186–187, 192–193.

26. Joe Orton, *Between Us Girls,* intro. by Francesca Coppa (London: Nick Hearn Books, 1998), xii–xiii; Clive Fisher, *Noël Coward* (London: Weidenfeld and Nicolson, 1992), p. 244; Noël Coward, "A Song at Twilight," in *Suite in Three Keys* (Garden City, N.Y.: Doubleday, 1967), pp. 86–87; John Osborne, *Inadmissible Evidence* (London: Faber and Faber, 1965), pp. 96–100; *A Patriot Life for Me* (London: Faber and Faber, 1965), p. 63.

27. *New York Times*, June 21, 1960, p. 28:2; June 28, p. 26:1; Andy Medhurst, "'Victim': Text as Context," *Screen* 25 (July–October 1984): 22–35; Richard Dyer, *The Matter of Images: Essays on Representations* (London: Routledge, 1993), pp. 93–109; Anthony Aldgate, *Censorship and the Permissive Society: British Cinema and Theatre, 1955–1965* (Oxford: Clarendon, 1995), pp. 134–135; *Times* (London), Aug. 30, 1961, p. 11c; see also *New Statesman*, Sept. 8, 1961, p. 319; *Spectator*, Sept. 8, 1961, pp. 321–322; John Hill, *Sex, Class, and Realism: British Cinema, 1956–1963* (London: BFI Publishing, 1986), pp. 90–94.

28. Gordon Westwood, *A Minority: A Report on the Life of the Male Homosexual in Great Britain* (London: Longman, 1960), pp. 147–149; Michael Schofield, *Sociological Aspects of Homosexuality: A Comparative Study of Three Types of Homosexuals* (London: Longman, 1965), pp. 175–194.

29. Michael Kettle, *Salome's Last Veil: The Libel Case of the Century* (London: Granada, 1977), pp. 7–8; Higgins, *Heterosexual Dictatorship*, pp. 306–308, 319; Rebecca West, *The New Meaning of Treason* (New York: Viking, 1964), pp. 316–333.

30. Lord Denning, *The Denning Report: The Profumo Affair* (London: Pimlico, 1992), p. 102; see also Christine Keeler, *Scandal* (London: Xanadu, 1989).

31. Wolfenden, *Turning Points*, p. 140; Grey, *Quest for Justice*, pp. 85–87; Higgins, *Heterosexual Dictatorship*, pp. 130–141.

32. Jeffrey-Poulter, *Peers, Queers and Commons*, pp. 82–88, 124.

33. See Grey's review of Higgins's *Heterosexual Dictatorship* in *Gay and Lesbian Humanist*, Spring 1997, http://www.galha.freeserve.co.uk/glh163b2.htm.

34. Noel Annan, *Our Age: Portrait of a Generation* (London: Weidenfeld and Nicolson, 1990), p. 124; J. W. M. Thompson, "They Walk in the Shadow of Fear," *Evening*

Standard, Feb. 22, 1962, p. 7; Ian Harvey, *To Fall Like Lucifer* (London: Sidgwick and Jackson, 1971), p. 142.

318 35. Robert Fabian, *The Anatomy of Crime* (London: Pelham Books, 1970), p. 52; see also Robert Fabian, *Fabian of the Yard* (London: Naldrett Press, 1950), pp. 40–44; Robert Fabian, *London after Dark* (London: Naldrett Press, 1954), p. 66; Westwood, *A Minority;* N. L. Thompson, D. J. West, and T. P. Woodhouse, "Socio-Legal Problems of Male Homosexuals in Britain," in D. J. West, ed., *Sexual Victimization* (London: Gower, 1985), pp. 126, 155–157.

36. Higgins, *Heterosexual Dictatorship,* p. 96.

10. THE GAY MOVEMENT'S ATTACK ON VICTIMIZATION

1. *Time,* Aug. 26, 1966, p. 20.
2. *New York Times,* Feb. 18, 1966, p. 19:4; Mar. 3, p. 1:2.
3. *New York Times,* June 1, 1966, p. 95:2; Aug. 17, p. 23:3.
4. *New York Times,* July 1, 1966, p. 2:2; Aug. 19, p. 33:1; Dec. 9, 1967, p. 54:7.
5. *New York Times,* July 12, 1967, p. 31:5; *United States v. Hughes,* 389 F. 2d 535 (2d Cir. 1968); *New York Times,* Feb. 16, 1968, p. 23:6; *United States v. Hughes,* 411 F. 2d 461, 463 (2d Cir. 1969); *New York Times,* Sept. 28, 1967, p. 39:8; Jan. 14, 1978, p. 25:4.
6. *United States v. Hughes,* 411 F 2d 461 (2d Cir. 1969); *United States v. Burke,* 278 F. Supp. 711 (D. Penn. 1968); *United States v. Nardello,* 393 U.S. 286 (U.S. 1969).
7. *New York Times,* June 1, 1966, p. 95:2.
8. John d'Emilio, "The Homosexual Menace: The Politics of Sexuality in Cold War America," in Kathy Peiss and Christina Simmons with Robert A. Padgug, eds., *Passion and Power: Sexuality in History* (Philadelphia: Temple University Press, 1989), pp. 226–240; Randy Shilts, *Conduct Unbecoming: Lesbians and Gays in the United States Military, Vietnam to the Persian Gulf* (London: St. Martins, 1993), p. 105; John d'Emilio, *Making Trouble: Essays on Gay History, Politics, and the University* (New York: Routledge, 1992), p. 60.
9. Robert W. Merry, *Taking on the World: Joseph and Stewart Alsop, Guardians of the American Century* (New York: Viking, 1996), p. 361; John Loughery, *The Other Side of Silence: Men's Lives and Gay Identities, A Twentieth-Century History* (New York: Henry Holt, 1998), p. 212; Jack Lait and Lee Mortimer, *Washington Confidential* (New York: Crown Publishers, 1951), pp. 90–96; Barbara Epstein, "Anti-Communism, Homophobia, and Construction of Masculinity in the Postwar United States," *Critical Sociology* 20 (1994): 32–44.
10. Loughery, *The Other Side of Silence,* p. 202; Benjamin Karpman, *The Sexual Offender and His Offense* (New York: Julian Press, 1954), pp. 466, 611–612.
11. Jim Kepner, *Rough News, Daring Views: 1950s' Pioneer Gay Press Journalism* (New York: Harrington Park Press, 1998), pp. 229–230; Allen Drury, *Advise and Consent* (New York: Doubleday, 1959); *Mattachine Review,* February 1960, pp. 21–24.
12. Colin J. Williams and Martin S. Weinberg, *Homosexuals and the Military* (New York: Harper and Row, 1971), p. 24; *People v. Ardito,* 431 N.Y.S. 2d 311 (Sup. Ct.

1980). For an unusual 1952 Pennsylvania case in which both the man and the woman were charged with sodomy, see *Commonwealth v. Young*, 92 A. 2d 445 (Penn. Super. Ct. 1952).

13. Kepner, *Rough News, Daring Views*, pp. 80, 93–94, 107–108, 123; *Mattachine Review*, July 1956, p. 7; July 1958, pp. 5–6; Kepner, *Rough News, Daring Views*, pp. 236, 341, 381.

14. Kepner, *Rough News, Daring Views*, p. 342; *Mattachine Review*, April 1960, pp. 6–8; June 1961, p. 21; "A Plea for Perversion?" *Time*, Feb. 23, 1962, p. 59; *Mattachine Review*, February 1958, p. 29; April 1963, pp. 8–10.

15. Alfred C. Kinsey, Wardell B. Pomeroy, and Clyde E. Martin, *Sexual Behavior in the Human Male* (Philadelphia: W. B. Saunders, 1948), pp. 249, 636–651; Epstein, "Anti-Communism," 21–44.

16. John Gerassi, *The Boys of Boise: Furor, Vice, and Folly in an American City* (New York: Macmillan, 1966), pp. 30–35; Estelle B. Freedman, "'Uncontrolled Desires': The Response to the Sexual Psychopath, 1920–1960," in Peiss and Simmons, *Passion and Power*, pp. 203–216; J. Paul de River, *The Sexual Criminal: A Psychoanalytic Study* (Oxford: Blackwell, 1949), pp. xii, 88; see also *Newsweek*, Oct. 10, 1949, pp. 52–54.

17. Allan Berubé, *Coming Out under Fire: The History of Gay Men and Women in World War Two* (New York: Free Press, 1990), p. 259.

18. Edmond Bergler, *One Thousand Homosexuals* (Paterson, N.J.: Pageant Books, 1959), p. 65.

19. David Ehrenstein, *Open Secret: Gay Hollywood, 1928–1998* (New York: William Morrow, 1998), pp. 90–103; *Newsweek*, May 16, 1960, p. 110; Ernest Haveman, "Scientists Search for the Answers to a Touchy and Puzzling Question: Why?" *Life*, June 26, 1964, pp. 76–80; Paul Welch, "The 'Gay' World Takes to the Streets," *Life*, June 26, 1964, pp. 66–75; Lee Edelman, "Tearooms and Sympathy, or, The Epistemology of the Water Closet," in A. Parker, ed., *Nationalisms and Sexualities* (New York: Routledge, 1992), pp. 263–284; *New York Times*, Oct. 18, 1964, sec. E, p. 11:1; "The Homosexual in America," *Time*, Jan. 21, 1966, pp. 42–43.

20. *Time*, Aug. 26, 1966, p. 20; "The Wicked and the Weak," *America*, June 3, 1967, pp. 310–311.

21. Hans von Hentig, *The Criminal and His Victims: Studies in the Sociology of Crime* (New York: Schoken, 1979 [first ed. 1948]), p. 433; Alfred A. Gross, *Strangers in Our Midst: Problems of the Homosexual in American Society* (Washington, D.C.: Public Affairs Press, 1962), pp. 37, 84, 138; Karpman, *The Sexual Offender*, p. 452; Gerhard Mueller, *Sexual Conduct and the Law* (New York: Oceana, 1979 [first edition 1961]), p. 10; Wainwright Churchill, *Homosexual Behavior among Males: A Cross Cultural and Cross Species Investigation* (New York: Hawthorn, 1967), pp. 226–227.

22. Laud Humphreys, *Tearoom Trade: A Study of Homosexual Encounters in Public Places* (London: Duckworth, 1970), pp. 83, 89, 91–93.

23. James T. Sears, *Lonely Hunters: An Oral History of Lesbian and Gay Southern Life, 1948–1968* (Boulder, Colo.: Westview Press, 1997), pp. 243–248; Ronald Bayer, *Homosexuality and American Psychiatry: The Politics of Diagnosis* (Princeton: Prince-

320

ton University Press, 1987), pp. 70–81; Jeffrey Weeks, *Coming Out: Homosexual Politics in Britain, from the Nineteenth Century to the Present* (London: Quartet, 1977), pp. 185–200; Stephen O. Murray, *American Gay* (Chicago: University of Chicago Press, 1996), pp. 60–63; "The Homosexual: Newly Visible, Newly Understood," *Time*, Oct. 31, 1969, pp. 48–56.

24. Donal E. J. MacNamara and Edward Sagarin, *Sex, Crime, and the Law* (New York: Free Press, 1977), pp. 157–158.

25. Walter Barnett, *Sexual Freedom and the Constitution: An Inquiry into the Constitutionality of Repressive Sex Laws* (Albuquerque: University of New Mexico Press, 1973), p. 294; John H. Gagnon and William Simon, *Sexual Conduct: The Social Sources of Human Sexuality* (Chicago: Aldine, 1973), p. 140; Alan P. Bell and Martin S. Weinberg, *Homosexualities: A Study of Diversity among Men and Women* (New York: Simon and Schuster, 1978), pp. 189–190, 192–193; Joseph Harry, "Derivative Deviance: The Cases of Extortion, Fag-Bashing, and Shakedown of Gay Men," *Criminology* 19 (1982): 557.

26. *New York Times*, Apr. 21, 1970, p. 45:8; *People v. Arena*, 411 N.Y.S. 2d 466, (Sup. Ct. 1978).

27. *New York Times*, June 16, 1988, p. 1:4; Paul Rosa, "Gays and the Security Myth," *Washington Post*, July 10, 1988, sec. C, p. 5:1; Gregory B. Lewis, "Lifting the Ban on Gays in the Civil Service: Federal Policy toward Gay and Lesbian Employees since the Cold War," *Public Administration Review* 57 (1997): 387–395.

11. FROM BLACKMAIL TO TABLOID EXPOSÉ

1. *New York Times*, Sept. 27, 1963, p. 1:4; Oct. 10, p. 17:5; Feb. 11, 1964, p. 31:2; Apr. 4, p. 20:5; *Newsweek*, Oct. 7, 1963, p. 42.

2. *New York Times*, Jan. 19, 1952, p. 13:3; *Monthly Film Bulletin* 23 (1956): 91; *New York Times*, Jan. 26, 1945, p. 16:4; Dec. 30, 1949, p. 13:2; *Time*, Aug. 5, 1960, p. 64; *New York Times*, July 28, 1960, p. 19:1; Raymond Chandler, *The Little Sister* (London: Hamish Hamilton, 1949).

3. *Times* (London), July 21, 1975, p. 3h.

4. Alfred C. Kinsey, Wardell B. Pomeroy, and Clyde E. Martin, *Sexual Behavior in the Human Male* (Philadelphia: W. B. Saunders, 1948), pp. 199, 325; Alfred C. Kinsey, Wardell B. Pomeroy, Clyde E. Martin, and Paul H. Gebhard, *Sexual Behavior in the Human Female* (Philadelphia: W. B. Saunders, 1953); Dorothy Dunbar Bromley and F. H. Britten, *Youth and Sex* (New York: Harper, 1938).

5. Erich Fromm, *The Art of Loving* (New York: Harper, 1956); Kinsey et al., *Sexual Behavior in the Human Male*, p. 587; Eustace Chesser, *The Sexual, Marital, and Family Relationships of the English Woman* (London: Hutchinson's, 1956), p. 517.

6. Kinsey et al., *Sexual Behavior in the Human Female*, pp. 432–436.

7. David Allyn, "Private Acts/Public Policy: Alfred Kinsey, the American Law Institute, and the Privatization of American Sexual Morality," *Journal of American Studies* 30 (1996): 405–428; Arthur H. Hirsch, *Sexual Behavior of the Upper Cultured: A Mid-*

Century Study of Behavior in the United States since 1930 (New York: Vantage Press, 1955).

8. Barbara Ehrenreich, *Hearts of Men: American Dreams and the Flight from Commitment* (New York: Anchor Books, 1983), pp. 42–51; Linda R. Hirshman and Jane E. Larson, *Hard Bargains: The Politics of Sex* (New York: Oxford University Press: 1998), p. 201.

9. *People v. Tarantino*, 290 P. 2d 505 (Calif. Sup. Ct. 1955); *New York Times*, June 3, 1957, p. 16:2; "Gutterdammerung," *Time*, Mar. 11, 1957, p. 67; Neal Gabler, *Winchell: Gossip, Power, and the Culture of Celebrity* (New York: Knopf, 1994), pp. 504–505; *New York Times*, Aug. 13, 1957, p. 53:1; Thomas K. Wolfe, "*Confidential Magazine*: Reflections in Tranquillity by the Former Owner, Robert Harrison, Who Managed to Get Away with It," *Esquire*, April 1964, pp. 87–90, 152–157; "Success in the Sewer," *Time*, July 11, 1955, pp. 90–92; Steve Govoni, "It Can Be Told," *American Film* 15 (February 1990): 28–33, 43.

10. *New York Times*, Aug. 4, 1957, p. 7:5; Aug. 10, p. 13:5; Aug. 28, p. 21:6.

11. "Clean and Otherwise," *Newsweek*, Aug. 26, 1957, pp. 60–61; *New York Times*, Jan. 17, 1957, p. 34:4; July 1, 1958, p. 36:2; June 28, 1957, p. 29:2.

12. Ezra Goodman, *The Fifty-Year Decline and Fall of Hollywood* (New York: Simon and Schuster, 1961), pp. 50–53; Christopher Browne, *The Prying Game* (London: Robson Books, 1996).

13. David Allyn, *Make Love Not War: The Sexual Revolution, an Unfettered History* (Boston: Little, Brown and Co., 2000); *New York Times*, July 3, 1970, p. 23:5; David J. Garrow, *The FBI and Martin Luther King, Jr.* (New York: Penguin, 1983), pp. 158–167; Athan Theoharis, *From the Secret Files of J Edgar Hoover* (Chicago: Ivan R. Dee, 1991), pp. 315–316, 346–356; Seymour M. Hersh, *The Dark Side of Camelot* (Boston: Little, Brown, 1997), p. 129.

14. *People v. Ramsey*, 83 Cal. App. 2d 707, 189 P. 2d 802, 713–714 (Calif. Ct. App. 1948).

15. Rickie Solinger, *The Abortionist: A Woman against the Law* (New York: Free Press, 1994), pp. 189–190; *New York Times*, July 3, 1951, p. 9:4; *People v. Beshany*, 252 N.Y.S. 2d 110 (Sup. Ct. 1964); *New York Times*, July 9, 1965, p. 15:1; July 10, p. 26:2; July 13, p. 12:2; July 14, p. 75:1; July 15, p. 59:4; July 16, p. 56:1; July 17, p. 26:5; July 20, p. 18:1; July 22, p. 23:1.

16. *Times* (London), July 13, 1954, p. 5c; Jan. 11, 1964, p. 6b; Dec. 1, 1967, p. 9c; Mar. 21, 1968, p. 4c; Mar. 29, p. 4f; see also Apr. 4, 1968, p. 15h.

17. Rosalind Pollack Petchesky, *Abortion and Woman's Choice: The State, Sexuality, and Reproductive Freedom* (New York: Longman, 1984), pp. 100–132; *New York Times*, June 17, 1960, p. 35:5; Leslie J. Reagan, *When Abortion Was a Crime: Women, Medicine, and Law in the United States, 1867–1973* (Berkeley: University of California Press, 1997), pp. 224–227; Laura Kaplan, *The Story of Jane: The Legendary Underground Feminist Abortion Service* (New York: Pantheon, 1995).

18. Stevi Jackson, *Christine Delphy* (London: Sage, 1996), pp. 15–19; Gloria Steinem, *Outrageous Acts and Everyday Rebellions* (New York: Holt, Rinehart and Winston, 1983), pp. 18–19.

19. Stephanie Coontz, *The Way We Never Were: American Families and the Nostalgia Trap* (New York: Basic Books, 1992).

322   20. Christie Davies, *Permissive Britain: Social Change in the Sixties and Seventies* (London: Pitman, 1975); Hirshman and Larson, *Hard Bargains*, pp. 229–232.

21. Stuart Hall, "Reformism and the Legislation of Consent," in National Deviancy Conference, ed., *Permissiveness and Control: The Fate of the Sixties Legislation* (London: Macmillan, 1980), pp. 1–44; Beth Bailey, *Sex in the Heartland* (Cambridge, Mass.: Harvard University Press, 1999); Jane Lewis, *Women in Britain since 1945: Women, Family, Work, and the State in the Post-War Years* (Oxford: Blackwell, 1992), p. 41.

22. *Times* (London), Mar. 20, 1970, p. 3d; Mar. 21, p. 3h; Mar. 24, p. 5c; Mar. 25, p. 2d; Mar. 26, p. 2c; *News of the World*, June 6, 1971, p. 1; *Times* (London), Mar. 22, 1974, p. 4d; Mar. 23, p. 3b; Mar. 26, p. 3a; Mar. 27, p. 3a; Mar. 29, p. 3a; Apr. 3, p. 3a; Apr. 5, p. 3a; Apr. 9, p. 4f; Apr. 10, p. 5a; Apr. 19, p. 1d; Dec. 17, p. 3d; "Y, oh Lord, oh why . . . ," *Socialist Worker*, Apr. 13, 1974, p. 5; "If the Law Doesn't Fit, Make It Up," *Socialist Worker*, Oct. 26, 1974, p. 7; *Times* (London), Oct. 17, 1974, p. 6e; Oct. 18, pp. 4g, 15b; Oct. 19, pp. 1b, 14e.

23. *New York Times*, Apr. 7, 1978, sec. 2, p. 2:4; Apr. 8, p. 51:1; Apr. 12, sec. 2, p. 20:4; Apr. 19, sec. 2, p. 4, p. 23:4; Apr. 22, p. 47:1; Apr. 29, p. 27:1; Mar. 17, 1979, p. 22:1; Jan. 12, 1980, p. 22:1.

24. Catharine A. MacKinnon, *Sexual Harassment of Working-Women: A Case of Sex Discrimination* (New Haven: Yale University Press, 1979); Susan Estrich, *Real Rape* (Cambridge, Mass.: Harvard University Press, 1987); *Times* (London), Aug. 8, 1975, p. 3d; Aug. 9, p. 3a; Stephen J. Schulhofer, *Unwanted Sex: The Culture of Intimidation and the Failure of the Law* (Cambridge, Mass.: Harvard University Press, 1998).

25. *New York Times*, Oct. 3, 1980, p. 12:6; Oct. 4, p. 6:3; Robert E. Bauman, *The Gentleman from Maryland: The Conscience of a Gay Conservative* (New York: Arbor House, 1986), pp. 3–25.

26. *New York Times*, Oct. 9, 1980, p. 27:1; Oct. 19, p. 26:3; Nov. 5, p. 19:6; *Newsweek*, Oct. 20, 1980, p. 32; *Time*, Oct. 13, 1980, p. 34; *New York Times*, Oct. 26, 1980, sec. 4, p. 3:1. On Eagleton see *New York Times*, Aug. 5, 1980, p. 8:6; Oct. 23, sec. 2, p. 12:5; Oct. 25, p. 11:2; Aug. 15, 1981, p. 6:6; Sept. 17, p. 22:4.

27. Jeffrey Archer, *First among Equals* (London: Hodder and Stoughton, 1984), pp. 80–81; *Time*, Nov. 10, 1986, p. 49; *Times* (London), July 19, 2001, p. 1a; *New York Times*, Mar. 21, 1987, p. 1:1; Mar. 28, p. 27:1; Aug. 26, p. 15:5; Oct. 21, sec. 2, 3:1.

28. *New York Times*, Nov. 8, 1992, p. 8:13; Alan M. Dershowitz, "Justice on Trial," *New York Times*, Nov. 18, 1992, p. 27:2; Sol Wachtler, *After the Madness: A Judge's Own Prison Memoir* (New York: Random House, 1997); see also John M. Caher, *King of the Mountain: The Rise, Fall, and Redemption of Chief Judge Sol Wachtler* (New York: Prometheus, 1998).

29. Tamara Jones, "Sex, Lies, and Audio Tapes," *Washington Post*, Feb. 22, 1998, sec. W., pp. 10, 25–29; Alan Dershowitz, *Sexual McCarthyism: Clinton, Starr, and the Emerging Constitutional Crisis* (New York: Basic Books, 1998), p. 274.

30. "The Gay Vice Squad," *National Review,* Oct. 19, 1992, p. 19; Richard Cohen, "Schlafly's Silence," *Washington Post,* Sept. 24, sec. A, p. 29:6; see also Sept. 19, 1992, sec. D, p. 1:5.

31. *Los Angeles Times,* Mar. 22, 1990, p. 1, sec. E, p. 2; *Time Magazine,* Jan. 29, 1990, p. 50; Edward Elwood, *Straight News: Gays, Lesbians, and the Media* (New York: Columbia University Press, 1996), pp. 265–286; *New York Times,* June 8, 1989, p. 1: 3; Aug. 26, p. 1:3; *Times* (London), Mar 21, 1995, p. 1d; Mar. 22, p. 2f.

32. Carolyn M. West, "Leaving a Second Closet: Outing Partner Violence in Same-Sex Couples," in Jana L. Jasinski and Linda M. Williams, eds., *Partner Violence: A Comprehensive Review of Twenty Years of Research* (Thousand Oaks, Calif.: Sage, 1998), pp. 169–170.

33. Nancy Fraser, "Sex, Lies, and the Public Sphere: Some Reflections on the Confirmation of Clarence Thomas," *Critical Inquiry* 18 (1992): 610.

34. Robert H. Bork, *Slouching towards Gomorrah: Modern Liberalism and American Decline* (New York: Regan Books, 1996), pp. 103, 106, 112–114, 174; William J. Bennett, *The Death of Outrage: Bill Clinton and the Assault on American Ideals* (New York: Free Press, 1998), p. 19.

35. Gertrude Himmelfarb, *The De-Moralization of Society: From Victorian Virtues to Modern Values* (New York: Alfred A. Knopf, 1995), p. 236; James D. Twitchell, *For Shame: The Loss of Common Decency in American Culture* (New York: St. Martin's Press, 1997), p. 1.

36. Coontz, *The Way We Never Were,* pp. 116–119.

37. Joshua Gamson, *Freaks Talk Back: Tabloid Talk Shows and Sexual Nonconformity* (Chicago: University of Chicago Press, 1998).

CONCLUSION

1. Stuart Hall, "Notes on Deconstructing the 'Popular,'" in Raphael Samuel, ed., *People's History and Socialist Theory* (London: Routledge and Kegan Paul, 1981), p. 233; David Vincent, *The Culture of Secrecy: Britain, 1832–1998* (Oxford: Oxford University Press, 1998).

2. Nicola Lacey, *Unspeakable Subjects: Feminist Essays in Legal and Social Theory* (Oxford: Hart Publishing, 1998), p. 102; Rosemary Hunter and Kathy Mack, "Exclusion and Silence," in Ngaire Naffine and Rosemary J. Owens, eds., *Sexing the Subject of Law* (London: Sweet and Maxwell, 1997), p. 182.

3. Lee Edelman, *Homographesis: Essays in Gay Literary and Cultural Theory* (New York: Routledge, 1994), pp. 148–172; Philip Brian Harper, *Private Affair: Critical Ventures in the Culture of Social Relations* (New York: New York University Press, 1999).

4. Joan Smith, *Moralities: Sex, Money, and Power in the Twenty-First Century* (London: Allen Lane, 2001).

5. *In re Yao,* 680 N.Y.S. 2d 546 (Sup. Ct. 1998).

INDEX